MODERN CHILDREN'S LITERATURE

7

Related titles from Palgrave Macmillan

Suman Gupta, *Re-reading Harry Potter*

Jacqueline Rose, *The Case of Peter Pan: Or the Impossibility of Children's Fiction*

Brian Rosebury, *Tolkien: A Cultural Phenomenon*

David Rudd, *Enid Blyton and the Mystery of Children's Literature*

Jack Zipes, *The Brothers Grimm: From Enchanted Forests to the Modern World*, 2nd edition

Modern Children's Literature

An Introduction

Edited by Kimberley Reynolds

First published 2005 by
PALGRAVE MACMILLAN
Houndmills, Basingstoke, Hampshire RG21 6XS and
175 Fifth Avenue, New York, N.Y. 10010
Companies and representatives throughout the world

PALGRAVE MACMILLAN is the global academic imprint of the Palgrave
Macmillan division of St. Martin's Press LLC and of Palgrave Macmillan Ltd.
Macmillan® is a registered trademark in the United States, United Kingdom
and other countries. Palgrave is a registered trademark in the European
Union and other countries.

ISBN 1–4039–1611–X hardback
ISBN 1–4039–1612–8 paperback

This book is printed on paper suitable for recycling and made from fully
managed and sustained forest sources.

A catalogue record for this book is available from the British Library.

Library of Congress Catalog-in-Publication Data

Modern children's literature : an introduction / edited by Kimberley Reynolds.
      p. cm.
    Includes bibliographical references and index.
    ISBN 0–4039–1611–X – ISBN 1–4039–1612–8 (pbk.)
    1. Children's literature, English–History and criticism. 2. Children's literature,
American–History and criticism. 3. Children–Books and reading–English-speaking
countries. I. Reynolds, Kimberley.

PR990.M63 2004
820.9′9282′0904–cd22

                                                                    2004056196

10   9   8   7   6   5   4   3   2   1
14   13   12   11   10   09   08   07   06   05

Printed and bound in China

Contents

List of Contributors

Noga Applebaum is a freelance writer and reviewer in the field of children's literature as well as a professional web designer. She is currently working on her doctorate in children's literature in the National Centre for Research in Children's Literature (NCRCL) at the University of Roehampton.

Peter Bramwell is a freelance lecturer, critic and researcher in children's literature for the Open University, the University of Sunderland and the NCRCL, from where he gained his MA.

Sarah Godek is a freelance children's literature lecturer and critic and a graduate of the MA in Children's Literature run by the NCRCL.

Judith Graham is a freelance specialist in picturebooks and children's reading, associated with the NCRCL.

Susan Hancock is a Senior Lecturer in the NCRCL. She convenes and teaches on the MA in Children's Literature by Distance Learning course.

Gillian Lathey is Reader in Children's Literature in the NCRCL. She also administers the Marsh Award for Children's Literature in Translation.

Pat Pinsent is Senior Research Fellow in Children's Literature at the University of Roehampton.

Kimberley Reynolds is Professor of Children's Literature at the University of Newcastle.

Lisa Sainsbury is Senior Lecturer in Children's Literature in the NCRCL.

List of Boxes

List of Figures

Acknowledgements

The editor and publisher wish to thank the following for permission to use copyright material:

Mitsumasa Anno, for the illustration *January 1* from *All in a Day*, and illustration no. 7 in *Anno's Counting Book*;

The Children's Book Council, Inc., for the Children's Book Week poster, reproduced by permission of The Children's Book Council, Inc.;

Frances Lincoln Ltd, for the illustration from *Sunshine* by Jan Ormerod, published by Frances Lincoln Ltd, © Jan Ormerod, 2004. Reproduced by permission of Frances Lincoln Ltd, 4 Torriano Mews, Torriano Avenue, London, NW5 2RZ;

Hodder and Stoughton Ltd, for the illustration from *Whose Afraid of the Big Bad Book?* by Lauren Child, reproduced by permission of Hodder and Stoughton Ltd;

Jane Nissen, for the illustration from *Mistress Masham's Repose*; reproduced with permission of Jane Nissen;

Penguin Books Ltd, for the illustration from *Fungus the Bogeyman* by Raymond Briggs (Hamish Hamilton, 1977), copyright © Raymond Briggs, 1977; the illustration from *Gentleman Jim* by Raymond Briggs (Hamish Hamilton, 1980), copyright © Raymond Briggs, 1980; the illustration from *The Family from One End Street* by Eve Garnett (Puffin Modern Classics, 1942), copyright © Eve Garnett, 1942; the front cover from *The Final Journey* by Gudrun Pausewang (Viking, 1996), copyright © Gudrun Pausewang, 1996; the illustration from *The Snowman* by Raymond Briggs (Hamish Hamilton, 1978), copyright © Raymond Briggs, 1978; all reproduced by permission of Penguin Books Ltd;

Random House Group, for the cover from *Child of the May* by Theresa Tomlinson (Random House); the illustrations from *The Bear* by Raymond Briggs (Jonathan Cape); the illustrations from *The Man* by Raymond Briggs (Julia MacRae); the illustration from *Ethel and Ernest* by Raymond Briggs (Jonathan Cape); the illustration from *Beegu* by Alexis Deacon (Hutchinson Children's Books); all reproduced courtesy of the Random House Group Ltd;

Ravensburger Buchverlag, for the cover illustration from *Reise im August* by Gudrun Pausewang; cover illustration Gabie Hilgert © 1997 by Ravensburger Buchverlag Otto Maier GmbH, Ravensburger

Every effort has been made to trace the copyright holders but if any have been inadvertently overlooked, the publisher will be pleased to make the necessary arrangement at the first opportunity.

Introduction

Kimberley Reynolds

Background

This book is based on a course run by the National Centre for Research in Children's Literature (NCRCL) at the University of Roehampton, London, since the 1970s. The Centre is part of the School of English and Modern Languages, and it follows that this is a book about children's literature as literature, not how to use books with children, or children as readers. While based on a taught course and designed to be useful for anyone engaged in the formal study of the subject, *Modern Children's Literature: An Introduction* provides a general introduction to current debates in Children's Literature Studies, illustrated with examples from children's books and related material produced in the English-speaking world, including some translated from other languages. Its origins in a British university mean, however, that there is a preponderance of British texts, so those teaching and studying children's literature outside the UK may want to add or replace the recommended key texts with examples from their own countries or that they have found effective for teaching particular subjects or critical approaches.

In the 1970s, when the course was initially designed, there were many fewer resources for those interested in studying children's literature than there are today, and many fewer primary texts as well, given that in the UK alone the number of children's books published annually has exceeded 6000 for many years. Some of the questions that exercised those trying to establish children's literature as a *bona fide* area of academic study have been thoroughly rehearsed in the books and articles about the subject that have appeared in the intervening years, and especially in the last decade, which saw a significant increase in the number of academic studies, courses, conferences and publications relating to children's literature. To avoid repetition, this Introduction will not rehearse in detail questions such as 'What is children's literature?' 'What status is it given in academia?' 'How is the child constructed in children's literature?' and 'Has children's literature come of age?' It is, however, important to an understanding of the field to be familiar with the debates that have taken place and the conclusions critics have drawn; texts that cover these areas thoroughly are listed in the suggestions for Further Reading at the end of the Introduction. It is a good idea to read at least one of these alongside this volume, since here we are concerned with applying and advancing thinking about the subject rather than going over well-trodden ground. There are also many websites and discussion lists covering the field which provide valuable background information and resources as well as generating topical debates. While details of standard, print-based resources are provided at the end of this

Introduction, because Internet addresses and sites are prone to change, they are not listed here, but many useful links can be found on the NCRCL website: www.ncrcl.ac.uk.

Studying children's literature

Those who have not ventured into the field of children's literature may assume that it is in some ways easier than the study of 'adult' literature. Nothing could be further from the truth. A key reason for this can be seen in the fact that no academic, teacher or researcher would be described as an expert in 'adult literature'. There are specialists in periods, movements, individual authors, categories, genres and forms. Some academics are primarily interested in the tools of literary scholarship, such as literary criticism and research methodologies; others concentrate on bodies of work such as postcolonial writing. Although academics and students are often interested in more than one of these areas, to say that someone specialised in adult literature would mean that they were expected to know about everything that has ever been published for adults to read. This, in fact, is the situation for those working in the field of Children's Literature Studies, creating both unique opportunities and significant demands.

While individuals will have particular areas of interest and expertise, as a rule, the subject encompasses everything from the earliest literature such as myths, legends, folk and fairy tales to the latest work for teenage readers. Its audience ranges in age from newborns to those who are preparing to leave school (in the UK these are normally the years up to the age of 16), with their very different needs, interests and abilities. In order to combine excitement and affordability, publishers, writers and illustrators for the young have always pushed back the boundaries of technology and design; children's books often venture into new formats, new media and innovative design well ahead of adult publishing – if adult books experiment with these elements at all. Again, this creates both opportunities and challenges for the student of children's literature.

Not only does the study of children's literature require knowledge of the texts in all their forms, but, as for the study of other areas of literature, knowledge of periods, genres, literary criticism, key figures, audiences, markets and so on is required – all complicated by the fact that there are effectively no borders or boundaries around the subject. This means that, for example, knowledge of Puritan writing and early forms of printing may be required for some texts, while understanding of teenage fathers, the Internet, substance abuse, or current patterns of adolescent sexual activity is needed for others. This volume is concerned with relatively recent writing – that produced from the twentieth century to the present – yet, as the following chapters show, even in a comparatively brief time span, the range of texts, issues and possible ways of making readings is vast. While in putting together *Modern Children's Literature: An Introduction* it has been necessary to be selective, the choice of texts, approaches and issues explored in the following chapters provides a good introduction to the breadth and quality of work generated in response to fictional texts produced for children (constraints of space mean that it was not possible to include sections on information books and other forms of non-fiction).

What will certainly become apparent in the course of reading this book and the texts it discusses, is that children's literature is both a crucial and a dynamic part of culture. The books children encounter provide them with the images, vocabularies, attitudes and structures to think about themselves, what happens to them, and how the world around them operates. The inclusion of illustrations in a large proportion of books for young people (and with the rise of graphic novels this extends to the upper age limits) means that books lay down ideas about aesthetics – such things as colour, design, and style. Together these factors mean that books read in childhood affect the adults we become at many levels, and so studying children's literature in some ways involves renegotiating the children we were as readers. *The Child that Books Built* (2002), a very successful recent book by Francis Spufford, provides an interesting exploration of this process.

Related to the role children's books play in acculturating children by introducing them to the manners and mores of society – not forgetting that learning to read, and encounters with books, are integral to the experience of schooling – is what they reveal about the assumptions of the writers as well as the societies and periods in which they were written. Because, with the exception of some young adult (YA) fiction, most children's books are written for less experienced readers who also represent the next generation, they tend at some level (whether or not they are aware of this) to encourage readers to subscribe to their view of what children/childhood and society should be like. In this way they participate in what John Stephens calls 'the struggle for young people's minds' (1992: ix). At the same time, the nature of the audience means that writers may be less subtle in conveying these agendas than would be the case for older readers. Because it has interfaces with so many areas, children's literature can be a valuable resource for revealing ideological assumptions across a wide spectrum, including areas such as pedagogy, racism, sexism, classism, religion, environmental issues, nationalism and more. Overall, it is important to remember that children's literature is a uniquely focused lens through which children and young people are asked to look at the images of themselves made for them by their societies. For this reason, it is important that both children's literature and Children's Literature Studies are alert to changing constructions of childhood and to the impact of trends such as commercialization, globalization, and the way the media treat children.

Just as many people assume that studying children's literature is less demanding than studying adult literature, so it is a common assumption, not least among members of the British royal family and some pop stars, that writing children's books is simple. In fact, creating books for children poses a number of challenges to writers and writer–illustrators. Jill Paton Walsh, who writes for both adults and children, sees the difference in this way:

> the children's book presents a technically more difficult, technically more interesting problem – that of making a fully serious adult statement, as a

good novel of any kind does, and making it utterly simple and transparent.
... The need for comprehensibility imposes an emotional obliqueness, and
indirection of approach, which like elision and partial statement in poetry,
is often a source of aesthetic power.   (Meek et al., 1977: 192–3)

As Paton Walsh explains, writing for children creates technical demands that
require original solutions, yet one of the most contentious pieces of writing
about children's literature of recent years, Jacqueline Rose's *The Case of Peter
Pan, or, The Impossibility of Children's Fiction* (1984), describes children's
literature as innately conservative at the levels of style, content, and the way
it frames the adult–child relationship. While there are certainly many books
that match Rose's description, the following pages will show that across
formats and ages there are many groundbreaking and radical children's
books that do more than imitate what is happening in adult fiction. Indeed,
Juliet Dusinberre's *Alice to the Lighthouse* (1987) argues that the children's
books of one age prepare the way for the adult books of the next so, for
example, Virginia Woolf's generation grew up after the great Victorian
fantasies such as *Alice in Wonderland* (1865), which took their literary
imaginations on paths leading towards Modernist experimentation. This is an
idea worth keeping in mind as you work through this book, as is the possibility
that children's literature is a safe-house and incubator for literary modes
that are temporarily out of fashion. All of these ideas are explored further in
the following chapters.

Organization

The book is designed to provide a sense of period and chronology, but since
this is in many ways an artificial and limited way of looking at texts, historical
development is not the central organizing principle. Instead, the chapters are
structured in various ways: some are primarily concerned with genre, others
with critical approaches, and others with themes or topics. Because certain
genres and tendencies, notably fantasy and realism, span the period and have
not only attracted many important writers but have also evolved in significant
ways, these are covered in more than one chapter. It may be productive to read
related chapters in succession rather than working through them in order.
Similarly, if you are interested in a topic such as the family or history, or a
particular critical orientation, bringing together chapters that cover the same
topic from different angles may be the best way for you to use the material
here. The individual chapter introductions flag up instances where material is
common to chapters. Often this will be in the form of the boxed information,
separate from the main text, which develops key concepts, critical approaches
or other background information. You may find it helpful to look at these
boxes before, as well as during, the reading of a chapter. A complete list of the
information boxes provided appears after the List of Contributors.

Primary texts

With tens of thousands of possible texts to choose from, the selection of primary texts for an introductory work such as this poses particular problems. The NCRCL course was originally confined to British children's literature, and though in recent years the syllabus has been expanded to include texts from other English-speaking countries and those in translation, it continues to be dominated by books that are produced and/or widely read in the UK. In turning the taught course into a book, the contributors agreed that it was important to include texts that we have taught over the years and which demonstrably stand up to critical scrutiny. At the same time, we wanted to include texts from outside the UK, both to stimulate comparison and to broaden readers' knowledge of world children's literature. Books from Australia, New Zealand, North America, and Europe are discussed in most chapters, as is some of the work of critics and scholars from these countries. Since Britain has one of the longest traditions of producing children's literature, and the children's literature of all of these countries has been substantially influenced by it, however, much can be learned from comparing British children's literature with that produced elsewhere. Those using this book outside the UK may find this a particularly productive way to proceed.

Other factors contributors agreed to keep in mind when choosing key texts for chapters were age range and visual elements. Having worked through the whole of this study, readers will have considered books for all stages and ages of readers from 0 to 16, including picturebooks, short chapter books, classic fiction, and YA novels. They will also have learned to look at texts from a variety of perspectives and using a range of critical approaches.

The course on which this text is based consists of a twelve-week programme of seminars and some formal lectures. Different universities have different teaching patterns, however, and after some experimentation, we found that including more than twelve chapters allowed for the greatest flexibility. Courses that concentrate on genre or chronology or issues, for instance, can make up programmes of appropriate length by concentrating on those chapters most appropriate to their own aims. Those who have more time at their disposal and are able to undertake a comprehensive introduction to the subject will find that this book allows them to engage with a very wide range of critical and topical debates, though again, it may be necessary to select or combine chapters to make a coherent programme of the required length. Ultimately, chapters aim to do three things. First, they provide a sound introduction to the conceptual material covered, in combination with selected background information about texts, authors and contexts as appropriate to each chapter's approach. Then, they offer sample discussions which can be used to stimulate readers to re-apply and extend the methodology to other texts. Finally, they point the way to more in-depth study of texts, approachs and topics through suggestions for further reading.

While the key texts chosen for each chapter have been proved to be effective, there are certainly many others that could be read alongside or substituted for them. It is, for instance, often illuminating to look at picturebooks in combination with longer fiction, as Gillian Lathey does in her chapters on children's literature of war. Whatever the final selection of primary texts, the critical approaches, contextual material and case studies provided in *Modern Children's Literature: An Introduction* will make a sound basis for individual thinking and group discussions.

FURTHER READING

At the end of each chapter, there is a list of books and resources for taking topics further. These include selected primary texts and critical reading, including material mentioned in the chapters. To keep lists from becoming too diffuse and cumbersome, only those materials that are directly relevant to the subject of the chapter are listed in this section; other sources appear in the References and Bibliography at the end of the book.

There are a few key resources that you will find helpful at various stages in your studies.

Books about Children's Literature

Carpenter, H. and Prichard M., *The Oxford Companion to Children's Literature* (Oxford and New York: Oxford University Press, 1984).

Egoff, S., Stubbs, E. T. and Ashley, L. F. (eds), *Only Connect: Readings on Childern's Literature*, 2nd edition (Toronto: Oxford University Press, 1980).

Lurie, A., *Don't Tell the Grown-Ups: Subversive Children's Literature* (London: Bloomsbury, 1990).

Meek, M., Warlow, A. and Barton, G. (eds), *The Cool Web: The Pattern of Children's Reading* (London: Bodley Head, 1977).

Nodelman, P. and Reimer, M., *The Pleasures of Children's Literature*, 3rd edition (New York: Allyn and Bacon/Longman, 2002).

Pinsent, P. *Children's Literature and the Politics of Equality* (London: David Fulton, 1997).

Reynolds, K., *Children's Literature in the 1890s and 1990s* (Plymouth: Northcote House, 1994).

Reynolds, K. and Tucker, N. (eds), *Children's Book Publishing in Britain since 1945* (Aldershot: Scolar/Ashgate, 1998).

Rose, J., *The Case of Peter Pan, or, The Impossibility of Children's Literature* (Basingstoke: Macmillan, 1984).

Rustin, M. and M., *Narratives of Love and Loss: Studies in Modern Children's Fiction* (London and New York: Karnac, 2001).

Spufford, F., *The Child that Books Built* (London: Faber & Faber, 2002).

Townsend, J. R., *Written for Children* (London: Bodley Head, 1990).

Tucker, N., *The Child and the Book: A Psychological and Literary Exploration* (Cambridge: Cambridge University Press, 1981).

Watson, V. (ed.), *The Cambridge Guide to Children's Books in English* (Cambridge: Cambridge University Press, 2001).

Books about Children's Literature and Critical Theory

Hunt, P. (ed.), *Children's Literature: The Development of Criticism* (London: Routledge, 1990).

Hunt, P. (ed.), *Literature for Children: Contemporary Criticism* (London: Routledge, 1992).

Hunt, P., *An Introduction to Children's Literature* (Oxford: Oxford University Press, 1994).

Hunt, P. (ed.), *International Companion Encyclopedia of Children's Literature* (London: Routledge, 1996).

Lesnik-Oberstein, K., *Children's Literature Criticism and the Fictional Child* (Oxford: Clarendon Press, 1994).

McGillis, R., *The Nimble Reader: Literary Theory and Children's Literature* (New York: Twayne, 1996).

Nikolajeva, M., *Children's Literature Comes of Age: Toward a New Aesthetic* (New York and London: Garland, 1996).

Rudd, D., *Enid Blyton and the Mystery of Children's Literature* (Basingstoke: Macmillan, 2000).

Shavit, Z., *The Poetics of Children's Literature* (Athens, GA: University of Georgia Press, 1986).

Stephens, J., *Language and Ideology in Children's Fiction* (Harlow: Longman, 1992).

Wall, B., *The Narrator's Voice* (London: Macmillan, 1991).

Journals

Bookbird
Canadian Children's Literature
Children's Literature Association Quarterly
Horn Book Magazine
The Lion and the Unicorn
New Review of Children's Literature
Papers
Signal (now defunct but still valuable)

Theories of Genre and Gender: Change and Continuity in the School Story

Pat Pinsent

KEY TEXTS

E. Blyton, *The O'Sullivan Twins* (1942)
E. Brent-Dyer, *Exploits of the Chalet Girls* (1933); *The Wrong Chalet School* (1952)
A. Forest, *Autumn Term* (1948); *End of Term* (1959)
J. K. Rowling *Harry Potter and the Philosopher's Stone* (1997)

This chapter approaches the study of school stories largely through the lens of genre theory, yet it also keeps in mind the fact that as fictional representations of the culture and experience of schooling, this body of writing is also concerned with aspects of socialization – including gender, education, friendship, attitudes to institutions, and the inculcation of ideas about the values, mores and power structures of society. By focusing on the girls' school story, in this chapter Pat Pinsent is able to consider both the contribution made by women writers, and the effects of sex and gender on the evolution of the genre. The broad timeframe of the chapter makes it possible to chart developments in the dialogue between the school story and the changing nature of schools as institutions reflecting prevailing social and educational philosophies. Related to this and also highly visible because of the genre's conventions, is the way schools themselves are used to create places outside of normal time and space. As this chapter shows, at the centre of the school story lies the school itself, superficially known and familiar, but in fact fraught with contradictions. The school in school stories functions both as a microcosm of the world and as an alternative to it; as a place of socialization and of subversion, and as an educational establishment in which the lessons learned generally take place outside the classroom. Significantly, during its long history, the school story has not merely reflected the world of school, but by preparing and shaping readers' understanding of what it means to go to school and what schools are and do, it has also influenced schools as institutions.

More than most varieties of literature, the school story can be described as a *genre*, (see Box 1.1) not entirely confined to children's literature, though most of its best known exemplars clearly presuppose an audience at least partly made up of young people. The genre of school fiction has certain character-istics, though not every individual novel featuring a school automatically displays these. Some of these characteristics appear in the earliest examples of school stories, while others emerge during the course of the school story's long history; this chapter sets out to display these with particular reference to the work of one of the most popular twentieth-century writers of school fiction, Elinor Brent-Dyer (1895–1969).

Since the school story can legitimately be termed a genre, it is tempting for writers about children's literature to indulge in generalizations about its health, or indeed its continued existence. In recent years, a number of critics have claimed school fiction to be in terminal decline, as the subtitle of P. W. Musgrave's *From Brown to Bunter: The Life and Death of the School Story* (1985) bears witness. This forecast has demonstrably proved to be false, given the fact that literally hundreds of children's novels with a school setting have been published since the mid-1970s. Nevertheless, it could be claimed that during the last third of the twentieth century, the genre underwent a paradigm shift. As a result, this chapter has two centres of interest: the girls' school stories characteristic of the first two-thirds of the twentieth century, focusing

---

BOX 1.1 GENRE

This term, of which the literal meaning is 'kind, sort or variety', is rather loosely used in contemporary literary criticism, though in the past, writers clearly distinguished between genres, paying attention to such things as style, conventions, and narrative rules for each genre category. In contemporary literary criticism, it is generally applied in a much broader way than in linguistics and educational theory, where it tends still to be applied specifically to text-type. Texts that share certain themes, moods or approaches to writing tend to be referred to as belonging to the same genre (or, occasionally, sub-genre). Examples from both adult and children's litera-ture might include the Western, the historical novel, tragedy, the epic, science fic-tion, the detective novel, or, as in the current instance, the school story. Sometimes even such large areas as realism and fantasy are referred to as 'genres', but the utility of the term is reduced if it is used too inclusively. Novels belonging to the same genre tend to have certain qualities in common, though they are unlikely to be uniformly present in all the books. (See Box 1.2 for discussion of one of these aspects, the chron-otope, and Chapters 6 and 12, which consider the genres of fantasy and romance, respectively.)

The fact that the school story can legitimately be termed a genre is borne out by the existence of two volumes: *The Encyclopaedia of Girls' School Stories* (2000), edited by Sue Sims and Hilary Clare, and *The Encyclopaedia of Boys' School Stories* (2000), edited by Robert Kirkpatrick.

on the work of three of the most notable writers, Elinor Brent-Dyer, Enid Blyton and Antonia Forest; and the developments in the school story genre in the last third of the century, ending with a reference to the recent development of the genre in the Harry Potter books.

Any discussion of twentieth-century school fiction needs, however, to be set in perspective by a brief glance at the earlier development of the genre, not only to contextualize the books considered, but also to justify the fact that, despite the prestige of boys' fiction, none of the novels examined below is set in an exclusively male school. Since the majority of the stories I examine are set in girls' schools and written by women authors, another critical stance that inevitably comes to the fore is that of gender studies, particularly with a feminist emphasis.

The history of the school story

The relative merits and respective primacy of boys' and girls' school stories have been much disputed. For some critics, it would seem, only the boys' story is truly canonical. In her introduction to *The Encyclopaedia of Girls' School Stories* (2000), Sue Sims quotes the comments of such otherwise sensitive critics as Elizabeth Bowen and Margery Fisher, revealing their hostility to the girls' stories. Nevertheless, it is generally agreed that the predecessor of the entire school-stories genre is the eighteenth-century work by the sister of the better known author of *Tom Jones*. Sarah Fielding's *The Governess, or The Little Female Academy* (1749) is set in a girls' school which has only nine pupils; as Sims goes on to remark, it was not until the work of the girls' school pioneers had been validated in 1868 that the 'full-blown' girls' school story could emerge (2000: 3). Nevertheless, other early writers, such as Maria Edgeworth (1767–1849), Elizabeth Sandham and Mary Hughes (dates uncertain but both were writing in the early 1800s), produced stories which anticipate the much more considerable achievement of L. T. Meade (1844–1914), whose over 200 titles include a number set in schools and other places of education.

Be that as it may, the school story whose title is likely to be most familiar, even with those who haven't read it, is Thomas Hughes's *Tom Brown's Schooldays* (1857). Like this text, other well-known Victorian examples of the genre, such as Talbot Baines Reed's *The Fifth Form at St Dominic's* (1887) and Rudyard Kipling's *Stalky & Co* (1899), tend to be set in schools where the only females to be glimpsed are Matron and possibly the Headmaster's wife. It was in boys' texts such as these that many of the conventions of the genre as we see it today were established, though it also needed their development in twentieth-century school stories, for both boys and girls, fully to determine what we now recognize as the typical school story.

When Angela Brazil (1868–1947) produced the first of her nearly fifty novels about girls' schools, *A Terrible Tomboy* (1904), she began in fact to build on the solid achievement of a considerable number of earlier writers in the girls' sub-genre, although she also incorporated features more characteristic of the boys' school story, notably the emphasis on games and the use of distinctive slang. Her books were extremely popular with girls, including many who were not of the social class likely to attend boarding schools themselves. Brazil was followed fairly swiftly by the authors whom Rosemary Auchmuty (in Tucker and Reynolds, 1997: 79) terms the 'Big Three': Elsie Oxenham (1880–1960), best known for the Abbey School; Dorita Fairlie Bruce (1885–1970), author of the 'Dimsie' stories; and Elinor Brent-Dyer, whose Chalet School novels are examined in more detail in the next section.

Elinor Brent-Dyer and girls' school stories up to 1970

The Chalet School Series

According to the *Encyclopaedia of Girls' School Stories*: 'Elinor Brent-Dyer [writing between 1922 and 1970] is probably the best-known and the most popular author in the field of the girls' school story, the standard by which all others are judged' (Sims and Clare, 2000: 75). I shall refer most closely to *Exploits of the Chalet Girls* (1933), a relatively early text, and *The Wrong Chalet School* (1952), a novel from the middle of Brent-Dyer's writing career, since these fairly typical Chalet School books are not only representative of Brent-Dyer's *oeuvre*, but also fit very closely into what might be termed the paradigm of the girls' school story. As there are so many books in the series by Brent-Dyer, Blyton and Forest, each section includes brief plot summaries of the relevant texts.

Exploits of the Chalet Girls
This book is the ninth in the series, its action occurring four and a half years after the foundation of the Chalet School in the Austrian Tyrol by Madge Bettany, later Mrs Russell. Her younger sister, Jo, is now headgirl, with seven fellow prefects all of whom have been at the school for several years. There is little over-arching plot, but the incidents described tend towards building up a sense of what might be termed the wholesomeness of the life of the girls at the school: speaking English, French and German; enjoying walks up the local mountains; eating home-made food; and staging concerts which both display their musical and dramatic talent and celebrate festivals, notably Christmas. The main discordancy arrives in the form of a new pupil, Thekla von Stift, the daughter of a Prussian Graf [Count]. She thinks herself superior to girls whose parents are in trade or manufacturing, and also has no notion of the schoolgirl code of conduct, displaying herself as a 'sneak' when she informs the staff about some pupils who have interfered with the school clock. By the end of the book, however, 'the atmosphere of the School was doing its duty and she was already a nicer girl than the one who had come in September' (136).

The Wrong Chalet School
The 24th volume of the 58 (see Sims and Clare, 2000: 76–81) is largely set in postwar Wales, where the main section of the Chalet School is now located on

a small island near the Swansea coast. Katherine Mary Gordon's aunt Luce, a stereotypically vague artist, having arranged for her niece to enrol at a different Chalet School in Pembrokeshire, arrives with her at Paddington from where the pupils of both schools are departing, and is confused by similarities in the colour of the uniforms. Inevitably, to the reader's satisfaction, Katherine joins 'our' Chalet School. This situation is compounded by the unlikely coincidences that both schools have teachers with the surname Wilson, and THE Chalet School is expecting a pupil called Mary Katherine Gordon. The reader familiar with Brent-Dyer's work is hardly surprised to discover that the incorrect choice turns out to be absolutely right as far as Katherine is concerned, fostering her ability at games and providing the kind of caring environment much needed by a girl whose parents are lost somewhere in Communist China. The contrast between the two schools allows the author to expound her values: 'our' girls have better manners, a nicer uniform, and a set curriculum, unlike the flamboyant colours and free choice of subjects allowed to the pupils at the other Chalet School. As usual, the value of speaking three languages, playing sports, and being creative, is emphasized.

An aspect common to both these Chalet School books and to most of the others is the frequent incidental mention of prayer and trust in God. In *The Wrong Chalet School* this trust is fulfilled when Katherine's parents are ultimately liberated, and at the end she is awaiting reunion with them.

The girls' boarding-school story paradigm

It is apparent from the brief summaries of these books that certain elements often recur, as indeed they do throughout Brent-Dyer's output, and in the work of the other girls' school story writers named above. Similarly, they are frequently to be found in the school stories of Brent-Dyer's younger contemporaries, Enid Blyton (1897–1968) and Antonia Forest (1915–2003). I am not claiming that Brent-Dyer established these characteristics of the genre by herself, nor indeed that all of them are to be found in each of her books. If, however, there is any truth in the claim that she created a standard by which other writers may be judged, it is scarcely surprising that her novels have features which frequently recur in other novels of the genre. Some but not all of these are also to be found in boys' school stories. The list below sets out characteristic features found in, but not always exclusive to, the girls' stories.

1   School novels tend to start with a train journey during which new girls are introduced and friendships between old pupils are renewed. The journey marks the boundary between home and school territory; when parents are allowed to appear at the school, it is clear that they are present by permission of the authorities, in what is virtually an alien country where their daughters and the staff are the inhabitants. It is interesting to observe that in spite of the likelihood that pupils in more recent times will have been delivered by car to their schools, a contemporary writer, Anne Digby, maintains the 'train' tradition in at least some of her 'Trebizon' books.

BOX 1.2 CHRONOTOPE AND KENOTYPE

The term *chronotope*, defined by Mikhail Bakhtin as 'the intrinsic connectedness of temporal and spatial relationships that are artistically expressed in literature', and more concisely translated by Maria Nikolajeva (1996: 121) as the indivisible 'unity of time and space' in a work of literature, is seen by Nikolajeva as providing 'an appropriate approach to genres', since 'specific forms of chronotope are unique for particular genres.' The use of the train to boarding school is particularly characteristic of the school story of the first two-thirds of the twentieth century, as well as having been adopted by J. K. Rowling in her 'Harry Potter' saga. The train marks the transition between the parental territory (as it exists in time and space) of the home, and the teacher/pupil territory of the school. It is a kind of liminal time–space zone, in which, by the inevitably scattered nature of authority, no one is in total control and associations of characters are provisional. The chronotope of the school story, then, normally encompasses three distinct domains of time and space: home (often also holiday), train journey and school.

Another term used by Nikolajeva (1996: 145–6) is *kenotype*, a concept suggested by another Russian critic, Mikhail Epstein. In contrast to the archetype, seen by Jung (see Chapter 3) as an enduring feature of the collective unconscious, the kenotype is a structure from modern history, signified by such things as objects/artefacts and places, which reflects 'a new system of human notions and experience'. Well-established as the school is, it is nevertheless a relatively modern institution, and has some claim to be classed as a kenotype, as a contemporary version of archetypal *milieus* of ritual and initiation.

This characteristic use of the train could be described as a *chronotope* (see Box 1.2 and the discussion in Chapter 10).

2 The school itself often becomes a kind of additional character in the book, moulding its pupils almost in spite of themselves, or of the efforts of the staff, into its own ethos. It is easy to see the attractions of a strong sense of place and ethos embedded in the school-as-character in providing writers with an element of continuity, as well as a setting that they will not need constantly to describe in detail. Most of the best known school writers for both girls and boys tend to use the same school for a number of different books.

3 Many books in the genre begin with the introduction of one or more new pupils, providing a way in for the reader not familiar with the series, while readers who are already knowledgeable can feel a sense of superiority to the character(s) concerned and enjoy a kind of vicarious meeting of old friends.

4 Much of the plot hinges on events internal to the school, such as selection for sports teams, preparations for dramatic or musical productions, and relationships between pupils and staff. The world outside may impinge through mention of past pupils, parents' situations, or even, in general terms related to the school, a war, but because of the boarding-school

environment, pupils themselves are not generally directly involved in activities outside the school.

5   Particularly characteristic of the world of the Chalet School, but also found in other girls' school books to a greater extent than in boys' books, is an advocacy of tolerance for others' differences and abilities, together with a fostering not only of sport but also of artistic ability.

6   Teachers in these girls' schools frequently display a high degree of care for their pupils, all of whom they seem to know well. This does not mean that they are perfect, or never become objects of comedy; some indeed, notably the French teachers, could be seen as 'stock characters'. On the whole, however, even in Blyton's work, there is rather less stereotyping than in the boys' stories. The same is not always true of the school fiction from later in the twentieth century.

7   Brent-Dyer's books, like those of the school-story genre as a whole, adhere to a school 'code of honour', involving the avoidance of 'meanness' or 'sneakiness' and a hatred of snobbery, whether this arises from social class or academic excellence. The wrongness of taking advantage of being related to those in positions of power, whether in the school or outside, is also emphasized.

8   There is often an ambivalence about gender, possibly reflecting something of the situation actually extant within 'real' boarding schools during the period concerned. These single-sex female environments allow girls to excel at both sport and schoolwork, yet the girls are often told that they must prepare for their roles as wives and mothers. The only Brent-Dyer character who seems capable of combining all these qualities is Jo Bettany, who, as Mrs Maynard, manages to have eleven children while being a successful writer and standing as a model to later generations of Chalet School girls. Her first name, possibly recalling that of Louisa May Alcott's heroine in *Little Women*, is androgynous, as indeed is that of another idealized Chalet School character, 'The Robin'. The use of boyish-sounding names is prevalent in many girls' school books, whereas any use of feminized names for characters in boys' stories is invariably derogatory.

9   As with the vast majority of boys' school stories of the period, these books tend to be set in boarding schools which are not only detached from ordinary society, but also by their nature patronized by the upper class and the upper middle class, even though their readership certainly included a good many children from 'lower' classes. Because of the relatively stable class structure which obtained prior to the Second World War, this element drew little comment at the time; children who did not attend single-sex schools, let alone boarding schools, were nevertheless prepared to take these not only as the norm, but also as an unattainable ideal. Consequently there is very little social criticism in the majority of school books before the 1950s.

10   As with those for boys, the girls' school stories often focus on friendships within a fairly small subgroup of pupils.

11   A feature particularly evident in Brent-Dyer's work is the *bildungsroman* aspect; the characters grow up as we progress through the series, and

indeed are succeeded by further generations of schoolgirls. While boys are also seen as maturing in many novels, notably *Tom Brown's Schooldays*, character development throughout a series seems less characteristic of the boys' series than of the girls' (contrast Buckeridge's 'Jennings' books with the majority of the books by Brent-Dyer, Bruce and Oxenham).

In what follows, the presence of some of these features in two other prominent, slightly younger, contemporaries of Brent-Dyer will be examined, before a consideration is undertaken of the changes in the paradigm as far as more recent schools fiction is concerned.

Enid Blyton

The school stories of this most prolific of children's authors have often been unfavourably compared both with those of the 'Big Three' and with Blyton's own adventure stories. Yet they have remained popular even during a period when boarding school education declined, and while their readers, unlike those of Blyton's other books, are likely to be almost exclusively female, there is no doubt that these books have introduced a number of readers to the genre, since Blyton's work is less demanding than that of many other school authors.

Blyton's three school series: 'The Naughtiest Girl', 'St Clare's' and 'Malory Towers', were published between 1940 and 1951, a relatively short period during a writing career which stretched from 1922 to the mid-1960s. Auchmuty (in Tucker and Reynolds, 1997: 82–5) puts forward several possible reasons for Blyton's choice of this genre at this time, ranging from commercial factors and her own family situation to the changes in society, particularly with respect to the situation of women.

The text discussed here is the second volume of the St Clare's series, which is broadly representative of Blyton's school stories. *The O'Sullivan Twins* (1942) has as its leading characters Pat and Isabel O'Sullivan, who have been at St Clare's for a term when they learn that their cousin Alison is going to join them there. There is the usual scene at the railway station, allowing the author to introduce both old and new characters. Once she is at school, Alison, who is much too concerned with her appearance, is slow to accept that she has to wait on the older girls in what can be seen as a continuation of the 'fagging' tradition, so important in *Tom Brown's Schooldays*.

The main plot theme, however, is about the character of Erica, who 'sneaks' on the girls having a midnight feast, and later meanly ruins Pat's knitting. She is eventually rescued from a fire by Margery, a girl whom the other pupils have suspected of the misdeeds perpetrated by Erica. Readers have already been given a clue that Margery cannot really be so unpleasant because she is very good at games. In due course it appears that the less attractive traits of both Erica and Margery have been triggered by their family situations, unexpectedly bringing in an element of social comment fairly rare in Blyton. Margery is able to reform and stays on, but Erica, too weak in character to remain in an environment where her faults have been discovered, has to leave St Clare's, though she is not expelled.

It is easy to see the extent to which this novel displays many of the paradigmatic features listed above. A notable scene is that where the headmistress, Miss Theobald, makes her views about morality clear; she is addressing the girls who have been discovered feasting in the music-room: 'Although you have broken the rule forbidding any girl to leave her dormitory at night, your escapade is not in the same rank as, for instance, meanness, lying, or disloyalty. Those are serious things; ... [yours is] silly mischief' (45).

A technique which Blyton uses extensively is that of creating similarities and contrasts between pairs of girls. Here the two girls who have been affected by family situations, Margery, who is bad-tempered but basically honest, and Erica, who is underhand, are contrasted. Similarly Pat and Isabel, ideal schoolgirls, are contrasted with their cousin Alison, who is 'full of airs and graces' (5) and, ultimate depravity, has had her hair permed at the age of fourteen. (Twenty-first-century readers are likely to feel that all the girls, some of whom are as old as sixteen, appear very young for their age – adolescence does not appear to have happened to them!) Sport features very significantly, acting as an indicator of Margery's basic goodness, while art too is given status by the fact that a very popular girl, Lucy, is an excellent artist. Some assumptions about the feminine role also occur; Matron tells Alison that it is likely that her mother has sent her to the school because she will have to learn to mend sheets: 'You hope to be happily married one day, don't you – and run your own home? Well, you must learn to take care of your own linen and mend it, then' (13).

Antonia Forest

Sims and Clare (2000: 140) describe Forest as 'widely regarded as one of the best – if not the best – writers of girls' school stories,' yet she has only produced four books in this sub-genre, all dealing with the adventures of the Marlow family (subjects also of another seven books not set in schools). I shall focus here on the first of her school books, *The Autumn Term* (1948), which introduces the characters of Nicola and her twin sister Lawrence (apparently so named because her parents hoped that she would be a boy). They are first seen when they are on the train to Kingscote School, travelling with their elder sisters, Karen (headgirl), Rowan (in the netball team), Ginty (in the second eleven hockey team) and Ann (a patrol leader in the Guides), all of whom have already distinguished themselves at the school. Forest uses the train chronotope more creatively than some writers; not only do the protagonists have the chance to identify themselves to the reader and to meet another new girl (Thalia Keith, known as Tim, niece to the headmistress) who will feature significantly in the text, but also Nicola pulls the communication cord and stops the train, because her new sixteen-bladed penknife has dropped out of the window.

Forest's twins are united in their desire to distinguish themselves at school, a desire initially thwarted by two factors: their poor academic performance, which results in their being placed in the Third Remove rather than 3A or even 3B, and their suspension from the Guides because they are unjustly blamed for an incident occurring on a hike. The climax of the book comes when they both do exceptionally well in a play staged by their form, and written and produced by their friend Tim.

Anyone reading this brief account of *Autumn Term* will no doubt have observed Forest's use of male names for Lawrie and Tim, while Nicola is usually known as Nicky. Certain values of the school story, prevalent in those for both sexes, are also to the fore in this book. The reader is left in no doubt that when Tim capitalizes on her relationship to the headmistress she is going against the unwritten ethos of the school, while Lawrie and Nicola are frequently tempted to make use of their family connections with more senior forms, though at times they also find the Marlow name works against their interest. A worse crime is to be dishonest, like Marie, 'a timid child, who still fled panic-stricken from dark landing to lighted hall', to whom it has never occurred that 'for the sake of her own self-respect she should confront her personal hobgoblins' (112–13). It is her lie which gets the twins into trouble, resulting in their being suspended from the Guide company, but although her perfidy is ultimately detected, they are not reinstated during the course of this novel, nor indeed are they promoted to a higher form. Forest seems to be rejecting the possibility of too facile a happy ending, while ensuring that the twins emerge with a due degree of recognition.

It is not difficult to understand the reasons for the high rating given to Forest's novels by those familiar with a large range of school fiction. Sims and Clare comment on 'her remarkable gift for character ... characters are individualized not only by their actions and their thoughts but also by their extraordinarily vivid dialogue' (2000: 140–1). Two later novels in the Kingscote School series, *The Cricket Term* (1974) and *The Attic Term* (1976), are relatively little known, perhaps because both were written in a period when the boarding-school story, in both its male and female manifestations, was declining in popularity – a situation which, in hindsight, can be seen to be only a temporary 'blip' before the revival most amazingly signalled by J. K. Rowling's Harry Potter saga (started in 1997).

Schools fiction since 1970

Changes in society frequently act as the triggers of changes in literature written for children, though children's books may often be relatively slow in their incorporation of such changes. As Jeffrey Richards comments in his study of the public schools in English fiction, 'It is generally acknowledged that popular culture holds up a mirror to the mind set of the nation' (1988: 1). If school takes a different form in the real world, the books and indeed the films and television dramas featuring it tend also to change. Even during the period of greatest popularity of boarding-school fiction, the majority of British school children were attending day schools, but because of the social cachet attached to the boarding school, as well as the advantage given to the author by the virtual 'island', remote from urban society, that this kind of school provided, in particular the removal of the young characters from their parents, boarding-school fiction lingered on well past what might have been seen as its 'sell-by' date. By the 1970s, in a society made conscious in particular of equality issues, embracing race and gender as well as class, 'issues-led' fiction began to dominate the children's market, to the detriment of the sales of books set in a single-sex environment where, inevitably, working-class and non-white characters had been few. As a result, during this period, day-school fiction, once very much the 'poor relation' of the genre, became supreme. By its nature, such fiction allows, or even demands, the incursion of the outside world, to an extent less appropriate to the boarding-school novel. As a consequence of their departure from the boarding-school genre, most of the authors to be discussed here are not mentioned in either the girls' or the boys' encyclopaedias of school stories.

Realism and 'issues-driven' school fiction

As has been evident in the previous discussion, morality has been a very important theme of the school story from its beginnings. The qualities which make for good relationships in a small community, such as leadership, friendliness and concern for others, are inevitably singled out for praise, while those which could lead to the breakdown of relationships, such as dishonesty, telling tales, and snobbery, are censured, either implicitly or explicitly. While this standard of values is certainly not abandoned in later fiction, it is set within a larger context. Because school, now almost always co-educational, is less of a closed community, wider values have more impact. The paradigm of school as a microcosm of society perhaps becomes more obvious when the school is set in the wider community, an aspect particularly appropriate to Robert Cormier's *The Chocolate War* (1974), which, as well as providing a severe critique of the practices of an American day school run by a fictional Catholic religious order, can be read as something of a satire on Mafia-like organizations within wider society.

The section on further reading includes several British novels from the last third of the twentieth century in which social issues such as racial prejudice, gender roles, and bullying are tackled, usually within a day-school context. Recent school-based novels are also prepared to take on questions concerning such problems as drugs and teenage pregnancy. While several of these books are clearly governed by a feminist agenda, and the causes they plead are not yet universally won, even in Britain, a weakness of their position is that in the attempt to redress the gender balance, they often portray being female as something of a disadvantage. It has even been suggested that the single-sex environment of the earlier school books allowed the writers to present a more positive aspect of femaleness, though not necessarily of femininity. Auchmuty (in Sims and Clare, 2000: 29) quotes Gill Frith (1985), who observes that:

> the school story presents a picture of what it is possible for a girl to be and to do which stands in absolute contradistinction to the configuration of 'femininity' which is to be found in other forms of popular fiction

addressed specifically to women and girls ... in a world of girls, to be female is *normal* and not a *problem'*.   [italics Frith's]

It is apparent that even within the category of realism, school books from the last one-third of the twentieth century can by no means be classified into the kind of paradigm appropriate to the earlier girls' school books, though aspects such as stereotyping and the 'code of honour' are still evident. Fantasy school fiction, a variation on the genre which became more numerous in the last third of the twentieth century, tends, however, to revert to a significantly greater extent to the typology of the earlier school novels, often including the setting of a boarding-school environment.

Fantasy school fiction: the Harry Potter phenomenon

School fiction in the past has nearly always been seen as belonging to the category of the realistic novel. In talking of F. Anstey's 1882 novel *Vice Versa* (where a father and son find that their bodies, and consequently their roles, have been interchanged), Robert Kirkpatrick claims that, 'The number of school stories which rely for their central premise on magic and the super-natural can even today be counted on the fingers of two hands' (2000: 29). Such texts often tend to be regarded as outside mainstream school fiction; although the first three of the Harry Potter books are discussed in Kirk-patrick's *Encyclopaedia of Boys' School Stories* (2000), neither Sims and Clare nor Kirkpatrick mentions Robert Swindells, Jill Murphy or Anthony Horowitz, while Sims explicitly comments on the omission by Sims and Clare of both Gillian Cross and J. K. Rowling from their reference book. (See the Further Reading section for more information about these writers.)

Several recent writers, however, have chosen boarding schools as the location for fantasy novels, and books by Anthony Horowitz and Jill Murphy in particular support the claim that the originality of J. K. Rowling's work does not lie specifically in her creation of a School of Wizardry. To say that Harry Potter was not the first child to go to boarding school to learn magic in no way reduces the achievement of J. K. Rowling, whose popularity is ample evidence of her success in 'taking the genre to its extreme edge' (Kirkpatrick, 2000: 286).

It is not difficult to locate within the Harry Potter books so far published many instances in common with the traditional exponents of the school-story tradition. As Sims (2000: 17) admits, Hogwarts 'departs from the traditional only in two small points: it is mixed; and it is magical'. While *Harry Potter and the Philosopher's Stone* (1997) does not actually begin with the train chronotope, when it does occur (Chapter Six), once Harry has managed to arrive at the magical platform Nine and Three-Quarters, everything becomes very familiar. Fond farewells are being taken from families, trunks being stowed away, twins are in evidence and the prefects have compartments to themselves. Ron Beasley's family background at Hogwarts is uncannily similar to that of the twins in Antonia Forest's *Autumn Term*. He tells Harry that he has a lot to live up to: 'Bill was Head Boy and Charlie was captain of Quidditch. Now Percy's a Prefect. Fred and George mess around a lot, but they still get really good marks. ... Everyone expects me to do as well as the others, but if I do, it's no big deal, because they did it first' (75).

This introduction of the boy who is to become one of Harry's two best friends immediately launches the reader into an environment in which success at sport and winning for your House are key factors. Like many series about girls' schools but fewer of those set in boys' schools, Rowling's books, at least at the point to which the series has reached at the time of writing, can be seen as affording an element of *bildungsroman* in their gradual development of Harry's character. Nevertheless, in some respects Rowling's boarding-school world has more affinities with the boys' school sub-genre than with the girls'. While the headmaster, Dumbledore, is undoubtedly a sympathetic figure, many of the teachers are so stereotyped as virtually to become comic figures, and on the whole they lack the empathy with pupils which is characteristic of some of the best writers for girls. So far in the series, there has been little emphasis on a musical or dramatic entertainment as the climax of an extended period during which the pupils' creativity is being developed.

The major difference between Rowling's work and the traditional 'realist' school story lies in the fact that in each book Harry is presented with situations which pose a threat to his own life and, increasingly, to the future of the world. Such life-and-death issues are far more the province of fantasy than of the stories which have been considered so far in this chapter. As a result, while the kind of behaviour which is censured in the traditional story, such as 'sneakiness', meanness and snobbery, is certainly not advocated (Draco Malfoy is constantly presented as an example of someone far too conceited about his distinguished background), the key virtues which in Dumbledore's speech at the end of the first volume are shown as winning Gryffindor House the house cup are: skill at chess as exhibited by Ron; logical thinking on the part of Hermione; and, most important of all, 'pure nerve and outstanding courage' as displayed by Harry himself (221). The other books in the series also suggest that Rowling wants her reader to be aware in particular of the importance of courage and integrity.

Conclusion

It would be rash to come to any overall conclusions after what has had to be a selective treatment of only a small group of the very considerable number of books within the sub-genre of the girls' school story. However, one thing does appear to be beyond challenge: the school story is far from being either dead or in terminal decline. It has, however, undergone considerable changes. While it has never been as monolithic as the selective treatment here might make it appear, any semblance of uniformity has now vanished. The traditional girls' boarding-school story still attracts twenty-first-century readers, though its popularity is inevitably less than that of Hogwarts, Harry Potter's mixed and magic boarding school. The day school is a pervasive setting in the genres of both realism and fantasy, allowing the writer to incorporate themes from the everyday world while retaining the authorial advantages of an environment free from the presence of parents. It is impossible to forecast future developments within this genre, but it is likely that, as in the past, they will continue to both reflect and subvert the society which the schools are at the same time within and outside.

WORKS CITED AND FURTHER READING

Primary Texts

Blyton, E., *The O'Sullivan Twins* (London: Atlantic Book Publishing, 1967; first published 1942).

Brent-Dyer, E., *Exploits of the Chalet Girls* (London: Collins, 1972; first published 1933).

Brent-Dyer, E., *The Wrong Chalet School* (London: May Fair Books, 1970; first published 1952).

Forest, A., *Autumn Term* (Harmondsworth: Penguin, 1977; first published 1948).

Rowling, J. K., *Harry Potter and the Philosopher's Stone* (London: Bloomsbury, 1997).

Critical Texts

Auchmuty, R., *A World of Girls: The Appeal of the Girls' School Story* (London: Women's Press, 1992).

Cadogan, M., *Chin Up, Chest Out, Jemima* (Haslemere: Bonnington Books, 1989).

Cadogan, M. and Craig, P., *You're a Brick, Angela: The Girls' School Story, 1879–1975* (London: Gollancz, 1986).

Kirkpatrick, R. J., *The Encyclopaedia of Boys' School Stories* (Aldershot: Ashgate, 2000).

Musgrave, P. W., *From Brown to Bunter: The Life and Death of the School Story* (London: Routledge, 1985).

Richards, J., *Happiest Days: The Public Schools in English Fiction* (Manchester: Manchester University Press, 1988).

Sims, S. and Clare, H., *The Encyclopaedia of Girls' School Stories* (Aldershot: Ashgate, 2000).

Tucker, N. (ed.), *School Stories: From Bunter to Buckeridge* (London: NCRCL, 1999).

Tucker, N. and Reynolds, K. (eds), *Enid Blyton: A Celebration and Reappraisal* (London: NCRCL, 1997).

Whited, L., *The Ivory Tower and Harry Potter: Perspectives of a Literary Phenomenon* (Missouri: University of Missouri Press, 2002).

Children's Books

Ashley, B., *The Trouble with Donovan Croft* (Oxford: Oxford University Press, 1974).

Blyton, E., *Claudine at St Clare's* (London: Atlantic Book Publishing, 1967; first published 1944).

Brent-Dyer, E., *A Genius at the Chalet School* (London: May Fair Books, 1969; first published 1956).

Cross, G., *The Demon Headmaster* (Oxford: Oxford University Press, 1982).

Digby, A., *Second Term at Trebizon* (London: Penguin, 1988; first published 1979).

Fine, A., *Bill's New Frock* (London: Methuen, 1989).

Forest, A., *End of Term* (London: Faber, 1959).

Horowitz, A., *Groosham Grange* (London: Walker Books, 1995; first published 1988).

Kemp, G., *The Turbulent Term of Tyke Tiler* (Harmondsworth: Penguin, 1981; first published 1977).

Leeson, R., *Grange Hill Rules OK?* (London: Collins, 1980).

Murphy, J., *The Worst Witch* (London: Penguin, 1988; first published 1974).

Swindells, R., *Room 13* (London: Doubleday, 1989); *Inside the Worm* (London: Doubleday, 1993).

Ure, J., *Jam Today* (London: Hutchinson, 1992).

Sociology, Politics, the Family: Children and Families in Anglo-American Children's Fiction, 1920–60

Kimberley Reynolds

KEY TEXTS

J. Lankester Brisley, *Milly-Molly-Mandy* (1928)
B. Cleary, *Beezus and Ramona* (1955)
D. Edwards, *My Naughty Little Sister* (1951)
E. Garnett, *The Family from One End Street* (1937)
N. Streatfeild, *Ballet Shoes* (1936)
L. Ingalls Wilder, *Little House in the Big Woods* (1932)

---

*Writing in the sixteenth century, the essayist Montaigne noted that 'There is scarcely any less bother in the running of a family than in the running of an entire state (*Essais, book 1, chapter 39*). Four centuries later, Dodie Smith likened the family to a 'dear octopus from which we never quite escape' (*Dear Octopus, 1938*). Ideas about the family may change, but from the earliest examples of writing for children, the family has played a central role. This makes it a useful topic for identifying changing social attitudes in children's literature over time. In this chapter, Kimberley Reynolds combines a focus on representations of the family with a broadly political reading of mid-twentieth-century texts to show how the interactions between ideological, psychological and economic constructions of the family affect the kind of texts produced for children at all levels. Specifically, the analyses here illustrate how ideas about what a child 'should' be like, how they 'ought' to be parented, what happens inside their minds, and appropriate ways of imaging them in texts for child readers are affected by current thinking about families and aspirations on the part of adults for future generations.*

In 1945, the poster advertising Children's Book Week (an event launched in the United States in 1919 to encourage reading and enjoyment of children's books) featured a family gathered together in what appears to be the father's study or den (see Figure 1). They are surrounded by books, and are clearly consulting an atlas and other information books to help them find out about some location on the globe at which they are all gazing. Given that the oldest

Figure 1   Gertrude Howe's Children's Book Week poster (1945)

son of the family, which consists of mother, father and three children, is wearing a navy uniform and the date advertises the week of 11–17 November, the image is recognizable as a narrative painting; 11 November is, of course, the anniversary of the armistice of the First World War, and in November 1945, the end of World War II was still fresh in the mind. Presumably, the family has come together to say goodbye to the son, who has enlisted in the navy, and they are looking up the location of his first port of call. Significantly, however, this is an image of peace, not war. The Children's Book Week theme, which dominates the top of the image, is 'United Through Books', and powerfully associates children's reading with efforts to achieve a lasting peace and a secure future. The word 'united', indeed, not only refers to the family itself, but conjures up images of the United Nations, which was to replace the League of Nations a few months after the 1945 Book Week.

This image usefully encapsulates many of the issues that will be developed in this chapter. First, it presents in an unquestioning way, a very particular construction of the family; a construction that dominated children's literature in the English-speaking world for the first half of the twentieth century. Although many of the characteristics and values associated with the pictured family still pertain at the start of the twenty-first century, much about it clearly belongs to a by-gone world. Interestingly, although many of the best known children's books of all time were written between 1920 and 1950, it is a period that has received very little critical attention, perhaps in part because of the view of the child, and particularly the child in the family, that the books of this period tend to provide. This view generally paid little attention to the child's feelings and emotional responses; readers today tend to be more sympathetic to the presentation of childhood in children's books after 1950, which is much more alert to children's psychological and emotional development and well-being. The reasons for this difference will become clear in the course of this chapter, which takes as its focus the depiction of children in family fiction between 1920 and 1960.

Families past and present

The term 'family' is so *familiar* (a word that shares the same Latin root, *familia*, which refers to people and things known intimately) that we rarely stop to consider what it means: *of course* we know what a family is. In fact, in the twenty-first century, most of us probably use the term loosely, to signify a number of relationships. Biologically, we use the word 'family' to mean those who are related to us by blood or through marriage, but socially and legally other definitions are also accepted. For instance, someone who is not a blood relative may legally be incorporated into a family through the process of adoption, and titles such as 'aunt' and 'uncle' are often conferred on family friends to acknowledge a special relationship with the children of another household. Similarly, saying someone 'is family', connotes a special, insider relationship with members of a group, whatever their biological relationships.

In the west today, families are usually described as 'nuclear' (mother, father and child[ren]), 'extended' (parents, child[ren] and other relatives), 'lone parent' (when children are largely or entirely raised by one of their biological parents) or 'blended' (families comprised of parents and children from previous relationships). Some children experience more than one kind of family, either serially or simultaneously. Clearly, the composition of present-day families is neither given nor permanent.

In the same way, the social meaning of 'the family' is constantly being revised and reconstructed. Currently we tend to think of families as important emotional units – the way you feel about and interact with the people you live with tends to be regarded as more important than a shared gene pool. But this has not always been the case; for much of history, the family was more important as an economic unit and power base than as a source of emotional strength and gratification. Before state benefits and other forms of social provision, your family was your security: you worked for your family and your family looked after you, for better or for worse. This was not simply a practical arrangement for individuals; the family has been an increasingly important social tool for governments, particularly in the transition from early economic systems such as feudalism through the various forms of capitalism that succeeded one another over the past two hundred years.

According to Frederic Jameson (1991: xviii–xxii), there have been three waves of capitalism:

- market capitalism (late eighteenth to early nineteenth centuries): driven by the Industrial Revolution in tandem with Romantic philosophy and aesthetics;
- monopoly capitalism (late nineteenth to mid-twentieth centuries): associated with technology, electricity, the creation of the consumer and the rise of modernism as an intellectual and artistic mode;
- consumer capitalism (mid-twentieth century to the present): shaped by information technologies, service industries, multinationalism, and marketing, and resulting in what is termed postmodernity.

Each of these stages has affected our understanding of the family. We live in an era of consumer capitalism, and critics such as Jack Zipes maintain that its values are putting the family under severe strain. In *Sticks and Stones* (2001), Zipes argues that as a direct consequence of the incessant urge to consume and to develop brand loyalties, many young people feel a stronger sense of belonging to corporate culture – say, to groups of consumers of Nike or Coca-Cola products – than to their families. Indeed, among the most popular television programmes of the 1990s was *Friends*, in which families are incidental: the things that count are your friends, and the lifestyle you can create together. Your friends become your family of choice.

These values are very much at odds with those expressed in children's literature written during the first half of the last century. In texts such as Joyce Lankester Brisley's Milly-Molly-Mandy books (1928–67), Laura Ingalls Wilder's Little House series (1932–43), Eve Garnett's *The Family from One*

End Street and its sequels (1937–62), Dorothy Edwards's My Naughty Little Sister stories (1952–74), and Beverly Cleary's books about the Quimby family (1955–) all aspects of the child's life are bound up in and shaped by the family. In the absence of a biological family of your own, necessity requires you to seek out or make one for yourself, as Noel Streatfeild's Fossil 'sisters' do in *Ballet Shoes* (1936). Not only do the three orphan girls – one rescued off a ship, one from Russia, and one the daughter of an impoverished ballerina – choose their own family name of Fossil (because the old gentleman they refer to as Great-Uncle Matthew, or Gum, collected them on his travels as he had previously collected fossils), but they devise a ceremonial vow for birthdays and special occasions which unites them in the determination to make their chosen name meaningful (see Chapter 3, 'The Fossil Family make a Vow').

In postmodern culture, the family may be said to have degenerated to the condition of a commodity, but this attitude only serves to highlight the relationship between the family and the prevailing economic system. Postmodernity is a condition of affluence, created largely through the idea of choice. It also depends on high proportions of double-income families, which inevitably make the home and any children in it less central to daily life than was the case for earlier generations. The consequent change in attitude to the family, which has led successive British governments to emphasize the need to return to 'family values', is a marked departure from constructions of the family under earlier forms of capitalism, when money tended to be generated and/or controlled by a single, usually patriarchal, figure in each family unit. This figure, accordingly, exercised considerable power, both practically and emotionally.

Before the end of the Second World War, however, there was a strong and forcefully articulated ideology of the family. This held that the family:

- was indispensable for emotional security;
- was fundamental to the creation of responsible citizens;
- and acted as a conservative force against the cultural degeneration some people believed was inextricably linked to the rise of modernism, with its links to *ennui*, anxiety, women's rights and less manly men.

The Children's Book Week poster epitomizes this ideology, placing father at the centre of the family, his oldest son preparing to go out into the world and do his duty, while mother stands behind and supplements the lesson. Not only is this family patriarchal, it is also white and middle class; all of these values and attributes characterize Anglo-American children's fiction of this period. As a corollary to them, there arose an equally influential belief system based on the centrality of the wife (usually also a mother) in the home.

This situation did not arise accidentally; rather, it was in many ways a conscious social project designed to improve the lives and living conditions of the masses – or put another way, to improve the physiques of the workforce and, through improved health and education, make them less costly to governments. It is important to be alert to the two sides to this endeavour; it is easy – and not inaccurate – to construct the policies that brought about such changes positively, and to show how the most vulnerable and dependent in society could benefit from them. Research at the time, such as B. Seebohm Rowntree's *Poverty: A Study of Town Life* (1901), showed that large numbers of the children in the UK were living in poverty, indicating that the need for social change was urgent. This chapter is concerned with the period beginning in the 1920s; however, it is impossible to forget that an ideology of human perfection with a concentration on bodily perfection, often achieved through regimes of health and fitness, flourished at this time. Debates about the pros and cons of eugenics, which studied how the human race could be improved physically and mentally, were rife, and eventually mobilized by the Nazi party to justify the extermination of whole social and ethnic groups on the grounds that the Nazis were building a 'master race'.

In the majority of the English-speaking world at this time, the family was the basic unit of society and the lynchpin of social change. It was assumed that children would be taught to become responsible and productive citizens by their families. As symbolized by the American family pictured in the Children's Book Week poster, the family represented the centre of the world, and everything the child[ren] needed was provided within it.

Mothers were regarded as particularly important in shaping the next generation in accordance with the needs of society, but for much of the period under discussion it was not assumed that all women were naturally or equally good mothers. This meant that a variety of checks on the development of children (Were they the right height? The right weight? Were their ears, eyes and lungs working properly?) were put into place, creating both a mass system of monitoring children and, though this was not discussed publicly, a means of checking on how well individual mothers were raising their children. Reactions to such interventions were mixed, and often perceived differently by the different classes, as will be seen in the contrasting attitudes of the carers in *Ballet Shoes* and the Ruggles parents in *The Family from One End Street*. In more remote areas, such as the back woods and vast farmlands of early twentieth-century North America and Australia, such systems of surveillance were not practical, but mothers there – and everywhere – were encouraged to consult the growing number of experts, whose guidance echoed government concerns about the need for a healthy population. Perhaps more significantly, their views on proper parenting shaped parent–child relationships and social attitudes to the child for generations to come. Indeed, dependence on baby and child-care gurus continues; however, from the 1920s to the 1950s, the new *science* of parenting, designed to produce healthy, able-bodied, educable and governable subjects, was in its heyday. Throughout these decades there was a general tendency to look to science for answers to virtually every question or problem in circulation, and what looks now like a rather naive trust in scientific opinion; meanwhile, science, medicine and the media energetically promoted the virtues of responsible, trained parenting. However, what was taught was not consistent throughout the period, and perhaps nowhere is the fact that both childhood and parenting are social constructs made more clear than in the shifting views on what comprised good parenting, 'normal' childhood, and the ideal family.

Children's literature and social constructions of the child and the family

Two series that typify the dominant construction of the family at this time appeared at almost the same moment and continue to be popular today. First on the scene was *Milly-Molly-Mandy* (1928), written and illustrated by Joyce Lankester Brisley and set in a rural village in England. Four years later, Laura Ingalls Wilder's hugely successful *Little House in the Big Woods* (1932) commenced the series of books plotting the life and travels of the Ingalls family, whose head (Pa) couldn't resist the persistent call to 'go West!' While superficially these books are very different, in that Milly-Molly-Mandy's world is entirely based on the known, the civilized, and the routine, while Laura's is the unknown, the wild wilderness, and the vagaries of nature, they are united in their constructions of what a family is and does. Both, for instance, are set during what is technically part of Jameson's epoch of monopoly capitalism, but both actually create a world which seems much older – even pre-industrial.

The two girls grow up in rural environments, and though for Laura nature is often so extreme and demanding that it doesn't function as a metaphor for the innocence and creativity of childhood in the way it is often thought to do in children's literature, it nevertheless teaches her and her siblings lessons that shape their characters. In *Milly-Molly-Mandy*, nature is much more benign and forms part of an overall view of children as innocent and childhood as an idyll. In the Milly-Molly-Mandy stories, it is almost perpetually summer, a point the illustrations emphasize, for one of the first things we learn is that Milly-Molly-Mandy wears a short pink-and-white-striped cotton frock in summer and a red serge one in winter, but only one picture shows her bundled up in warm clothes. Even the descriptions of her winter garments make the seasonal change nothing more than the opportunity for wearing her 'nice warm woolly gloves that Grandma had knitted for her, and Aunty's best nice warm woolly scarf, lent for the occasion' (93). By contrast, winter for Laura is a time of retreat. Like the animals around them, the Ingalls family stays inside as much as possible, and when they do venture out, elaborate preparations have to be made. After a Christmas visit from her cousins, Laura watches them put on their travelling clothes for the journey home. The clothing they don to keep them warm for the journey requires them to be wrapped up by the two mothers:

> They pulled heavy woollen stockings over the woollen stockings and shoes that they were already wearing. They put on mittens and coats and warm hoods and shawls, and wrapped mufflers around their necks and thick woollen veils over their faces. Ma slipped hot baked potatoes into their pockets to keep their fingers warm, and Aunt Eliza's flatirons were hot on the stove, ready to put at their feet in the sled. The blankets and the quilts and the buffalo robes were warmed, too. (81–2)

Clearly, the practical relationships between children and nature in these two texts are different, but much of their enduring appeal undoubtedly lies in the sense that both are set in 'natural' worlds. The pressures associated with industrialization and technology, modernity and postmodernity, are entirely absent from both books and their protagonists' experiences. This is a major source of the feelings of security and harmony that characterize the texts, and it underpins the view of the family they offer. Both Lankester Brisley and Ingalls Wilder treat it as 'natural' that children grow up with two parents, that there are strong connections with relations, and that every member of the family will be productive. Milly-Molly-Mandy and Laura spend much of their time, and derive much of their pleasure from, helping other members of the family with daily chores. On the first page of the first Milly-Molly-Mandy story, readers are told:

> Now everybody in the nice white cottage with the thatched roof had some particular job to do – even Milly-Molly-Mandy. ... Milly-Molly-Mandy's legs were short ... but they were very lively, just right for running errands. So Milly-Molly-Mandy was quite busy, fetching and carrying things, and taking messages.   (9–10)

In the same way, we learn that, 'Laura and Mary helped Ma with the work', and then follow not only detailed descriptions of daily tasks, from wiping the dishes to making the beds, but also the litany of never-ending chores that females are required to do in the home while the men are labouring elsewhere:

> Wash on Monday,
> Iron on Tueday,
> Mend on Wednesday,
> Churn on Thursday,
> Clean on Friday,
> Bake on Saturday,
> Rest on Sunday.   (29)

Though both live in times after electricity, trains and other 'modern' inventions are available in towns and cities, virtually every form of work described is done by hand; even when a 'wonderful machine' comes to the Big Woods (Chapter 12) to thresh the grain, its power is supplied by horses.

Another assumption of both texts is that parental authority is unquestioned, because parents are invariably loving and wise, and make decisions that are in the best interests of the family as well as of individual children. Milly-Molly-Mandy is in fact the only child in an extended family (reflecting the shift to smaller families in the early twentieth century), and all the adults who surround her are given equal love and respect. Just as the weather is always mellow in Milly-Molly-Mandy-Land, so no one ever gets cross, and there is no need to discipline any of the children. The Ingalls children, with only each other to play with and very few diversions, do occasionally sulk and disobey – Pa keeps a strap on the wall for precisely this purpose – but whatever Ma and Pa decide to do with or to their children is shown as right, proper, and their duty. This difference is important, too, for what it tells us about the kinds of texts these are. Despite its grounding in the ordinary – even repetitive – experiences of an ordinary child, and its rejection of all things fantastical or psychological, *Milly-Molly-Mandy* is a fantasy of perfect childhood. It not only promises that Milly-Molly-Mandy will eventually become a valuable member of society, but shows her already taking her place in her little community by successfully doing the kinds of jobs that the women around her do: she minds the shop, helps in the home, and with Little Friend Susan, looks after the local baby. It is worth noting at this point that almost all the children featured in the texts discussed here are female, and most of the work they do is associated with the home and traditionally female roles such as nurturing and cleaning. There are exceptions: Milly-Molly-Mandy's friend Billy Blunt is asked to do jobs such as painting the gardening equipment and weeding, and Milly-Molly-Mandy is not averse to helping him, but on the whole, childhood is constructed as part of the feminine domain.

In both texts, the parents treat the job of parenting as important, but significantly, never require the intervention of an 'expert': parenting is shown to be as natural as childhood. In many ways, the construction of the family as a self-sufficient, loving and successful unit in a stress-free, often rural or semi-rural environment, pervaded English-language children's literature for most of the twentieth century (significantly, a very different tradition pertained in parts of Europe). However, developments in the world beyond children's books were not ignored by writers and illustrators as the century matured, especially as these related to views of the child in the family, and outside intervention in child-rearing.

Women and children first

In the 1920s, the role played by the family – and especially by mothers – in what was regarded as 'proper' socialization was paramount. The *Mothercraft Manual* (published between 1922 and 1954), for instance, taught that 'Self-control, obedience, the recognition of authority, and, later, respect for elders are all outcomes of the first year's training' (Cunningham, 1996: 175). That training, it was assumed, would be provided by the family. Of all the parenting experts from this period, one in particular stamped his view on how infants should be handled by their parents – a New Zealand doctor, Truby King. King's message to parents was often interpreted as a warning against spoiling children. He spelled out the dangers of kissing and cuddling babies and small children, and emphasized the importance of strict routines covering every aspect of child behaviour, from sleeping and feeding to crying and nappy changing.

To be fair to Dr King, his advice grew out of a culture in which infant mortality was extremely high: when he first began practising in New Zealand, 1 baby in 40 died each year of infant diarrhoea, but his strictures on cleanliness and reduced contact rapidly helped reduce this to 1 per 1000 (Cunningham, 1996: 175–6). However, as interpreted by the media and over time, the King method seemed to drive a wedge between parents and children, and in its claims that doctor (or more broadly science) knows best, it questioned the very validity of the family. Once society was sufficiently organized, the thinking went, children could be taken out of the limited environment of home and raised in purposely designed, excellently resourced environments under the guidance of experts. When every child had a balanced diet, regular routines, abundant and educational toys, and plenty of fresh air, exercise and space, it was argued, the fullest expression of human potential would be achieved, and criminal behaviour effectively eliminated. With the backing of the International Infant Welfare Movement, this view of child-rearing lasted into the 1940s. Though ultimately this view presumed that the family would become obsolete, until that event, parents were encouraged to raise their children according to widely circulated precepts and guidelines.

But not everyone accepted this socially orientated model of child-rearing and its attitude to the family. An alternative, more individual model, also presented as 'scientific', was offered by those who believed the child's *psychological* rather than physical needs were paramount. As psychoanalysis became increasingly familiar to the professional classes, experts began to offer more child-centred models of parenting; its advocates went so far as to claim that the rise of fascism in Europe could be linked to overly controlling and oppressive child-rearing practices which resulted in such feelings as rage and the desire for omnipotence (176). Accordingly, during the 1930s and 1940s, alternatives to the Truby King method emerged. These stressed the enjoyment to be found in parenting, the need to understand the world from the child's perspective, and the centrality of the family in the child's life and psyche. They also took care to reassure parents that their children would not be spoiled by expressions of affection and the creation of strong bonds, but that this was a natural part of parenting. In an obvious refutation of the King philosophy, which undoubtedly contributed to its phenomenal success, Dr Benjamin Spock's *Baby and Child Care* (1946) asserted:

> Your baby is born to be a reasonable, friendly human being. ... *He doesn't have to be sternly trained.* You may hear people say that you have to get your baby strictly regulated in his feeding, sleeping, bowel movements, and other habits – but don't believe this. (19–20)

In part, this shift was possible because of the reduction in family size. By the beginning of the twentieth century, families in which six or seven children survived (usually from several more pregnancies) were common; by the 1930s, most households, like that in the Children's Book Week poster, consisted of father, mother and two or three children. Single-child families such as Milly-Molly-Mandy's were also on the increase, and were attracting the attention of child psychologists.

With the exception of the war years, this emphasis on parenting as a pleasure and a creative opportunity tended to prevail. Women in particular were encouraged to embrace motherhood as their vocation, and accordingly even those who could afford it, began to scorn professional care. This change was reflected in children's literature with the demise of the nanny as a character, being replaced by that of the mother-at-home. In tandem with this shift was the rise of an ethos that is now generally associated with late twentieth-century legislation stimulated by the United Nations Convention on the Rights of the Child. The spirit behind the UN Convention, however, has its origins in debates about childhood earlier in the last century, when the view that all children are entitled to a proper childhood first began to appear.

As childhood began to be valued and respected, there was also an effort to prolong and define it – once again creating roles for scientists and other experts. For instance, attempts were made to understand children's minds, asking questions about how they learned and how they acquired language, or trying to ascertain the difference between instinct and intelligence. Inevitably, such considerations led to tests and measurements, and new definitions of what was 'normal' and 'abnormal'. These ideas are treated with varying degrees of respect in the literature of this period. Two contrasting examples are provided by Noel Streatfeild's *Ballet Shoes* (1936) and Eve Garnett's *The Family from One End Street* (1937).

Despite the fact that the three Fossil girls come from very different backgrounds and know virtually nothing about their parentage, the Cromwell Road household in which they grow up is undoubtedly middle class. Even when Gum has been away for longer than anticipated and money is short, the establishment includes the old family nanny and a cook (in 1936 the nanny figure had not yet been replaced by the mother-at-home). To make ends meet, their guardian, Sylvia, takes in lodgers, but these too are entirely middle class: two female academics, a dance teacher, and an affluent young married couple. The household combines middle-class acceptance of the law and of all government interventions, with an equally middle-class network of connections, ownership of property and respect for individuality. Accordingly, when Pauline, the oldest of the Fossils, obtains her first paid role in a ballet and is required to go to County Hall to be examined by the Education Officer in order to obtain a licence permitting her to work, the text offers three equally telling reactions. First, all the adults accept the procedures without question, and regard them as necessary to protect the well-being of the children. Significantly, Noel Streatfeild learned about the legal and financial controls relating to child performers during her brief career as an actress. Although she based the training the girls received on an elite academy run by 'Italia Conti', she was more impressed by the working-class girls who made up the dancing troup in a pantomime in Newcastle. According to Streatfeild's biographer, she was impressed by the way such girls were 'rescued' from overlarge and inadequate families by the state. The legislation that required the Fossils to obtain licences also required real children to be taken into care, and to be given the kind of nutritional meals and regulated lives and access to education that their families could not afford to provide (Bull, 1984: 95–6).

The second reaction also relates to the various adult characters responsible for the children; all fear that they will be found inadequate by the official measures, and because they believe in them, it is implied they will accept the judgement. Thus Nana worries about the children's health and growth, Dr Jakes and Dr Smith 'fussed inside themselves in case [Pauline] should not be up to the required standard' (*Ballet Shoes*: 159), and Sylvia is terrified that she will be looked at 'with scorn as one trying to make money out of an adopted child' (160). The most telling reaction, however, is that of the narrator, who assures readers that, 'There could be no doubt that Pauline was in the most bounding health, and rather ahead of her age from an educational point of view' (159). The fact that the children have been educated at home is given unstinting approval when Pauline comes through every test and proves herself to be 'a most highly educated person' in the judgement of the Education Officer (162). She is also in robust health, and not only are the children's earnings protected by law, but their guardian intends to refuse their contributions to the household coffers.

In all ways, then, *Ballet Shoes* both accepts the views of 'experts' on child development, and vindicates middle-class child-rearing practices which grow from them. A rather different perspective was offered the following year in *The Family from One End Street*. Undoubtedly one reason for this difference is that Garnett chose to write about a working-class family. Having spent her childhood reading Victorian children's literature, in which waifs, orphans and the children of the poor feature prominently, Garnett was struck by their absence in twentieth-century children's fiction. Her career as an artist began in the 1920s, a time of high unemployment and low wages, which reached a crescendo following the General Strike of 1926. In 1927 she was invited to illustrate Evelyn Sharp's *The London Child*, which required her to look closely at the lives, lifestyles and children of the poor. What she saw and learned stimulated her to begin writing and illustrating her own books, frequently featuring working-class characters and especially children, culminating in the short series of books featuring the Ruggles family: *The Family from One End Street, Further Adventures of the Family from One End Street* (1956) and *Holiday at the Dew Drop Inn* (1962).

Critical reaction to Garnett's books has been mixed, and over the years there has been a tendency to move away from celebrating her for breaking the mould of children's literature by choosing to feature working-class family life, and instead to find her depiction of working-class life patronizing. When *The Family from One End Street* first appeared, however, her efforts were loudly applauded. It was widely translated, and in 1937 was the second book to be awarded the prestigious Carnegie Medal.

While the adult characters responsible for the Fossil sisters accede to the authority and wisdom of officialdom without demur, the Ruggleses are considerably less impressed with bureaucrats and their experts – especially when it comes to raising a family. One reason for their attitude is that the Ruggles parents, and particularly Jo the father, are often bemused by the forms and language that represent authority for them. When their daughter Kate is awarded a scholarship to attend the secondary school and Mr Ruggles is required to complete various forms to secure it and money to help with the costs of the school uniform, it not only 'take[s] more out of him than two days' hard work' (33), but his handwriting is so poor that the authorities believe he has only one child instead of seven, and turn him down. Eventually the mistake is resolved satisfactorily, but in the Ruggles household, attitudes to the State are very mixed.

The book was written just before the Second World War, and though there was as yet no comprehensive Welfare State in the UK, Jo at least is a firm believer that it is the government's responsibility to provide a safety net ('The government'll do summat towards it ...', 32). At the same time, the closing chapters of the book adopt a sympathetic line towards trade unions, which the government had so firmly put down in 1926, with the family going to London to ride with the children's Uncle Charlie in the city's Cart Horse Parade. Uncle Charlie, whose prize-winning horse is named Bernard Shaw [Shaw was a well-known Fabian Socialist], plans to go to night school to take up political debating.

While Jo's attitude to authority may be ambivalent, his wife's views on the experts who want to impose their opinions on the way she raises her family are unambiguous. This is implicit in the size of the family, which is of Victorian proportions at a time when, as we have seen, advice on health and home economics was resulting in families with many fewer children. In chapter 6, 'The Baby Show', Rosie Ruggles discounts the opinions of 'the Welfare', and is outraged by the mystique of the doctor, who offers platitudes about when baby William's teeth will come through, seems to question the authenticity of

Figure 2   Mothers and children as drawn by Eve Garnett for
The Family from One End Street

his birth certificate, 'and then he writes no end of things in a little book' which he won't let Rosie see. Worst of all, Rosie tells her friend, are the two uniformed nurses who have come to help judge the baby contest, in which William has been entered. Their attempts at conversation and advice she dismisses as, 'just talk it is, they learns it them at the Hospital – it don't mean nothing' (103).

Rosie's dismissive attitude to the experts is given a very specific context: the local baby show. As early as 1912, as part of international attempts to improve the health and reduce the mortality of babies, such competitions became widespread. Beginning in the USA, they soon spread to the UK and Europe, and not long after began to find their way into children's fiction. While the authorities began the competitions to encourage better standards of hygiene and child-rearing, in Garnett's text at least, their efficacy is questioned. As a mother, Rosie Ruggles has proved to be as effective as all the women involved in rearing the Fossil children put together. The Ruggles children, while occasionally succumbing to the ordinary round of childhood diseases, are healthy, active, willing to work, and have a strong sense of family unity. They get the kind of love and individual attention they need, and their individual characters and talents are recognized by their proud parents. Baby William wins first prize in his category, and Rosie suspects if she'd paid a little less attention to hygiene and more to her husband (Jo proposed giving the baby dog biscuits to help him cut the crucial first teeth), William would have been the overall winner.

While *The Family at One End Street* undoubtedly celebrates family values, it is also a radical text in its willingness to critique the wisdom of authority, and its recognition that many parents resented heavy-handed state intervention, seeing it as questioning their ability to look after their families properly. Rosie Ruggles' confidence in her mothering may have looked challenging in 1937; shortly, however, new views on mothering would vindicate her. In the 1940s and 1950s, experts such as Benjamin Spock and D. W. Winnicott rejected the scientific and interventionist efforts to teach women how to mother (many of which had been found wanting), and espoused the doctrine of the 'good enough' mother. According to Winnicott, 'the best mothering comes out of natural self-reliance. ... Administrative tidiness, the dictates of hygiene, a laudable urge towards the promotion of bodily health ... and all sorts of other things get between the mother and her baby' (1957: 9). The new child-care experts were distinctly on the side of the mother – but the attitudes they were combating were becoming more and more complex as increasingly critical analyses of the role of the family were finding their way into society, not least through fiction.

New theories, new families: towards the 1950s

Thus far, this chapter has concentrated on real families, real policies, and fictional works that largely reflect them, but there was a very strong and popular antidote to this official version of the family provided in the literature –

including some of the children's literature – produced between 1920 and 1960. In 'Eccentric Families in the Fiction of Adolescence from the 1920s to the 1940s', Nicola Humble points out that very often the central characters of popular books written by women from the 1920s to the 1950s are adolescent girls. Such books have tended to be read by teenagers as well as women, making them an early example of what is now called 'crossover fiction', or books that appeal equally to audiences of adults and children. Indeed, it could be argued not only that these books appealed to two audiences, but that they also helped to shape the new genre generally referred to as Young Adult (YA) fiction.

It is certainly the case that in the family paradigms outlined above and in most children's literature of this period, childhood was presented as white and (almost invariably) middle class; it was associated with rural, or possibly suburban, environments; it involved plenty of exercise and fresh air, usually taken in the company of loved siblings, and the consumption of vast quantities of healthy food. All this was provided by families headed by two loving parents (though father was frequently absent for work-related reasons). Moreover, the children in such books, typified in the works of Enid Blyton and Arthur Ransome, take their lifestyles for granted: they have no anxieties about money, and never contemplate the need for waged work. (No doubt this security is fundamental to the ability of such fictional children to leave home and family behind in pursuit of mystery and adventure.) All the central children are presented as happy and well adjusted, and the implied expectation is that they will grow up to become productive and responsible citizens, like their parents. The model is unquestioned, and seems to assume that all children and all families are broadly the same – that these are vignettes of what is normal.

By contrast, in both middlebrow novels by women, typified by Nancy Mitford's *The Pursuit of Love* (1945) and Dodie Smith's *I Capture the Castle* (1949), and later works dealing with teenage life, quite different pictures of childhood and family life are provided. Far from taking family life for granted and pushing it safely to the background, such novels focus on the family – especially the children in the family – and show them as *unlike* the world outside. As Humble argues, these works show families as 'profoundly eccentric organisations; idiosyncratic rather than normative' and as forums where 'social values are challenged rather than inculcated' (1998: 79). Precisely because of their eccentricity, the children in these families are self-conscious and develop a fortress-family mentality (us versus the world), created in part through private games, invented languages, and a complex insider culture (77). Another notable difference between the standard children's book and these popular female creations is that the families featured are usually very large; the numerous offspring are haphazardly raised by the usually vague if not neglectful adults around them, and the children tend to be critical or even 'mutinous' (79). They long to leave their families behind and try to make their ways in the world unencumbered by the unfashionable clothes and bizarre behaviour of their relatives.

In their adult forms, such families anticipate and, indeed, may have fuelled the thinking behind the work of R. D. Laing in the 1960s, who suggested that families, far from promoting stability and normality, were likely to be the source of mental illness, and Edmund Leach, who was later to argue that the family, 'with its narrow privacy and tawdry secrets, is the source of all our discontents' (Jonathan Dollimore, in Sinfield, 1983: 61). While such ideas were being articulated with increasing force in the culture at large by 1960, in children's literature they were strongly resisted. Indeed, seminal works of the 1950s, including Dorothy Edwards's series about My Naughty Little Sister, and Beverly Cleary's Beezus and Ramona books, owe much to earlier ways of representing the family, stressing stability, normality, daily routine, and confidence that most children are happy and will grow up to be well adjusted. Nevertheless, between 1920 and 1960, several notable children's books featuring 'eccentric' families appeared and were extremely popular. Undoubtedly the leading exponent of such stories was Noel Streatfeild, and many of the elements Humble identifies can be found in her first children's book, *Ballet Shoes*. Subsequent Streatfeild novels, including those published in the 1960s and 1970s, elaborate on this view of the family, perhaps reflecting growing recognition that family life is more complicated than earlier models had presented it (see the section on Further Reading). Streatfeild's eccentric families are usually large, usually in financial difficulties, and the parents who head them are usually charming but decidedly out of touch.

A child's world

All of the texts discussed so far were written either before, between or during the war years. *My Naughty Little Sister* (1952) and *Beezus and Ramona* (1955) are distinctly postwar in tone, preoccupation, and their view of the child in the family. Both feature two-child, nuclear families living in friendly, predictable communities. Both texts are narrated through the persona of the older sister, and though both narrators regard their siblings as embarrassingly wilful and badly behaved, there is nothing eccentric about their families.

In these ways *My Naughty Little Sister* and *Beezus and Ramona* maintain the traditional prewar view of the family seen in *Milly-Molly-Mandy*, but there is a notable difference. Milly-Molly-Mandy is an uncomplicated child. She gets up and goes about her business in a way that all can observe, and she never succumbs to fears, moods, or the confusion produced by the contradictory behaviour of adults. Edwards's and Cleary's characters, however, are given internal worlds signalled by references to play and imagination, but also clearly explained in terms of motivation and action. For instance, one day when the family plans an outing to a fair, My Naughty Little Sister refuses breakfast, calls her food 'nasty' and spills her milk. The narrator immediately steps in to explain *why* her sister behaved in this way (and by extension, to the child listening to the story why s/he has done similar things in the past): 'Shall I tell you why my naughty little sister hadn't wanted to eat her breakfast? *She was too excited.* And when my naughty little sister was excited, she was very cross and disobedient' (8). Similarly, when Ramona has been particularly naughty one afternoon, Beezus's aunt (a primary school teacher) explains how best to deal with the behaviour in a way that demonstrates knowledge of child psychology:

> 'I wouldn't say anything more about it,' said Aunt Beatrice. 'Lots of times little children are naughty because they want to attract attention. I have an idea that saying nothing about her naughtiness will worry Ramona more than a scolding.' (98)

Unlike Milly-Molly-Mandy, then, these children are not perfect, but 'naughty', a mild term that is very different from the charges of sinfulness and wickedness made against disobedient and badly behaved children in early children's literature, such as Mrs Sherwood's *The Fairchild Family* (1818), which regarded children as the products of original sin. By contrast, 'naughty' children are seen as normal children who behave as they do for understandable reasons, including sibling rivalry (Beezus learns that it is normal not to love her little sister all the time), boredom, anxiety, illness, mistaken beliefs, and as part of elaborate imaginary games. In other words, naughtiness, like play and creativity, is an expression of the child's inner world, a world which Milly-Molly-Mandy seems never to have visited.

As in *Milly-Molly-Mandy*, each chapter in Edwards's and Cleary's books recounts an incident in the daily life of their child-protagonists, but the world is seen and understood from the child's point of view, reflecting the widespread assimilation of psychoanalytic ideas about childhood in society, and the related rise of developmental psychology. The thrust of the books is to explain their own behaviour and feelings to the children who read or hear the stories, and to reassure them that the mistakes they make and the bad feelings they sometimes have are normal and forgivable, and that they are lovable and loved. This psychoanalytic emphasis is the seminal difference between children's literature before and after World War II.

Another way in which these texts construct a view of the family is in their notion of audience. The Naughty Little Sister stories first appeared as stories read aloud on the BBC radio programme *Listen with Mother*. The very name conjures up an image of mother at home, listening with her child[ren] as part of the daily routine. It seems significant that shortly before, the BBC's *Woman's Hour* had broadcast D. W. Winnicott's series of talks about the child, which were also published in 1952 under the title *The Child and the Family*. The following year Dr John Bowlby's very popular *Child Care and the Growth of Love*, in which he stressed the importance of the mother figure in providing affection and security, appeared. Together these new experts reinforced the postwar ideology, so evident in the Children's Book Week image, that women should be in the home fulfilling their roles as wives and mothers; their failure to do so, warned Dr Bowlby, was likely to result in their children becoming juvenile delinquents rather than sailors. Ramona Quimby and My Naughty Little Sister may get into trouble, but the constant presence of their mothers, who manage their daughters lovingly and consistently, ensures that as an adolescent, neither will be found in the juvenile court!

Conclusion

These stories of solidly respectable families headed by parents who clearly understand the importance of their roles, the need for division of labour (fathers at work and mothers at home), and the fact that their offspring have internal worlds which encompass negative feelings such as guilt, anger, greed and resentment as well as more attractive qualities usually associated with childhood, strike an appropriate note on which to end this chapter. The 1950s were years when a great many 'naughty' children turned into rebellious teenagers, and though it took some time for children's literature to start incorporating elements of youth culture, by the end of the decade an impressive new generation of writers had begun to articulate deeper, darker, and considerably more complex views of children, families and society.

WORKS CITED AND FURTHER READING

Primary Texts

(Where primary texts are available in a number of editions, only the original date of publication is given.)

Cleary, B., *Ramona the Pest* (1968); *Ramona the Brave* (1975); *Ramona and her Father* (1977); *Ramona and her Mother* (1979); *Ramona Quimby, Age 8* (1981); *Ramona Forever* (1984); *Ramona's World* (1999).

Edwards, D., *More Naughty Little Sister Stories*; *My Naughty Little Sister and Bad Harry*; *When My Naughty Little Sister was Good*; *My Naughty Little Sister's Friends*.

Garnett, E., *Further Adventures of the Family from One End Street* (1956); *Holiday at the Dew Drop Inn* (1962).

Streatfeild, N., *Apple Bough* (1962); *The Grey Family* (1956); *The Growing Summer* (1966); *The Painted Garden* (1949); *Party Frock* (1956); *Tennis Shoes* (1937); *A Vicarage Childhood* (1963); *White Boots* (1951); *The Years of Grace* (ed.) (1950).

Wilder, L. Ingalls, *By the Shores of Silver Lake* (1940); *Little Town on the Prairie* (1942); *The Long Winter* (1941); *On the Banks of Plum Creek* (1938); *These Happy Golden Years* (1944).

Critical Texts about the Period

Bull, Angela, *Noel Streatfeild* (London: Collins, 1984).
Jameson, F., *Postmodernism: or, The Cultural Logic of Late Capitalism* (London: Verso, 1991).
Marwick, A., *British Society since 1945* (London: Penguin, 1996).
Molloy, T., *Eve Garnett: Artist, Illustrator, Author* (Lewes: Book Guild, 2002).
Mowat, C. L., *Britain Between the Wars, 1918–1940* (Cambridge: Cambridge University Press, 1955).
Sinfield, A., *Literature, Politics and Culture in Britain* (Oxford: Basil Blackwell, 1989).
Sinfield, A. (ed.), *Society and Literature, 1945–1970* (London: Methuen, 1983).
Stevenson, J., *British Society, 1914–45* (London: Penguin, 1984).

Critical Texts about Childhood and Children's Literature

Bowlby, J., *Child Care and the Growth of Love* (Harmondsworth: Penguin, 1953; first published 1951).

Cunningham, H., *Children and Childhood in Western Society since 1500* (London and New York: Longman, 1996).

Humble, N., 'Eccentric Families in the Fiction of Adolescence from the 1920s to the 1940s', in K. Reynolds (ed.), *Childhood Remembered* (London: National Centre for Research in Children's Literature, 1998; republished by Pied Piper Publishing, 2003).

Hunt, P., *An Introduction to Children's Literature* (Oxford and New York: Oxford University Press, 1995).

Hunt, P., 'Retreatism and Advance (1914–1945)', in P. Hunt (ed.), *Children's Literature: An Illustrated History* (Oxford and New York: Oxford University Press, 1995), pp. 192–224.

Martin, J., ' "Get Well Soon!" Representations of Illness in Children's Literature', unpublished MA dissertation, University of Surrey Roehampton, 2001.

Spock, Benjamin, *Baby and Child Care* (New York: Pocket Books, 1946).

Townsend, J. R., *Written for Children: An Outline of English-language Children's Literature* (Harmondsworth: Kestrel, 1983; first published 1965).

Winnicott, D. W., *The Child and the Family* (London: Tavistock, 1957).

Winnicott, D. W., *The Child, the Family and the Outside World* (Harmondsworth: Penguin, 1976; first published 1957).

Fantasy, Psychology and Feminism: Jungian Readings of Classic British Fantasy Fiction

Susan Hancock

Fantasy is one of the most important genres (see Box 1.1) in children's literature. It has attracted high-profile writers across the centuries, and currently the work of fantasy writers such as J. K. Rowling, Philip Pullman and J. R. R. Tolkien is attracting considerable media attention. For this reason, fantasy is discussed in some detail in more than one chapter in this book; Chapters 6 and 9 are also concerned with fantasy, and you may find it helpful to read them alongside this discussion by Susan Hancock of two well-known British fantasies.

Since at least the last century, critics and educationists in particular have been ambivalent about the status of fantasy. Many regard it as an inferior, regressive literature, which perhaps explains why it is so strongly associated with children's literature. Yet in the closing decades of the twentieth century, versions of fantasy such as Magic Realism and highly regarded examples of postmodern fiction such as the novels of Salman Rushdie have spoken importantly about contemporary issues. Indeed, it could be argued that some modern novelists have turned to fantasy to find an appropriate idiom for contemporary fiction, pointing to an important function of children's literature in culture. When genres fall out of favour in mainstream fiction they are frequently relegated to the nursery (as is the case with myths, legends, folk and fairy tales, and nonsense as well as fantasy), where they are preserved for future use. While in the realm of children's literature, however, they are not languishing, but, through interaction with juvenile audiences and often illustrators as well, subtly metamorphosing into modes suitable for new audiences of different ages. As this chapter shows, in the case of fantasy, this laying down of material is closely related to what Jung called the collective unconscious, resulting in forms that are rich in archetypes and resonances.

Particularly at times of anxiety, transition and upheaval, writers are likely to turn to fantasy to find ways of exploring disturbing material, both for themselves and for the historical moment in which they are working. While the texts used in this chapter are by two white, male, British writers, the approach explained and applied here can be very widely employed, and some provocative readings made by comparing different kinds of writers and texts specifically with those by Tolkien and Lewis discussed here.

> Fantasy is reality. Aristotle says that music is the most realistic of the arts because it represents the movements of the soul directly. Surely the mode of fantasy (which includes many genres and effects) is the only way in which some realities can be treated.
>
> (Russ, 1995: xii)

There are many ways of approaching fantasy fiction written for children, and because they are so well known, the classic fantasy texts examined in this chapter have been subjected to most of them. Here I have chosen to conduct a psychoanalytical examination (Box 3.1) on the grounds that fantasy narratives are woven from the strands of multiple 'realities': strands which bind such

---

BOX 3.1 PSYCHOANALYTIC CRITICISM

Literary critics may employ techniques and concepts derived from psychoanalysis to make readings of texts. It should be stressed that they are interpreting the text, not the author. However, when an author's complete work is considered in this way, certain patterns, silences, recurring motifs and so on may seem to reflect on her or his personal preoccupations.

Psychoanalytic criticism sees the text in the same way that analysts see the mind: as being made up of both conscious and unconscious elements. The analogy can be taken further by seeing the reader and text as being in a similar relationship to that of the analyst and patient.

Freud saw similarities between creative writing and day-dreaming, though he warned that if a writer's work were to be of interest to others it had to be given form and meaning beyond the personal. Just as the unconscious, which is not allowed to communicate its concerns directly, finds ways of breaking through the controlling conscious through such things as slips of the tongue and dreams, so material is filtered by writers, both knowingly and unconsciously. For this reason, certain explanations about the way the psyche works can usefully be applied to literary texts. Among these are displacement and condensation, in which repressed fears are disguised, often by combining them with elements from daily life and making a single, condensed image or dreamscape, which fools the conscious into allowing repressed material to be expressed. Because they are disguised and condensed, such images work like symbols and metaphors in literature – they require interpretation – underlining the similarities between the analytical and the critical processes.

The theories of three key thinkers are usually associated with psychoanalytic criticism: Sigmund Freud, Carl Jung and Jacques Lacan. The work of all three can usefully be employed in the readings of children's literature, though in this study Jungian theories predominate.

texts to their eras, their creators and, ultimately, their audiences. For the purposes of this discussion, what's interesting about these strands is the way they can be unpicked to reveal the underlying psychological dimensions of all such levels of reality.

The choice of Jungian, rather than Freudian, psychoanalytical theory arises from an important difference in dynamic between the two, a difference which arguably makes the former more suited to examining children's literature. Jungian analysis (Box 3.2) has a forward-looking momentum in its processes; it examines the drive towards integration of the conscious and unconscious as a

BOX 3.2   JUNGIAN THEORY

Carl Gustav Jung (1875–1961) was a complex thinker, who, in addition to the insights he adduced from the case-studies arising from his practical work in the field of psychoanalysis, allowed many other streams of thought to influence his writings on the psyche. These included a lifelong involvement with spiritualism, a lengthy period of self-analysis, extensive scholarship in the fields of comparative religion and mythology and a fascination with alchemy. At one time he was a disciple of Freud, and seen as Freud's natural successor, but their relationship broke down over Jung's insistence that sexuality was not at the base of *all* neurosis. He argued that Freud had confined himself to the insights offered by one myth, the 'Oedipus' myth, and had failed to recognize those that could be attained by examining the metaphorical images offered by all myths.

Key Concepts: The ego, collective unconscious, archetypes and archetypal images

Jung constructs a model of the psyche which comprises both conscious and unconscious levels. The '**ego**' is seen as the centre of the conscious personality, represented to the world by a '**persona**', or social mask, but it is not the total sum of the personality and is in a constant and fluctuating relationship with the unconscious. In addition to what he terms the '**personal unconscious**', Jung argues that there is a deeper, 'inborn' layer – something he terms the '**collective unconscious**' (1990: 299). This, he suggests, is common to and identical in all human beings, being composed of structuring patterns that predispose us to image a range of archetypal situations and figures. Such '**archetypes**' are without gender or shape; the forms they ultimately take within a given individual, Jung refers to as '**archetypal images**'. They may manifest themselves as positive and/or negative, 'shadow' (see below) images, and, modulated by culture and personal experience, may appear in a plurality of forms – as human beings, animals or even inanimate objects. In Jung's view, myths offer compelling evidence of archetypal imaging in progress (see 1990: 299–344).

Important **archetypes** include:

- **Anima** – appearing in a man's unconscious as anything from an 'angel of light' to a 'daemonic' being, the anima is the experience of 'otherness', or, as Jung puts it, the 'not-I' (323) in man. Due to the male (and presumed masculine) nature of the 'I', this is usually manifested as a woman, or in other 'feminine' form. Jung also calls this the '**soul-image**', suggesting that it arises first in the figure of the Mother archetype (see below).
- **Animus** – the equivalent figure, and therefore usually arising as 'masculine', in women. Jung does not devote much space to enlarging on this, and much of what he does write is unhelpful, being both negative and dismissive.
- **Child** – appearing as anything from divine to monstrous in form. Jung stresses that this motif represents both beginnings and ends, recalling human origins – 'the pre-conscious childhood aspect of the collective psyche' (1995: 33) – but speaking to futurity and new beginnings through rebirth and images of the 'child god' as 'mythological saviour' (36).
- **Mother** – the first appearance of the feminine 'other' in the psyche, and may appear in forms as disparate as the 'Queen of Heaven' or a devouring witch, as 'Mother Church' or a 'terrifying animal' (1990: 349).
- **Shadow** – the archetypal potential for chaos and evil, present within the personality and *all* archetypes. The process of individuation entails consciously coming to terms with the shadow, so that it does not break out destructively.
- **Trickster** – an unreflective joker, shape-shifter and (false) saviour, with a dual nature, bestial and divine. Jung associates the trickster with the world-turned-upside-down of carnival, and 'the alchemical figure of Mercurius' (1980: 255).
- **Wise Old Man** – as 'superior master and teacher' (1990: 331), this archetypal figure functions as a spirit guide, paradoxically sometimes seen as father, sometimes son of the anima.
- **Wise Old Woman**, Grandmother – wise and mysterious, a witch/fairy/goddess figure with both benevolent and malevolent aspects (1980: 102).

In the process that Jung names '**individuation**', the conscious and unconscious elements of the psyche are integrated, through realization of the '**Self**'. According to Jung, the **Self** is the **governing archetype** of the unconscious (1990: 275) and it ultimately 'expresses the unity of the personality [that is, including conscious and unconscious elements] as a whole' (274).

way of moving toward psychic 'wholeness' for the maturing subject. Freudian analysis, on the other hand, has a retrospective quality, as it investigates the early causes of the neuroses (all, in Freud's view, relating to repressed aspects of sexuality) that surface in the adult subject. As Brian Attebery comments in *Strategies of Fantasy*, 'Whereas Freud looks to origins, Jung looks to ends: not where we came from but what we may grow into' (1992: 30).

Calling on Jungian theory provokes consideration of the deepest and oldest realities, for underlying Jung's work is the idea that there is an unconscious layer within the psyche that all human beings share and have shared since the beginnings of human time. Jung terms this the 'collective unconscious', claiming that it is this which provides human beings with the propensity to form certain images in their 'personal unconscious', the form of these images being tied to and influenced by each individual's own location in time and space. The structuring potentialities arising in the collective unconscious Jung names 'archetypes', while the forms they ultimately take he refers to as 'archetypal images'. In Jungian terms, the tendency of the psyche to produce archetypal images arises in the universal unconscious, but the final forms these take are mediated by the surrounding personal and socio-historical context of their creation.

The first strands that bind a fantasy to era and creator, arise from the fact that the minds of inventors of fantasies are inescapably rooted in their own lived experiences, both general and personal. All writers strive to imbue their work with the mystery and intrigue associated with fantastical creations using everyday words, ideas and concepts from that experience. The prime resources available to fantasy writers in their attempts to defamiliarize the familiar (at least, familiar to their contemporary readers – time and space may lend their own forms of defamiliarization to texts read at a distance from their creative source) are their own imaginations and dreams: the fertile workings of their own conscious and unconscious minds. Tolkien describes his ideas about the process, and the power he felt it conveyed, in his lecture 'On Fairy-Stories':

> When we can take green from grass, blue from heaven and red from blood, we have already an enchanter's power upon one plane; and the desire to wield that power in the world external to our minds awakes. . . . We may put a deadly green upon a man's face and produce a horror; we may make the rare and terrible blue moon to shine; or we may cause woods to spring with silver leaves and rams to wear fleeces of gold and put hot fire into the belly of the cold worm.   (1983: 122)

In drawing on the deeper resources of the unconscious, however, more realities can creep in, not least writers' own hidden or repressed reactions to the events that comprise their lived experiences – the material that makes up the unconscious elements of their psyches. Fantasy may tend to use the metaphorical spectrum as a mode of writing, yet it is the happenings of the 'real' world that are cloaked in fantasy dress.

Just as myth and fairy tale may be viewed as fantasy narratives that symbolically convey deep universal truths from the dawn of time, so later fantasy texts, whether consciously or unconsciously drawing on such underlying prototypes, can be said to clothe these earlier fundamentals in images from more recent times and places. The effect of this is to compel the more modern texts to reflect and give form to the concerns and assumptions of their own age, including responses to tragedy and trauma. It is significant that the texts discussed in this chapter span the most traumatic events of the last century; a psychoanalytic approach to reading them shows how such experiences find form and expression through fantasy.

Real and disturbing issues certainly abounded through most of the twentieth century; there is a reason why historian Eric Hobsbawm named the forty years between the outbreak of World War I and the years immediately following World War II an 'Age of Catastrophe' (1994: 7). In between periods of transient stability and apparently civilized living, the century was torn apart by a series of the most cataclysmic events, including two world wars. When discussing the work of J. R. R. Tolkien (1892–1973) and C. S. Lewis (1898– 1963), it is salutary to remember that during the horrific trench warfare of World War I (1914–18), in which both fought, millions of soldiers perished; British losses included half a million men under the age of thirty (1994: 26). Commenting on attempts by readers and critics to draw parallels between his later work, *The Lord of the Rings* (1954–5), and the Second World War, Tolkien was quick to point out:

> One has indeed personally to come under the shadow of war to feel fully its oppression; but as the years go by it seems now often forgotten that to be caught in youth by 1914 was no less hideous an experience than to be involved in 1939 and the following years. By 1918 all but one of my close friends were dead. (1968: 11)

But is awareness of trauma and potential trauma sufficient reason for looking in and beneath the words of fantasy texts, using psychoanalytical criticism to search for layers of meaning which engage with such ills? Attebery focuses on the process as a means of self-analysis, suggesting that 'Jung's archetypes … [as] narrative functions … within fantastic narratives … help us comprehend our own perceptions and motives (1992: 30–1). For readers, the interplay between the collective unconscious, the images created by a writer from a distanced temporal and spatial location, and those readers' own interpretations of the metaphorical dimensions underlying fantasy texts, offers simultaneously the opportunity for self-analysis and a sense of what such narrative functions suggest about the underlying personal and collective angst of life earlier in the last century. This does not preclude the possibility that different readers may produce differing interpretations, but it is the process that is revealing – the propensities of the text rather than its actualized realities, its archetypal images rather than its concrete events. As Jung comments, 'The most we can do is to *dream the myth onwards* and give it a modern dress. And whatever explanation or interpretation does to it, we do to our own souls as well, with corresponding results for our own well-being' (in Abrams, 1995: 31–2).

Anima and Mother images in *The Hobbit* and *The Lion, the Witch and the Wardrobe*

Analysing any narrative using Jungian theory involves interpreting the text as the metaphorical representation of a functioning psyche. At a conscious level, one of the characters, usually the hero, can be seen as representing the ego – from whose perspective the text is focalized. Other characters or settings, whether represented as human, animal or inanimate objects, form archetypal images which enact elements of the unconscious. The goal of the text as psychodynamic process is 'individuation', that is, the integration of the conscious and unconscious elements, through realization of the 'self'. Jung speaks of 'divesting the self of the false wrappings of the persona [the outward 'social' face of the ego] on the one hand, and of the suggestive power of primordial images on the other' (1990: 148). In other words, realization of the self-image draws and holds together the 'other' of the unconscious and the ego of the conscious. Marie Louise von Franz is certain that 'all fairytales endeavor to describe one and the same psychic fact. ... This unknown fact is what Jung calls the Self, which is the psychic totality of an individual and also, paradoxically the regulating center of the collective unconscious' (1996: 2). The self-image ultimately 'expresses the unity of the personality [that is including conscious and unconscious elements] as a whole' (Jung, 1990: 274).

Susan Rowland (2002) gives a useful and compact summary of common archetypes in *Jung: A Feminist Revision* (see also Box 3.2):

> Jung refers to ... individual archetypes as the feminine in man (the anima), the masculine in woman (the animus), the mother, the wise old man/ woman, the trickster and rebirth. They are all plural and androgynous, meaning that they can have many shapes and can be equally in feminine or in masculine. Archetypes are bipolar in that they contain their own opposites, so that the mother archetype can be manifested as a caring female form, yet will also be able to produce a devouring monster image: it all depends what the ego needs at the time.   (2002: 30)

Unpacking this as part of a psychoanalytical exploration of *The Hobbit* and *The Lion, the Witch and the Wardrobe*, I want specifically to explore the ideas of the 'feminine' that exist within these texts, as evidenced by the particular images in which the archetypes of 'woman' – the 'mother' and the 'anima' – appear, and of their relationship as 'other' to the conscious masculine ego of the narrative as psychodynamic process. This approach does not entail essentialist usage of the terms 'feminine' and 'masculine', which would suggest that these are unvarying categories with a fixed underlying reality; rather, the labels are used to signify a set of culturally defined (and so not fixed) characteristics.

The process of analysis involves relating narrative functions (characters, settings and objects) to underlying archetypes and examining the possible significances of the forms in which they appear. Awareness of the ways in which these may be represented in separate, oppositional forms (the 'good' and the 'shadow' versions, see Box 3.2) is a significant aspect of this. It should also be remembered that discovery of such forms in no way implies that the writers intentionally and consciously included these elements in order to create a metaphorical interpretation of the process of 'self' realization.

Superficially it is difficult to see *The Hobbit* as a source of aspects of 'woman', whether mother or later anima; there is a complete lack of overt female characters, with even the legendary adventuress Belladonna Took, Bilbo's long dead mother, introduced as an absence: present in the central hobbit character's genes (it is Bilbo's late father who is the respectable 'solid and comfortable' (15) part of the partnership), but no longer in person. Here is a story, one which grew into life as an oral tale told by Tolkien to his young sons, with an overtly all-male cast. Yet, Terry Eagleton suggests that the psychoanalytical examination of a text is capable of revealing a sub-text which is 'visible at certain "symptomatic" points of ambiguity, *evasion* or overemphasis, and which we as readers are able to "write" even if the novel itself does not' (1983: 178; emphasis added). Evasion is revealing; the lack of overt presence may be seen as a strong indicator of a more deeply hidden female presence.

Looking away from the characters, toward the setting of the text, reveals that surface evasion *does* mask a deeper female presence, that of the lands in which the tale is set. For convenience, these can be referred to under the collective name of 'Middle-earth', though Tolkien did not use this collective name for them until *The Lord of the Rings* (1954–5) was in progress. Nature and the earth are frequently personified in female terms, and the image of the earth mother is sufficiently common for it to be reasonable to see in 'Middle-earth' the archetypal mother image of Tolkien's story. As an image, Middle-earth has the advantage of offering both 'good' mother and 'shadow' destructive mother forms. Jung suggests that, 'The [mother] archetype is often associated with things and places standing for fertility and fruitfulness: the cornucopia, a ploughed field, a garden' (1990: 345). Middle-earth encompasses all of these.

The language of the text is strongly supportive of such an interpretation since it is redolent with imagery of the female anatomy, particularly the mothering function. Middle-earth supplies a polymorphic, multifaceted, occasionally dark, but fecund image of 'woman': loving and motherly in Hobbiton, mysterious in Mirkwood, and dark in mountain caverns. 'She' is portrayed as running with waters [Jung lists 'deep water' (346) as an important feature of the mother archetype]: rivers swollen with rains (Tolkien, 1981: 40); giving 'birth' to a river, which issues out 'of a dark opening in a wall of rock' (229). 'She' is possessed of 'deep places' (5) in which gems may be found, with hidden areas that are spoken of softly, in terms that could be suggestive of female anatomy – 'the secret valley of Rivendell' (55) – while the dark tunnel entrance to Mirkwood invites travellers to penetrate the forest via a path towards yet another dark internal river, one that 'carries enchantment and a great drowsiness and forgetfulness' (132).

Bilbo is referred to as a 'child of the kindly West' (270) in the text. As ego image, he is depicted as being initially smothered by the 'good' mother of Western Middle-earth within his cosy hobbit hole, constantly surrounded by domestic detail. Gandalf, who may be interpreted as an image of the Wise Old Man archetype (Box 3.2) and is intriguingly linked with Tolkien as storyteller – the text advises that 'Tales and adventures sprouted up all over the place wherever he [Gandalf] went' (15) – comes to wrest Bilbo Baggins away from this womb-like space, to propel him down a 'tube-shaped hall like a tunnel' and out through 'a perfectly round door' (13) to join a band of all-male companions on the road to adventure.

In delivering Bilbo from the womb of the Shire for the delight of the tale's original audience of male children, Tolkien's character, Gandalf, speaks to the need for eventual separation from the mother image. Despite being a 'good' mother, the Shire offers a delightfully regressive and passive existence, and must give way to the search for the anima, the future feminine 'other' for the maturing subject. In Jung's words:

> The first bearer of the soul-image [Box 3.2] is always the mother; later it is borne by those women who arouse the man's feelings, whether in a positive or negative sense. Because the mother is the first bearer of the soul-image, separation from her is a delicate and important matter of the greatest educational significance. Accordingly among primitives we find a large number of rites designed to organize this separation. (1990:171)

Applying Jungian psychoanalytical theory at this point, with all its focus on imagery associated with the maternal body and on separation from it, might seem to indicate that there is little difference between Jungian and Freudian ideas. However, the reverse can be seen as true when potential interpretations of the episode are compared. Looking at the story events from a Jungian perspective maintains the forward momentum of Bilbo, from mother, through birth canal, toward anima, a 'delicate' separation and rebirth assisted by the wisdom and care of Gandalf, as image of the 'Wise Old Man' archetype, the 'superior master and teacher' (1990:331) of the unconscious. In contrast, a Freudian perspective might cast Gandalf as a father figure, an adult male intruding into the dyadic mother–child idyll. Attention would be focused on the male child's desire to possess the mother – and here the birth canal becomes vagina and the movement wished for turns inward – and on the child's fear of castration at the hands of the father, making the desired act effectively tabooed. It is difficult to carry the Freudian interpretation forward beyond this specific moment, however, for the intrusion of the father gives rise, in Freudian terms, to the 'Oedipus complex', through which Bilbo would be seen as desiring Gandalf's death, something that would be difficult to support in relation to this text. Freud regarded 'falling in love with the mother and jealousy of the father ... as a universal event of early childhood' (Mitchell, 2000:61). Writing to his friend Fliess, Freud went so far as to claim that

> the Greek Legend [*Oedipus Rex* – in which Oedipus kills his father and copulates with his mother] seizes on a compulsion which everyone recognizes because he feels its existence within himself. Each member of the audience was once, in germ and phantasy, just such an Oedipus, and each one recoils in horror from the dream-fulfilment here transplanted into reality, with the whole quota of repression which separates his infantile state from his present one. (in Mitchell, 2000:61)

As conscious ego, Bilbo has multiple 'shadow' images in the metaphorical unconscious of the text. These are given form as Middle-earth's more monster-like children – from warlike goblins to trolls wrested from the mountains; from poison-dealing spiders to ferocious wolves or wargs; from devious, cold, possessed Gollum to the greedy and death-dealing dragon Smaug. It is not too difficult to see spilling out of these specifically masculine shadow creations symbolic representations of the ills of the early part of the twentieth century.

The horrors of war are evident in the trolls and spiders who mercilessly murder their victims, and in the goblins, of whom the text suggests: 'It is not unlikely that they invented some of the machines that have since troubled the world, especially the ingenious devices for killing large numbers of people at once' (Tolkien, 1981: 69). Similarly the greed and acquisitiveness of Smaug can be conceptually linked to capitalism:

> Dragons steal gold and jewels, you know, from men and elves and dwarves, wherever they can find them; and they guard their plunder as long as they live … and never enjoy a brass ring of it. Indeed they hardly know a good bit of work from a bad, though they usually have a good notion of the current market value … (32)

On this score, even the dwarves can be seen, at least partially, as shadow children, easily overcome by greedy lust for treasure and willing to fight to control it. Thorin, in particular, is portrayed as so possessed by these feelings that he refuses to accede even a small part of Smaug's plunder to those who have a just claim for a share.

Capitalism was under severe pressure in the era into which *The Hobbit* was born. The world was only just in the process of recovering from the Great Slump, in which the global collapse of the free markets was spectacularly highlighted by the New York Stock Exchange crash of 29 October 1929. Economic disaster on such a scale in the 1930s was responsible for driving millions into poverty and some to death through suicide. Hobsbawm suggests that it 'confirmed intellectuals, activists and ordinary citizens in the belief that something was fundamentally wrong with the world they lived in' (1994: 102), that 'an economy increasingly dominated by huge corporations [had] made nonsense of the term "perfect competition" and economists critical of Karl Marx could observe that he had been proved right, not least in his prediction of the growing concentration of capital' (103). The concentration of capital in Smaug's lair, and the desolation surrounding him, the wanton killing and destruction surrounding the goblins and wargs, are convincing images of an intratextual sense of the obscenities arising from what might be seen as the shadow side of a rampant masculinity, out of touch with the 'feminine other' of the unconscious.

A sense of the need to repress aspects of the shadow 'masculine' emphasizes the importance of a successful transfer from early relationships with the internally-realized mother to images of 'women who arouse the man's feelings' (Jung, 1990: 171), the ultimate bonding with the anima. Again, however, the text offers no overt female character in which such an image could be located. In *The Individuated Hobbit*, O'Neill (1980) suggests that this archetype could be represented by the image of Belladonna Took, in the 'Tookishness' that Bilbo carries with him on his adventures (1980: 67). This is a convincing possibility; however, it is also feasible to see the anima as located in another inanimate object, symbolically and supra-sexually present as the treasure Bilbo finds: the Arkenstone, 'fairest of all' (1981: 220) gemstones; the beauteous object at the heart of Smaug's lair. Again the language used within the text draws attention to this as a potent anima symbol: 'It was like a globe with a thousand faces; it shone like silver in firelight, like water in the sun, like snow under stars, like rain upon the Moon' (200), connecting the Arkenstone with the natural world, and specifically, with silver, water and the often feminized moon.

Bilbo, as ego, is shown to be maturing during his engagement with archetypal figures from the unconscious, but ultimately he does not go the whole way to possessing the fully sexualized 'other' of the anima in this form. Though seduced by her and in thrall to her beauty, he hides her away:

> The great jewel shone before his feet, of its own inner light ... it took all light that fell upon it and changed it into ten thousand sparks of white radiance shot with glints of the rainbow.
>
>   Suddenly Bilbo's arm went towards it drawn by its enchantment. His small hand would not close about it, for it was a large and heavy gem; but he lifted it, shut his eyes, and put it in his deepest pocket ... 'I think I would choose this, if they took all the rest!' (225)

Yet later, in giving up this manifestation of an attractive anima image, Bilbo shows himself possessed of what Jung would define as 'feminine' qualities, for, in pursuit of peace and negotiated settlements, Bilbo takes the stone, concealed in a rag, to the camp of Bard and the Wood-Elves, drawing 'her' covering away to reveal to them (and again note the moon imagery): 'the Arkenstone ... [i]t was as if a globe had been filled with moonlight and hung before them in a net woven of the glint of frosty stars (256).

This is not the end of the story of Bilbo's encounter with feminized beauty, however, for the Arkenstone image is sublimated in the text to the stars in the night sky as Bilbo hears the elves sing 'The *stars are far brighter / Than gems* without measure / The moon is far whiter / Than silver in treasure' (277 [emphasis added]). Moon and stars are re-figured as natural anima images of feminized night as the song continues: 'The stars are in bloom, the moon is in flower and bright are the windows of night in *her* tower' (279 [my emphasis]).

In being sublimated to an untouchable, almost 'goddess-style' image, the revised anima in the narrative aligns intriguingly with ideas in circulation when Tolkien was writing *The Hobbit*. These ideas, based on M. Esther Harding's 1935 study of *Women's Mysteries*, are usefully summarized by Susan Rowland and could almost have been written specifically about this aspect of *The Hobbit*:

> This fascinating work amplifies Jung's identification of the female psyche with Eros, the function of relatedness, and with the signification of the

moon in alchemy. . . . [It] is a marvellous elaboration of moon goddesses as active authors of the feminine principle. Such femininity is regarded as native to women, but present in the psychology of men in the anima. (Rowland, 2002:49)

The image of the 'self' arises from the successful process of individuation. In Jungian theory, this is regarded as the governing archetype of the unconscious, linking the conscious ego with the underlying unconscious. Jung offers a range of potential images for the Self:

Empirically, the self appears in dreams, myths, and fairytales in the figure of the 'supraordinate personality' . . . such as a king, hero, prophet, saviour, etc., or in the form of a totality symbol, such as the circle, square . . . cross, etc. When it represents a . . . union of opposites, it can also appear as a united duality.   (1990:275)

The character in *The Hobbit* who most clearly answers all the descriptions 'supraordinate personality', 'hero', 'saviour' and 'union of opposites' is Beorn, and it is this unusual character, a union of human and animal, of love and violence that seems the most likely of possible 'self' images in the text. Significantly, coming into his own as the final element of the final battle with the 'shadow' children of Middle-earth, Beorn resolves the violent conflict in godlike fashion – a 'larger than life' hero/saviour figure, who is the ultimate destroyer of evil in its multiple forms. When all else has failed, and even the late-arriving eagles have not managed to turn the tide, Beorn, alone and in the shape of a gigantic bear, is depicted entering the fray, crushing the Goblin leader, Bolg of the North, and scattering the immense host of goblins and wolves almost single-handedly (Tolkien, 1981: 271).

Beorn offers a goal to the individuating psyche of *The Hobbit* in that ideas of masculinity and femininity are drawn closely together in this power-ful and ambivalent figure. In the bipolar fashion so loved by Jung, whose work focuses on the tension between opposites – e.g. the feminine in the male; the masculine in the female; the shadow versions of archetypes – Tolkien's Beorn is portrayed as being, simultaneously, a gentle *and* a warlike figure. The combining of man and bear is not a simple Jekyll and Hyde duality; it is presented as a much more complex blend of vegetarian, animal lover, and vengeful killer. The honey and cream eater and sharer is the same, yet paradoxically different, creature who, discovering a wandering warg and goblin, kills and displays them as trophies (131). This paradox is emphasized by Gandalf's frequent warnings of the dangers associated with Beorn's animal state, which is too terrible to be 'safe' even for a Hobbit. The 'shadow' side of the Self, rampant in the unconscious, is not to be encountered lightly in the night realm by the as yet unready ego. The possibilities are there, however, in the manner in which Beorn is portrayed as a caring figure, loving his animals as if they were his children (135), supplying the adventurers with loaves, butter, honey, clotted cream and mead (128), and offering them safe passage, on his own beloved ponies, as far as his immediate territories extend.

Beorn is presented as a metaphorical representation of a union of opposites, offering, as governing archetype, a godlike self that is capable of uniting the ideas of fighting, strength and violence, with loving, caring and nurturing, joining together roles more traditionally and stereotypically assigned to separated masculine and feminine spheres at the time of his creation.

Tolkien's narrative can be interpreted as idealizing and sublimating aspects of the feminine, though recognizing a dark, destructive potential in mothering. In the creation of Beorn, the goal of individuation is fully recognized as offering the fruitful potential of a conjunction of feminine and masculine qualities in the male subject. By contrast, a lack of reconciliation between male and female is very evident in C. S. Lewis's *The Lion, the Witch and the Wardrobe*. Taking Edmund as the ego of the conscious psyche, the character's seduction by the White Witch emphasizes that there will be no sublimation of the mother here. The White Witch is imaged as a destructive taker of life, draining it away as she uses her magic to turn creatures to stone, rather than a life-giver, a role controlled by the 'divine' and 'wise' male Aslan, the only one depicted in the text as being capable of revivifying her petrified victims. Resembling Hans Andersen's Snow Queen, the White Witch is the absolute shadow of a 'good' mother image. Her mark is absence, she is stripped of colour, 'not merely pale, but white like snow or paper or icing-sugar' (1965: 34) – apart from the vivid red of her mouth, a symbol of bloodshed. She is presented as being 'proud and cold and stern' (34), with 'white fur up to her throat' (34) and 'eyes flaming' (37). She epitomizes the fairy-tale witch figure, with 'witch' being the first on Jung's list of 'evil symbols' (Jung, 1990: 345) of the mother archetype.

As evil, barren mother, the White Witch creates magical sweetmeats to suborn Edmund with oral gratifications that are the reverse of 'mother's milk'. Unlike the nourishing meal which Edmund's siblings consume at the Beavers' house – fresh fish, 'creamy milk', potatoes and 'deep yellow butter' (Lewis, 1965: 72) – her offerings are addictive, a 'very sweet' drink and 'sweet and light' Turkish Delight (38–9). The lone false-mother figure seduces the ego with enchanted fare and promises of power, fulfilling Jung's description of a negative mother archetype as 'anything that devours, seduces, and poisons, that is terrifying and inescapable like fate' (Jung, 1990: 346).

The Witch's 'long straight golden wand' (Lewis, 1965: 34) speaks to intimations of death, as, weapon-like, it delivers her power to transform animate to inanimate:

'Oh, don't, don't, please don't' shouted Edmund, but even while he was shouting she had waved her wand and instantly where the merry party had been there were only statues of creatures (one with its stone fork fixed forever half-way to its stone mouth). (108–9)

The shape and colour of the wand suggest the idea of feminine misappropriation of phallic power. (A Freudian analyst *would* probably be inclined to agree with the possibility of seeing the wand as phallic, acquired by the Witch as compensation for penis envy; however, this would necessarily form part of an analysis of the Witch as female subject and thus detach this moment from the dynamic of the story as a whole.)

The only other image that could possibly be interpreted as a mother figure in Lewis's text is that of Susan, Edmund's sibling, as she attempts to 'mother' her brothers and sister. However, the image is figuratively, if not actually, colourless and denigrated as a pseudo-mother, a shadowy and inadequate recollection of the absent birth mother, trying to adopt their mother's tone of voice and telling her younger siblings what to do (10). In the framing text, outside the alternate world of Narnia, the mother is absent or, in the traces of her carried by Susan, undesired, so that, deprived of an adequate maternal female figure, the children receive the 'best' guidance and wisdom from a male, the Professor with whom they stay, and who can be seen as an image of the Wise Old Man archetype as he supports Lucy and encourages the children to believe in her account of an alternate reality. Inside Narnia, the mother archetype is imaged as wholly evil and seductive, repressing all idea of adult females as repositories of wisdom or even as offering appropriate maternal care.

The image of the anima in *The Lion, the Witch and the Wardrobe* can easily be interpreted as Lucy, Edmund's younger sibling, from whom he is initially alienated by the seductive intervention of the negative mother archetype. Guroian draws attention to the character's name, and its 'Latin root *lucer* which means "to shine"' (1998: 163), and connects this to his idea of Lucy as a 'Heroine of Faith and Courage' (140–76). However, although she is portrayed as a healer, her function is only made possible by the gift of a life-saving cordial from the patriarchal figure of Father Christmas (possibly another image of the Wise Old Man archetype, this time located in the inner story) (Lewis, 1965: 102–3).

Lucy is clearly an instrument rather than a source of the power, and in using the gift is firmly controlled by Aslan (the divine). In the moment of possible joining between anima–Lucy and ego–Edmund, when she is restoring him after he has been wounded, Aslan disrupts, distances and controls events. He sternly reminds Lucy of the needs of others, as she lingers with Edmund to await some sign of his recovery. Finally the divine patriarchal figure chastizes Lucy for her excessive focus on Edmund: ' "Daughter of Eve," said Aslan in a graver voice, "others also are at the point of death. Must *more* people die for Edmund?" ' (165).

Aslan dons the mantle of the Self in Lewis's text, the goal of individuation. Jung suggests that Christ is the 'self' image for Christians, and here Aslan can be seen as the allegorical representation of the Christ figure. Yet the self image, manifest in Aslan and controlling the link between ego and anima, does not appear to promise a resolution to the lack of union between the male subject's masculine and feminine elements, as envisaged in the text. Unlike the situation which is metaphorically suggested by the union of opposites in *The Hobbit*, the psychodynamic processes of *The Lion, the Witch and the Wardrobe* seem to negate the idea of a fruitful union of masculine and feminine qualities, emphasizing separation in connection with representations of war. Lewis's Father Christmas pronounces firmly: 'battles are ugly when women fight' (103) – thus presumably *not* when men fight, a symbolic reiteration of traditional images of the noble, righteous and wholly masculine warrior. Through its inability to accommodate union with the mother or anima, and by rigidly controlling what is represented as feminine, the text, in this interpretation, shows symptoms of the angst of the era and represses recognition of the disturbances occasioned by delineating and separating feminine and masculine spheres.

Conclusion

These Jungian readings of early to mid-twentieth-century classic fantasies for children inevitably relate to my own personal and socio-cultural context, a context I share, at least in part, with many contemporary readers of Tolkien's and Lewis's fictions. Post-9/11 and in the aftermath of another war in Iraq, their fantasies speak to contemporary concerns about men and war, while feminism has alerted us to historically-dated essentialist views on men's and women's roles, and 'appropriate' models of 'femininity' and 'masculinity'. In my readings, Tolkien's text is shown to grapple with ways in which 'feminine' and 'masculine' qualities may fruitfully be reconciled to explore ideas of a 'goddess' or 'nature-related' feminine as a way for men both to regard women and to reconcile 'femininity' within themselves, while also positing the existence of evil and the legitimacy of fighting. At the same time, it accepts negotiation, generosity, and a hatred of unnecessary killing as valid responses for male subjects whose soul-image resides in nature and beauty. Lewis's text, by contrast, is revealed as a more rigid apologia for patriarchy and the 'masculine' soldier, aligning Christianity with honour and the necessity for men to fight and women to remain outside war – obedient, pure, loving and childlike. Both texts, however, ultimately hand on underlying archetypal material for contemporary and future creators of fantasy to re-image in their own contexts – something Jung himself envisaged when he suggested that:

> active fantasy is the chief mark of the artistic mentality, the artist is not just a reproducer of appearances but a creator and educator, for his [sic] works have the value of symbols that adumbrate lines of future development. (1990: 255)

WORKS CITED AND FURTHER READING

Primary Texts

Lewis, C. S., *The Lion, the Witch and the Wardrobe* (London: Collins, 1965).
Tolkien, J. R. R., *The Hobbit* (London: Unwin, 1981).

Critical Texts

Abrams, J. (ed.), *Reclaiming the Inner Child* (London: HarperCollins, 1991).
Attebery, B., *Strategies of Fantasy* (Bloomington: Indiana University Press, 1992).
Carpenter, H., *The Inklings* (London: HarperCollins, 1978).
Eagleton, M. (ed.), *Feminist Literary Theory: A Reader* (Oxford: Blackwell, 1996).

Eagleton, T., *Literary Theory: An Introduction* (Oxford: Basil Blackwell, 1983).

Guroian, V., *Tending the Heart of Virtue: How Classic Stories Awaken a Child's Moral Imagination* (Oxford: Oxford University Press, 1998).

Hobsbawm, E., *Age of Extremes: The Short Twentieth Century, 1914–1991* (Harmondsworth: Penguin, 1994).

Jung, C., *The Archetypes and the Collective Unconscious*, trans. R. F. C. Hull (Princeton, NJ: Princeton University Press, 1980; first published 1968).

Jung, C., *The Basic Writings of C. G. Jung*, trans. R. F. C. Hull, ed. V. S. de Laszlo (Princeton, NJ: Princeton University Press, 1990; first published, 1959).

Jung, C., 'The Psychology of the Child Archetype', trans. R. F. C. Hull, in J. Abrams (ed.), *Reclaiming the Inner Child* (London: HarperCollins, 1991).

Mitchell, J., *Psychoanalysis and Feminism: A Radical Reassessment of Freudian Psychoanalysis* (Harmondsworth: Penguin, 2000: first published 1974).

O'Neill, T., *The Individual Hobbit* (London: Thames & Hudson, 1980; first published 1979).

Rowland, S., *Jung: A Feminist Revision* (Oxford: Polity Press, 2002).

Russ, J., 'Introduction', to A. Williams and R. Jones (eds), *The Penguin Book of Modern Fantasy by Women* (Harmondsworth: Penguin, 1995).

Scott Littleton, C. (ed.), *Mythology: The Illustrated Anthology of World Myth and Storytelling* (London: Duncan Baird, 2002).

Tolkien, J. R. R., 'On Fairy-Stories' (pp. 109–61) in C. Tolkien (ed.), *The Monsters and the Critics and other Essays* (London: George Allen & Unwin, 1983; originally the Andrew Lang Lecture, given at the University of St Andrew's, 8 March 1939).

Tolkien, J. R. R., 'Foreword', to *The Lord of the Rings* (London: George Allen & Unwin, 1968; first published 1954–5).

von Franz, M., *The Interpretation of Fairy Tales* (Boston, MA: Shambhala Publications, 1996; first published 1970).

Children's Books

Other books in C. S. Lewis's 'Chronicles of Narnia' sequence: *Prince Caspian* (1951); *The Voyage of the Dawn Treader* (1952); *The Silver Chair* (1953); *The Horse and his Boy* (1954); *The Magician's Nephew* (1955); *The Last Battle* (1956).

Tolkien, J. R. R., *The Lord of the Rings*.

Autobiography and History: Literature of War

4

Gillian Lathey

KEY TEXTS

N. Bawden, *Carrie's War* (1973)
I. Dische, *Between Two Seasons of Happiness* (1998)
J. Kerr, *When Hitler Stole Pink Rabbit* (1971)

To introduce the topic of war as it has been explored in texts for children, Gillian Lathey combines historical overview with techniques derived from studies of autobiographical writing. The study of autobiography necessarily touches on ideas drawn from psychoanalysis and psychoanalytical criticism (see Box 3.1), demonstrating both how difficult and artificial it can be to draw firm boundaries between critical approaches, and the strengths of allowing different approaches and methodologies to complement and extend each other. For younger readers, many of the issues and events associated with war stories – from historical background to violence – can be problematic. Nevertheless, as this introduction shows, the literature of war makes up a substantial section of the juvenile bookshelf, and is used for a variety of purposes. In war stories a range of discourses converge – those arising from history, opposing ideologies, masculinity, heroism, loss, grief and mourning, comradeship, danger, and survival – and they fulfil a variety of functions. They transmit the didactic imperative to ensure that cultures do not forget the sacrifices and atrocities of the past, define and redefine what it means to be a hero, work through the meaning behind everyday words such as 'friend' and 'enemy', and generally engage young readers with key issues and historical moments that have shaped present-day life and culture.

The last decades of the twentieth century saw a marked increase in the number of children's books offering a realistic treatment of war. War is now an accepted, even common, subject in children's books – but why should adults choose to write about war for children? Surely we should protect children from the inhumanity of war for as long as possible? Such questions and arguments arise in western cultures seeking to exploit a sanitized construct of childhood, one that cocoons children from the realities of the political world. Yet throughout history children have been the unwilling victims of war as well as enthusiastic wartime propagandists and even combatants. It was, for example, the sight of child victims – the war orphans and refugees who roamed across Europe in the wake of the Napoleonic Wars in the early nineteenth century – that drove the Swiss educationalist Pestalozzi (1746–1827) to create his children's villages. In more recent times, the fates of children displaced by the Third Reich or made homeless by combat in the Second World War are the subject of numerous fictional and autobiographical accounts.

These children were also the targets of wartime propaganda that prepared them for adult combat. In Germany, young people who were enthusiastic members of the Hitler Youth in the 1930s went straight into the armed forces (or, for girls, non-combatant war service) as soon as they reached adulthood; Hans-Peter Richter's trilogy *Friedrich* (1987), *I Was There* (1987) and *The Time of the Young Soldiers* (1978) charts the deadly momentum of this progress. To find evidence of active participation in wars by children, we only have to look to the examples of young men falsifying their ages to join the army in World War I, or contemporary television images of child soldiers in a number of conflicts in Africa and elsewhere. It is simply not possible to keep children entirely protected from war; even those who are sent away from likely danger to distant places are deeply affected for the rest of their lives by that experience. Moreover, war frequently acts as a catalyst in accelerating progress to maturity, even though, as some of the texts discussed in this chapter and Chapter 5 will show, the necessary but premature acceptance of adult responsibilities can exact a high personal cost.

For both these reasons – to acknowledge the inescapable reverberations of war in children's lives and its significance for the central preoccupation of children's fiction with growing up – children's authors have readily turned to war as a fitting subject for their audience. Over the years, writers of historical fiction have often focused on distant conflicts, such as the Roman conquest of Britain in the work of Rosemary Sutcliff, but it is the wars within living memory that have inspired the largest volume of children's fiction. Before investigating what is at stake for adult writers, and where the child reader's interest lies in these texts, a brief account of changing perspectives in children's literature about war in the twentieth century will provide a context for the discussion of Second World War texts at the centre of these two linked chapters.

The First World War

Children's books featuring war written in the early decades of the twentieth century largely follow a clear-cut gender division in addressing either girl or boy readers, and the protagonists are often adults. The principal characters in children's fiction set in the First World War (1914–18), for example, are either male combatants demonstrating their physical courage and guile, or plucky young women sent to the Front (the battlefields of northern France and Belgium) as nurses, where they succeed in maintaining respectability and decorum in the most trying circumstances. Such fortitude was not confined to longer prose fiction; stories in the British companion magazines *The Girl's Own Paper* and *The Boy's Own Paper* maintained a patriotic stance and emphasized

Figure 3   Captain W. E. Johns's *Biggles Goes to War*

The plane came screaming down on him as Biggles crouched in the ditch

courage and duty in combat and on the home front respectively. In their survey of war fiction for the young, Kate Agnew and Geoff Fox (2001) cite examples of First World War texts that appealed to girl and boy readers respectively: for example, the independent and active heroines created by Bessie Marchant and the early RAF stories of Percy F. Westerman. Perhaps the most popular of all these heroic wartime series, read by generations of boys in the twentieth century, are the Biggles stories by Captain W. E. Johns. These stories span the First and Second World Wars, although Biggles, shown in typically forceful mode in Figure 3, did not make his first appearance until 1930 in the pages of the magazine *Popular Flying*.

Between the World Wars

British children's literature published during and between the World Wars served an ideological purpose that was often made explicit. Germans are usually represented negatively, and there is little explanation of the historical and political causes of war beyond simplistic messages of propaganda. It is surprising, given the young audience and the humanistic and didactic intentions that normally underpin children's literature, that there are very few children's books published in the interwar period offering an unequivocally pacifist message. Two significant exceptions are both translations into English: André Maurois's fable *Fattypuffs and Thinifers* (published in France in 1930 and in English in 1945), and Rudolf Frank's First World War novel *No Hero for the Kaiser* (first published in Germany in 1931; an English edition did not appear until 1986). Frank's fourteen-year-old Polish hero, Jan Kubitzky, disappears rather than participate in a military ceremony at which he is to be honoured. In contrast to Frank's realist tale set in an embattled village, Maurois chooses an amusing allegory of a war between a nation of thin, orderly people and their rotund, easy-going enemies, in order to highlight the absurdities of war and to offer an optimistic way forward.

World War II

Children's stories published during World War II and in the early postwar period maintained the patriotic tradition of First World War fiction. As illustrated in boys' comics, the division between Allied troops and 'the enemy' – primarily the Germans and Japanese – is apparent in physical appearance and uniforms, and in representations of language: most boys growing up in the 1950s and 1960s acquired a smattering of German, 'Schweinhund', 'Achtung' and the like. Adult combatants were the central figures in such comic strips, just as they were in many early World War II stories written for boys. Biggles continued his perilous air force career, and Captain Charles Gilson, who wrote First World War stories for *The Boy's Own Paper*, created additional adult heroes in titles such as *Out of the Nazi Clutch* (1940) and *Through the German Hordes* (1941). For girl readers, some of the popular school series discussed in Chapter 2 temporarily took on a war setting as child protagonists responded to the urgencies of the international situation, as in *Dimsie Carries On* (1946) by Dorita Fairlie Bruce and *The Chalet School in Exile* (1940) by Elinor Brent-Dyer. Children become resourceful sleuths in other adaptations of existing genres: the adventure story, for example, transmutes into the spy story in the work of Malcolm Saville. Whether battles are conducted on land, in the skies, or by groups of astute and fearless children, the tone of wartime propaganda prevails in the majority of these stories, with the German enemy presented as one-dimensional, caricatured figures. As Agnew and Fox (2001) point out, Elinor Brent-Dyer makes a rare distinction between Germans and Nazis in a speech the headmistress delivers to her Chalet School girls in *The Chalet School Goes To It* (1941).

The postwar era

As the postwar era settled into a prolonged period of peace, marked by the international tensions of the Cold War, children's literature of war embarked on a sea change in written mode, content and purpose. Ian Serraillier's *The Silver Sword* (1956) marked a turning point from the popular, patriotic appeal of earlier war stories and genre fiction. Serraillier's story of refugee children searching for their families in the postwar devastation of central Europe addressed serious issues with an implicit didactic intention. Although he does not explicitly promote pacifism in the text, Serraillier was a Quaker who had a close, carefully researched knowledge of his subject. His presence in the narrative is that of the knowledgeable and wise adult, an omniscient narrator who, in the final pages of the novel, demonstrates to his readers that the emotional shock waves of war reverberate far into the future in the lives of his protagonists. In this respect, *The Silver Sword* set the tone for the many retrospective novels to come, since a preoccupation with the affective consequences of war characterized war literature in the decades that followed.

New dimensions of psychological insight into children's responses to wartime trauma are apparent in stories told from the child's perspective. Indeed, there is an extension of what counts as 'war' fiction. Children's literature addresses both the prewar persecution of the Jews, leading to the Holocaust, and the reverberation of wartime events in the period. In addition to an increased chronological range, there is a shift in the setting of wartime fiction to the private domain. In British children's fiction it is the domestic setting that registers the most profound effects on children's lives, with evacuation as the most popular single theme: two of the best known examples are Nina Bawden's *Carrie's War* (1973), and Michelle Magorian's *Goodnight Mr Tom* (1981). The absence and return of fathers in the armed forces is a strand common to many novels (Nina Bawden, *Keeping Henry*, 1988; Michelle Magorian, *Back Home*, 1985), as is the fear and disruption of family life caused by air raids (Robert Westall, *The Machine-Gunners*, 1975, and *The Kingdom by the Sea*, 1990; Susan Cooper, *Dawn of Fear*, 1974; and David Rees, *The Exeter Blitz*, 1978).

Representing the 'enemy'

Children's authors are also increasingly concerned to stress the humanity of all sides in the conflicts they address. There is a corpus of Second World War novels dating particularly from the 1970s in which an opportunity is engineered for children to meet the German enemy. German pilots fall from the skies or sailors are washed up on British shores with unlikely regularity. In Westall's *The Machine-Gunners*, Michael Morpurgo's *Friend or Foe* (1977) and, more recently, James Riordan's *The Prisoner* (1999), it is German pilots the children befriend, while young Simon in David Rees's *The Missing German* (1976) tends and hides a German sailor discovered on a Devon beach. In a rare acknowledgement of Allied culpability, Riordan takes the opportunity to convey the terror of the bombing of Hamburg, his pilot's home town, to his young readers. In Bette Greene's *Summer of My German Soldier* (1973), set in the southern USA, the central relationship is that between a Jewish girl and the escaped German prisoner of war she hides.

The hiding of an enemy alien is a plot device that adds suspense to a wartime story; it also enables writers to create a dialogue between children and an adult they had been taught to mistrust or even to hate. Inevitably these encounters with 'the enemy' lead child protagonists, and ultimately child readers, to question the wartime propaganda fed to them by adults and, as in the anarchic scenes at the close of Westall's *The Machine-Gunners*, adult values generally. The urge to present children with a range of points of view continues in fiction set in more recent conflicts. Westall adds political edge to his psychic representation of a young Iraqi soldier in *Gulf* (1992), while in Els de Groen's *No Roof in Bosnia* (1997), translated from the Dutch, five young people – two Serbs, a Croatian, a Bosnian Muslim girl and a Romany boy – are given shelter by a wily old woman, who keeps them alive by stealing supplies from the United Nations force UNPROFOR. All five teenagers are clearly delineated characters whose wartime experiences constitute a tapestry of encounters with different ethnic and religious groups; the bond they form with each other transcends past allegiances.

Picturebooks on war

Visual images have been significant in children's literature of war since the beginning of the twentieth century, from the line drawings that illustrated First World War fiction to the comic strip adventures of numerous combatants from all participating nations and their stereotyped 'enemies' in the Second. After World War II, developments in picturebooks about war have made use of the image to convey aspects of war with the visual immediacy that engages children, whatever their levels of literacy. Picturebooks for younger children tend to mediate the harshness of their subject matter by couching a pacifist message in an allegorical tale; for example, in Elzbieta's gentle animal allegory *Go Away War!* (1994, translated from the French), or through the use of colour and tone, as in the controversial concentration camp setting of *Let the*

Celebrations Begin! (1991) by Australians Margaret Wild and Julie Vivas. Another Australian picturebook, *My Dog* by John Heffernan and Andrew McLean (2001), takes an elliptical approach to the brutality of ethnic cleansing in the former Yugoslavia by depicting events from the viewpoint of a young Bosnian child: only an older child or adult would 'read' the suggestion of rape in the image of the abduction of young Alija's mother and an emphasis in the text on her beauty. On the other hand, the impact of images is given free reign in expressive paintings of burning human flesh in Toshi Maruki's *The Hiroshima Story* (1983), or of concentration camp inmates in Roberto Innocenti's *Rose Blanche* (1985). Finally, picturebook representation of war reaches a high degree of sophistication in *La Petite Marchande d'Allumettes* (1999), illustrated by Georges Lemoine, a version of Hans Christian Andersen's story of the little match girl set in Sarajevo, Yugoslavia, in the 1990s. Artwork is based on photographs taken at the time, while the text is a combination of Andersen's narrative with phrases taken from a poetic commentary on the devastation of Sarajevo by Ozren Kebo. The pathos and simplicity of Kebo's text echoes that of the match girl's story in a book dedicated to the child victims of barbarity across the world.

The diversity of children's literature on World War II

Given the vast range of literature about war written for children that has been outlined above, a more probing approach to a limited number of texts is essential in order to uncover the conflicting ideological and national perspectives that underpin them. I have chosen to focus on the Third Reich and the Second World War (1933 to 1945 and beyond), because it is the historical period that has generated and continues to generate the most extensive and varied body of children's literature. The Second World War inspired new directions in at least two genres of children's literature. In addition to picturebooks devoted to war themes, memoirs of wartime childhoods represent a new development in autobiographical writing for children, as writers reflect on personal experience and changing national perspectives on the past. Texts discussed in these chapters on war, including picturebooks, have a strong autobiographical emphasis.

Children's literature set in the period 1933–45 also reflects the ways in which writers have gradually extended the boundaries of what is acceptable in children's books. Not only are injury, loss, death, and child refugees the subjects of fiction and autobiographical writing, but – in a trend that would have been unthinkable even in the first three decades after the war – there is now a proliferation of children's books on the Holocaust. Whereas Eric Kimmel, writing in 1977, was able to cite only one children's book that addressed the 'ultimate tragedy' of the death camps, since then many children's writers and artists have done so in a range of forms. Jan, the protagonist of Pam Melnikoff's novel *Prisoner in Time: A Child of the Holocaust* (1992), for example, survives life in Theresienstadt concentration camp with the help of a German protector, only to find at the end of the novel that he is to be transported to the east, probably to Auschwitz. In recent decades the international injunction to remember the Holocaust has been inscribed in a large corpus of literature for children, encompassing novels, personal memoirs by Jewish writers and both fictional and non-fictional picturebooks.

In addition to the range and new directions of texts on the subject, the second major reason for addressing children's literature on the Third Reich and World War II is the potential for a comparative approach to children's books originating from a number of countries, including those on opposing sides of the conflict at the time. Fortunately, a varied corpus of children's literature on World War II from across the world is available in English, from the UK and the US, from Australia (Max Fatchen, *Closer to the Stars*, 1981), or set in the Far East (Meindert de Jong, *The House of Sixty Fathers*, 1956). Fiction set in the Second World War selected for discussion in these two chapters originates from a number of nations and languages and ranges from familiar texts to the less well known. Authors such as Nina Bawden, Robert Westall and Michael Foreman have remained rooted in one country, whereas others have migrated at different times in their lives. Judith Kerr left Germany for Britain as a child; Irene Dische moved from the USA to Berlin but continues to write in English; German author Gudrun Pausewang lived for many years in South America, and Tomi Ungerer has lived for long periods in Alsace, the USA and Ireland.

Whatever the experience, literary strategies offer similar patterns. A child in one particular setting in wartime is the focalizing character in each case; young readers share the protagonist's flawed understanding of events and the impact of domestic disruption caused by war. In the first set of texts to be discussed, those by Bawden, Kerr and Dische, the focus will be on the personal and domestic impact of war in texts written in English, while a comparative approach to English-language and translated texts in Chapter 5 will reveal ideological differences at international and collective levels.

Reconfiguring the family: the impact of the Third Reich and World War II

In view of the psychological significance of the family and its dynamics in children's literature, discussed in Chapter 2, it is not surprising that much of the fiction on World War II written for children has been constructed in terms of family relationships. In the transition from war stories in the adventure story mould to a realistic treatment of war, the domestic repercussions of evacuation, family separation, persecution, and the dangers and readjustments of a refugee existence have dominated children's literature on the subject. Children searching for their parents; children taking on the parenting role; children finding adoptive parents; children forced into exile with or without their families; the impact of historical circumstance on family dynamics – these are the recurring motifs of children's books set in the period 1933 to 1945. A reconfiguration of the family takes place so that new family units are formed: one sibling becomes parent to another (*Carrie's War*); the family is extended by taking in refugees or evacuees (Gabriel Alington, *Evacuee*, 1988); grandparents take charge of their grandchildren (Gudrun Pausewang, *The Final Journey*) or children form their own family group as in Serraillier's *The Silver Sword*, where young Ruth adopts the role of mother.

The potential or actual fragmentation of the family is central to an interpretation of war from the child's point of view. Political information reaches children in piecemeal fashion in many Second World War texts, but overheard snatches of radio broadcasts or worried conversations between adults are brought into sharp focus by the impending departure of a father, or plans for evacuation or a journey into exile. In each of the texts under discussion in this section, family relationships are tested and irrevocably altered by historical events: all three are written by women who have a personal interest in the Second World War, its prehistory and aftermath. Nina Bawden's *Carrie's War* (1973) and Judith Kerr's *When Hitler Stole Pink Rabbit* (1971) are the work of near contemporaries (Bawden was born in 1925, Kerr in 1923); Bawden was evacuated from Ilford in Essex to Wales as a child, and Judith Kerr left Germany at the age of nine in 1933. Bawden weaves aspects of her own wartime childhood into a literary novel, whereas Kerr offers a chronological account of her own family's exile years – albeit with her own interpretation of family interaction.

The third writer in the trio, Irene Dische, was born in 1952 and draws on the experiences of her parents' generation. She grew up in New York's Washington Heights district, the daughter of Viennese Jews; she then chose to emigrate to Germany, where she has lived since 1980. Her novel, *Between Two Seasons of Happiness* (1998), is undoubtedly inspired by this family history of migration. Comparison of Bawden's and Kerr's semi-autobiographical texts with Dische's entirely fictional novel reveals a tension between artistry and personal need.

Autobiographical fiction

When considering Bawden's and Kerr's autobiographical fiction and that of several of the authors to be discussed in Chapter 5, questions arise as to the accuracy of the experiences represented in each text. It is now a commonplace assumption that memory is deceptive, especially when several decades separate an event from its imaginative reconstruction. In theoretical writing on autobiography, too, the conscious or unconscious recasting of memory is now recognized.

Critical discussion of autobiography as a literary genre is relatively recent: George Gusdorf's influential essay 'Conditions and Limits of Autobiography' (1956), and Roy Pascal's seminal study *Design and Truth in Autobiography* (1960), were two of the earliest studies. Whereas Gusdorf emphasized the affirmation of individualism in autobiography and argued that: 'there is a oneness of the self, an integrity or internal harmony that holds together the multiplicity and continual transformations of being' (1956: 6), later studies have taken a radically different approach. Far from considering the self as an essentially stable and unchanging core, there is an assertion that the self is a construct that changes according to psychological need, social and historical circumstance and ideological pressures.

The image that an author wishes to present to an audience at the time of writing an autobiography is only the most recent in a chain of multiple identities, just as individuals change their behaviour, actions and even their spoken language to a lesser or greater degree when interacting with different social groups. In his introduction to a collection of essays representing new directions in the study of autobiography, James Olney summarizes this critical trend as follows: 'The self, then, is a fiction and so is the life ...' (1980: 22). Such an extreme position is untenable if tested against events in a life history witnessed by others and corroborated by evidence, but the underlying point that autobiography is an imaginative re-creation of personal experience governed by personal interest and changing ideologies is one that should lead readers to guard against accepting personal accounts of wartime childhoods at face value. When, as is the case in the texts by Bawden and Kerr, authors set out to write a work of fiction with an autobiographical strand, this act of re-creation is effectively acknowledged. A psychoanalytical approach to these texts (see Box 3.1) can reveal different levels of storytelling as the adult writer fictionalizes and reframes childhood memory. Whether autobiographical material is presented as authentic or woven into an explicitly fictional work, it is often possible to detect the adult's review of childhood identity and family relationships.

Nina Bawden: *Carrie's War*

In both Nina Bawden's *Carrie's War* and Judith Kerr's *When Hitler Stole Pink Rabbit*, the author's own younger self is the focalizing character, although in each case personal experience is distanced by the adoption of another name and persona. Bawden deliberately disassociates her childhood self from the fictional character at the centre of her novel. In the afterword by Julia Eccleshare to the Puffin Modern Classics edition of *Carrie's War*, she is cited as denying that Carrie's story is her own, stating that *Carrie's War* is only 'loosely' based on her wartime childhood. Yet there are many parallels between the novel and Bawden's description of evacuation in her autobiography, *In My Own Time* (1994). These range from the description of hanging around in a school hall waiting to be chosen by host families, to the houseproud 'auntie' who would not allow Bawden and her friend Jean to go upstairs more than twice a day in case they wore out the stair carpet. This auntie's mutterings of 'Up and down ... humbugging about' are attributed verbatim to Mr Evans in the novel. Both these instances have particular significance for a child: the sense of powerlessness during the selection process and the urgent anxiety of not being able to reach the first-floor toilet would not easily be forgotten.

It is the underlying emotions of Bawden's own experience, however, that suffuse the narrative. Both the tension in Carrie between a sense of loss and the exhilaration of freedom from parental control, and the guilt resulting from her attempt to decipher and even determine family ties between Mr Evans and his sister, have their roots in Bawden's childhood. Bawden's guilt had a different cause, but her autobiography reveals that its impact also lasted into adulthood. A letter the young Bawden wrote to her mother complaining of hunger had an unintended consequence: she was moved to a different Welsh family and felt the 'taste of guilt' (1994: 59) at the slight to her former hosts. In the novel, Carrie's emotional confusion as a pre-adolescent evacuee is finally resolved in a retrospective narrative framework, as the widowed adult revisits the scenes of her wartime childhood.

In her autobiography, Bawden is anxious to avoid any trace of sentimentality when she quickly dismisses the 'tear-jerking piece about the sadness of a wartime child torn from her loving family' (37) that she wrote at the time for publication in a local newspaper. Similarly, in *Carrie's War*, she does not represent Carrie and her younger brother Nick as homesick evacuees pining for their parents. Like Bawden, Nick and Carrie travel with a photograph of their mother, but they rarely look at it. Their mother 'didn't belong there. Like their father . . . she belonged somewhere else' (in Eccleshare, 1993: 171). Both children are preoccupied with their integration into their new extended family of the Evans and Gotobed households. Yet this suppression of loss is registered in the novel both literally – the children who do not look at the photograph – and metaphorically, in the legend of the screaming skull. Carrie is very affected by the story of the skull, alleged to be that of a young African boy taken from his home and placed in the wealthy Gotobed household at a time when black page-boys were fashionable. He is described as crying 'as any child might cry, taken from his mother' (59); he remained inconsolable and died of a fever during his first winter in England. Bawden offers further insights into Carrie's need for family security in her envy of Nick as he sits on the lap of the motherly Hepzibah, and in her preoccupation with the estranged relationship between Mr Evans and his sister Mrs Gotobed. Carrie both creates an imaginary, sentimental scenario of reconciliation between the siblings, and seeks reassurance from Nick that he and she would never quarrel in such a manner.

Although the text acknowledges the sense of loss that accompanies family separation in the emotional undercurrents of *Carrie's War*, Bawden also draws on memories of liberation from family constraints and the sense of autonomy she gained as a young evacuee. Carrie is eager to embrace new responsibilities as she assumes the role of parent to her younger brother, Nick. At the same time, she seeks and finds attachment to the new, complex set of family relationships that link Mr Evans's shop with Hepzibah's kitchen, and is keen to analyse and interpret (sometimes mistakenly, as it turns out) the motivations of the adults around her. These new bonds are so tenacious that Carrie is reluctant to leave when the time comes; once again this is reminiscent of Bawden's own experience of crying on leaving her first billet: 'as I hadn't cried leaving my mother and brothers in London' (1994: 41). Carrie's guilt at misjudging her host Mr Evans, the loss of her new family, and the impending return to her own mother all combine to induce a state of extreme nervous confusion in her mind as she and Nick leave the Welsh valley by train. Carrie catches sight of a fire at the Gotobed house, blames herself for activating the curse of the screaming skull, and breaks down in a paroxysm of guilt and misery. Many years later that emotional crisis acts as a channel for the grief of the bereaved adult Carrie who appears in the retrospective narrative framework of the book.

In *Carrie's War*, Bawden has taken her own wartime childhood as the starting point for a subjective novel about a young girl's highly charged preoccupation with family relationships. She chooses not to engage with war at an ideological level, or with its history or politics, beyond the fact of evacuation that sets events in motion. War plays a metaphorical rather than a literal role in signifying the internal struggle of the protagonist as she measures the relationships she encounters against her romanticized notion of family ties – hence the ambiguity of the title. One of the few direct references to war simply reinforces Carrie's self-absorption. In comparing the bombing that has been taking place elsewhere to adult conversation going on over children's heads, Carrie both acknowledges the remote reality of war and takes refuge in a child's powerlessness. War is little more than a backdrop and catalyst in the novel, but the family separation it so frequently caused was of sufficient significance in Bawden's own life for her to write about it three times in fictional form: in *Carrie's War*, *Anna Apparent* (1972; a novel for adults) and *Keeping Henry* (1988). Bawden's need to rework personal experience a number of times suggests a therapeutic purpose to her writing on wartime childhood; such a pattern is common to the work of a number of children's writers to be discussed in these chapters.

Judith Kerr: *When Hitler Stole Pink Rabbit*

Unlike Nina Bawden, Judith Kerr did not set out to write literary fiction for children, nor was she separated from her parents for more than short periods; yet she shares with Bawden a preoccupation with the immediate and long-term effects of historical events on family interaction. Kerr was already an established author of picturebooks (*The Tiger Who Came to Tea*, 1968; and *Mog the Forgetful Cat*, 1970) when she was inspired by questions from her own children to write an account of her refugee childhood for a child audience. Judith Kerr is the daughter of Alfred Kerr, an eminent Jewish theatre critic and essayist in prewar Germany. As a leading public figure, Kerr knew that his public prominence was likely to lead to an early arrest, so in 1933 he left the Third Reich with his family, escaping via Switzerland to Paris and eventually to London. Judith Kerr was nine when the family left Germany.

When Hitler Stole Pink Rabbit (1971), the story of the family's first two years in exile, necessarily includes more historical information than *Carrie's War*, since the family's fate is determined at every step by political events. Kerr takes care to introduce the historical context in a form accessible to her child reader, so that child protagonists comment on a poster of Hitler in the street, or a playground fight echoes street battles between Nazis and Socialists. The

Reichstag fire in Berlin and the possible election of the NSDAP (Nationalso-
zialische Deutsche Arbeiterpartei, the Nationalist Socialist Workers' Party of
Germany; the title was shortened to 'Nazi' as a label for individual members)
to power provide the impetus for the family's exile; the parents in the novel
discuss these political events openly with their children. *When Hitler Stole
Pink Rabbit* is the first volume of a trilogy: the following two volumes take the
reader into Kerr's adolescence and adult life and were published for adults.
In Kerr's case, the autobiographical impulse led to a continuation of the story,
as the adult seeks to revise the child's understanding of radical changes in
family dynamics caused by the exigencies of exile.

Kerr, who renames her fictional younger self Anna in *When Hitler Stole
Pink Rabbit*, presents family separation as Anna's greatest fear throughout the
novel. Whenever a temporary parting is mooted – in order for her parents to
find accommodation in England before sending for the children, for example –
Anna is adamant that she does not mind being a refugee as long as the family
stays together at all costs. Anna is the focalizing character, who registers and
reflects family anxiety and neurosis. While her brother Max appears to adapt
readily to any new situation, Anna is held back by concern for the physical and
emotional welfare of her father. On hearing of a famous anti-Nazi professor
who was forced to live in a dog kennel in a prison camp, she imagines that the
phrase 'a price on his head', used in connection with her father, must indicate
a similar torture – one where heavy gold coins would fall on him from a great
height. Kerr depicts the fears of an imaginative child surrounded by distant,
half-understood, dangers with a sure touch; a child of Anna's sensibility might
easily interpret an idiom literally to feed existing fears. As a powerless child
whose only recourse is to the games of an overwrought imagination, Anna
prays desperately that her father's nightmares should visit her at night instead
of him. Like Carrie, Anna takes on a parenting role, but hers is a reversal of
roles and remains purely imaginary, at least until she is able to supplement the
family income in the second volume of the trilogy. Anna's desire to protect
stems from a keen awareness that her father is a writer without a language: the
critic who had enjoyed the power of consigning any Berlin theatre production
to success or failure is reduced to impotence.

If Kerr allows free reign to her childhood sympathies by allowing Anna to
register her father's moods and anxieties in *When Hitler Stole Pink Rabbit*, a
reassessment of the situation becomes the central strand in the next two
volumes of her trilogy. Kerr becomes more self-critical; she represents herself
at the beginning of *The Other Way Round* (1975; republished in 2002 under
the title *Bombs on Aunt Daisy*) as a self-indulgent and naive adolescent who
finds her mother increasingly irritating. And in the final volume, *A Small
Person Far Away* (1978), the fundamental realignment in the family caused by
her father's failure to find work is viewed in a new light. Anna is now an adult,
visiting her mother in a Berlin hospital after she has made a suicide attempt.
In passages of dialogue and reflection, Kerr allows Anna to acknowledge her
mother's impetuosity, as well as her practicality and the rigours of the menial
work she undertook in order to keep the family afloat. She also admits to a
degree of resentment at her brother's ability to distance himself from family

tensions. This reappraisal of family dislocation is the impetus that drives Kerr's trilogy to its conclusion. When Anna revisits the family home in Berlin, she suddenly finds herself asking for her mother in German, thus simultaneously regaining the dormant German language and the close, dependent relationship with her mother that she enjoyed in childhood. Freud's theories on the repression of painful experience and the triggers that may cause it to resurface in the mind are now common knowledge, and a familiar feature of the literary landscape. In this instance, an instantaneous reconnection with childhood seems rather too neatly Freudian, and reflects the author's desire for a satisfactory resolution to a personal history.

Judith Kerr recast her childhood in fictional form, with the initial intention of informing the young about the lives of wartime refugees. As she continues her story and begins to write for an adult audience, the adult seeks to reinterpret childhood and present it as a life story by which she can live. *When Hitler Stole Pink Rabbit* is not as aesthetically satisfying as *Carrie's War* – it does not have the same metaphoric coherence or structural balance – but it is the first step towards the reconstruction of a life history and a remarkable representation of a child's insight into the vagaries of a refugee existence.

Irene Dische: *Between Two Seasons of Happiness*

Like Bawden, Irene Dische's intentions are writerly in the first instance. Although there is a surface simplicity to her writing, Dische expects a degree of literary sophistication and historical knowledge from her audience. *Between Two Seasons of Happiness* (1998) is a novel for experienced young readers; it follows the fortunes of young Peter, his father Laszlo and grandfather Dr Nagel in Hungary and Berlin during the prewar period and throughout the Second World War. Peter's father Laszlo, a 'good-luck man', is appointed to a diplomatic post in Berlin by the Hungarian government. Laszlo takes Peter to live with him in Berlin in the early days of the Third Reich, but eventually has to tell his son of the family's Jewish identity and send him back to his grandfather in Hungary. Peter conducts a relationship with his father by letter; when the letters no longer arrive because Laszlo has been executed for forging passports for Jews, Dr Nagel secretly continues the supply of letters to Peter by writing them himself.

Historical circumstances in prewar Europe dictate the changing pattern of this particular family constellation. The narrator in Dische's novel ensures that the reader is in no doubt as to the temperamental clash between Peter's father and grandfather, and Peter's pivotal position between the two. Dr Nagel's emotional distance and orderly existence and Laszlo's spontaneous hedonism are clearly delineated, albeit in a detached manner. After crashing his fast car and killing Peter's mother in the process, for example, Laszlo is described as escaping: 'with bumps and scratches on his handsome exterior' (13). Such elliptical irony confounds the reader's expectations of grief and remorse while hinting that the 'handsome exterior' may be more important to Laszlo than the death of his wife. In the second half of the novel, focalization places Peter's reactions to events centre stage, but the reader still has to read between the lines. Dische's narrator allows her reader to deduce six-year-old Peter's longing, hesitancy and misunderstandings from an apparently objective description of the sterile routine to which he politely submits in his grandfather's house. This narrative strategy is made explicit when Peter suddenly sees a photograph of his father and is overcome by a sense of longing: 'If he had known how to name his feeling he might have said "love" (21). There is a sophisticated irony in the hypothetical qualification of this statement by a knowing narrator, an irony that implies an audience considerably older than the child protagonist.

Peter's loss is intensified as war breaks out and he has to endure the longest period of separation from his father that he has ever known. At the same time, the reader discovers an unsuspected tenderness in Dr Nagel. He adopts his son Laszlo's lighthearted persona in writing to Peter, just as he gives all his household employees six months' wages in advance to reassure them that the Germans are not about to invade. No more is said about Dr Nagel, but the reader can begin to reappraise this fastidious, uncommunicative man and conclude that he is, at heart, not so very different from his son after all.

Dische is adept at making the historical context a part of the fabric of the novel in a limited number of telling instances. First, Laszlo attempts to explain to his young son – not yet six – that Germany is changing its shape and size just like the flooding river Danube he has taken him to see. Dische's intention is to demonstrate Laszlo's humanity in making comparisons that his small son can apprehend, but at the same time, the reference to Germany's expansionism situates the novel historically for the reader. Later, a child's unknowing interpretation of events becomes an implicit commentary. Peter's appropriation of the swastika on the 'pretty red flags'; his love of drawing them all over his Hungarian picture books, and his inability to get the direction of the hooks right, indicate that for a small boy the swastika is a challenging pattern rather than a sinister symbol. Similarly, Peter regards Hitler, the Führer, as 'obviously a dear, but cranky man' (52) who is always cheered for his hectoring and scolding. Dische's irony demands a response from her historically aware reader, in contrast to Kerr's account in *When Hitler Stole Pink Rabbit*, where historical references are evaluated within the text.

Kerr devotes considerable space to the learning of new languages, which taxed her as a child, whereas Dische glosses over Peter's adaptation from Hungarian to German in a few lines. Dische underplays the language-learning process in the interests of the artistic whole: the interlude in Berlin with his father is a carefree time for Peter, a time of emotional stability when all difficulties can be overcome. The role of language in migration is registered in the form rather than the content of the novel. As the child of immigrants to the United States, Dische's own written style has occasional dissonances that add to the quality of alienation that permeates the text for the American or British reader. Phrases such as 'a well paying job' (12), or 'I'm a good-luck man' (reminiscent of the German *Glückskind*, 'lucky child'), carry echoes of the German language, and therefore act as reminders both of the book's setting and of Dische's heritage.

Conclusion

The novels of Dische, Kerr and Bawden form one strand of the shift in emphasis that has taken place in the latter half of the twentieth century in the purpose, as well as the content, of children's fiction on war. From the entertainment value and patriotic intent of many early twentieth-century war stories to the interiority of *Carrie's War* and the psychoanalytical probing of Kerr, children's literature of war has become a site for the representation of childhood trauma and its aftermath and, in Irene Dische's novel, for the literary expression of a cultural and political legacy. All three writers have chosen to focus on the disruption of adult–child relationships in the context of war, in texts that are autobiographical or concerned with personal and individual responses to war. Only Kerr and Dische demonstrate any underlying didactic intention in relation to the broader ideological, historical and moral issues of the period: there is an implicit criticism of the absurdity and cruelty of persecution in the early pages of *When Hitler Stole Pink Rabbit*, just as Laszlo's clumsy attempt to counteract the anti-Semitism experienced by his son in a Berlin school conveys a definite message to the reader. In texts to be discussed in the next chapter, didacticism and collective memory move into the foreground in narratives conveying a reinterpretation of the wartime period to the next generation.

Please note: To avoid duplication, the Works Cited and Further Reading sections for this chapter are combined with those for Chapter 5.

WORKS CITED

Primary Texts

Bawden, N., *Carrie's War*, with an Afterword by Julia Eccleshare (London: Puffin, 1993).
Dische, I., *Between Two Seasons of Happiness* (London: Bloomsbury, 1998).
Kerr, J., *When Hitler Stole Pink Rabbit* (London: Collins, 1971).

Comparative and Psychoanalytic Approaches: Personal History and Collective Memory

5

Gillian Lathey

KEY TEXTS

M. Foreman, *War Boy* (1989)
G. Pausewang, *The Final Journey* (1996)
T. Ungerer, *Die Gedanken sind frei: Meine Kindheit im Elsass* (1993); *Tomi: A Childhood under the Nazis* (1998)
R. Westall, *The Machine-Gunners* (1975)

Still addressing the topic of war, in this chapter Gillian Lathey introduces and applies techniques derived from two related critical approaches: translation studies and comparative literature. While she shows how a topic such as war can help focus a comparison of texts written in different languages and cultures, she also highlights the tendency for the children's literature in English-speaking countries to be parochial; while world rights to children's books written in English tend to be sold readily, very few books originally written in other languages find their way into the children's book markets of Britain, North America and Australia. This not only limits the insights into other cultures for young people who speak no language other than English, but it also encourages them to assume that theirs is the dominant 'normal' culture, not least in the way it constructs childhood and adolescence. As the comparisons below show, in many ways, and for a variety of reasons, at least on the subject of war, English-language children's literature tends to soften the experience and deal in less direct and challenging ways with ethical issues and the facts of history than does children's literature written in other languages; not least in the presentation of children's role in war as heroic and 'good'. In the twenty-first century, however, such interpretations of wars, past and present, are clearly inadequate; a comparative approach seems increasingly relevant for this and a range of topical issues now given expression in world children's literature.

BOX 5.1 COMPARATIVE LITERATURE

What scholars and critics who study literature comparatively do:

■ They trace cross-cultural influences between national literatures, whether written in the same or different languages. Scholars have, for example, examined the historical influence of *Household Tales* collected by the German Grimm Brothers on the literatures of a number of countries, and the impact of the *Harry Potter* series on developments in children's literatures across the globe is currently a fruitful area for comparative investigation.

■ They examine literature written in the same period in different cultures and countries to expose and contrast the social, political and ideological content of literatures at a given historical moment.

■ Comparatists who work in the field of Translation Studies undertake close analysis of source (the original) and target (the translation) texts to discover evidence of the manipulation of stories, poems, plays and novels as they cross cultural and national boundaries. In children's literature, abridgement, censorship, and cultural context adaptation (changing foreign food, coinage etc. to their British, North American or Australian equivalents) reveal a great deal about differences in constructions of childhood in the source and target cultures.

■ They raise awareness of difference and alternative literary forms, genres, and thematic content in literatures across the world.

■ They reveal patterns of similarity in world literatures, for example the motifs common to folk tales internationally.

■ In a branch of comparative study known as Imagology, scholars explore the representation of one nationality in the literature of another. The representation of the French 'mademoiselle' in the British school story, for example, raises questions about the image of the French in young British minds in the first half of the twentieth century.

Collective memory dictates the popular perception of turning points in history; recollection crystallizes in the national psyche into familiar patterns. From legendary heroism in combat to the construction of memorials to the dead, different national and ethnic groups across the world have developed a collective interpretation of the events of World War II. Yet such interpretations are constantly challenged by both insiders and outsiders, and children's literature has become a significant site for both the perpetuation and the interrogation of national perspectives on the past. In Japan, for example, children are introduced from an early age to picturebooks on the terrible loss of life and injuries caused by the atomic bombs dropped on Hiroshima and Nagasaki; the national emphasis on the Japanese as victims is replicated in children's literature. One of the very few texts to interrogate the role of the Japanese armed forces is Miyoko Matsutani's *Yaneurabeya no Himitsu* (*The Secrets of the Attic*, 1988), an account of the testing of biological weapons on Chinese captives by 731 Unit of the Japanese army. Germany's reckoning with its past, on the other hand, has produced both evasive texts for children, where collective guilt remains unacknowledged, and others that embody an act of atonement. Comparative readings of texts originating from such widely differing circumstances and interpretations of the past can unlock new understandings of national literatures on the subject of war.

Comparative literature

Although a common academic discipline in continental European universities, where staff and students are accustomed to reading across cultures and languages, comparative literature (see Box 5.1) has until recently been a neglected area of study in the USA and remains so in the UK. This is regrettable, since to pursue influences across national and linguistic borders, to trace the manipulation of stories as they travel, and to place texts from different cultures side by side, can be a most illuminating approach to literary studies. Susan Bassnett, one of the few leading British comparatists, offers the definition that comparative literature 'is concerned with patterns of connection in literatures across both time and space' (1993: 1). These 'patterns' may be recurring similarities, as in motifs common to folk tales across the world, or may result from direct cross-cultural influences; the fairy tales of Oscar Wilde, for example, particularly *The Happy Prince* (1888), are undoubtedly indebted to the work of the Danish children's author Hans Christian Andersen.

In addition to direct cross-cultural influences, the connection to be made between cultures may be one of contrasting developments. For instance, in the 1930s, at a time when British children's literature was deeply conservative in approach and subject matter, there was a political polarization in German children's fiction. Texts for children reflected the radical politics of the Weimar republic, from the urban proletarian novel to the fascist sentiments of a novel such as *Hitlerjunge Quex* (1932) by Karl Alois Schenzinger. Such contrasts highlight the ideological content and historical context of the children's literature of both cultures: an examination of the children's books of a particular period in one country or language can throw into relief qualities previously taken for granted in another.

Since the Second World War was, by definition, an international event, both comparative literature and translation studies have much to offer anyone embarking on a study of the period in children's literature, just as child readers can only benefit from reading literature written from different points of view. Scholars and critics who take a comparative approach can begin to unravel the web of national mythology, ideological revision and personal psychology that supports any one text in comparison with others arising from different historical circumstances. A significant comparative project on war fiction for children organized by three European countries, Belgium (Flanders), Portugal and the UK, has already produced two informative publications that include many texts set in World War II: *War and Peace in Children's Books* (1998), a trilingual annotated list of children's books on war in Dutch, English and

Portuguese, and an anthology of translated texts, *In Times of War* (2000), that facilitates comparative insights for those who only read English.

Although comparatists read across languages, it is possible to begin to study cultural and socio-historical difference by reading translated texts without any knowledge of the source language. A number of children's books on the Second World War from mainland Europe are available in translation. Anne Holm's allegorical *I am David* (1965), translated from the Danish, offers a decontextualized account of a young boy as archetypal victim and refugee, while Tatiana Vassilieva, in *A Hostage to War* (1996, translated from Russian via German), has written a diary account of her transportation from Russia to a labour camp in Germany at the age of thirteen. Hans-Peter Richter's trilogy, Gudrun Pausewang's *The Final Journey* (1996) and Reinhardt Jung's *Dreaming in Black and White* (2000) are inscribed with the agonized signs of what has become known as 'the German question' – the problem of how to address collective national guilt for the crimes of the Holocaust. Reading a translation opens new perspectives on the historical period in which it is set, but it is important to bear in mind that a translation is a text that reaches the reader through the medium of a translator.

Translators and publishing houses frequently adapt books to meet the assumed expectations of readers in the target language (the language into which the text is translated), a process that may be immediately visible in the marketing and packaging of a book. The German paperback edition of Pausewang's *The Final Journey* (original title *Reise im August*, which translates literally as 'Journey in August'), for example, has a stylized representation of a railway line leading into the entrance of a death camp, a muted, sombre image with no human beings in sight (see Figure 4). As can be seen in Figure 5, Puffin produced a collage for a British audience, where a large red swastika (the lettering of the title is also red) is superimposed on an archive photograph of Jews wearing stars. The initial impact of the British cover is undoubtedly greater, in line with the jacket text recommending a story that: 'reveals the atrocities of Nazi Germany during the Second World War'. Images of swastikas (on front and back covers) and hints of 'Nazi atrocities' attract the young British reader, whereas such sensationalism would be likely to alienate German readers already aware of national guilt.

In this chapter a cross-cultural, comparative discussion of Pausewang's book and the work of Robert Westall, as well as of picturebook accounts of wartime childhoods by British artist Michael Foreman and Tomi Ungerer (born in Alsace), will reveal the interplay between personal need and changing national perspectives on the past in the 60 years since 1945. When writing about wartime childhoods, the ideological starting points for British and German authors could hardly be further apart. Although certain experiences were shared by British and German children – air-raids, absent fathers, the gleaning of political information from adult conversation and radio broadcasts – others, such as the Hitler Youth rallies and persecution of Jews in Germany, were not. Above all, the subsequent sifting, sorting and reconstruction of childhood memory by adult writers takes place in response to a sense of national pride on the one hand, and collective national guilt on the other.

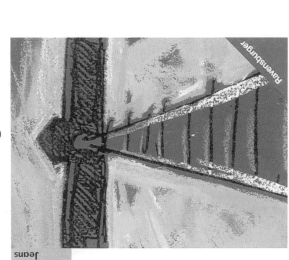

Figure 5   The 1998 British cover for Pausewang's
The Final Journey

Figure 4   Gudrun Pausewang, *Resie im August*; cover
illustration by Gabie Hilgert (© Ravensburger Buchverlag
Otto Maier GmbH, Ravensburg)

Robert Westall: *The Machine-Gunners*

Robert Westall grew up on Tyneside during the Second World War. He witnessed the bombing of what was an area of great strategic importance, and shared with his family and neighbours the constant fear of air-raids. Westall decided to write about this childhood for his own son, so that he could communicate the heady sense of danger and excitement which he once expressed in an interview with a *Guardian* journalist (28 March 1991): 'For a ten-year-old to be lightly bombed – we're talking of five bombers a night – is enormous fun. I've never had an adventure like it, which is perhaps why I tend to return to it.' As Westall's comment indicates, war was to become a major theme in a career of writing for children that began with *The Machine-Gunners* (1975).

In *The Machine-Gunners*, Westall successfully conveys children's responses to events that break the monotony of daily routines and introduce a welcome note of danger and fear. Like Nina Bawden in *Carrie's War* (see Chapter 4), he incorporates the tiniest of remembered details into his fiction. In both the novel and a memoir (*Children of the Blitz: Memories of Wartime Childhood*, 1985), Westall compares the sound of approaching bombers to the sound of a stick dragged along iron railings, and flattened bullets found on the street to silver mushrooms. By selecting these authentic childhood sensations, writing in realist mode and including elements of the adventure-story genre, Westall creates in *The Machine-Gunners* fiction that has pace, suspense, and affective power. Westall's protagonists also adopt the values of his childhood. Charles McGill's pride at being a 'Britisher' is manifest, and the image of Germans in the novel is at first that promoted in cinema newsreels of jackbooted troops marching through the countries of Europe. Yet when the German pilot, Rudi, is found and given shelter by Charles and his friends, the ambivalence of Westall's purpose becomes apparent and begins to change the direction of the novel.

Westall was well aware of the need to temper the anti-German sentiments and unquestioning patriotism of his own childhood for a child audience reading the book thirty years after the events depicted, and at a time of changed relations with Germany and different attitudes to war. By introducing the figure of Rudi, Westall increases tension in the plot of the novel, allows his child protagonists to develop autonomy and, most significantly, creates an opportunity for an insight into the German experience. In passages of self-doubt, Rudi expresses his disenchantment with the Third Reich:

> Besides, he realized sadly, he just didn't want to escape. His patriotism towards the Fatherland was dead. He tried to coax it back to life: thought of the Fuehrer; thought of his old father and mother and how ashamed they'd be of his cowardice.   (140)

Rudi is a sympathetic German who confounds all expectations of a 'Nazi'. But the ambivalence inscribed in the character of Rudi goes further. He utters German phrases that echo the popular war comics and stories of the time and that Westall represents inaccurately. 'Dumkopf' loses an 'm', for example, and 'Hände hoch' its umlaut, while Rudi sends the verb to the end of the sentence at every opportunity when speaking English – even where this would not be necessary in German. Rudi, conceived as a figure to counteract a stereotype, nevertheless bears the linguistic hallmarks of one: his language matches readers' preconceptions, even though his sentiments do not. It may well have been Westall's intention to meet his audience's expectations in order to undermine them all the more effectively when Rudi is critical of the Nazi regime, but Rudi is never as convincing a creation as the salt-of-the-earth Geordies Westall drew from experience. His indecisiveness and introspection are likely to alienate the very readers Westall wished to convert.

Despite his didactic intentions in creating Rudi, Westall cannot quite free himself from the nostalgia for the clear-cut value system of wartime Britain, which lends the novel its panache and resurfaces in later texts set in World War II (*Fathom Five*, 1979, *A Time of Fire*, 1994). Even in the novel *Gulf* (1993), set in a late twentieth-century conflict, there are traces of Westall's childhood perceptions of the national enemy of the time. A signal that Andy, a young British boy, has assumed the alternative persona of the thirteen-year-old Iraqi soldier, Latif, is a switch to: 'that strange guttural language' (54). The term 'guttural' has a long history of negative association with German in particular (O'Sullivan, 1990), but it has become a cypher for the alien in language generally. Latif, who represents the 'enemy' in this text, utters the same kinds of sounds as the Germans of Westall's childhood imagination. That childhood, with its imaginary scenarios of loss and devastation as well as extraordinary and memorable events, is the origin of Westall's preoccupation with war in many of the texts he wrote for children, from the entertainment and suspense of *The Machine-Gunners* and its sequel *Fathom Five*, to the lonely and frequently disturbing journey of a young air-raid victim in *The Kingdom by the Sea* (1990).

German writers and the legacy of the Third Reich

If Robert Westall is at pains in *The Machine-Gunners* to attempt a revision of his childhood allegiances, what might be the position of German writers who were members of the Hitler Youth and gave their support to a regime that was responsible for the Holocaust? How do they now view the exhilaration of a mass movement that was cleverly orchestrated to appeal to the insecurities of the young? Westall addresses personal and national history by drawing on the adventure-story genre; such a choice was not open to his near contemporary Hans-Peter Richter, who grew up in Germany in the 1930s, became a member of the Hitler Youth, and served as a young soldier in the Wehrmacht. Richter's trilogy based on his own Nazi childhood and youth (*Friedrich* was first published in Germany in 1961, *I Was There* in 1962, and *The Time of the Young Soldiers* in 1976) belongs to a first wave of German writers to address the persecution of German Jews. Adults have seized on *Friedrich* as a text that enables the young to understand the causes of the inhumanity of the Third Reich: it was for many years recommended reading in German schools, and had by 1989 sold one million copies. *Friedrich* was regarded in its time as an ideal text for reshaping the historical consciousness of a nation even though, as prominent Israeli critic Zohar Shavit has pointed out (1988: 20–1), there is an unnaturally positive representation of the Jewish family in the novel.

Such over-compensation is an early stage in the interrogation of Germany's past that has found new directions and emphases since *Friedrich* was first published. Children's literature on the subject is almost exclusively auto-biographical. Many texts suppress any responsibility for the policies and crimes of the Third Reich by, for example, adopting the uncomprehending point of view of a young child or attributing all blame to Hitler and the Nazi hierarchy (Lathey, 1999), while in others there is an attempt to acknowledge complicity. It is against this background that Gudrun Pausewang wrote *The Final Journey* (1996; first published in Germany in 1992), a book that represents a watershed in her own crusade to inform the young and to write her way towards personal and collective atonement.

Gudrun Pausewang: *The Final Journey*

During her childhood in a German-speaking area of what is now the Czech Republic, Gudrun Pausewang belonged to the generation of young people who idolized Adolf Hitler. At the end of the war, after her father – an ardent Nazi – had been killed on the Russian front, Pausewang, her mother and five younger siblings had to flee the family homestead to escape reprisals by local Czechs. With nothing more than a handcart on which to transport their belongings, the Pausewangs made their way on foot to Hamburg, some three hundred miles away. It was during this journey that the seventeen-year-old Pausewang first began to confront the vacuum created by the collapse of a value system that had led to the Holocaust. All of her subsequent work as a children's writer has been driven by a desire to warn and politicize the young, a desire that arises from her own youthful transgression. Protagonists in Pausewang's novels are frequently one-dimensional figures whose fate is set against the broader, more compelling canvas of human suffering and the collapse of the social order, as is the case in her two dystopian novels (see Box 12.3) based on nuclear catastrophes *The Last Children* (1989) and *Fall-out* (1994).

In a number of autobiographical texts (as yet only available in German) that address the legacy of the Third Reich directly, Pausewang treads a fine line between the recollection of personal trauma and the didactic impulse to acknowledge collective culpability. These are self-conscious narratives, addressed initially to her son and interrupted by passages of retrospective commentary. Pausewang gradually moves through this autobiographical writing towards the reconciliation of a friendship with the Czech family now living on the smallholding her family had left behind in 1945. In *The Final Journey*, written after the completion of her autobiographical odyssey, Pausewang turns to fiction in depicting the last days of a young Jewish girl, Alice, as she travels to Auschwitz. In her writing about the Third Reich up to this point, Pausewang circled ever closer to the ultimate guilt of the German nation, which she finally addresses directly in this novel.

Any German writer who represents the last journey of Jewish prisoners on their way to Auschwitz is open to critical attack by survivors or their relatives and descendants, but Pausewang's own history compelled her to take that risk. When reading *The Final Journey* in translation, it is important to remember that Pausewang wrote the book for the generation of young Germans of the late 1990s. She assumes that her readers know about the policies of the Third Reich. In the second instance of the mediation of this text in the process of translation, the British version includes an afterword that provides the reader with a bare historical outline of the fate of the Jews.

The narrative in *The Final Journey* is designed to provoke reflection as well as disgust in the young reader. Pausewang orchestrates a number of narrative strategies to achieve both of these aims. The intensity of aggressive human interaction and foetid living conditions in the wagon is punctuated by flashbacks to the period when Alice was in hiding, thus offering some respite to the reader. By creating a protagonist who has been both over-protected and deceived by adults, Pausewang elicits empathy in her young reader. Alice is almost twelve, yet she has only limited knowledge of sexual behaviour and childbirth, of the anti-Semitic policies of the regime that dictates her fate, and even of the likely destination of her absent parents. As she quickly learns about life by witnessing the birth of a baby and the physical intimacy of couples, and from conversations with her peers, Alice begins to reject her family's values. She confronts her grandfather, demanding to know why she is ignorant of information about the concentration camps that is common knowledge to others of her age. In a line that might be taken as a justification for addressing the subject at all in children's fiction, Alice expresses a sense of outrage with which many adolescent readers can sympathize: 'Do you think I can't stand the truth?' (72). Alice's progress towards adolescence is accelerated; in a few short days she rejects past values, revises her understanding of national identity, gains a degree of political understanding, and begins her first period as she enters the gas chamber. The narrative function of Alice's passage to maturity is entirely different from that of Carrie in Bawden's novel. Carrie's reflection and perceptions are the subject of Bawden's novel; Alice is a conduit, a narrative strategy to enable the reader to understand historical issues of persecution and ethnic or national allegiance.

The title journey in Pausewang's novel is therefore a metaphor in the familiar sense of a voyage of self-discovery, but it also suggests another common analogy between travel towards a destination and the trajectory of an individual or a social group towards death. Within the confined space of a cattle truck, Pausewang presents a microcosm of society that includes representatives of different age groups, social classes, family constellations and occupations. Although such social engineering may seem artificial, it enables Pausewang to achieve a number of objectives. First, hers is not the idealized portrait of Jews of which Zohar Shavit is critical. Ruth Mandel's husband, for example, divorced his Jewish wife because he was only half Jewish and wished to save himself.

There is even an indication that the persecuted have the potential to become persecutors, when the 'trench-coat woman', irritated by the behaviour of the mentally retarded adult Ernstl, suggests that 'that sort should be in a special truck' (80). Secondly, different points of view enable Alice, and through her the reader, to interrogate concepts of national and ethnic identity and responsibility. Alice thinks of herself as German rather than Jewish, in line with her grandfather's opinions: he instructs her to clench her teeth to suppress the pain of an upset stomach and reminds her that 'A German girl is not afraid' (47). Ruth Mandel, on the other hand, responds angrily to such a display of the nationalistic interpretation of all aspects of behaviour that was propagated during the Third Reich. Both Ruth's daughter, Rebekka, and the young Jewish boy, Aaron, express pride in their Jewishness and avoid any mention of their German nationality. Aaron also predicts Germany's future as a pariah nation.

What is immediately striking in comparing Pausewang's Second World War fiction with that of Robert Westall, is that Westall subordinates any didactic or therapeutic purpose to the desire to tell a good story with direct appeal for a child audience. Westall has described reading chapters of *The Machine-Gunners* aloud to his son: 'Twelve spoke to twelve, without interruption' (Westall, 1978: 37). Westall's son represents the young reader he wishes to transport to a time when life was permanently spiced with fear; times were hard but never dull. Pausewang's autobiographical account of her refugee trek, too, was written for her son, but both there and in *The Final Journey*, her intention is to use harrowing stories to educate and to warn. Nostalgia and the representation of positive memories have no place in the writing of those who inherit the legacy of a Nazi childhood. Pausewang's memoirs and novels are part of a long-term national, as well as personal, process of reassessment; she writes against a background of national guilt that places moral and historical expectations on texts for the young.

The historical development from entertainment to a more reflective, morally responsible approach to war fiction for children is nowhere more apparent than in Germany, where children's literature has played an essential role in the process of personal and national catharsis. From self-indulgent stories of Germany's postwar devastation to the implicitly confessional writing of Gudrun Pausewang, German children's books register the denial as well as the troubled conscience of postwar Germany. Educational policy makers have also turned to children's literature: accounts of childhood experience during the Third Reich by both German and Jewish writers have long been required reading in the school curricula both of the Federal Republic of Germany and of the former German Democratic Republic before reunification in 1989. In this instance, and in the work of all writers addressing the legacy of the Holocaust, children's literature becomes a potential channel for atonement. British children's fiction on World War II, although taught in schools, is not part of such a high-profile national programme of reconciliation. British authors are therefore free to address a range of imaginative purposes, from a focus on the subjective consequences of war, to the fond backward glance. In the picturebook memoir, too, there are parallel contrasts between culturally determined visions of the past.

Images of wartime childhoods: Michael Foreman's *War Boy* and Tomi Ungerer's *A Childhood Under the Nazis*

Of the many picturebooks set in the Second World War published in recent decades, most take the fate of a particular child as the *leitmotif* through scenes of chaos, destruction, displacement and death. In the texts to be discussed next, that child is the author–illustrator of the book, who balances text and image to achieve the dual purpose of expressing affective memory, and informing an audience about the past. Michael Foreman and Tomi Ungerer have produced texts that are ambivalent in their implied audience. Both are primarily artists, who represent memories of the war years in a hybrid of the picturebook and illustrated information book forms usually associated with a child audience. Foreman's *War Boy* (1989), however, has been enjoyed by many of his reminiscing contemporaries, and a review of the French version of Ungerer's book in *Le Monde*, after pondering the question of audience, had to conclude that it was a book about childhood for all. Such initial points of contact between the two artists only emphasize the divergence in the narrative and visual stance towards the past adopted in each case.

War Boy is set on the east coast of Britain in the rural village of Pakenfield near Lowestoft. Foreman's vision of early childhood is suffused with the positive memories of a loving and secure domestic setting. In a series of images that delight the eye at the turn of every page, he mixes exact technical drawings copied from original sources with humorous vignettes and glowing watercolours. The reader recognizes the ultimate danger of war as Foreman's mother flees from an incendiary bomb with her son in her arms, and in a core of sadness for the soldiers the young Foreman met who did not return, that runs through the book. Nevertheless, the general impression is that of a childhood savoured by the adult, who presents the ideology of the period uncritically. The written text closes with a paraphrase of the popular song, frequently performed by singer Vera Lynn, that epitomized the British patriotic spirit, 'There'll be bluebirds over the white cliffs of Dover'. Foreman's personal recollections culminate in a reaffirmation of adult belief in a victorious outcome for Britain: 'So it was true, all the things the grown-ups had said during the dark days. Now the war was over everything would be all right, there'll be blue birds over the white cliffs, not barrage balloons. And men with rainbows on their chests would, like my kite, come home' (95).

Tomi Ungerer's *A Childhood Under the Nazis* is, in contrast, an uncomfortable, self-conscious text caught between the languages and cultures of France and Germany in Alsace. Ungerer's conscience is troubled on behalf of those French nationals who collaborated with the German occupying forces, and his own part-German cultural heritage. In line with his bilingual upbringing and its political connotations, Ungerer first published his autobiography in French (as *À la guerre comme à la guerre*, 1991), then 'reconceived' the book in German (*Die Gedanken sind frei*, 1993) and, finally, wrote an English edition for the US market in 1998 (references are from the American edition unless stated otherwise). This account of a childhood in German-occupied Alsace opens on an apologetic note as Ungerer regrets that his childhood perception of war as a great spectacle might: 'appear to be a trivialization of the great dramas of misery, torture and violence' (1998: vii). Indeed, Ungerer even questions the text's authenticity by claiming to mistrust childhood memories (German edition, 1993: 82). A chronological gap between text and pictures intensifies this ambivalence towards the past: the images are those drawn at the time by Ungerer between the ages of nine and fourteen, but the text was written by the reflecting adult.

Ungerer's view of humanity is marked by a wartime childhood that compels him to eschew sentimentality and to assume a pragmatic, even cynical attitude to childhood events. In the German edition, he reflects on the consequences of his own successful, if subversively critical, adaptation to life under the aegis of the Third Reich. Ungerer's description of being caught up in the Nazification process and the necessary development of 'chameleon-like' (German edition, 1993: 57) qualities lead him to acknowledge a degree of moral flexibility. The child who was a French boy at home, a German at school and an Alsace lad with his friends, made two sets of cards for playing Old Maid featuring, respectively, French and German figures. In drawings indicative of his outstanding graphic talent, Ungerer satirizes both sides: the naive-looking French boy scout is juxtaposed to the sweating member of the Hitler Youth banging his drum (1998: 80–1). But Ungerer also conformed to a school exercise to draw a Jew (1998: 42), producing a caricature on his mother's advice that would meet the expectations of his teachers. In what can be read as an artistic act of atonement, Ungerer later (1948) drew a bleeding and despairing concentration camp inmate with the caption 'Dachau Buchenwald Ausschwitz' (1998: 162). Throughout this text he conducts a process of moral self-examination that can never be fully resolved. *Fascination*, a television documentary on Ungerer made for the British Channel 4 in 1996, revealed that he admires the visual acumen of Nazi propagandists, and is to this day a keen collector of Nazi memorabilia. Yet he also appears on screen weeping during one of his frequent visits to the concentration camp of Struthof in Alsace.

The most telling point of contrast between the ambiguity of Ungerer's response to his wartime childhood in an enemy-occupied area and the national pride evoked by Foreman, can be found in the closing lines of both texts. Whereas Foreman expresses a retrospective confidence in the words spoken to him in childhood by adults – 'it was true, all the things the grown-ups had said' – Ungerer's experience has taught him to rely on no one. Only the immensity and incorruptibility of the sea, first glimpsed on a visit to Normandy for his sister's wedding, is capable of cleansing and reviving him: 'enough water to rinse my despair, wash out the past, drown my rancor' (1998: 174). Changes in cultural heritage from French to German and back again before, during and after the German occupation, and the accompanying reversals in political ideology, have made this narrator wary, mistrustful and introspective in his review of wartime adventures. Personal and national accommodation to the occupation resulted in a disillusionment that contrasts sharply with Foreman's retrospective glow. Foreman retains, in the apparently unified vision of child and adult, the positive British national perspective on the war years, whereas Ungerer's text is troubled by knowledge of French collaboration with the

Germans, and an underlying personal guilt at his ability to adapt to changes in historical circumstances so readily. Both Foreman's and Ungerer's views of history are inevitably partial, but comparison raises questions about the interpretation of history presented to the young in picturebook form.

Conclusion

Writing on the Second World War will soon cease to be informed by personal experience. Even those who were children at the time have now reached old age, so that an expression of the experiences that marked the childhoods of Bawden, Kerr, Westall, Pausewang, Ungerer and Foreman will soon no longer be possible. As the number of eye-witnesses to wartime events dwindles, writers have to rely on family memories or research; this is already the case, for example, in Irene Dische's *Between Two Seasons of Happiness* (see Chapter 4) and the Second World War novels of Michelle Magorian. There will be new developments in children's fiction on the subject, and we can only speculate on how the war that dominated the twentieth century will be regarded across the world in the next decades. It is already apparent that the response by children's writers to recent conflicts is more immediate and uncompromising in its representation of the full impact of war than earlier texts that mediated the subject for the young reader. From Robert Westall's Iraqui boy soldier in *Gulf*, to George Lemoine's little matchgirl in Sarajevo, and Els de Groen's mixed group of adolescents in Bosnia, authors introduce young readers to the plight and the prejudices of their contemporaries in ways that demand a reaction to the injustice and horror of war. The postwar vision of Jella Lepman, founder of the International Board of Books for Young People, that children's books could be the foundation of international understanding and peace, has proved to be over-optimistic. War goes on, but it is no longer the stuff of patriotic adventure yarns for the young. In addressing war, children's literature has come of age.

WORKS CITED AND FURTHER READING FOR CHAPTERS 4 AND 5

Primary Texts

Foreman, M., *War Boy* (London: Pavilion, 1989).
Pausewang, G., *The Final Journey*, trans. Patricia Crampton (London: Viking, 1996).
Ungerer, T., *Die Gedanken sind frei: Meine Kindheit im Elsass* (Zürich: Diogenes, 1993).
Ungerer, T., *Tomi: A Childhood Under the Nazis* (London: Roberts Rinehart Publishing, 1998).
Westall, Robert, *The Machine-Gunners* (London: Macmillan, 1975).

Critical Texts

Agnew, K. and Fox, G., *Children at War: From the First World War to the Gulf* (London: Continuum, 2001).

Bassnett, S., *Comparative Literature: A Critical Introduction* (Oxford: Blackwell, 1993).

Batho, B. *et al.*, *War and Peace in Children's Books: A Selection* (Brighton: University of Brighton, 1998).

Fox, C. *et al.* (eds), *In Times of War: An Anthology of War and Peace in Children's Literature* (London: Pavilion, 2000).

Lathey, G., *The Impossible Legacy* (Berne: Peter Lang, 1999).

O'Sullivan, E., *Friend and Foe: The Image of Germany and the Germans in British Children's Fiction from 1870 to the Present* (Tubingen: Gunter Narr Verlag, 1990).

Westall, R. 'How Real do you Want your Realism?', *Signal*, 28 (1979): 39–46.

Children's Books

Alington, G., *Evacuee* (London: Walker Books, 1988).

Andersen, H. C., *La Petite Marchande d'Allumettes*, trans. P. G. La Chesnais, illus. Georges Lemoine (Paris: Éditions Nathan, 1999).

Bawden, N., *Keeping Henry* (London: Gollancz, 1988).

Cooper, S., *Dawn of Fear* (London: Gollancz, 1988).

de Groen, E., *No Roof in Bosnia*, trans. P. Crampton (Barnstaple: Spindlewood, 1997).

de Jong, M., *The House of Sixty Fathers* (New York: Harper and Brothers, 1956).

Elzbieta, *Go Away War!*, trans. not credited (London: Hamish Hamilton, 1994).

Foreman, M., *After the War Was Over* (London: Pavilion, 1995).

Frank, R., *No Hero for the Kaiser* (New York: Lothrop, Lee and Shepherd, 1986).

Greene, B., *Summer of My German Soldier* (New York: Dial Press, 1973).

Heffernan, J. and McLean, A., *My Dog* (New South Wales: Margaret Hamilton Books, 2001).

Holm, A., *I am David*, trans. L. W. Kingsland (London: Methuen, 1965).

Johns, Capt. W. E., *Biggles Goes to War* (Oxford: Oxford University Press, 1938).

de Jong, R., *Dreaming in Black and White*, trans. A. Bell (London: Egmont, 2000).

Kerr, J., *Bombs on Aunt Daisy* (London: Collins, 2002; first published in 1975 as *The Other Way Round*).

Kerr, J., *A Small Person far Away* (London: Collins, 1978; revised 1989).

Magorian, M., *Goodnight Mr Tom* (Harmondsworth: Kestrel, 1981).

Magorian, M., *Back Home* (London: Viking, 1985).

Maurois, A., *Fattypuffs and Thinifers*, trans. N. Denny, illus. F. Wegner (London: Bodley Head, 1968).

Melnikoff, P., *Prisoner in Time: A Child of the Postwar* (London: Blackie, 1992).

Morpurgo, M., *Friend or Foe* (London: Macmillan, 1977).

Rees, D., *The Missing German* (London: Dobson, 1976).

Rees, D., *The Exeter Blitz* (London: Hamish Hamilton, 1978).

Richter, H. P., *Friedrich*, trans. E. Kroll (London: Puffin, 1987; first published in the USA, 1970).

Richter, H. P., *I Was There*, trans. E. Kroll (London: Puffin, 1987).

Richter, H. P., *The Time of the Young Soldiers*, trans. A. Bell (Harmondsworth: Kestrel, 1978).

Riordan, J., *The Prisoner* (Oxford: Oxford University Press, 1999).

Serraillier, I., *The Silver Sword* (London: Jonathan Cape, 1956).

Ungerer, T., *Otto* (Paris, L'École des Loisirs, 1999).

Vassilieva, T., *A Hostage to War*, trans. A. Trenter (London: Hamish Hamilton, 1996).

Westall, R., *Fathom Five* (London: Macmillan, 1979).

Westall, R., *The Kingdom by the Sea* (London: Methuen, 1990).

Westall, R., *Gulf* (London: Methuen, 1992).

Westall, R., *Children of the Blitz: Memories of Wartime Childhood* (London: Macmillan, 1985).

Westall, R., *A Time of Fire* (London: Macmillan, 1994).

Wild, M. and Vivas, J., *Let the Celebrations Begin!* (London: Bodley Head, 1991).

Fantasy – Postwar, Postmodern, Postcolonial: Houses in Postwar Fantasy

Sarah Godek

> **KEY TEXTS**
>
> L. Boston, *The Children of Green Knowe* (1954)
> M. Norton, *The Borrowers* (1952)
> N. Wheatley, *The House that was Eureka* (1981)
> T. H. White, *Mistress Masham's Repose* (1946)

This chapter deals with themes and approaches that are discussed elsewhere in this book. It would be helpful to read it alongside Chapters 3, 8, 11 and 12 particularly, to develop greater understanding of fantasy; ways of reading derived from colonial and postcolonialism; the transition from Modernism to Postmodernism; understanding of Utopianism, and the concept of the chronotope. The chapter is organized around the topic of houses, which enables Sarah Godek to avoid the tendency to link fantasy and psychoanalytic criticism, offering instead readings that focus on period and place. It would, of course, be equally possible to place the house at the centre of a psychoanalytic reading of the same texts: according to Freud, in dreams 'the one typical . . . representation of the human figure . . . is a house' (1963: 149). Attempting such a reading after completing this chapter could be illuminating.

    Here discussion of fantasy is extended to think specifically in terms of the impulse to fantasy: why certain kinds of fantasy prevail at particular historic moments, for instance? Whose need is served by these fantasy texts – writers? characters? readers? Is fantasy better suited to some topics than realism – or can it treat the same topics to promote different understandings? Do adolescent readers (a new concept in the postwar period) require different fantasies from younger children? Is there a correlation between children's play and fantasy texts? All of these questions are raised in the course of – or surface in response to – this chapter.

    Three of the key texts in this chapter are British, reflecting the impact of World War II on British life and, related to this, the need to address child readers.

> A house constitutes a body of images that give mankind proofs or illusions of stability. We are constantly re-imagining its reality: to distinguish all these images would be to describe the soul of the house.
>
> (Bachelard, 1994: 17)

In the years that followed World War II, housing was a subject on the minds of many. With the population boom caused by rising birth rates combined with the return of soldiers to their home countries and the rebuilding of war-torn towns, housing was in short supply. But the importance of houses went far beyond the need for shelter from the elements. In a social climate where nothing seemed certain, the house became, as Bachelard points out, a symbol of stability, or at least of the appearance of stability. With Modernism in full effect and Postmodernism on the rise, many postwar thinkers perceived the crumbling of social institutions such as empire, church and family.

It should come as no surprise, then, that many postwar fantasies use houses as central images. T. H. White's *Mistress Masham's Repose* (1946) involves a plot to prevent an old manor from being passed down to the rightful heir of the family that owned it; Mary Norton's *The Borrowers* (1952) presents a family under threat as the secret location of their home is compromised, and Lucy Boston's *The Children of Green Knowe* (1954) is set in an ancient house that allows characters to slip though time in order to learn more about past generations. That these books arise from and reflect concerns of the postwar era becomes clear when they are compared to later texts in which houses are used for similar purposes. A useful contrast is provided by Australian writer Nadia Wheatley's *The House that was Eureka* (1981), making the point that fantasy, just as much as realism, is a product of and responds to cultural and historical conditions. Fantasy may depict worlds that play with time or seem to operate outside real times and places, but it is inevitably and inescapably dependent on them.

Approaching fantasy

Before turning to specific fantasies and their use of houses, it is useful to set out some of the central characteristics of the fantasy genre (see Box 1.1). Fantasy can be difficult to discuss academically because it is a term that lacks a clear definition. The word comes from the Latin *phantasticus*, derived from the Greek *phantastikos*, which literally means an appearance, or the result of something being made visible. Common usage encompasses many different senses of the word; it can be used as a synonym for dream, ghost, desire, or imagining. The multiplicity of definitions in common use contributes to the confusion over the definition of fantasy as a literary genre. It overlaps other types of literature, and it is debatable whether types of stories such as science fiction, ghost stories, and fairy tales are indeed separate genres, or are merely sub-sets of fantasy.

Many critics define fantasy by contrasting it with realism, but this binary opposition is unsatisfying. First, it leaves no place for realistic texts that contain elements of fantasy, but perhaps more importantly, it assumes that the meaning of the term 'reality' is stable across different cultures. Because experience varies from person to person, even people who share similar cultural backgrounds often disagree about what is or is not realistic. Another common definition, which describes fantasy as literature that depicts the 'impossible', contains the same ethnocentric assumptions – in other words, it views its own culture as the norm by which all things are measured, ignoring the fact that what is impossible to a western, English-speaking culture may not be the same as what is impossible to other cultures.

In the absence of a satisfying alternative, however, or a set of conventions analogous to those identified as characteristic of the school story (see Chapter 1), for the purposes of this discussion, which deals with fantasy writing from English-speaking, western societies, fantasy is defined as 'texts depicting the impossible and/or involving the supernatural or some other unreal element'. Although this definition still leaves room for debate, there is enough of a consensus on what is real or impossible within western societies for it to be a useful starting point in determining the boundaries of fantasy.

Even having established a working definition of the term, fantasy is still a sticky subject. As a genre, it is often given a lower status than literature that could be described as 'realism' (Box 6.1). Believed by many to be of lesser

---

BOX 6.1   REALISM

It is important to distinguish between realism and what the critic Catherine Belsey (1980) has termed the 'classic realist text'. Belsey is concerned with the narrative conventions that encourage readers to accept that the world of the text is an analogue for the real world, which, of course, it can never be. She highlights three main strategies for achieving this: *illusionism* (creating the illusion of a real world), *interpellation* (drawing readers into that world) and a *hierarchy of discourses* (the arrangement of sources of information, which is normally presided over by an omniscient narrator with whose opinions/values/world-view the reader is encouraged to agree). Significantly, the writer of fantasy also depends on these strategies: the reader of fantasy too is drawn into the world of the narrative, accepts that world as 'real' while reading, and is subject to narratorial manipulation. Realism and fantasy differ in that:

- In a realistic text, the world of the narrative resembles and follows the natural laws of the world as we know it: supernatural events are excluded.
- Realistic texts tend to be more interested in the physical world than the inner world (whether mental or spiritual).
- Realistic texts often deal with difficult issues or problems, demanding that characters (and readers) acknowledge and deal with these directly rather than through the kinds of disguises employed in fantasy.

importance than most realistic texts, fantasy is frequently attacked as being escapist and thus reflecting a reluctance to deal with or prepare for the real world. Writing about Lewis Carroll's *Alice in Wonderland* (1865) and *Through the Looking Glass* (1871), for instance, Francis Molson celebrates the shift away from didacticism in children's books. He writes that 'the publication of the Alice books ... marked the first time juvenile fiction was written for the express purpose of 'wasting' its young readers' time instead of "improving" it' (1981: 19). Of course, this was not seen as what children's books *should* do, and a debate sprang up over whether or not it was appropriate.

The debate over whether children should read fantasy texts is still alive. Although the belief that children's books must be instructive has waned somewhat since the time of Lewis Carroll, many parents, teachers and librarians underestimate the ability of children to distinguish fact from fiction and argue that introducing children to such fantasy staples as witchcraft and magic, or mythological creatures and monsters, is potentially damaging.

The low status of the fantasy genre has caused even more confusion in determining what qualifies as fantasy, since some writers are reluctant to be associated with it. For example, the British writer David Almond, whose books contain magical elements, asserts: '[my] books are realistic. When people try to describe them as fantasy I say: They're not. They're not fantasy. Because they're all set in a very real world that I could take you to and show you where each of these stories took place' (Richards, 22/09/03). Similarly, Philip Pullman, whose *His Dark Materials* trilogy features witches and travel to alternate worlds, claims that he 'can't read fantasy' and calls his trilogy 'stark realism' (Fried, 14/10/03).

While some writers retreat from the fantasy label, others feel the need to defend the genre. Ursula LeGuin argues:

> There are different ways of thinking, being, and doing things. Both science fiction and fantasy offer more options. They let you think through an alternative without actually having to do it. Which, I think, is really one of the functions of all fiction – to let you live other lives and see what they're like. It widens the soul.   (Justice, 22/09/03)

Many critics have also penned books in defence of fantasy. The difficulty in limiting and defining the genre can be seen as an advantage rather than a problem. The most common objection to fantasy is that it does not relate to what readers may experience, but the many kinds of fantasies mean that it can be related to the 'real' world in many different ways. Although the four texts examined in this chapter share some similarities (*Mistress Masham's Repose* and *The Borrowers* are both about little people, and *The Children of Green Knowe* and *The House that was Eureka* are both time-slip stories), each has a unique approach to fantasy. For that reason, a broadly socio-historic approach to the texts – that is, a way of reading that sets the texts in the context of the period in which they were written – is useful (see Boxes 11.1 and 11.2). As will become apparent in the course of this chapter, such an approach shows that despite superficial similarities, the texts vary widely in their responses to contemporary events, issues, and prevailing attitudes, and construct both children's literature and childhood very differently.

Fantasy as satire: T. H. White's *Mistress Masham's Repose*

Mistress Masham's Repose follows ten-year-old Maria in her adventures at Malplaquet, her dilapidated ancestral home. The central image of this crumbling house, described at great length by White throughout the book, reflects his dissatisfaction with the state of his world. At the level of plot, the book presents two main problems. The first arises when, while exploring the grounds of Malplaquet, Maria discovers a colony of Lilliputians who were brought to England by Captain Biddel, who rescued Gulliver in Jonathan Swift's *Gulliver's Travels*, and have since been forgotten. Maria must save these little people, both from her own tendency to treat them as toys, and, after their presence is discovered by Maria's caretakers, Miss Brown and Mr Hater, from the prospect of captivity. The second problem of the novel is the fact that Maria's greedy caretakers are embezzling money meant for the

---

BOX 6.2 POSTCOLONIAL CRITICISM AND *MISTRESS MASHAM'S REPOSE*

Emerging in the 1990s, postcolonial criticism has done for minority cultures what feminism has done for females. It examines the representation of cultures treated as 'other' by literary texts and denies the possibility of universals such as 'human nature' existing across cultural boundaries. Postcolonial criticism focuses on the relationship between native populations and colonizing forces, celebrating the cultural diversity created by such situations while simultaneously highlighting the problematic structures of control that rise out of the attempted assimilation of one culture into another.

While T. H. White does satirize British colonialism, postcolonial critics would point out that he is still a man of the Empire and his thinking is clearly influenced by it. Though he suggests that the Lilliputians are a civilization and should not be taken advantage of, he nevertheless feels the need to prove that the little people are indeed 'civilized' in a very British sense of the word. He does so by making their culture more familiar to his English readers. As proof that they are 'civilized', White describes their 'painters, who did wonderful formal pictures of old-fashioned shepherds and shepherdesses in pannier skirts and ribbons' (p. 82), and their writers, who produce poetry, essays and five-act tragedies, which are acted out by the opera company and accompanied by the orchestra and harpsichord (p. 83). While some of this similarity to British culture is undoubtedly due to the Lilliputians' transportation and acclimatization to England, there still lurks behind White's descriptions the assumption, now seen as spurious, that all civilizations should be measured against British culture (cf. Box 11.2).

maintenance of Maria and Malplaquet, and plotting to prevent Maria from receiving her inheritance. The Miss Brown–Mr Hater plotline provides narrative drive, but White employs the Lilliputians to carry on the Swiftian tradition of using fantasy in the service of satire.

T. H. White was born in British-colonized India, and the publication date of *Mistress Masham's Repose*, just four years after the granting of Indian independence, makes it clear that one of the institutions White is satirizing is the crumbling British Empire. Readers should not, however, directly equate the crumbling family home with the Empire. It is a complex signifier, allowing the writer to critique a number of institutions and social practices.

After she befriends the Lilliputians, Maria learns about their history as a conquered people, and part of the significance of the run-down stately home should be connected with the oppression of colonized peoples (see Box 6.2). The Lilliputians, like many native populations of colonized areas, were seen as amusements rather than people, and were forced to play tiny instruments (56). Captain Biddel treated them as 'Creatures not possessed of human Rights, nor shelter'd by the Laws of Nations' (58). Even after hearing about their past, however, Maria acts as yet another conqueror of the little people:

> The more she adored and wondered at the doings of her six-inch People, the more she wanted to take control of them. She wanted to play with them, like lead soldiers, and even dreamed of being their queen. She began to forget what the Professor had said, about not being an owner. (82)

Here White's target is not just the imperialist attitudes of the British, but also the educational system that both failed to prevent and fostered them; both concerns are reflected in Fritz Eichenberg's illustrations for the text, as can be seen in Figure 6. Maria is consistently excused for her indiscretions on the grounds that she is young and inexperienced, but the Professor himself shows the failure of education to prevent ethnocentric colonialism. As educated as he is, the Professor still fantasizes about capturing, not the Lilliputians, but a giant Brobdingnagian (also encountered by Gulliver on his voyages). In his daydream, he shows himself to be no better than Maria's greedy caretakers, who attempt to sell the Lilliputians in Hollywood. He dreams of housing his captured giant in the Albert Hall and charging admission for people to watch him eat his dinner. His daydream is a strange mix of his secret desires tempered by what he knows is humane. He imagines telling the giant:

> 'We will feed you and house you and treat you with respect, and we will carry you home after one year.'
>
> He considered this for half a mile, before concluding: 'Perhaps it would be wise to keep the gun pointed at him. . . . We would not tell him about it of course, for fear of hurting his feelings.'
>
> 'Also,' added the Professor later, still feeling a little uncomfortable, 'we would pay him a commission of ten per cent.' (179)

**Figure 6   Illustration by Fritz Eichenberg for *Mistress Masham's Repose*,
showing the Lilliputian army on their march to save Maria
(their banners reflect the book's concern with both colonial attitudes
and the educational system)**

White's strongest indictment of the educational system is the very character of the Professor. Just as the crumbling Malplaquet represents the problems of the community at large, the disorder of the Professor's cottage illuminates his shortcomings. He is overly erudite, messy, easily distracted and clearly has his priorities all wrong. He spends most of the novel worrying about the proper translation of the ancient Latin word *Tripharium*, even when Maria is in great danger. His behaviour shows how an education and lifestyle like the Professor's can result in the neglect of many areas of life, and the consequent if slow demise of many institutions. The Professor has good intentions, but is generally inept, impractical, and even ludicrous:

> He was a failure, but he did his best to hide it. One of his failings was that he could scarcely write, except in a twelfth-century hand, in Latin, with abbreviations. Another was that, although his cottage was crammed with books, he seldom had anything to eat. (29)

White's concern over education was shared by his contemporaries. Many changes were made both to the educational system and to general attitudes toward education, in the 1940s. The postwar years saw a boom in education and 'a genuine social tendency of parents to seek further training for their children' (Gillis, 1974: 134). The Education Act of 1944 made secondary education mandatory and increased the school-leaving age from 14 years to 15. It was during this period that a new professional class was forming in England and, as Gillis points out, 'The mode of upward mobility of this group was no longer the time-honored ladder of the trades and private enterprise, but education, at first secondary but later at university as well' (169).

Many aspects of *Mistress Masham's Repose* show that White had great hopes for the children for whom he was writing, if only they were educated properly. Each of the adults in the novel has a failing: Miss Brown and Mr Hater are underhanded and cruel; the Professor is wrapped up in himself and his obscure academic interests; the Cook, Mrs Noakes, is probably the most positive adult character in the book, but even she is still sadly uneducated. Meanwhile, the only child in the book, Maria, is bright, resourceful, and always thinking ahead of her adult persecutors. The optimistic ending of the book shows that Maria has fulfilled her potential. The crumbling house, which had reflected White's dissatisfaction with the present, is restored, suggesting a more stable and better ordered future.

By contrast, the Lilliputians, who are adult yet allied with children because of their small size, give a positive example of what child-rearing and education should be. Their dwelling place, in contrast to Malplaquet, is tidy and well kept. The orderliness of their home reflects their community, which, aside from the threat posed by human adults, is a Utopia, owing to their pragmatic systems of upbringing and education:

> They believed that the most important thing in the world was to find out what one most enjoyed doing, and then do it. ... Their children were never taught a word about Algebra, but were, on the contrary, educated

in the various sciences of life: that is to say, in Natural History and in their own History and in Oeconomy and in anything else which dealt with being alive. (70)

White uses children's fantasy to satirize the practices of his day, and uses the central image of the house as a measuring stick of the health of the community that dwells within and around it. In *Mistress Masham's Repose*, not only is fantasy used to call attention to the problems T. H. White perceived in the world around him, but also to suggest an alternative way of life that would become a solution to those problems.

Postmodern fantasy: Mary Norton's *The Borrowers*

Mary Norton also presents a sophisticated narrative to a child audience, but *The Borrowers* neither offers, nor presents as desirable, the restoration of stability that marks the closure of *Mistress Masham's Repose*. Norton's novel is about a family of little people – called Borrowers because they exist by 'borrowing' food, tools and housing from humans – and their attempt to co-exist with humans. It presents this small community, not as a Utopia and a model for the solution of problems, but as a society in decline. This can be read as giving form to the shift from Modernism, which was the dominant mode of art from 1880 to 1940, to Postmodernism, which was coming to prevalence in the postwar era (Box 6.3). As in *Mistress Masham's Repose*, the house in *The Borrowers* is a metaphor for stability; the Borrowers' home coming under threat, their futile attempts to make it more settled and permanent by bringing in dolls' furniture, and their eventual eviction from the house, reflect the unstable, Postmodern world-view. Norton uses her fantasy to reflect the impossibility of attaining the stability that the house represents.

Fantasy as a genre is particularly well suited to the Postmodern mode. While not all fantasy could be categorized as Postmodern fiction, Lance Olsen makes a convincing point about the similarities between Postmodernism and much fantasy:

BOX 6.3   MODERNISM VERSUS POSTMODERNISM

Because Postmodernism developed largely out of the Modernist movement they share many attitudes toward life and sometimes are confused with one another. Two key differences between Modernism and Postmodernism should be stressed. First, while both modes are based on the perceived lack of stability of the modern world, Modernists view literature and language as a means of coping with this problem, while Postmodernists do not offer any sense that there may be a 'solution'. Secondly, Modernism and Postmodernism can usually be distinguished by their respective registers. While Modernist texts generally adopt a serious tone, Postmodern texts can often be more playful (cf. Box 11.1).

> [C]ontemporary fantasy ... is a mode which interrogates all we take for granted about language and experience, giving these no more than shifting and provisional status. It is a mode of radical skepticism that believes only in the impossibility of total intelligibility; in the endless displacement of 'meaning'; in the production of a universe without 'truth'; in a bottomless relativity of 'significance'.   (1987: 3)

From the outset, Norton deconstructs the illusion of reality created in mimetic storytelling. She highlights the constructedness of the text by changing its details as she tells the story. The book opens: 'It was Mrs May who first told me about them. No, not me. How could it have been me ... ? Kate, she should have been called. Yes, that was it – Kate' (2003: 1). But the opening chapter is just a frame story, and the story of the Borrowers is a story within that story, at least twice removed from lived experience. The structure of the text is reflected in its house imagery, for the Borrowers' home is a house within a house, just as their tale is a story within a story. Mrs May, before telling Kate what her brother had told her about the Borrowers, sets up their story as a very postmodern text by questioning not so much its veracity, but whether it is ever possible to determine the 'truth'. She tells Kate: 'Oddly enough I remember it better than many real things which have happened. Perhaps it was a real thing. I just don't know' (9).

Norton also plays with the slipperiness of language throughout the book, negating the stability of linguistic meanings. Occasionally, words will appear in scare quotes, as in 'For the next three weeks Arrietty was especially "good"' (71). This device calls attention to the fact that the word 'good' does not have a consistent meaning, requiring readers to consider the meaning of the word, drawing them away from the mimetic qualities of the story, and reminding them that they are reading a text where significances are not stable.

The end of the story within a story is abrupt and leaves the Borrowers' situation unresolved. Mrs Driver has discovered the Borrowers, the boy is locked in his room, the police have been called and the threat of exterminators looms over the tiny family, when Mrs May stops telling the story. That is the point at which the boy, Mrs May's younger brother, was forced to leave the house, so there can be no more to his story. The rest of the story consists of Norton/Kate telling readers what Mrs May told her. This information was told to Mrs May by her brother, who had had it from an unknown source. With so many tellers of the story, its veracity is made questionable, but, of course, the 'truth' does not matter. 'Truth' is a false concept, for it suggests a stability of meaning that cannot exist. Significantly, then, the end of the book gives a detail that throws the whole story into doubt when Mrs May reveals that Arrietty had the same handwriting as her brother; however, by this point the postmodern elements of the text have already shown the audience that truth, stability, and consistency are unattainable, and therefore unimportant. What matters is the ability to adapt to new circumstances and make the self anew in the world that was being refashioned in the second decade of the twentieth century.

Fantasy, because it is only ambiguously related to lived experience, is open to a multiplicity of meanings, and, appropriately for a postmodern text, the symbolism of the Clock family is open to many interpretations. They can be read as representative of the British Empire, which was dependent on its colonies just as the Borrowers are dependent on humans, and which, like them, was under threat. The fear of the annihilation of the entire race of Borrowers may reflect either residual anxieties caused by World War II or new ones arising from the Cold War, a source of great unease in the 1950s. Another interpretation could be that the Borrowers represent the British aristocracy, who for decades had been 'emigrating' out of their stately homes and into more modest housing. Concern over the destruction of Britain's aristocratic country houses is also a theme in *Mistress Masham's Repose* and can be seen in White's loving descriptions of the many rooms of Malplaquet. But perhaps nowhere in children's literature is this theme more prevalent than in Lucy Boston's *Green Knowe* series.

Fantasy and continuity: Lucy Boston's *The Children of Green Knowe*

Although Postmodernism was becoming an influential force in literature in the postwar period, children's literature, which many argue should be stylistically conservative (see the Introduction), was widely associated with books such as *The Children of Green Knowe*, which were based on pre-modern conceptions of the world. Whereas very little seemed stable in the world of *The Borrowers*, just as little seems susceptible to change at the manor at Green Knowe. So little, in fact, that Mrs Oldknow believes that, 'The world doesn't alter every day. As far as I can see, it's always the same' (2000: 17). The house reflects this stability, as it has stood, virtually unchanged, since the time of the Black Plague, which had killed all three little children who now inhabit it as ghosts. Family names are passed down from generation to generation, so the main character, Tolly, whose real name is Toseland, is not the first boy by that name to live at Green Knowe. In fact, the name is so old that it is shared, not only by family members, but also by places in the surrounding area. The stability of the house extends beyond its grounds to the local community. When Tolly tells the women on the train his name, they exclaim, 'Toseland! That's a real old-fashioned name in these parts. There's Fen Toseland, and Toseland St Agnes and Toseland Gunning' (2).

Tolly is connected to the place by his name, and the connection between people and places is a major theme in the book, as it is in much postwar British children's fiction. The three ghost children, Toby, Alexander and Linnet, are so connected to Green Knowe that they continue to inhabit it after their deaths, not because of a horrible injustice, as is the case in many ghost stories, but simply because they belong there. The difference between the friendly supernatural elements of *The Children of Green Knowe* and the ominous ghosts of other stories highlights the idyllic feeling of Boston's book.

Tolly's great-grandmother, Mrs Oldknow, is perhaps more connected to the place than anyone else. She has the same air of mystery as the house, with all of its mirrors and shadows. Tolly connects Mrs Oldknow with the house when he sees her in her dressing gown without her teeth: 'She looked so old that Tolly could easily believe she was as old as the house' (50). Moreover, when Tolly is in the house without her, the place feels quite different. The house feels as if its spirit has left it, and the garden is filled with a feeling of menace: 'For some reason he felt convinced that until his great-grandmother returned, not so much as a marble would move in the house. He felt no such assurance about the garden' (94).

As Tolly notices here, Green Knowe is so connected with the people who have lived there, that it takes on a life of its own and is almost another character in the story. Linda Hall writes of the significance of the house:

> The house that is both the setting and the subject of Boston's novels seems almost more important than the people who have lived within its walls, if only perhaps because it transcends their individual mortality by its lasting power and so can become the symbol as well as the receptacle of that community without which all human effort seems purposeless. (1998: 226)

The theme makes a strong argument for the preservation of historic manor houses, an issue that Boston certainly cared about, having lovingly restored her own home, the original for the manor in the book, with the help of her son Peter, who illustrated the Green Knowe series.

Another sign that *The Children of Green Knowe* is rejecting the forces of Postmodernity and fighting the decline of social institutions is its incorporation of a Christian framework. St Christopher is an important figure in the text and appears several times. Not only does the miraculous statue of him walk on Christmas Day in Linnet's time and protect the house from the cursed topiary of Green Noah in Tolly's, but his influence is felt elsewhere in the book as well. St Christopher is known for carrying the Christ child across a stream. As he crossed, the burden of his load grew heavier, but he did not give up. St Christopher, therefore, is the patron saint of travellers and is a protector against floods and lightning, both of which play important roles in *The Children of Green Knowe*.

This chapter's interest in the relationship between texts and historical contexts makes Boston's use of St Christopher significant for the way it illuminates the view of children taken in the novel. Because they are under the protection of St Christopher, as was the Christ child, all of the children in the text, ghosts or fully alive, are linked to Christ. Like Christ, they represent innocence and hope for the future. They are not clever and resourceful like Maria; in this novel, the hope for the future rests entirely on the innocence of children. That the children are forces of good and agents of redemption is repeatedly symbolized as, for instance, in their relationships with animals: they tame them so well that the fox does not chase the rabbit, a powerful image of peace in Boston's postwar world. Boston not only places her child characters in a peaceful and stable world, she also presents them as both its heirs and its guardians; defenders of Church, family, aristocracy – all the institutions that were, in fact, under threat. Hers is a wishfulfilment fantasy on the part of traditionalists, who believed the damage and disruptions caused by two world wars could only be permanently healed by renewing and maintaining links with the past.

As disparate as these postwar British fantasies may appear, their fundamental similarities may be seen by comparing them with a fantasy from a different time and place.

Nadia Wheatley's *The House that was Eureka*: Fantasy as new realism

The 1960s–70s saw a great many changes to youth cultures all over the English-speaking world. The 'sexual revolution' meant that adolescents were allowed, and occasionally encouraged, openly to discuss previously taboo sexual topics. The rise of mass media also opened up other issues to child audiences as parents found it difficult to censor their children's radio listening and television viewing (see also Chapter 8 and compare with attitudes to the Internet in Chapter 15). Teenagers became more involved socially and politically, and were granted greater privileges in these spheres, largely because of the military enlistment expected of teenage boys throughout the Cold War. By the 1980s, children's literature reflected these changes. No longer were children seen as innocent, and a new kind of realism dominated children's fiction. Writing in 1981, Francis Molson observed, 'Juvenile fantasy is thriving at present in spite of a current emphasis on the new realism which purports to introduce youngsters to the "real" world of sex, drugs, abortion, homosexuality, and similar problems' (29).

The 'new realism' to which Molson refers is the trend in children's literature, begun in the 1970s, of using fiction to explore the grittier and more unpleasant aspects of life. Sometimes called 'issue-books', these texts often focus on a specific social concern and explore how that issue affects the protagonist's life. This marks a departure from earlier children's realism, which usually depicts an idyllic, protected and generally middle-class existence for children.

Lance Olsen notes that fantasy tends to be popular 'at times of cultural unease' (1987: 22), and this may explain the rise of realism in the middle decades of the twentieth century, which were relatively peaceful and prosperous for much of the English-speaking world; as a consequence, fantasy was not in the ascendant. Perhaps paradoxically, the end of the Cold War and the wave of optimism generated by *Glasnost* and German reunification in fact ushered in a period of political uncertainty and instability, the focus of which is currently in the Middle East, and fantasy is undoubtedly having a resurgence, with the work of Rowling, Pullman and Tolkien dominating the bestsellers charts for books, films and their various electronic spin-offs. Between the Cold War and

Glasnost – roughly the 1980s – when fantasy was perhaps less needed culturally and was certainly less well received, there nevertheless appeared some strong and revealing fantasy texts with very different world-views and ways of constructing individuals' needs and identity formation. Instead of responding to vast conflicts between countries, for instance, they operate at more personal levels. The rise of the AIDS virus, the effects of drug addiction and the widening gap between rich and poor were just some of the issues that were causing concern, and were explored both in the new realism and in a fantasy–realism hybrid that could equally be called 'new fantasy'.

Australian writer Nadia Wheatley's *The House that was Eureka* is one such example. The story follows sixteen-year-old Evie in her adjustments to a new house. The house, however, influences Evie's dreams, and she begins to have nightmares in which she is transported back in time and lives out the life of the house's previous inhabitant, Lizzie. Evie's fifteen-year-old neighbour, Noel, who is the grandson of Evie's landlady, also gets caught up in the house's past, and lives out in his dreams the life of his uncle Nobby, who was in love with Lizzie. The contrast between the time-warping nature of the house at Green Knowe and Evie and Noel's houses on Liberty Street foregrounds the differences between children's fantasy of the 1940s and 1950s and the kind of fantasy being written in the 1980s. Where Boston's time travel was exciting and magical, Wheatley's version comes in nightmares and saps Evie and Noel of their energy.

Wheatley's book is an example of a fantastic text as described by Rosemary Jackson in *Fantasy: The Literature of Subversion* (1981). Although Jackson sometimes seems to use 'fantastic' and 'fantasy' interchangeably, they should not be confused, for the fantastic is a specific genre that has developed out of the broader fantasy mode. Jackson defines the fantastic in terms of a spectrum. At one extreme is the marvellous, at the other the mimetic, with the fantastic floating somewhere between the two. Jackson gives fairy tales as an example of the marvellous, which consists of texts that describe an ideal and are built on the assumption that there exist in the world some universal truths. The mimetic, on the other hand, is concerned with the concrete world with all of its flaws, but still believes that that world functions under stable and consistent laws. The fantastic, in the middle, plays these separate modes off against one another, using the tension between their differing types of stability to create instability and slippage. Jackson explains that in a fantastic text, the

> means of establishing its 'reality' are initially mimetic ('realistic', presenting an 'object' world 'objectively') but then move into another mode which would seem to be marvelous ('unrealistic', representing apparent impossibilities), were it not for its initial grounding in the 'real'. (1995: 20)

The fantastic balances the 'real' with the 'unreal' in a discomforting mix, and Jackson points out that because of this discomfort, the fantastic has subversive potential where other, more comfortable forms of fantasy may not: 'The presentation of impossibility is not by itself a radical activity: texts subvert only if the reader is *disturbed* by their dislocated narrative form' (1995: 23). The initially threatening nature of the house and the time-shifts it causes, give Wheatley's text a subversive power entirely different from the more comfortable types of fantasy written in the immediately postwar period.

The House that was Eureka uses the subversive potential of the fantastic to tackle social issues affecting its young audience. The book's social consciousness explores the plight of the working class both through Lizzie and Nobby's story, which is set in 1931 during the Great Depression, and in Evie and Noel's story, set in 1981, another time of economic hardship in Australia. Both stories show adolescents as socially and politically active. Lizzie's is a working-class family, hit hard by the depression and struggling to keep their landlady, Nobby's mother, from evicting them. All of the children in Lizzie's family, who range in age from toddlers to teenagers, are involved in the fight, which becomes violent when police are called in to break up their demonstration and evict the family. This story is fictional but borrows heavily from Australian history, and the often overlooked story of the violent evictions of the poor which actually did take place (see Boxes 11.1 and 11.2 for information on the relationship between history and fiction).

Evie and Noel are less directly involved in the political activism of their time than Lizzie and Nobby, but it is present none the less. Evie has finished school, is out of work and goes to a governmental organization called the CYSS in order to convince her mother that she is trying to find employment. The CYSS, though, is under threat of having its funds cancelled, and the workers there organize protests in an attempt to save it. When they discover the history of Evie's house, they insist on re-enacting Lizzie and Nobby's story. During the re-enactment, the two time frames cross, and Evie and Noel act out the parts of Lizzie and Nobby instead of just dreaming them.

In addition to the book's concern with socio-political issues, it shares with the new realism a willingness to explore issues of teenage sexuality. One aspect of Evie's life that would not have been included in earlier children's fantasies is the struggle with her attraction to her stepfather Ted, and her eventual escape from those taboo desires through the acceptance of her attraction to Noel, a socially acceptable sexual partner.

Evie's relationship with Ted is highly conflictual. They fight continually, but behind Evie's dislike of her stepfather there can be seen hints of her attraction to him. In describing their family photo, Evie describes Ted as: 'blond, smiling too much for Evie's taste, with a shirt over his slacks to hide his beer gut, but still not too bad (Evie gave him that) for forty three' (3). Evie admits that she did not always dislike Ted, and 'when he'd first married mum he'd tried to be nice to Evie and she'd been jealous of him and started to fight' (27). Her behaviour suggests that her way of dealing with the situation has been to repress her inappropriate attraction to her stepfather and replace it with anger.

Fifteen-year-old Noel, by contrast, is a socially suitable object for her affections. They connect on an emotional level when Noel takes Evie to his favourite spot in the city:

It was good there, peaceful and happy. A change from the tension of the two houses in Liberty Street. Evie and Noel sat for a long time dangling their legs over the suburbs, comfortable for once at simply being who they were. (31)

But Evie resists her feelings for Noel because he is not the type of boy to whom her best friend Roseanne would be attracted. Instead, Evie develops a crush on Roger, who runs the CYSS. Roger has the perfect exterior appearance, but Evie is shy of him and does not understand his political fervour.

When Roseanne visits her, Evie begins to tell her friend about Roger as if he is her boyfriend, but her feelings for Noel begin to show when she begins to mix the qualities of the two boys in her description. Eventually she slips and mentions Noel by name, not even noticing until her friend Roseanne points it out. Evie is not yet ready to accept her feelings for him, though, and when he comes over and introduces himself to Roseanne she is mortified.

Evie's daydreams about her imaginary boyfriend are fantasies within a fantasy text, as was the Professor's daydream of capturing a giant in *Mistress Masham's Repose*. Although these are fantasies in a non-literary sense of the word, comparing them can help illuminate the differences between postwar fantasy and the new fantasy that was rising alongside the new realism. Evie's daydreams, like Wheatley's book overall, are based around lived experience. She fantasizes about two people she has met, and her fantasies help her take control of a problem which affects her life directly, that of her own sexuality. Wheatley clearly belongs to a post-Freudian world with a deeply embedded sense of how the psyche works and can be worked upon. By contrast, White's Professor has less personally motivated – and less personally useful – daydreams. White's concern is not with helping the Professor to understand himself and overcome obstacles to his social adjustment, but with commenting on the social problems caused by the legacy of outdated colonial attitudes.

In another type of dream, not a daydream but a sleeping dream, Evie's feelings for both Ted and Noel get mixed up with Lizzie's story. This new fantasy trope, in which are found the chronotopes from the primary and secondary worlds (see Box 1.2 and Chapter 10), is used with increasing frequency in end-of-century fantasy, and generally, as here, to create feelings of unease (see discussion of the uncanny – Box 8.1 and Chapter 10). Evie dreams a scene from Lizzie's life. Originally Lizzie is trying to put some nails into wood to make a sign for their protest, and her father is laughing at her, but in Evie's dream she is banging on the wood:

Bang
Ted was there, but in the dream he was her father.
Bang.
Noel was there, but he wasn't quite Noel. (26)

Even her nightmares are closely connected to fact, showing how tightly woven realism and fantasy are in Wheatley's book. This is one of Evie's early dreams, and before she knows Lizzie's story, she cannot understand it. Living through

Lizzie's life, however, helps Evie realize that she should not push Noel away merely because he does not fit the picture of what she had thought would be her ideal partner. Lizzie had refused the love of Nobby because he, unlike her, was middle class, and because Lizzie thought that being in love would weaken her in her social crusade. After Evie sees Lizzie's regret at spurning Nobby, Evie herself can begin to accept her attraction to Noel.

Once she has accepted a socially acceptable partner, Evie's dislike for Ted disappears. He shares with her that he has been laid off, and Evie feels comfortable enough to joke with him:

> 'You secret dolebludger!' Evie said, trying to make her voice pretend to be someone on talk-back radio, but it just wouldn't, she was laughing too much.
> 'I *reckon*, pal,' Ted said. 'Will you give me an in, down the club?' (187)

Ted notices the difference in Evie, then, thinking, 'Everything's so much easier now I've my troubles off my chest. And Evie suddenly doesn't seem to buck against me any more' (187). She has conquered her sexual feelings, and he no longer has to pretend he is still working. They both had been living out fantasies, Evie in her dream merging of past and present, and Ted by pretending he had not been fired. After they have dealt with their problems, and their fantasies are no longer useful to them, Evie and Ted can be friends.

Conclusion

While White's use of fantasy is satirical, Norton's fantasy introduces some key concepts of postmodernity, and Boston uses fantasy to create an ideal existence, the function of the fantasy elements in Wheatley's book is to explore the psychological workings of her characters and to help solve the problems within them. Her fantasy elements, unlike any of the previously discussed postwar fantasies, create an uneasy feeling, and sometimes even seem threatening and painful, both to the characters who experience the time-shift and to the reader of the novel. As painful as Wheatley's fantasy may be, it is eventually cathartic and helpful. Through experiencing the house's painful past, Evie can better understand her present and can see how to make her own pain bearable. Wheatley makes another subtle point about fantasy, which distinguishes it from some of the best-known fantasies in the juvenile canon: whereas classic texts such as *Alice in Wonderland* and *Peter Pan* leave the fantasy world open, allowing the possibility of infinite return, Wheatley subtly ensures that readers recognize that while fantasy can be a useful activity, it mustn't become a permanent state, or, instead of promoting growth, it will arrest development.

It is also worth recognizing that some of the differences between *The House that was Eureka* and the earlier fantasies can be accounted for by the difference in the ages and contexts of their implied audiences. At sixteen, Evie is the oldest protagonist of any of the four novels, but Arrietty, only three years younger than Evie, is also technically a teenager. Clearly, the perception of what it means to be a 'teenager' changed significantly between 1952 and 1981. While all of the protagonists face terrible situations, Evie's problems are the ones most closely connected to historical events and to her day-to-day life. They therefore seem the most 'realistic.' Certainly the levels of violence and sexuality seen in *The House that was Eureka* speak of an entirely different conception of childhood from the relative innocence of the children in the fantasies of the 1940s and 1950s. The willingness to depict these previously taboo themes also reflects a change in the uses of fantasy. While the fantasy of the earlier period seemed at least partially to be about escape and the possibility of a better world, the new fantasy exemplified by *The House that was Eureka* shows a willingness to grapple more directly with the problems faced by many young people both at home and in society.

The use of the house as a metaphoric image also changed between the postwar era and the advent of the new kind of fantasy seen in *The House that was Eureka*. While the prewar fantasies discussed above all use the house as a symbol of stability, or at least the impression of stability, the house in Nadia Wheatley's book does not provide feelings of structure and order. If anything, the house on Liberty Street is an agent of change, as it helps Evie and Noel confront and overcome the problems they face in the process of maturation. This shift from a focus on stability to a focus on growth, reflects a cultural shift away from sheltering children and toward exposing them to the problems of life in order to better prepare them for the instability that they will inevitably face.

WORKS CITED AND FURTHER READING

Primary Texts

Boston, L., *The Children of Green Knowe* (London: Faber and Faber, 2000).
Norton, M., *The Borrowers* (London: Puffin, 2003).
Wheatley, N., *The House that was Eureka* (Ringwood, Victoria: Puffin Australia, 1988).
White, T. H., *Mistress Masham's Repose* (London: Jane Nissen Books, 2000).

Critical Texts

Bachelard, G., *The Poetics of Space* (Boston: Beacon Press, 1994).
Barry, P., *Beginning Theory: An Introduction to Literary Cultural Theory* (Manchester and New York: Manchester University Press, 1995).
Carpenter, H. and Prichard, M., *The Oxford Companion to Children's Literature* (Oxford: Oxford University Press, 1995).
Cleverley, J. and Phillips, D. C., *Visions of Childhood: Influential Models from Locke to Spock* (New York and London: Teachers College Press, 1986).
Freud, S., 'Symbolism in Dreams' (1916), in the Standrd Edition of the Collected Works, vol. XV (London: Hogarth Press, 1963).
Fried, K., 'Amazon.com: Darkness Visible: an Interview with Phillip Pullman', http://www.amazon.com/exec/obidos/tg/feature/ (accessed 14 October 2003).

Gillis, J. R., *Youth and History* (New York and London: Academic Press, 1974).

Hall, L., 'The Pattern of Dead and Living: Lucy Boston and the Necessity of Continuity', *Children's Literature in Education*, 29(4) (1998): 223–36.

Justice, F., 'Steering her Craft: an Interview with Ursula LeGuin', Writing-World. com⟨http://www.writing-world.com/sf/leguin.shtml⟩ (accessed 22 September 2003).

Manlove, C. N., 'Fantasy and Loss: T. H. White', in *The Impulse of Fantasy Literature* (Kent, OH: Kent State University Press, 1983).

Molson, F., 'Children's Fantasy and Science Fiction', in M. B. Tymn (ed.), *The Science Fiction Reference Book* (Mercer Island, WA: Starmont House, 1981).

Olsen, L., *Ellipse of Uncertainty: An Introduction to Postmodern Fantasy* (New York and London: Greenwood Press, 1987).

O'Malley, A., 'Mary Norton's "Borrowers" Series and the Myth of the Paternalist Past', *Children's Literature*, vol. 31 (2003), pp. 71–89.

Richards, L., '*January* Interview with David Almond', *January Magazine* ⟨http://www.januarymagazine.com/profiles/almond.html⟩ (accessed 22 September 2003).

Children's Books

(Each of these texts is available in numerous editions so only the date of publication is given.)

Boston, L., *The Chimneys of Green Knowe* (1958); *The River at Green Knowe* (1959); *A Stranger at Green Knowe* (1961); *An Enemy at Green Knowe* (1964); *The Stones of Green Knowe* (1976).

Farmer, P., *Charlotte Sometimes* (1969)

L'Engle, M., *A Wrinkle in Time* (1962); *A Wind in the Door* (1973).

Lively, P., *The Driftway* (1972); *The Ghost of Thomas Kempe* (1973); *The House in Norham Gardens* (1974); *A Stitch in Time* (1976).

Norton, M., *The Borrowers Afield* (1955); *The Borrowers Afloat* (1959); *The Borrowers Aloft* (1961); *Poor Stainless* (1966); *The Borrowers Avenged* (1982).

Park, R., *Playing Beatie Bow* (1980).

Pearce, P., *Tom's Midnight Garden* (1958).

Storr, C., *Marianne Dreams* (1958).

Uttley, A., *A Traveller in Time* (1939).

Wheatley, N., *My Place* (1987); *The Night Tolkien Died* (1994); *Luke's Way of Looking* (2001).

White, T. H., *The Sword in the Stone* (1938); *The Witch in the Wood* (1939); *The Ill-made Knight* (1940); *The Book of Merlin: The Unpublished Conclusion to 'The Once and Future King'* (1977).

Feminism and History: Historical Fiction – Not Just a Thing of the Past

Peter Bramwell

KEY TEXTS

M. Furlong, *Wise Child* (1987); *A Year and a Day* (1990; retitled *Juniper*, 1992); page references are to the 1990 edition.

S. Jordan, *The Raging Quiet* (1999)

T. Tomlinson, *The Forestwife Trilogy* (2003; first published as *The Forestwife* (1993), *Child of the May* (1998), *The Path of the She-Wolf* (2000)); page references are to the original, separate volumes.

There are many reasons why writers for children and young people are attracted to the genre of historical fiction; in contemporary society, for instance, when children's movements are closely monitored out of fear for a variety of potential dangers (strangers, traffic, drug dealers), setting a text in the past can make it possible for child characters to move and behave freely. Related to this is the fact that the possibility for adventures seems greater in the past, which, perhaps paradoxically, is generally regarded as a time when life was more dangerous than it is now. But just as in fantasy the fantasy world and the real world are in a mutually dependent relationship, so any re-creation of the past is a product of its own time (see Box 11.2). In this chapter, Peter Bramwell is specifically concerned with the way contemporary historical fiction for the young is addressing the problem of how women have traditionally been written out of history. The novels chosen for discussion show particularly well how issues of female power and creativity are being explored for a generation of western children that has grown up in a world in which at least the discourse of equal opportunities is recognized at most levels in society. This world-view affects profoundly the sexual politics of the texts discussed below, and though writers use a variety of techniques to indicate that people from the past were not simply like us in different clothes (by, for instance, experimenting with archaic ways of talking or calling attention to differences in aspects of everyday life such as sanitation, medicine, and education), readers need to be alert to the fact that in many ways historical fiction is more about the present than about the history it purports to reflect. For this reason, as ideas of what history is mutate over time – no longer is it comprised of the dates of major battles or the names and successes of 'great' figures from the past (almost invariably white men) – so the subjects that appeal to writers of historical fiction change. If Peter Bramwell is right, and the historical novel is currently staging a revival, it is important to ask why this is and what gaps new historical fiction fills for readers and writers. It would be interesting to compare what this chapter says about history and women with issues raised in Chapter 11 about other groups whose history has previously not been told.

Historical fiction for children and young adults can be said to be 'not just a thing of the past' in a number of ways. First, the genre is currently in a vibrant state, as can be seen in the following analyses of historical novels by Theresa Tomlinson, Monica Furlong and Sherryl Jordan. Secondly, writers of historical fiction make it 'not just a thing of the past' by consciously addressing present-day issues; even when they make contrasts between the past and the present, this is done with the modern sensibility of exploring and embracing difference. This is in the context of changing perceptions of historiography (history writing) and historical fiction, from looking at how the past shapes the present, to an awareness that our present affects how we view the past.

History is 'an unending dialogue between the present and the past' (Carr, 1986: 30), and historical fiction inevitably retrojects the sensibilities of the writer's own context. What is accepted as historically accurate and convincing changes through time, so that what is realistic to one generation of writers and readers is incredible to another generation, and vice versa. Sometimes a change in the conventions of genre can be revolutionary; a good example is the work of Geoffrey Trease, whose historical and adventure novels from the 1930s onwards reacted against the conventions established in the jingoistic and hierarchical days of the expanding British Empire by using a modern style and a democratic point of view (Agnew et al., 2001: 335). This shift of interest from rulers to ordinary people is also apparent in the works of Leon Garfield and Rosemary Sutcliff. Most of Sutcliff's central characters are young men; apart from a few famous women, female characters and experience were rarely focused on in children's historical fiction until the last quarter of the twentieth century.

Theresa Tomlinson, Monica Furlong and Sherryl Jordan address current issues by depicting independent young women on the edges of convincingly imagined medieval societies. It is notable that these historical novels share the 'generic characteristics and plot structures [...] symptomatic of cases of *the feminine* in children's literature' as defined by Wilkie-Stibbs, referring to the work of Margaret Mahy and Gillian Cross:

all the texts feature a central, focalizing character, either male or female, who, though central to the narrative, is always positioned at the margins of their particular social milieu. S/he is, in some way, either physically and/or mentally displaced from 'home' into another elsewhere [...] which becomes their transformational space.   (2002: xiii)

The complaint that 'Current trends to depict early cultures as feminist havens ... sit uncomfortably against a medieval background' (Maund, 1997: 469) misses the point. Since the pioneering work of Eileen Power (1922), historians have increasingly been bringing medieval women's lives out of hiding, inevitably mirroring modern concerns in the process. Some historical novelists, including Tomlinson, Furlong and Jordan, have been doing the same, so that we are in the midst of a shift in what is perceived as accurate in historiography and historical fiction. The 'medieval background' against which the portrayal of autonomous women sits 'uncomfortably' is, then, the outdated one from which they were written out.

Mainly through the lens of feminist deconstruction, this chapter will look at the ways in which the authors of *The Forestwife Trilogy*, *Wise Child* and *A Year and a Day*, and *The Raging Quiet* consciously question and redefine constructions of gender difference. The focalized young women in these stories gain independence within the context of friendships and collaboration, and are nurtured by mentors from an older generation. In *The Forestwife Trilogy*, *Wise Child* and *A Year and a Day*, the friends and mentors are female, but in *The Raging Quiet* they are male. Indeed, redefining women's roles in these novels has an inevitable impact on men, implicitly or directly – either by parodying rigid masculinities, or by presenting 'feminized' male characters. As Wilkie-Stibbs stresses, *the feminine* cannot be reduced to the sex of authors, characters or readers, but is an order of discourse, a socially embedded system of signification, which is more fluid, plural and egalitarian than the historically dominant social order. Questions of gender identity in the work of Tomlinson, Furlong and Jordan are far-reaching, extending to religious difference, and the construction of narratives of history and story.

The women in the Greenwood: *The Forestwife Trilogy*

Theresa Tomlinson's novels have a consistent interest in women's history, and in the working lives of children and young adults in the past. Sometimes contact is made with the past through the device of a time-slip (*Night of the Red Devil*, 2000; *Scavenger Boy*, 2003), or by cross-generational friendships (*Summer Witches*; *Riding the Waves* – both 1989), or both (*Meet Me by the Steelmen*, 1997). Other novels, for older readers, are set entirely in the past: *The Moon Riders* (2003) tells the story of the siege of Troy from the Amazons' perspective, and *The Forestwife Trilogy* (2003) portrays the women of Sherwood. Theresa Tomlinson's first novel, *The Flither Pickers* (1987), contains a folk story of Robin Hood, and also includes a midwife and wise woman character, Miriam. These interests are developed much more fully in *The Forestwife Trilogy*. In the first book of the trilogy, Marian is focalized: the story stays with her, largely in the forest, while the exploits of Robert (Robin Hood), in his misguided loyalty to King Richard, are reported to her. It is Marian, rather than Robert, who takes up the cause of the sick and poor, and who acts on injustice. And it is Marian who confers the green hood upon Robert.

Marian starts out as Mary de Holt (Mary 'of the wood': her surname prefigures her destiny), of noble birth and subject to an arranged marriage. She escapes to the forest, where her nurse Agnes joins her. Mary has to adapt to an environment and people previously alien to her. The forest, and the Forestwife in her hidden clearing, are strange to outsiders, including Mary herself at first, who depends on received prejudices, saying that the forest 'is a place of evil' and that the Forestwife is 'a witch of the worst kind' (19). After Agnes becomes Forestwife, she renames Mary, Marian. With her new name, Marian develops a new identity: she becomes physically stronger, and intimately familiar with the forest. She also adopts the dialect of her new community. Marian eventually succeeds Agnes as Forestwife, and so moves from the question, 'But who am I? What part am I to play?' (35), to the knowledge 'I am Marian. I am the Forestwife' (161).

Tomlinson has created in the Forestwife a wise-woman figure, whose antiquity, continuity and femininity are signified by the girdle passed on from one Forestwife to the next. The role of the Forestwife is defined by Agnes thus: 'It is an ancient and sacred pact, an agreement, between the forest folk. It will bring us safety, for none will know or even ask our names. The Forestwife may keep her mysteries' (34). The Forestwife's skills and responsibilities include healing, midwifery, and offering food and shelter to the starving and homeless. The righting of wrongs associated with Robin Hood in more traditional retellings is, in Tomlinson's version, ascribed to Marian as Forestwife. The accent is on redressing injustices to women, and there is also a concern with overcoming prejudices about people with disabilities.

In *The Forestwife*, a woman is rescued from the scold's bridle, and the unorthodox Sisters of Mary Magdalen, stockaded for holding their own services, are liberated. Thereafter, the Sisters frequently work together with the Forestwife's enclave, and accept the forest people's nature religion, Mother Veronica affirming Marian's vocation as Forestwife. One of the Sisters, Margaret, was consigned to the nunnery as an unmarriageable daughter because of her harelip. She has her difference accepted and celebrated when the outlaw, Much, urges her not to cover her face as they dance together to honour the deer slain to feed the forest people through the winter.

There is a shift in emphasis in *Child of the May*, the second book of the trilogy, to the lives of aristocratic women, though the story of the plight of the noble Ladies of Langden is counterpointed by the development of Magda, born and raised in the forest. An aspect of Magda's growth is to overcome her aversion to disfigurement – Robert's facial scar, and the sores which lepers have. She learns from Mother Veronica, who was not harmed by the years she spent caring for people with leprosy. Furthermore, the historical Knights of Saint Lazarus, lepers who 'live in the wilderness as outcast as we' (89), play a significant part in the action of *Child of the May*. The Epilogue to this book enacts Magda's acceptance of physical difference: she and Tom, whose leg was permanently damaged by a mantrap in *The Forestwife*, dance together as May Queen and Green Man.

Magda and Tom's roles at the end of *Child of the May* echo Marian and Robert as Green Lady and Green Man in *The Forestwife*. Through Marian and Robert, gender polarities are not so much broken down as re-prioritized: while Robert roams wildly in the wider world, Marian is for the most part confined within the compass of the forest, but her role is privileged and focalized, and shown to be more effectual than his. The effect of presenting these characters in divine guises is to sanctify and universalize a reappraisal of gender and other individual differences. However, this universalizing tendency is constrained by the functions of disguise in the trilogy, and by the growing questioning and redefining of the Forestwife's role.

For Magda to go to Nottingham in *Child of the May*, she has to be disguised as a potter's lad. The implication is a feminist critique of the perceived necessity not to appear female to be an actor in the world, and accords with Lissa Paul's (1987) observation that women and children in literature tend to escape entrapment through trickery and deceit. At climactic moments in the third Forestwife story, *The Path of the She-Wolf*, Marian masquerades as the Hooded One. Marian's disguise enables her to act, but its form is also significant: by donning the hood she enters the male side of the binary opposition previously established between Marian/Green Lady/Forestwife and Robert/Green Man/Hooded One. There is little movement in the other direction, though – Robert still lacks Marian's competence and flexibility.

Marian comes to doubt her assumption that as Forestwife she could not be 'tied to a man', but she continues as before, having an intermittently intimate relationship with Robert, but refusing to marry him. By contrast, Marian's successor, Magda, does combine marriage and motherhood with the role of Forestwife, though Magda finds the forest confining, whereas for Marian it represents freedom. The choices available to many women in the West are clearly echoed in Tomlinson's presentation of alternative resolutions to the tensions between vocation, commitment to a partner, and different notions of freedom.

The concepts of both the Hooded One and the Forestwife are extended at the end of the trilogy. Robert's ageing is honoured and the Hooded One becomes, like the Forestwife, a role indefinitely passed on, as Tom, Magda's husband, takes over the hood. Marian's ageing is likewise hallowed, as she is identified with the Corn Goddess. The Forestwife's girdle splits in three, so that Gerta, Magda and Brigit are respectively 'The Old One, the Mother and the Maid' (128). This overt, capitalized reference to the three aspects of the pagan Triple Goddess deifies one model of the ages of woman.

It is possible to see the narrative structure, time-scheme and setting of *The Forestwife Trilogy* as an instance of Nikolajeva's female chronotope (Box 1.2). The structure and focus of the first book, *The Forestwife*, challenge the paradigms of historiography and historical fiction. The episodic nature of *The Forestwife* denies the teleology of historical narrative – that is, its goal-oriented, linear structure, which is a characteristic of the male chronotope. *The feminine* 'disrupts the linear temporality and logic of the [masculine] Symbolic [order]', according to Wilkie-Stibbs (2002: 28). The central characters of *The Forestwife* are liminal, living on the margins: legendary figures of contended historicity; women and working people largely written out of history until recently. The historian E. H. Carr claims:

> History begins when men [sic] begin to think of the passage of time in terms not of natural processes – the cycle of the seasons, the human life-span – but of a series of specific events in which men are constantly involved and which they can consciously influence. (1986: 134)

In *The Forestwife*, such 'his-story' is sidelined and subverted by 'her-story': men's actions are not purposive – kings act arbitrarily, and Robert signally fails to influence events. By contrast, women do influence events – Marian intervenes successfully to redress injustice. Furthermore, *The Forestwife* fore-grounds natural processes, and its sequels are structured around the cycle of the seasons.

Child of the May begins and ends with the festival of May Day, and is more precise than *The Forestwife* about the practices of nature religion, which celebrates the cycle of the seasons as the 'wheel of the year'. This is developed further in *The Path of the She-Wolf*, in which festivals are settings for rites of passage – girl to woman on May Day, marriages at Lammas. The novel opens and closes with Brig's Night, encompassing Magda's wish for a child and its multiple fulfilment. Magda's prayer, accompanied by ritually making a bower and a Biddy doll, is answered by twelve-year-old Brigit's arrival, by Magda's adoption of six homeless children, and by her having her own baby.

These details reveal a great deal about Tomlinson's female chronotope. First, the cyclic narrative embodies Magda's pregnancy, instantiating the generalization made by Trites that 'nested narratives can themselves become a child-of-the-mother image. ... The very structure of a nested narrative places a metaphorical value on birth [and] evokes the awareness of inter-personal connections' (1997: 113). Secondly, Magda's pagan ritual accords with the 'wheel of the year' structure of the narrative. The contrast between male and female chronotopes could be argued to have a spiritual dimen-sion, with the male chronotope corresponding to patriarchal, apocalyptic 'sky god' religion, and the female chronotope embodying female, cyclic 'earth goddess' religion. Thus, in incidents as well as at a whole-narrative level, *The Path of the She-Wolf* retrojects current interest in nature religion. Tomlin-son does this consciously in *The Forestwife Trilogy* and *The Moon Riders*: in interview (2003) she has revealed, 'I think the ancient mother goddess religions were based on respect for the earth and our environment and that many people do recognise the need for this today.'

Finally, Magda's prayer has a proleptic and hermeneutic function in the narrative – that is to say, it engages the reader in anticipating and guessing. It is also part of a wider pattern, in the last two Forestwife books, of visions, forebodings and prophecies, which self-consciously disrupt linear narrative. Tomlinson also consciously reflects her own storytelling in a scene in *The Forestwife*, in which present concerns are mirrored in the past: 'Sarah held them enthralled. Her stories [about Merlin and Arthur] told them of a time long ago, a time when hopes of justice had prevailed' (105). In these ways, *The*

Figure 7   The cover for Theresa Tomlinson's *Child of the May* shows clearly the centrality of the independent females featured in this historical novel

Forestwife Trilogy contradicts Stephens's assertion that 'Historical novels generally employ a realistic mode, and avoid any self-conscious reflections on their own narrative strategies' (1992: 236).

As with the characterization of Marian and Robert, the chronotope of *The Forestwife Trilogy* privileges the female side of the female–male binary opposition, rather than problematizing the terms of opposition. However, a tension in defining femaleness as both wild and domestic, which patriarchy solves by elevating the domestic and taming the wildness, is resolved in a different way in the Forestwife's clearing, which is simultaneously safe and wild.

This section is called 'The women in the Greenwood' as a deliberate riposte to the chapter in Stephens and McCallum (1998) on 'The Boys in the Greenwood: Stories of Robin Hood'. Stephens and McCallum find in Robin Hood retellings a predominance of male initiation and bonding. *The Forestwife*, despite being first published five years before their study, is apparently not known to them since they announce that 'we are still waiting for a *Robin Hood* in which Marian is principal focalizer' (181)! They do pay attention to Robin McKinley's *The Outlaws of Sherwood* (1988), and I would observe that much of what they find there is echoed by the later Forestwife trilogy: Sherwood is a refuge for oppressed women; female characters are focalizers; 'the patterns of male bonding [are] displaced by an emphasized social concern and conscience' (1998: 189); and Robin is 'a transformed and somewhat decentered character' (190).

The Forestwife Trilogy can be counted among the few exceptions to Stephens and McCallum's observation that the tendency of Robin Hood retellings 'towards socially conservative ideologies ... is unrelieved and systematically programmatic' (198). What particularly distinguishes *The Forestwife Trilogy* is the current resonance of its sustained exploration of gender roles, achieved through its female chronotope and through the figure of the Forestwife. *The Forestwife Trilogy*, together with, for example, Kevin Crossley-Holland's self-consciously border-crossing *Arthur* trilogy (2000–3), may be seen to represent a growing resistance to the culturally conservative 'Western metaethic' Stephens and McCallum regard as pervasive in retellings of traditional stories.

Becoming a Wise Woman: *Wise Child* and *A Year and a Day*

Although Monica Furlong also wrote a Robin Hood novel (*Robin's Country*, 1994), in order to maintain this chapter's focus on women's history and spirituality, I will look instead at her paired novels *Wise Child* (1987) and *A Year and a Day* (1990). *Wise Child* is set in seventh-century Scotland and depicts Wise Child's training by Juniper as a *doran*; its prequel, *A Year and a Day*, goes back in time to tell in turn of Wise Child's mentor's training. A *doran* is a wise person, male or female, Christian or Pagan, who has 'found a way of seeing and perceiving' (1987: 85), and lives 'in the rhythm'. Though a *doran* may be male, what is actually presented in both novels is wisdom being passed from older women to younger ones, making Furlong's *doran* comparable with Tomlinson's Forestwife. Conflict and dialogue between Christianity and

Paganism are prominent in *Wise Child* and *A Year and a Day*, as is an exploration of different models of female power.

From the outset, the presentation of otherness in *Wise Child* is multi-layered and shifting. 'Juniper was different from us' implies identity between the reader and the narrator, but then it becomes clear that not only Juniper, but also the narrator, lives in a world different from the reader's: 'In the first place she [Juniper] came from another country – Cornwall' (9). In fact, much of what makes Juniper different from Wise Child's community – and causes her to be both needed and feared as a 'witch' – makes her more like the present-day implied reader, in knowledge, beliefs and artefacts. Juniper is less superstitious and more knowledgeable than Wise Child. She has books and other technologies (a kaleidoscope, a magic mirror which may be a camera obscura) which open new ways of seeing; as she explains, 'What is difficult about learning ... is that you have to give up what you know already to make room for the new ideas' (44).

Wise Child does indeed adopt new ideas and a new way of life under Juniper's tutelage. Like Marian in *The Forestwife*, Wise Child becomes physically more strong and skilled; she learns to work with her hands and her mind. She loathes spinning and sewing, but Juniper insists on their value – thereby privileging what is disdained as 'women's work'. Juniper makes Wise Child confront and overcome her prejudice against people with leprosy, as Veronica does with Magda in *Child of the May*, and with the same generalized lesson for readers in the present about not rejecting but understanding people with illnesses such as HIV/AIDS. Though Wise Child grows more used to Juniper, Juniper's difference is maintained so that she can still surprise Wise Child, as she does at the Feast of Beltane: 'I felt separate, in awe of her, as if I didn't know her at all, she was so splendid' (156).

Similarly, in *A Year and a Day*, the 'prequel' to *Wise Child*, the young Juniper at first dislikes her mentor Euny and is 'afraid of her rags and poverty' (1990: 26), but she comes to understand and respect her, whilst maintaining a 'familiar sense of being surprised by Euny – of always being on the wrong foot yet of rather enjoying it' (128). Two months of Juniper's apprenticeship are spent at Angharad's, which is more colourful and comfortable than Euny's. Teaching Juniper to dye wool, Angharad subtly defends Euny: 'the vinegar ... is the biting acid that makes the colour fast' (73). When Juniper returns home after a year and a day, she feels 'as if nothing could console me for the loss of those hard days which, I now realized, had taught me a great deal' (109).

In both *A Year and a Day* and *Wise Child*, Monica Furlong experiments with mixing Christianity and nature religion. In *A Year and a Day*, Euny and young Juniper honour the Mother in the form of a black Madonna by a well, and the trainee *dorans*, Juniper and Trewyn, share bread and wine with their mentors at a stone circle. As in *The Forestwife*, some of the novel's concerns are epitomized in a brief reference to Arthur, whom Juniper's mother Erlain sees as a syncretizing figure – a figure used to reconcile contradictory elements: 'The Christians say that there is no magic – that the world is ruled by love. I cannot decide whether they are right. Our forebear Arthur was a Christian yet believed in magic' (27).

A rather schematic opposition is set up, in *Wise Child*, between the priest, Fillan, who represents a persecuting, punitive, patriarchal version of Christianity, and the *doran*, Juniper, who is tolerant and in touch with nature. This opposition makes Wise Child herself a site of conflict and resolution, as she declares, 'I want to be both a Christian and a *doran*' (1987: 170). This statement crystallizes two key moments in Wise Child's apprenticeship. First, under the influence of a hallucinogenic ointment, she experiences visionary 'flying', on a broom and accompanied by a cat. Wise Child interprets her vision with an ecstatic jumble of Christianity and Paganism by praying 'to God, to Christ, to that special, magic place, to the wild world about me, to St Brigid, St Michael, to Columba, to Finbar [her absent father], to Juniper, my most intimate saints' (82). Secondly, Wise Child's 'flying' vision is fulfilled when she joins a gathering of *dorans* at a stone circle for the festival of Beltane/May Day (ch. 15). Again, something apparently pagan is Christianized – there are echoes of the biblical story of Abraham and Isaac when Wise Child surrenders herself to be sacrificed, only for a deer (rather than a ram) to replace her. Then, in a ceremony like the Mass, everyone sips from a silver chalice and partakes of the sacrificial deer's flesh.

When Fillan contrives to have Juniper tried as a witch, her point of view is that:

> He thinks that I am working against the new religion but it is not so. I love and revere Jesus as he does – how could one not? But in the new religion they think that nature, especially in the human body, must be fought and conquered – they seem to fear and distrust matter itself, although in the Mass it is bread and wine that is used to show how spirit and matter are one. They think that those, like the *dorans*, who love and cherish nature, must be fought and conquered too. Jesus did not tell them to do this – it is all their own invention because they fear nature, their own and that of others. (199)

This contrast in religious outlooks is presented in terms of gendered binary oppositions, which the Christian priest Fillan's male side upholds by repressing the material, natural feminine, whereas the female *doran* Juniper destabilizes the opposition she describes.

In *Wise Child*, Furlong explores different models of women's power through the characters of Juniper and Maeve the Sorceress. Juniper is drawn from but also challenges stereotypes. She is witch as healer, and in adopting Wise Child she is a kind of Virgin Mother. She makes drudgery divine, giving value to women's work in the home, but she is not a stereotyped 'angel in the house', because she is not beholden to any man, and she comes and goes as she pleases. Juniper's spells of absence also make Wise Child more autonomous. Juniper is very much idealized, as a mature role model for Wise Child and the implied reader. She is still, silent, and watchful; she is full of laughter and she is slow to chide – she will not get angry or beat Wise Child; she is a marvellous storyteller; she has a house of her own, and she owns land and is kind to her tenants. Wise Child thinks of 'Juniper who did not think in terms of luxury and handsome husbands, but who lived as if everything in life ... was a joyful and wonderful treat, a source of amusement, of pleasure, of fascination' (176).

By contrast, Maeve, Wise Child's absent mother, is portrayed as the beautiful, seductive and cruel witch. Her hatred of Juniper derives from an old jealousy over a man. She too has independent means, but is cruel to her tenants and servants. Maeve is Wise Child's tempter, offering to spoil her and make her attractive to men. The stereotype which Maeve represents is not interrogated or redefined, it is simply there for Wise Child to reject.

Maeve's magic is evil, according to Juniper, because it is selfish and controlling – 'forcing you to do something cannot be right' (190). However, Wise Child is coerced into surrendering herself to others' control during the ordeals of her training. Juniper asks Wise Child, 'Would you trust me if I told you to do something you really hated? That scared you? ... Because you would be glad afterwards. It would be very good for you' (73). Juniper and her former mentor, Euny, proceed to make Wise Child fast, bathe and strip, and cover her with psychotropic ointment. 'Broken with faintness and nausea, [Wise Child was] too ill now to wonder or do anything but helplessly surrender' (79). What follows is the mystical revelatory experience of 'flying'. Later, Juniper remorselessly drills Wise Child in a magic language until tiredness sends her beside herself, or ecstatic. And at Beltane, as we have seen, Wise Child submits to be sacrificed. There is a tension between the value of Wise Child's experiences and the intimidating ways in which they are induced.

Furlong took the opportunity of the later book, *A Year and a Day*, to revisit and reappraise the issues of control that arise in *Wise Child*. This process is comparable with Tomlinson's redefinitions of the Forestwife's role as the trilogy progresses, and with Susan Price's questioning in later Ghost World novels of disempowering aspects of the shamanism presented in *The Ghost Drum* (see Chapter 9). Unlike Wise Child, young Juniper manifests signs of her gift before she is apprenticed: her birth is accompanied by portents, she is a natural dowser, she sees visions and dreams, and she has a healing gift. It is vocation that compels her: 'I knew that life was pushing me towards the peculiar sort of wisdom that Euny and Angharad had. I felt I had no real choice' (1990: 91). Juniper is forewarned more than Wise Child, and her trust of her mentors is repeatedly spelled out. Ordeals such as being locked in a smoke-filled hut are also somewhat mitigated by the companionship of Juniper's friend Trewyn.

It is also indicated that Juniper's apprenticeship to Euny is less oppressive than the life she has left behind as a marriageable princess, 'having no control over my life, of being a mere pawn, indeed a lost pawn, in the game being played between Meroot [her aunt] and my father' (135). The *dorans* represent a better alternative to patriarchy than Meroot's malevolent magic, as Angharad explains: 'Among the *dorans* we speak of people having power, you know. We don't mean power like kings or popes have power, of course, but power to bring things back into a sort of harmony' (72). Both *Wise Child* and *A Year and a Day* partake of *the feminine* by advocating a social order in which power is not about subjecting and marginalizing others but collaborating with them; not subduing nature, but living 'in the rhythm'.

Embracing difference: *The Raging Quiet*

New Zealand writer Sherryl Jordan's 'Author's Note' to *The Raging Quiet* (2000) reveals that she is consciously writing a story for our time about difference: 'This tale belongs to any time, even our own; it is about prejudice and ignorance, and a young woman wrongly accused, who is guilty of only one thing – the unforgivable crime of being different.' The 'young woman' is Marnie, who is 'wrongly accused' of witchcraft, because the villagers of Torcurra mistrust her autonomy and her companionship with Raven, a deaf young man with whom Marnie invents a system of sign language. Modern sensibilities enter into a medieval setting, both in the assumed wholesale intolerance of a small community of the time (for the most part presented as an undifferentiated, unnamed mass), and conversely in the very 'modern' traits of the main characters.

Marnie is an incomer, and Father Brannan, a man of vibrant and humane faith, warns her that the villagers 'feel threatened by newcomers, especially people they know nothing about' (61). What is more, Marnie lives in a remote cottage with an evil reputation: its former inhabitant was executed as a witch. Marnie herself is suspected of witchcraft when her wealthy and loathsome husband dies in an accident within two days of their moving into the cottage, leaving Marnie to lead a solitary and independent life.

Marnie is supported in her independence by Father Brannan, who is 'like her father … in his gentle manner and easy way of talking' (61). Marnie's father Michael is also the measure of her new friendships, and when she later visits him, she credits him with allowing her to gain the skills to be self-sufficient: 'You'd be so proud if you saw me! All those times you let me try things that were different, that women weren't supposed to do – I'm grateful for them, now' (183). Michael has been unable to talk since having a stroke, and Marnie perceives his similarity to Raven, who has 'the eyes of a caged animal, full of intelligence and pleading and pain. It was the same look her father had, since his affliction' (86).

Raven is portrayed as a wise fool – the significance of this theme is signalled by the name of Torcurra's inn, 'The Sage and Fool', mentioned at the beginning and end of the novel. Marnie sees that there is 'something ageless and unworldly about Raven, something akin to innocence. It was as if he were empty, pure, unspoiled by the world's guile and complexity' (85). This is the positive stereotype, but stereotype nevertheless, of the disabled person having extraordinary compensating abilities. Raven's inability to talk mirrors the way women are deprived of a voice in patriarchal society. It is Marnie who gives him a voice, by initiating inventing signs. The dramatic physicality of this form of communication writes large the feminist idea of gaining a voice through 'writing the body'. Appropriately, the sign for 'different' is the one that is most elaborately described (131–2).

The villagers of Torcurra fear and persecute Marnie and Raven, regarding their signs as sorcery, and are pruriently suspicious of Marnie taking homeless Raven under her roof, not long after her husband Isake's sudden death. Isake's brother Pierce, like Isake before him, refers to Marnie's physical beauty as 'bewitching', invoking the witch-as-seductress stereotype. Marnie is brought to trial as a witch, despite all the accusations against her being unfounded. Father Brannan cannot stop the excruciating trial by ordeal, but he takes control and limits the damage as far as he can. Raven knows 'well the voiceless pain, the raging quiet within' which Marnie endures (268). Father Brannan is convinced of her innocence, which is indeed proved, though the villagers' intolerance is unassuaged.

There are limits even to Father Brannan's tolerance: he thinks Raven and Marnie should marry as 'you're flying in the face of custom, and you'll be spurned for it' (282). Although Marnie responds by asserting, 'I'll not marry to please you, or to stop people's tongues wagging' (282), she does marry Raven, after they have made love for the first time. Marnie consents with Raven in a way she never did with Isake, but she is passive in bed: 'spellbound, powerless ... she gave herself to him' (289). Such submission reverts to romantic convention and fundamentally undermines the active subjectivity Marnie has gained in the rest of her life.

Like Wise Child, Marnie keeps her Christian faith throughout her experiences. She blesses the cottage when she moves in, and prays frequently. Father Brannan assures her that Isake's death is not a terrible answer to prayer. Her faith is tested by the horrors of wedlock to Isake and by her trial as a witch, but she continues to pray through both. Though she can accommodate the tradition of Midsummer Eve, 'dancing in the fields by huge bonfires, celebrating the summer and the sun' (174), Raven's instinctive paganism is at first strange to Marnie:

> Like ancient sentinels, the stones leaned dark and overpowering against the wheeling stars. The air seemed alive, the shining silence still ringing with the songs of bygone worshippers. Marnie shivered, remembering warnings she had heard about these places; warnings of heathen gods, spirit forces, and forbidden rites. But Raven embraced the stones, stroking them, sensing their primal force. (236)

And yet, again like Wise Child, she filters new experience through Christian perceptions: 'Longing for lost innocence, for that oneness with the perfect earth, she yearned to dance as Raven danced – as surely Adam and Eve had danced – in newborn Eden' (236). She does dance with Raven, and feels 'at one with the moonlight and the night, unaware of self, unaware of everything but this freedom, this cleansing unity with the earth and sky and God' (237). Raven's deafness and homelessness have removed him from socializing processes, so that his nature religion appears innate, though Father Brannan and Marnie think it is intuitive Christianity.

Marnie's independence is nurtured by her biological and spiritual fathers, and her closest friends are men with 'female' qualities: Raven is close to nature, and Father Brannan is tolerant and compassionate. Thus *the feminine* in *The Raging Quiet* involves change for both sexes, in terms of subjectivity, social relations and spirituality.

Conclusion

There has recently been a resurgence of medieval historical fiction, and given that 'settings implicate attitude and ideology' and are 'part of the process of signification' (Stephens, 1992: 209), it is worth trying to gain an overview of what this period offers today's writers and readers. This chapter has shown that medieval settings can be used to explore young adult character development, and a range of differences, including those of sex, gender and religion. Medieval historical fiction also appears to lend itself to a degree of self-conscious narration. While all these things may be achieved in other settings, they are currently being used in medieval settings in a distinctively complex and coherent way, permeated and integrated by a feminist concern with the construction of gender. Gender identity is not an issue exclusive to women novelists portraying female protagonists, as can be seen in Kevin Crossley-Holland's *Arthur* trilogy. Likewise, as a male reader myself, I maintain that the issue is not only of interest to female readers, though sadly it can be difficult to get boys to engage with the kinds of texts discussed here, since even after years of gender awareness, masculinity and femininity still tend to be defined against each other.

Young adults' choices are foregrounded in medieval historical fiction, because these choices, particularly for young women, are presented as being starker then than now. The present ideal of independence is, though, apparently more achievable in the past – when it was not so much the ideal. The novels discussed in this chapter supply what today's young adults may be viewed as lacking: autonomy, clear rites of passage, a sense of community and collaboration, and inter-generational friendships. Similarly, the depiction of nature religion reflects a current desire for the 'Old Religion' to have a history, and to place it in the rural context from which terms like 'pagan' and 'heathen' derive. Questions of faith are raised by portraying the uneasy co-existence of religion and magic, Christianity and Paganism, in medieval settings. Tomlinson presents an all-female Christian community of nuns working with the Forestwife and her people, whereas Furlong and Jordan have solitary male priests (though Jordan's Father Brannan is considerably more tolerant than Furlong's Fillan!). In both *Wise Child* and *The Raging Quiet*, women are brought to trial as witches; this has a bearing on the distrust and ignorance that continues today, both of independent women, and of people with misunderstood beliefs.

The connection between *the feminine* and nature religion is upheld and privileged at a whole-narrative level by the use of the female chronotope. The cause-and-effect, goal-oriented, hierarchical male chronotope is also disrupted by self-conscious and fantastic elements: reference to legendary figures, reflections on the telling of history and story, and the possibility of magic. Thus we can align the works of Tomlinson, Furlong and Jordan with Wilkie-Stibbs's

paradigmatic texts of *the feminine* [in which] there is a constant slippage and blurring of the logic in boundaries between fantasy and 'reality,' past and present, and a continuous interplay between psychic and everyday life, and between fantastic and realistic modes of narrative.   (2002: xiv)

Now, as ever, children's historical fiction is 'responding, adapting, and freely cross-breeding with other genres' (Rahn, 1991: 1), its range of viewpoints is wide, and ways of writing and reading it are in flux, including a growing consciousness, shared between contemporary writers and readers, that current concerns are inescapably inscribed in narratives of the past. Historical fiction for children is certainly not just a thing of the past.

WORKS CITED AND FURTHER READING

Primary Texts

Furlong, M., *Wise Child* (London: Gollancz, 1987).

Furlong, M., *A Year and a Day* (London: Gollancz, 1990; retitled *Juniper*, 1992).

Jordan, S., *The Raging Quiet* (London: Simon and Schuster, 2000; first published in 1999 in the USA by Simon and Schuster).

Tomlinson, T., *The Forestwife Trilogy* (London: Random House, 2003; originally published separately as *The Forestwife* (1993), *Child of the May* (1998) and *The Path of the She-Wolf* (2000)).

Critical Texts

Agnew, K. et al., 'Historical Fiction', in V. Watson (ed.), *The Cambridge Guide to Children's Books in English* (Cambridge: Cambridge University Press, 2001), pp. 335–8.

Collins, F. and Graham, J. (ed.), *Historical Fiction for Children: Capturing the Past* (London: Fulton, 2001).

Rahn, S., 'An Evolving Past: the Story of Historical Fiction and Nonfiction for Children', *The Lion and the Unicorn*, 15 (1991), pp. 1–26.

Stephens, J. and McCallum, R., *Retelling Stories, Framing Culture: Traditional Stories and Metanarratives in Children's Literature* (New York and London: Garland, 1998).

Tomlinson, T., 'An Interview with Theresa Tomlinson', by Peter Bramwell. http://improbability.ultralab.net/writeaway, 2003.

Children's Books

Branford, H., *The Fated Sky* (London: Hodder, 1996).

Crossley-Holland, K., *The Seeing Stone* (London: Orion, 2000); *At the Crossing-Places* (London: Orion, 2001); *King of the Middle March* (London: Orion, 2003).

Furlong, M., *Robin's Country* (Harmondsworth: Penguin, 1994).

Gavin, J., *Coram Boy* (London: Egmont, 2000).

Geras, A., *Troy* (London: Scholastic, 2000).

McKinley, R., *The Outlaws of Sherwood* (London: Macdonald, 1989; first published in the US, 1988).

Price, S., *The Wolf-Sisters* (London: Hodder, 2001).

Tomlinson, T., *Summer Witches* (London: Walker, 1989a; published in paperback as *The Secret Place*); *Riding the Waves* (London: Walker, 1989b); *The Flither Pickers* (London: Walker, 1990; first published in 1987 by the Littlewood Press); *Meet Me by the Steelmen* (London: Walker, 1997); *Night of the Red Devil* (London: Walker, 2000); *The Moon Riders* (London: Transworld, 2003); *Scavenger Boy* (London: Walker, 2003).

Childhood, Youth Culture and the Uncanny: Uncanny Nights in Contemporary Adolescent Fiction

8

Lisa Sainsbury

KEY TEXTS

G. Cross, *Wolf* (1990)
A. Garner, *The Owl Service* (1967)
J. Whedon, *Buffy the Vampire Slayer* (television series, 1997–2003)

In this chapter, Lisa Sainsbury organizes a series of oppositions – between youth culture and adult authority; familiar and unfamiliar; official and unofficial; waking and sleeping; living and dead – around the dynamic between night and day. This approach combines considering texts in their social and political contexts with an interest in the workings of the psyche. At its core lies the dichotomy that underpins contemporary thinking about childhood: on the one hand we cling to the pervasive myth off childhood as a time of innocence while on the other, children are increasingly cordoned off and made safe as if they were a social danger. Texts dealing with these issues fulfil an important role in helping juvenile readers think about what it means to be young in contemporary society, and as part of this, about the relationship between adolescence and self-identity. With its focus on adolescence and maturation, this chapter can usefully be read alongside Chapter 9.

While episodes of Buffy the Vampire Slayer have been novelized, this chapter refers to the original television series. Since the narratives of youth culture often find forms outside the mainstream of book publishing, this use of a popular television series can open up a range of debates about interactions between media, the impact of media on youth narratives, and issues relating to performing youth (all the main actors in the series are older than the roles they play), among other concerns.

Legislating the night

In 1999 the British government presented a Criminal Justice and Police Bill to the House of Commons which introduced curfew schemes for children up to the age of fifteen. It suggested that children and teenagers should be legally required to be off public streets by 9.00 pm and confined to their homes at night. The curfew law attempts to deal with a spiralling 'yob culture', and while the bill has only limited relevance to most young people, such legislation reflects the perennial tension between youth culture and adult authority. The controversy surrounding these curfews has elicited complex debates beyond the scope of this chapter (see, for instance, BBC's *Talking Point* website on Curfew and Yob Culture). However, some of the arising issues are directly related to literary constructions of adolescence, and the figurative significance of day and night associated with them.

Part of the controversy surrounding this bill is fuelled by the youth of potential offenders, as people cling to idealistic notions of childhood which offer its innocent inhabitants protection from the 'real world'. Commentators detect a rift between such constructions of childhood/family life and the lived reality of contemporary society. As one enraged participant in the BBC's *Talking Point* asks, 'Curfews! Why are these problem children on the streets? What's going on in their homes? What are their parents doing?' (Paul B, *Talking Point* Contributor, UK, 2001). The government's bill admits that children of a young age are transgressing the cultural codes which say that by early evening the young should be safely housed within the domestic sphere, or engaged in some sort of sanctioned activity such as an after-school club or sport. Similarly, consensus dictates that children should be tucked up in bed before their parents, and that evening or night-time experiences should be mediated by adults.

Having said this, it should be noted that the yob culture attacked by the curfew bill is more closely aligned to notions of adolescence than to those of early childhood. It also reflects a universal battle between adults and youths who are seeking to negotiate curfews and to establish experience outside of the home. Adolescence is, then, partly defined by the struggle to move out of sanctioned day-time experience into night-time experience shared with peers; to take charge of the nighttime world of mature, sexualized adulthood. In adolescent fiction, the transition between night and day frequently also works as a complex metaphor for the psychological domain of adolescent characters as, in an evocation of Freud's notion of the uncanny, the familiar world of childhood becomes defamiliarized during the journey to adulthood.

Adolescence and the uncanny

Before looking closely at examples of adolescent fiction, it is useful to consider constructions of adolescence in relation to Joseph Appleyard's developmental schema and Sigmund Freud's discussion of the uncanny (see Box 8.1). Adolescence is typically defined as a transitional stage between childhood and

---

BOX 8.1   THE UNCANNY

The notion of the uncanny is frequently traced to Sigmund Freud's seminal essay 'The Uncanny' (*Das Unheimlich*), which was first published in 1919. In 'The Uncanny' Freud attempts to identify and explain the particular type of fear or dread classified as uncanny. He suggests that 'the uncanny' is within the sphere of the frightening, but that 'a special core of feeling is present which justifies the use of a special conceptual term' (Freud, 1990: 339). Freud goes on to trace a fundamental relationship between the uncanny/unfamiliar (*unheimlich*) and familiar/canny (*heimlich*), finally concluding that the uncanny is related not simply to that which is weird or mysterious, but to that which is *strangely familiar* (Royle: 2003, back cover). Exploring a range of literature, Freud establishes that certain literary images, such as damage to eyes, the theme of the double, or dismembered limbs, elicit uncanny feelings which can then be attributed to various psychological anxieties. As Nicholas Royle observes in his recent study, *The Uncanny*, Freud's approach to the uncanny has influenced a range of contemporary theories from feminism to queer theory, but 'as a ghostly feeling and concept ... the uncanny has a complex history going back to at least the Enlightenment' (Royle: 2003, back cover). Several critics writing within the field of children's literature, for example John Stephens and Robyn McCallum (2001) and Claudia Nelson (2003) have identified uncanny motifs with literature for young people, suggesting that such feelings of dread are particularly common to adolescent experience.

---

adulthood, during which young people attempt to come to terms with themselves and society. In *Becoming A Reader* (1990), Appleyard explores various psychological accounts of adolescence, each of which suggests that the associated phenomena are 'manifestations of one central phenomenon: the discovery of the subjective self and of subjective experience as something unique' (Kohlberg and Gilligan, cited in Appleyard, 1994: 96). This discovery frequently leads to a divisive and polarized world-view, in which this new-found and highly prized inner self is valued over the external self that plays out social roles; a polarity which rejects pretence (external self) in favour of authenticity (internal self). This adolescent preoccupation with division and otherness can be connected to Freud's notion of the uncanny, but before exploring this relationship, it is useful to consider Erik Erikson's suggestion that, 'although adolescents undergo a rapid physiological maturation, society (especially a technologically advanced one) postpones their taking genuine adult roles by keeping them in school (in Appleyard 1994: 97–8). Society forces young people into a liminal space that lies somewhere between childhood and adulthood, but that is essentially distanced from both. It is a period of transition which, given its pre-disposition to thoughtful introspection (97), is obsessively aware of its status as such.

Of particular significance here, adolescence is frequently perceived as a time of dislocation; as a phase in which new-found self-consciousness leads to a reassessment of the familiar world, rendering it unfamiliar. It is this focus which links to Freud's notion of the uncanny. Freud's 1919 essay 'The Uncanny' attempts to uncover ways in which particular works of art produce *certain qualities of feeling* which, while related to the feelings of dread and horror aroused by that which is frightening, are not reducible to it (1990: 339). During the course of this exploration, Freud traces the linguistic development of the term, beginning with the German terms *unheimlich* (uncanny/unfamiliar) and *heimlich* (canny/familiar), finally providing a tentative definition which has parallels with prevailing constructions of adolescence. Freud concludes that the meaning of '*heimlich* develops in the direction of ambivalence, until it finally coincides with its opposite *unheimlich*' (347). There is a correlation between *heimlich* and *unheimlich*, in which meanings fuse and the familiar becomes unfamiliar.

The ambivalence Freud detects in his final definition of the uncanny is, then, applicable to modern conceptions of adolescence. As Nicholas Royle points out: 'the uncanny involves feelings of uncertainty, in particular regarding the reality of who one is and what is being experienced. Suddenly one's sense of oneself ... seems strangely questionable' (2003: 1). These feelings of uncertainty are central to each of the texts explored in this chapter, as adolescent characters embark on journeys which move within diurnal and nocturnal realms.

Constructing adolescence

Like many texts dealing with adolescent angst, Alan Garner's *The Owl Service* (1967) lends a mythic dimension to its preoccupation with youth. *The Owl Service* is set in a secluded Welsh valley and centres on the relationship between three adolescents: Alison, Roger and Gwyn. As Michael Lockwood explains:

> Alison and her step-brother Roger are English, staying in the farmhouse used by Alison's family as a holiday home for many years. Gwyn, who is Welsh, is the son of the cook, Nancy. The three are caught up in a re-enactment of one of the tragic and violent legends from the *Mabinogion* – as, it emerges, generations have been before them, often with fatal consequences. Some of the bruised participants in previous enactments of the legend are present as adults as this particular cycle of the frightening legend begins.   (1992: 83)

The legend Lockwood refers to is 'Math of Mathonwy', a story of betrayed love in which the enchanter Gwydion makes Blodeuwedd out of flowers as a wife for his son Lleu. However, Blodeuwedd falls in love with Gronw Pebyr, who is eventually killed by Lleu, while Gwydion transforms Blodeuwedd into an owl as a punishment for betraying his son. In Garner's 'expression'[1] of the tale, Alison becomes Blodeuwedd to Roger's Gronw and Gwyn's Lleu.

A useful way in to *The Owl Service* is first to consider *The Mabinogion*, the sequence of medieval Welsh tales through which Garner's complex text expresses itself. In his introduction to *The Mabinogion*, Jeffry Gantz explains that:

> Unfortunately, the *meaning* of the word *mabinogi* in the present context is still a problem. Professor Ifor Williams was able to show that *mabinogi* generally designates the story of someone's early years. . . . Alternatively, Rachael Bromwich has suggested that mabinogi came to signify 'a tale of descendants', and that the Four Branches actually deal with the children of the early Celtic deities. (1976: 31–2)

Whatever the precise etymology of *mabinogi*, there seems no doubt that it is concerned not only with stories of young people, but with their descent; with the relationship between generations and the tensions which arise as children come into adolescence. Gantz's etymology confirms that the adolescent psychodrama at the core of *The Owl Service* is inevitable if the myth, 'Math of Mathonwy', is to be given any sort of viable expression.

One of the clearest ways in which Garner approaches adolescence in *The Owl Service* is through the manifestation of the double. The inter-weaving of Garner's triple narrative involves a shifting and doubling of identity that permeates the book; for example, gazing from her bedroom window Alison sees 'herself mirrored among haloes that the sun made on the water' (1973: 83), representing a manifestation of the uncanny. According to Freud, the 'phenomenon of the "double"' is often,

> marked by the fact that the subject identifies himself with someone else, so that he is in doubt as to which his self is, or substitutes the extraneous self for his own. In other words there is a doubling, dividing and interchanging of the self. And finally there is the constant reference of the same thing – the repetition of the same character traits or vicissitudes, of the same names through several generations. (1990: 356)

Freud ponders the source of uncanny terror induced by such doubling, suggesting that the 'double' variously functions as 'an assurance of immortality', while also, in a typically uncanny contradiction of this idea, as 'an uncanny harbinger of death' (356). Freud's notion of doubling echoes Garner's construction of adolescent identity, which sees itself reflected in others more clearly than it recognizes itself. Garner's central characters are doubled with their counterparts in previous generations, and in this sense they are rendered immortal. It is, however, a blighted immortality, structured around death rather than birth. The children seem to be locked inextricably into past patterns, culminating in death and destruction; in owlish darkness rather than flowery sunlight.

If the subject of adolescence is essential to the mythic resonance of *The Owl Service*, it is equally central to the reworking of 'Red Riding Hood' in Gillian Cross's *Wolf* (1990). *Wolf* tells the story of Cassy's enforced departure from the home she shares with her grandmother; Cassy's journey to the London squat inhabited by her mother, her mother's boyfriend, and his son Robert; and Cassy's confronting of the 'wolf', which stalks her from the past and in her dreams: a wolf that seems inextricably linked to her absent father. Cassy's journey across London to find her mother is only the latest in a familiar, if unwelcome and perplexing, aspect of Cassy's childhood experience: 'Step by step, word by word, they would go through the same pattern as last time – and all the times before' (1992: 4). The journey is not in itself remarkable, but the conditions attributed to it are. That Cassy must make this trip alone is significant. Cassy's plea to her Nan, 'But you *always* take me,' is met with the rejoinder: 'Maybe it's time you were growing up, then' (6). Evidently this is a journey from childhood to adulthood.

It soon becomes apparent that Nan's controlling regime of over-protection, however well meant, has ill equipped Cassy for her adolescent adventure. She will have to unlearn the rules of childhood, in which she sees herself through Nan's eyes:

> Cassy shut the bathroom door tight and glared at her reflection in the mirror. Sensible brown eyes. Sensible short brown hair. You only had to look at that face to know she wouldn't do anything wild. *If everyone was like you*, Nan said, *the world would be a simpler, sweeter place.* Sometimes Cassy wished being sensible wasn't so important.   (6)

Cassy is propelled on a journey of self-discovery, initiated and defined by her grandmother at the outset. Her path leads from the sensible and ordered existence of life with Nan to her mother's emotional and instinctual world, in which Cassy's perception of reality and self are challenged. Throughout this process of defamiliarization, Cassy struggles to maintain links with the conditions of her childhood. 'Shocked' and 'frozen' by the distortions of her mother's mirrored room, Cassy 'gripped the handle of her suitcase, standing completely still as she worked out where the boundaries were' (14). Her response to this uncanny environment is to grip the familiar object: the suitcase which she associates with Nan. She reaches for the familiar to make sense of the unfamiliar, but must soon come to terms with the idea that she cannot have one without the other, as Freud's exploration of the uncanny suggests.

Joss Whedon's teen drama *Buffy the Vampire Slayer* (1997–2003) also draws on mythological sources in its witty integration of adolescent pre-occupations and heroic narrative structure. The central premise of *Buffy* is repeated at the beginning of each episode, 'In every generation there is a Chosen One. She alone will stand against the vampires, the demons and the forces of darkness. She is the Slayer.' Buffy Summers is the 'Chosen One', a high school student who must battle against evil by night and attend school by day. Significantly, she must act alone as, although she gathers a group of friends/ helpers around her, her position reflects the familiar adolescent anxiety of being alone (though not powerless) in an overwhelmingly cruel, adult world. Although individual episodes occasionally have self-contained plots, each series has a central story-arc that pits Buffy against an evil adversary, which is eventually destroyed, though not without cost to Buffy and her friends.

As Whedon observes, the show reframes 'the mythic structure of a hero's journey' through 'the growth of an adolescent girl. ... The things she has to go through – losing her virginity, dying and coming back to life – are meant to be mythic and yet they're meant to be extremely personal' (cited in Golden et al., 2000: viii). *Buffy* suggests that teenage concerns do have resonance in later life and in the world outside of individual experience. Buffy is thus able to try out for the cheerleading squad, run for Prom Queen and struggle with her studies, while simultaneously preventing Armageddon. This seems to be an exaggerated and often comic reworking of Erikson's observation (see Appleyard, 1994: 98) that adolescents are forced to play out adult roles from within the confines of school life.

That the primary setting for the first three seasons of *Buffy* is Sunnydale High School, confirms the show's preoccupation with teenage life. Indeed, the very first episode, 'Welcome to the Hellmouth', opens at night in Sunnydale High with the first of many vampiric slaughterings. However, as the Vampire Slayer, not only must Buffy attend school, but she must also prevent Sunnydale's (and by extension, humankind's) descent into the hellmouth. Like Alison in *The Owl Service*, Buffy leads a double existence, and the tension between these roles is frequently emphasized. In one episode (series 3, no. 16), titled 'Doppelgangland' ('*doppelgänger*' is the German word for 'double'), central characters are faced with mirror images of themselves, and in the comedic 'Intervention' (series 5, no. 18), a robotic replica of Buffy is created. Indeed, Buffy's double identity is the focus for much of the show's brand of uncanny horror and humour. As Nicholas Royle points out,

> the figure of the double is also a figure of humour. ... Such humour is inscribed in the very heart of Poe's work ... though his connection is intriguingly absent, or apparently absent, from Freud's account of the double in 'The Uncanny'. Freud suggests that the double, in the ancient past, 'wore a more friendly aspect' ... but his essay completely disregards, suppresses or represses the comic dimensions of this figure. The double is *funny* in the most strongly antithetical or duplicitous sense of 'funny'. (2003: 190)

While Garner's expression of the double in *The Owl Service* is closer to Freud's dark vision, *Buffy* specializes in Poe's brand of black humour; there is undoubtedly a duplicitous level on which *Buffy*'s teenage audience is asked to laugh at the superficial preoccupations of adolescent experience, while simultaneously being expected to take them seriously. However, *The Owl Service*, *Wolf* and *Buffy* each supports Robyn McCallum's observation that, 'the double, or *doppelgänger*, is frequently used in narrative to explore the idea that personal identity is shaped in dialogic relation with an other and that subjectivity is multiple and fragmented' (1999: 75). Garner, Cross and Whedon suggest that adolescence typically denies a unified and stable sense of self, offering instead a range of subject positions manifested in uncanny confrontations with the double.

Night into day

In each of these adolescent texts, the boundaries between childhood and adulthood are figuratively played out in the passage between night and day. Consequently, *The Owl Service* opens with Alison in bed during the day, which, while suggesting illness, might also imply that night-time behaviour is bleeding into day-time. With Gwyn's help, Alison attempts to locate the mysterious scratching above her bedroom, and we learn that her nights have been disturbed ever since she arrived in Wales, 'I heard it the first night I came', said Alison, 'and every night ever since: a few minutes after I'm in bed' (1973: 8). Alison's symptoms are connected to these nocturnal disturbances and it seems inevitable that she should see owls (since they are nocturnal hunters) in the pattern on the plates. One explanation is that Alison has internalized the anxieties brought about by her new familial structure and by the onset of adolescent sexuality.

Conversely, we first meet Roger among flowers, meadowsweet specifically (11), which is one of the flowers used to make Blodeuwedd, Alison's mythical counterpart from the *Mabinogion*. Roger is the child of the sun and light (as an amateur photographer, the only darkness he encounters is the artificial darkness of the dark-room) and it is logical that it is he who should finally see flowers in Alison at the moment of salvation. Roger is sun – 'he felt the sun drag deep in his limbs' (11) – to Alison's moon. Metaphorically, Alison is also 'in the dark' when it comes to reading the plates. She does not realize that there is a choice to be made between owls and flowers, while Roger sees the possibility of interpretation. Alison asks:

'Don't you see what it is?'
  'An abstract design in green round the edge, touched up with a bit of rough gilding.'
  'Roger! You're being stupid on purpose! Look at that part. It's an owl's head.'
  '– Yes? I suppose it is, *if you want it to be*.'   (15, my emphasis)

Roger recognizes that choice is possible; that what you see depends on how you look. Alison's approach is more instinctive, and she is unable to apply the logic which allows Roger to save her. Roger has apparently come to terms with the 'relativism of points of view', something with which Appleyard (1994: 97) suggests that adolescents typically struggle.

In *Wolf* the tension between night and day is played out primarily through its pervasive dreamscape. Indeed, the book opens epigraphically with Nan's denial of Cassy's nocturnal consciousness:

Of course Cassy never dreams, Nan always said. *She has more sense, to be sure. Her head touches the pillow and she's off, just like any other sensible person. There's been no trouble with dreams, not since she was a baby.* (2)

The fundamental problem with this observation is that Nan cannot know whether Cassy dreams or not. Cross implies that Nan's intervention in Cassy's capacity to dream is related to the effective brainwashing which has led to Cassy's mistrust of her mother and her suppression of the past. It is also unclear to whom Nan is addressing this observation. Nan could be talking to herself in an attempt to reinforce her conviction that Cassy's unconscious will not lead to any dangerous or disturbing memories. Alternatively, she might be speaking to Cassy's father, reassuring him that his daughter does not pose a threat; that she will not expose him as the Cray Hill bomber. Cross's refusal to identify Nan's addressee is significant, however, for it signals the uncertain nature of Nan's relationship with Cassy from the outset, and the level of engagement Cross expects from her readers; in many ways *Wolf* is a literary puzzle to be pieced together by both Cassy and the reader.

That Cassy's father first appears shrouded in mystery is not insignificant; Cassy mistakes him for some bestial creature as 'his feet padded along the balcony', in the middle of the night: 'He came in quickly, in silence, in the dark ...' (3). This nocturnal visitor has not yet been identified as Cassy's father, but the strange-yet-familiar figure soon pervades her dreams, lending an uncanny dimension to Cassy's journey of self-discovery at the squat. Cassy's impending access to her dreaming unconscious is signalled by the word emblazoned across Lyall's van: MOONGAZER (12). This refers, on one level, to Lyall's theatre company, but also to the figurative 'Wolf' of the title, and the new perspective from which Cassy will come to interpret her experiences. As moon-gazing suggests, Cassy is to be initiated into a way of life antithetical to Nan's, but it does not come as easily to her as it does to Lyall's son: 'Robert was sure-footed in the dark, but she had to feel her way very carefully' (17).

Cassy's nightly trips into the unconscious realm of her past, a re-casting of the Oedipal conflict (Reynolds, 1994: 59), in which Cassy must confront her father's predatory sexuality, are clearly disturbing. She ignores their presence for a time, attempting to return to the pre-pubescent denial which once rendered her sleep dreamless:

> Cassy sat up, wrenching her mind out of the dream. Whatever was the matter with her? She never dreamed. Never, never. But she knew, as she sat there with her heart thumping, that she had dreamed every night in that house.
>   Her mind scrabbled for a way to make sense of it. It must be the hard floor. (52)

Still under Nan's influence, Cassy gropes for logic, aligning the rational routines of daily life with security, well-being and familiarity, while her nocturnal dreamscapes represent fear, moral uncertainty and abnormality. It is Robert (like Roger in *The Owl Service*) who finally forces Cassy to accept that there are other ways of making sense of the world:

> 'What is this thing you've got about real life?' ... '*Real* life and *real* people? That doesn't mean anything. It's just a way of making walls, to

shut out what's uncomfortable. And it doesn't work you know. If things are there you have to admit it in the end.'   (82)

The problem with Cassy's/Nan's approach to life is that it over-simplifies experience, constructing a world of good and bad; a fairy-tale world in which justice is clear-cut.[2] As Cassy discovers, real life is more complex than Nan has led her to believe. Furthermore, she must accept her dreams and confront the knowledge that they bring if she is to make sense of her past and advance into the future.

Where Cassy only gradually comes to discover the importance of integrating experience of night and day, Buffy is forced to forge a relationship between night and day from the moment she accepts her calling. The premise of *Buffy* sets up an obvious tension between day and night, as the Sunnydale slayer is destined to destroy the creatures of the night. The daylight in *Buffy* is clearly that of Southern California, providing 'a day as bright and colourful as the night [is] black and eerie' (Whedon, cited in Tonkin, 2002: 37). As Tonkin points out, the setting of *Buffy* is crucial to the show's style of evil; seething beneath a seemingly innocent surface, it draws on a cultural, social and geographical heritage which indulges in a 'taste for didactic dualism. In "So Cal" [Southern California] shines the blinding light that hides sinister secrets', but *Buffy*'s day/night dichotomy is not as straightforward as it might first appear (Tonkin, 2002: 38). The intense daylight is ultimately treacherous and as the series progresses it becomes clear that day is not simply the morally correct foil to a sinister night.

This moral ambiguity is reflected in the central plotline of Seasons One to Three, in which Buffy falls in love with Angel, the vampire with a soul. In loving Angel, it seems that Buffy gives expression to the darkness within herself, recognizing and valuing the aspect of herself which she is born to destroy. Buffy is constantly torn between love and duty and finally turns her back on Angel in response to her calling as Slayer. However, Buffy's dalliance with the dark side is resurrected later in the series, when she takes Spike, another vampire, for a lover. The relationship causes more pain than pleasure and more guilt than relief from the responsibilities of her calling; her relationship with these creatures of the night is destructive, irresistible but finally necessary. As a sinister incarnation of Buffy's dead mother asks, 'Are you worried about the sun going down? Because there are some things you can't control ... the sun always goes down, the sun always goes up' (series 7, no. 10). Whether the sun is rising or falling, Buffy is destined to respond, but the ambivalence of her response – she is never sure whether to privilege day over night or her schoolgirl self over her role as Slayer – is precisely the point at which the series echoes the fragmented subjectivity and anxieties that permeate contemporary constructions of adolescence.

Curfew and transgression

It is clear, then, that the boundary between night and day is explored on thematic and figurative levels in each of the primary texts discussed. The ways in which this boundary leads to conflict between young people and parental authority, and the nature of transgression as adolescents breach imposed/ implied curfews, is equally revealing. *The Owl Service* is concerned less with the direct confrontation of parent and child than with the ways in which the older generation tries to contain the reactions of its offspring (and so repress the age-old tragedy underlying relationships in the present). While the oppressive atmosphere is partially explained by the hot summer that finally explodes into the book's climactic storm, it is also caused by parental silence and withdrawal. Nancy refuses to explain the significance of the dinner service, while Alison's mother is physically absent. Both attempt to exert authority over their children as, for example, Alison is forbidden from conversing with Gwyn, and Gwyn is prevented from speaking to Huw (the 'half-wit' who turns out to be his father).

Much of the action centres on the young people's attempts to break this silence and uncover the secrets they seem to have inherited. If they are to progress through adolescence and come to some sort of self-knowledge (quite apart from preventing the tragedy engulfing them) then these unspoken boundaries must be breached. The mere presence of the children in the valley seems enough to expose the patterned dinner plates in the attic and the mural of Blodeuwedd long hidden behind plaster; beyond this, however, it is the disruption of order represented by the various dichotomies (night: day; owls: flowers; self: other; child: parent; Welsh: English; working class: upper class) at work in Garner's text that finally challenges parental authority and lifts the curse of 'Math of Mathonwy'.

Of particular relevance here is a pivotal scene in which Gwyn and Alison break the parental curfew and sneak out of the house at night. Both are forced to confront fears which reflect their insecurities and troubled, double (or even multiple) identities. They deal with this fear in different ways, but it none the less draws them together into a violent, pseudo-sexual confrontation which alters their relationship and marks their initiation into adult experience.

When Gwyn first sees Alison (he thinks), she is half in shadow, dappled in the moonlight (64). This liminal, still and solitary figure does not prepare readers for the discovery of the real Alison. Cooped up in the hen hut, Alison approaches madness – she has lost herself at this moment and become the owls: 'All of me's confused the same way. I keep wanting to laugh and cry.' She cannot express herself, 'I haven't the words' (67). This is adolescent trauma at its most extreme and, like the disturbing *Buffy* episode, 'Normal Again' (series 6, no. 17), in which Buffy's identity as the Slayer is reduced to a psychotic delusion, powerfully conveys the psychological stress of adolescent insecurity. Although Buffy eventually breaks through the delusions induced by a demon's venom and embraces life in Sunnydale, the episode ends with a haunting image of her in an Asylum, staring vacantly at the walls. Furthermore, during a conversation with her best friend, Willow, Buffy explains that she was committed to a mental institution when she first started seeing vampires, and fears that she never actually left the clinic as she believed. Whedon thus leaves open the possibility that Buffy's role is no more than an absurd, psychotic fantasy; that her friends, vampiric lovers and Sunnydale itself are the projected anxieties of a disturbed teenager. And of course this is the point: *Buffy* is on many levels a figurative representation and exploration of adolescent experience, and thus the dark underside of its comedy can be interpreted as a manifestation of adolescent trauma.

Like Buffy, Alison is drawn to the darker side of her personality, symbolically represented by Garner's owls, though she is also frightened of the night-space in which they hunt. She refuses to leave the hut until sunlight, and Gwyn agrees to protect her from the night until morning. Garner's description of their departure from the hen hut suggests a post-sexual euphoria: 'They stepped from the hut into rainbow dew and walked together up to the house through the midsummer dawn' (69). Though the exact nature of their experience is unclear, Gwyn and Alison have certainly spent the night together, and Garner does not want us to miss this point. Huw watches them as they leave the woods and observes that: 'She's come' (69). Of course, Huw is also referring to Blodeuwedd, reincarnated in Alison, but whatever the cause of the change, Huw recognizes that in this act of transgression, Alison has started on the path towards adulthood. Although Alison eventually seems to bend to her mother's prejudice, abandoning Gwyn, it is clear that she is ready to challenge the confines of childhood. Manifest in Gwyn is the impulse both to protect and to destroy, and these conflicting urges are unresolved at the book's closure as finally he is unable to help Alison. Perhaps Garner is suggesting that Gwyn's problems transcend adolescence; that they are in some way beyond him. Of all the characters he is the most incapacitated by family and social circumstance and does not yet have the means with which to set himself free.

In *Wolf* the transgression of authority is complicated by the apparent role reversal of parent and child. This exchange is indicated by Cross's inversion of the traditional sequence of events, in which Red Riding Hood travels to her grandmother to deliver a parcel of food on behalf of her mother. In *Wolf*, Cassy is sent by her grandmother to stay with her itinerant mother, whom Cassy believes to be closer to child than parent. As Christine Wilkie observes:

> the children are rational, and the adults behave like fantasising children, '[t]alking to Goldie was like arguing with a nagging child' (28); 'Lyall and Goldie were like children after a party' (59); and, '[t]hat was Goldie's voice, giggly and excited' (14). Nan's 'sensible' voice echoes in Cassy's head as the internalised voice of the parent and is the only regulator of stability in her newly rootless and chaotic life. (1998: 94)

Goldie and Lyall invest in a child-like impetuosity, which seems chaotic and irresponsible to Cassy. Indeed, Goldie actually invites and encourages transgression (she lives in a squat, eschewing social convention), refusing to draw the sorts of boundaries that are the pre-requisite of curfew and which Cassy associates with Nan. However, the parental 'echoes' in Cassy's head are not entirely helpful, nor do they result in a successful or complete reversal of roles. Cassy plays at being Nan in order to cover her own discomfort: 'Cassy pulled a face, thinking of food and rubbish side by side. But she knew what Nan would have done so she did it' (1992: 20), but this role is only a short-term refuge from emotional insecurity. If she is to progress, Cassy must accept that her views of Goldie and Lyall are narrow; that they are founded on her grandmother's perceptions; that her own attempts at parental control are in themselves childish, naive and ill-informed. Cassy must challenge the ideological boundaries set by Nan and find middle ground between two conflicting lifestyles, in which she can come to know herself.

Cassy's rescue of her grandmother is another version of the Red Riding Hood journey, though this time she arrives without the traditional basket of goodies. Unable to locate the semtex demanded by her terrorist father, Cassy arrives empty handed, and is finally rescued by Goldie, who brings the package herself, demonstrating her capacity for maternal responsibility. This act now allows for the true progression of events (in which mother gives to daughter gives to grandmother), since it is this symbolic passing of love from mother to daughter which will allow an emotionally secure Cassy to care for Nan; as Robert points out, 'When Granny Phelan gets out of hospital, she's sure to need you back' (139).

That Cassy's transgression of Nan's childhood boundaries is a positive experience is confirmed in the final dream sequence. Cassy dreams of herself as a child no longer bound by fear; in her dream, Nan banishes a storybook wolf, but Cassy draws him back, writing to him in her head:

> *Dear Wolf, Don't vanish into the dark forest again. I still need to know about you. Perhaps I can come and visit you, or ... or ...*

> Slowly her eyelids drooped. She knew that she wouldn't finish the letter in this dream, but she wasn't worried.

> She would write it when she woke up. (140)

This is no longer an uncanny dreamscape, in which the familiar, everyday world is rendered frightening by its relationship with night-time fears. In letting herself dream, Cassy experiences a merging of night/unconscious and day/conscious, allowing for a more balanced, deep and complete under-standing of self.

In line with *Buffy*'s direct approach to adolescent experience, the issue of curfew is confronted early on in the series as Buffy is grounded by her mother, while on her way to prevent the opening of the hellmouth. In response to Buffy's expulsion from her previous school, Joyce Summers has clearly been taking lessons in parenting and chooses this crucial moment to exercise her tentative authority:

Buffy: Mom, I promise it is not gonna be like before, but I *have* to go.
Joyce: No.
Buffy: Mom!
Joyce: The tapes all say I should get used to saying it ... No!
Buffy: This is really, really important.

Joyce: I know ... if you don't go out it will be the end of the world.
          Everything is life or death when you're a sixteen-year-old girl.
                                                              (series 1, no. 2)

In the context of everyday teenage experience this exchange is unremarkable, but Joyce's closing line is played for ironic effect, making the most of her ignorance of Buffy's role as Slayer. Buffy subsequently escapes through her bedroom window, destiny dictating her the moral victor and rendering Joyce's curfew petty by comparison. This rejection of adult authority is surely part of the show's appeal for young audiences and is developed throughout the series: (Buffy's high school Principal is eaten by a pack of student-hyenas (series 1, no. 6); Buffy's potential stepfather is revealed as a murderous robot and destroyed (series 2, no. 11); and the Mayor, actually a snake-demon, is destroyed by Buffy and her friends (series 3, no. 22). This is not to say that Buffy and her friends operate in a licentious space void of authoritative structure. Buffy may be all-powerful, but she is disorientated to the point of dysfunction when her mother dies in the fifth series, and increasingly relies on her Watcher (the Slayer's mentor and guide), as a father figure.

Ultimately, it is Buffy's relationships with Angel and Spike, the vampires she is born to destroy, that really test her emotional and moral boundaries: 250 years her senior, Angel is perceived as a threat to Buffy the schoolgirl Slayer; Buffy's mother immediately recognizes Angel as a sexual predator, while her friends all have concerns about the Slayer's relationship with a vampire. However, Buffy is irresistibly drawn to Angel and eventually sleeps with him. Inevitably, in an American teenage drama (characteristically conservative in its treatment of teenage sex), she is punished immediately for her act of passion. By making love, Buffy and Angel unwittingly invoke a gypsy curse revoking Angel's soul and causing him to revert to his monstrous state. He torments Buffy until finally she is forced to kill her enemy/lover (who later returns to life in another twist in this complex plotline). This is a selfless act that concedes to the moral dictates of adult authority, but that proves devastating in terms of Buffy's well-being.

Conclusions

In *Becoming a Reader*, Appleyard provides a thumbnail portrait of young people between the ages of thirteen and seventeen:

Hall's romantic description of adolescence and its conflicts has combined with Erikson's darker but still optimistic picture of youth struggling to achieve a mature identity amid the problematic choices offered by adult society to give us our conventional image of adolescence and its characteristic features: sudden and erratic physical growth, intensified sexuality, idealism that is often grandiose as well as naïve, self-consciousness, romanticism, moodiness and ambivalence, ambition and drive, rebellion and crisis. (96)

Appleyard is quick to point out that, however familiar and accurate this description might be of many real young people, it constitutes a constructed notion of adolescence which expresses more about 'the conflicting attitudes of adult culture about its own experience' (Spacks, cited in Appleyard: 96) than it does about actual adolescent behaviour. Indeed, it might be argued that this perception of adolescence is now so embedded in cultural/social consciousness that it is almost impossible for young people to avoid acting out such behaviours. The texts discussed here all construct adolescent characters who, while psychologically complicated and rounded, display various character-istics described by Appleyard, and their success might well lie in a portrayal of adolescence which confirms social expectations of adolescent behaviour. It seems reasonable to suggest, therefore, not simply that young readers see themselves reflected in their texts, but that they are offered options as to *how* they might be themselves in a social context.

Social life usually starts within the family, and each of the texts discussed in this chapter opens with some sort of disruption of family dynamics, which instigates the adolescent journey to adulthood; this is regularly depicted in the figurative play of night and day. Furthermore, adolescent development is frequently confined or limited by social circumstance, often seeking to escape the conditions of restrictive or frightening environments; it is this impulse to transgress which relates to the notion of curfew and the associated tension between child/criminal and adult/law. *The Owl Service*, *Wolf* and *Buffy* each conveys a convincing social backdrop of contemporary life, exploring dark and complex issues from class difference, through terrorism, to drug abuse. While social conditions often act as a catalyst for individual development, it is the psychological conditions of adolescence which are really foregrounded here. Alison, Gwyn, Roger, Cassy and Buffy all project anxieties onto those around them and their environment, thus the familiar realities of contempor-ary life are rendered uncanny, strange and finally dislocated from recognizable experience into disquieting fantastic worlds. On some level, all of the adolescent protagonists are forced to confront the limits of experience, coming into near fatal conflict with authority at a metaphoric point of curfew: conflict, these texts imply, that is unavoidable and essential to growth into adulthood in the late twentieth and early twenty-first centuries.

WORKS CITED AND FURTHER READING

Primary Texts

Cross, G., *Wolf* (London: Puffin Books, 1992; first published 1990).
Garner, A., *The Owl Service* (London: Lions, 1973; first published 1967).
Whedon, J., *Buffy the Vampire Slayer* (television series: Warner Brothers, 1997–2003).

Critical Texts

Appleyard, J., *Becoming a Reader* (Cambridge: Cambridge University Press, 1990).
Freud, S., 'The Uncanny', *The Penguin Freud Library*, vol. 14, *Art and Literature* (London: Penguin, 1990; first published 1919), pp. 335–81.

Gantz, G. (tr.), *The Mabinogion* (Harmondsworth: Penguin, 1976).

Golden, C. et al., *Buffy the Vampire Slayer: The Monster Book* (New York: Pocket Books, 2000).

Lockwood, M., ' "A Sense of the Spoken": Language in *The Owl Service*', *Children's Literature in Education*, 23(2) (1992).

Nelson, C., 'The *Unheimlich* Manoeuver: Uncanny Domesticity in the Urban Waif Tale', in K. Mallan and S. Pearce (eds), *Youth Cultures: Texts, Images, and Identities* (London and Westport, CT: Praeger, 2003).

Royle, N., *The Uncanny* (Manchester: Manchester University Press, 2003).

Stephens, J. and McCallum, R., ' "There are Worse Things than Ghosts': Reworking Horror Chronotopes in Australian Children's Fiction', in A. E. Gavin and C. Routledge (eds), *Mystery in Children's Literature: From the Rational to the Supernatural* (Basingstoke: Palgrave Macmillan, 2001), pp. 165–83.

Tonkin, B., 'Entropy as Demon: Buffy in Southern California', in R. Kaveney (ed.), *Reading the Vampire Slayer: An Unofficial Critical Companion to Buffy and Angel* (London and New York: Tauris Parke, 2002), pp. 37–52.

Wilkie, C., 'The Garden, the Wolf and the Dream of Childhood: from Philippa Pearce to Gillian Cross', in K. Reynolds (ed.), *NCRCL Papers 3 – Childhood Remembered: Proceedings from the 4th Annual IBBY/MA Children's Literature Conference at Roehampton Institute London* (London: NCRCL, 1998), pp. 91–105.

Websites

Buffy programming details: www.upn.com/shows/buffy/ (accessed 18/11/03).
Buffy resources: www.slayage.com/index.html (accessed 18/11/03).
Talking Point: http://news.bbc.co.uk/1/hi/talking_point/1143408.stm (accessed 1/10/03).

Children's Books

Cormier, R., *In the Middle of the Night* (London: HarperCollins, 2002; first published 1995).
Farmer, P., *Charlotte Sometimes* (London: Puffin, 1972; first published 1969).
Mahy, M., *The Changeover* (London: Puffin, 1995; first published 1984); *Memory* (London: CollinsFlamingo, 2002; first published 1987); *24 Hours* (London: CollinsFlamingo, 2000).
Masefield, J., *The Midnight Folk* (London: Mammoth, 2002; first published 1927).
Pearce, P., *Tom's Midnight Garden* (London: Puffin, 1976; first published 1958).
Ransome, A., *Swallows and Amazons* (London: Red Fox, 1993; first published 1930).[3]
Westall, R., *The Scarecrows* (Harmondsworth: Puffin, 1983; first published 1981).

NOTES

1. Garner describes *The Owl Service* as 'an expression of the myth found in the Welsh *Math vab Mathonwy*' and, as are all his books, an example of his 'present-day activity within myth' (Garner, 1997: 110–11).

2. Cross's postmodern approach to fairy tale represents a challenge to the typically dualistic structure of fairy tales, which convey good and bad in simplistic terms and because of this are valued by commentators such as Bettelheim in *The Uses of Enchantment* (1975).

3. *Swallows and Amazons* might seem an unlikely suggestion for further reading in the context of this chapter, but the scenes which take place at night are in many ways a transgression of parental authority and can be seen as turning points in the development of identity for the characters involved.

Fantasy, Psychoanalysis and Adolescence: Magic and Maturation in Fantasy

Peter Bramwell

Fantasy is a major genre in children's literature and lends itself to a variety of critical approaches, though given the well-established links between fantasy and the activities of the psyche, foremost among these tends to be a version of psychoanalytic criticism (cf. Chapter 5, however). While in the domain of 'adult' fiction, ideas derived from the work of Freud tend to dominate, as was argued in Chapter 1, children's literature and its criticism are often more sympathetic to the theories of Jung. In the case of literature for and about adolescence, Jung's theories, with their emphasis on the heroic struggle of the individual for autonomy, accord closely with thinking about adolescence. At least since the 1950s and the publication of Erik Erikson's Childhood and Society, *adolescence has been seen as a time of alienation from and conflict with society, during which the young person is tried and tested in the manner of the ancient heroes of epic. All this is preparation for the moment when the adolescent becomes an adult member of the society that was rejected during the teenage years.*

In this chapter, Peter Bramwell too uses ideas associated with Jungian analysis to consider how two fantasy texts model the individual's acquisition of an independent, autonomous, identity. As you read the following discussion, it is worth considering what the Australian critic Robyn McCallum says about the 'ideology trap' that characterizes much of the fiction of adolescence. This is the kind of writing that promotes acceptance of the status quo and discourages readers from questioning the way society works. Is magic – especially the 'word magic' of metafiction – used in either or both of these texts to defamiliarize and critique the social order, or does it trick readers into accepting established values and codes of behaviour? Does magic have the same function in the two texts, or do they work differently? Finally, if you are familiar with some of the famous children's texts of the past, such as Peter Pan *or* Alice in Wonderland, *how do you think the attitude to growing up in these books compares with those earlier works, which place such importance on childhood? The close readings of two texts provided here are particularly useful for encouraging readings of the many other texts that employ magic and the supernatural as metaphors for adolescence, and can also be effectively compared with Lisa Sainsbury's discussion of the uncanny in Chapter 8.*

Fantasy fiction is set in another world – or a different version of this world – in which magic and the supernatural are treated as realities, magic often providing entry into that world (see Chapter 7). The novels explored here fit this definition. Susan Price's *The Ghost Drum* (1987) is set in a fantasy Czardom; Chingis is trained as a witch and shaman, and travels between three worlds: her austere northern home; the Czar's sprawling, opulent palace; and the Ghost World, the world of the dead. In Margaret Mahy's *Alchemy* (2002), Roland Fairfield undergoes magical experiences in the contemporary world, when he follows Jess Ferret to her house in 'The Riverlaw reserve, that unreliable country, its boundaries ... shifty and unresolved' (118).

While fantasy as a genre may be defined in terms of other worlds and magic, it is the ways these are used that gives fantasy its impact. The other worlds reflect and impinge upon the evolving inner worlds of fictional characters and, by implication, real readers. Stephens's distinction between 'fantasy as a *metaphoric* mode and realism as a *metonymic* mode' (1992: 248) is useful here: whereas realism presents aspects of the real world, 'a slice of life', fantasy suggests parallels, resemblances. Magic can, then, be regarded as a metaphor for maturation, the protagonists' magical development offering a model of growth for readers.

Through examination of magic and maturation in Susan Price's *The Ghost Drum* and Margaret Mahy's *Alchemy*, this chapter seeks to explain and apply aspects of Jungian psychoanalytic criticism (Box 3.1), paying particular attention to the significance of witch, shaman and magician figures. Ursula Le Guin has argued in her essay 'The Child and the Shadow' (1974, collected in 1995), and shown in the *Earthsea* sequence, how Jungian analytical psychology is relevant to adolescent development, as presented in fantasy and experienced by its readers. Jungian interpretations of the *Earthsea* sequence and Philip Pullman's *His Dark Materials* (particularly the daemons) are well established, but Millicent Lenz (chapters 2 and 4 in Hunt and Lenz, 2001) combines these with looking at patterns of 'male' heroic quest and 'female' initiation in ways that, as the discussion below shows, can prove equally fruitful for other fantasy texts.

Magic as a metaphor for maturation intersects with other uses of magic. The adolescent 'reader as thinker', to use the model developed by Appleyard in *Becoming a Reader*, can engage with the moral questions raised by the interplay of good, evil and false magic. The world-views offered in these novels tap into the 'opening up of the possible [that] allows an adolescent to think about the future, to construct theories and ideological systems, to develop ideals, to understand others' point of view' (1994: 97). Self-conscious narration, together with distinctions between 'true' and 'false' magic, can cause the reader as thinker 'to hesitate between a natural and a supernatural explanation of the events described': such hesitation is, for Todorov, what defines fantasy as a genre (1995: 33).

The Ghost Drum

Uses of magic

Like Monica Furlong's *Wise Child* and *Juniper*, and Theresa Tomlinson's *The Forestwife Trilogy* (see Chapter 7), Susan Price's *The Ghost Drum* depicts wisdom being passed through a female line to an adopted apprentice. In *The Ghost Drum*, the old witch trains Chingis in herb-lore, and then what she calls 'the three magics': word-magic, the magic of writing, and the magic of music. Thus definitions and functions of magic are foregrounded (Box 9.1, point 4).

The way word-magic is defined expresses an outlook which has the potential to empower young adults (Box 9.1, points 6 and 1). Word-magic is potent but mundane, in the literal sense of being of this world rather than supernatural. It can be found everywhere and everyday, at home and in public places. The sense in which it is 'magical' is that it is tricksy and alters perception. Chingis and the implied reader have their political consciousness and critical language awareness raised by learning the tricks of word-magic.

An aspect of the 'word-magic' of fantasy is that ' "true" or "secret" names command phenomena by expressing essences' (Stephens, 1992: 271). In a way consistent with the definition of word magic in *The Ghost Drum*, *Ghost Song*, the second Ghost World book, bases the magical power of knowing names on their everyday force: 'Others have power over you when they know your name. They call your name, and you are made to look up. And a shaman can use your name for greater magics than that' (36).

Born an unnamed slave, as a young adult Chingis in *The Ghost Drum* spontaneously names herself: *Chingis* is her true name, her name of power. *Chingis* is a variant spelling of *Genghis* (see Magnusson, 1990: 575), indicating Chingis's potential to threaten the Czardom. The name means 'universal' (575), which suggests that Chingis emblematizes a general empowerment of the oppressed. Chingis's mentor, the old witch, is never named. As John Fowles (2000: 33) has said, 'Naming things is always implicitly categorizing and therefore collecting them, attempting to own them' – the unknowability of the old witch's true name means she can never be dominated.

Naming is also used for satire in *The Ghost Drum*, maintaining the link between language and politics. The villainous Princess Margaretta, 'who dyes her hair blue and never says what she means' (8), declares when she becomes Czaritsa, 'I am God on earth in female form' (88). She has power without

---

BOX 9.1   USES OF MAGIC IN CHILDREN'S FANTASY FICTION

1 **Maturation**   Children's fantasy uses magic as a metaphor for personal development; the fictional protagonist's maturation offers a model for the reader's own growth.

2 **Imagination**   Magic is also a metaphor for the child's imagination and capacity to tell stories. While these abilities are defined and honoured as being characteristic of childhood, they are often presented as being important to preserve and adapt into adulthood.

3 **MacGuffin**   Magic may serve as a plot device, to get into and out of scrapes! But since magic is never *essential* to driving the plot, its presence upholds a magical view of reality (see point 6, below). The ambiguities of prophecy and divination thicken the plot, but they also disrupt its linearity, so they are an aspect of:

4 **Metafiction**   Authors of fantasy may foreground definitions and functions of magic, and 'spell out' analogies between magic and narration, both of which can play tricks with words and alter perception. Fantasy lends itself to self-conscious narration, alerting the reader to the artifice of fiction and alternate ways of telling.

5 **Morality**   Good, evil and false magic are differentiated in fantasy, though in a more blurred and complex way in writing for older readers. Good magic tends to be portrayed as communal, evil as solitary and divisive. Exposing false magic – trickery – lends credibility to 'true' magic.

6 **World-view**   Magical thinking need not be outgrown, because magic can be used in fantasy as a vehicle for an outlook on the world, including politics and spirituality. Magic is defined in terms of this world-view – often magic is used to confound distinctions between natural and supernatural, and to express a sense of wonder in nature. Fantasy at least implies, and often explicitly proposes, that there are many alternate realities, and many ways of perceiving the same reality.

---

accountability, and is subject to paranoid delusions; significantly, at the time of the writing and publication of *The Ghost Drum*, Margaret Thatcher was Prime Minister of Britain.

Word-magic is also at play in *The Ghost Drum* through self-conscious narration (Box 9.1, point 4). The story is told by a cat, which teases the reader about the reliability of its telling, and about what might happen next. Magical prophecy is used in a similar way, disrupting linearity of plot, such as when the old witch proclaims that the new-born slave girl 'will be a Woman of Power, and the son of a Czar will love her' (5). The effects on the reader accord with Stonehill's observation: 'The most engaging and rewarding self-conscious fictions ... are those which manage to combine a story that we care about with reminders that it *is* a story' (1988: 16). *The Ghost Drum*'s self-conscious narration compels readers to be active and reflective in the story's construction. Readers are neither put in their place as spectators, nor do they get lost as participants in the story – that is, subjected – but are attentive and critical subjects.

As Johnston (1995: 213) points out, since the cat is referred to in the third person ('says the cat'), there is another narrator of *The Ghost Drum*. I would suggest that this overarching narrator, the teller of the story within the story, is in fact Chingis, for the old witch exhorts Chingis to 'remember, it is your duty to write down all you learn, for our sisters and brothers in the future' (62). And so Chingis 'practised her arts and slowly, sentence by sentence, wrote her own book' (63), thereby exercising the power she gains by learning the 'second magic': reading and writing. The old witch explains that there is a 'magic' to reading:

> Every day, people who know nothing more of witchcraft, open books and listen to the talk of the dead. They learn from the dead, and learn to love them, as if they were still alive. That is strong magic.   (38).

Later, when Safa Czarevich is reincarcerated, Chingis's spirit can feel how cramped he is: 'She felt, saw, sensed all this faintly, but clearly – just as we, reading a book, see the scene painted thinly and faintly between our eye and the page' (132–3). The reader is made conscious of the power of reading, while reading.

The third magic, 'the strongest and greatest magic of all', is 'the power of music' (40). Although music magic can be a useful plot device (Box 9.1, point 3) – for example, when the old witch sings and drums for a year to make baby Chingis grow to 'a young woman of twenty years' (31) – it is much more than a plot device. The power of music is given the briefest description of the three magics, as it defies and surpasses words. When the old witch chooses to die, she sings 'of every step a spirit must take on the way to the ghost-world' (63).

Music magic is an aspect of the use of magic to convey a world-view (Box 9.1, point 6). *The Ghost Drum* offers an outlook on the living world – animistic, interconnected – as well as on the afterlife. There are no spirits or gods in *The Ghost Drum*, but all people and animals have souls. Chingis can conjure and converse with animal spirits, including a bear-spirit with 'stars of ice – or stars, perhaps – rippling in its fur' (99). The hut on chicken legs is a prime example of animism, and it and the ghost drum live on in the Ghost World.

The interconnectedness of all things is expressed by Chingis thus: 'Nothing can be altered without altering everything that touches it' (97). *The Ghost Drum* celebrates ordinariness and diversity. After Chingis has freed him from imprisonment in an onion dome, '[t]o Safa, the variety and beauty of the world were shocking; and the shock never ended. . . . The real, the ordinary, outdid all imagination. . . . Difference, difference in everything' (92–3). Thus *The Ghost Drum* evokes a sense of awe and wonder through the perceptions of the characters, without recourse to supernatural explanations. Such a humanist spirituality fits well in a Jungian frame: 'To Jung, religious experience is an authentic psychic event which does not necessarily imply a transcendent reality *external* to the psyche' (Rowland, 1999: 13). Through following Chingis's training in the three magics, and through the effects of self-conscious narration, adolescent 'readers as thinkers' are equipped as critical subjects to decide whether to accommodate the ideas encountered in *The Ghost Drum* into their own views of the world.

Shamanism and maturation

Susan Price makes a precise difference between witches and shamans (see Box 9.2) in *The Ghost Drum*: the former have learned magic and can soul-journey, while shamans have gained in addition the ability to travel to the Ghost World, the world of the dead – and to return from it. In this text, shamanism and the shaman's drum function as metaphors for maturation and imagination (Box 9.1, points 1 and 2). This section, therefore, starts by considering the relationship between Chingis's personality and her drum, and then presents a more specifically Jungian analysis of Chingis's shamanism as a metaphor for her development.

The magical object in fantasy can be regarded as a transitional object in two senses of the term. On the one hand, such objects may serve as developmental props, which give comfort at the stage when the child is learning to separate from its parents, but need to be outgrown. On the other hand, such magical

---

BOX 9.2   SHADES OF SHAMANISM

A shaman is someone who is capable of entering into a trance and journeying in spirit to other realms, from which s/he returns with knowledge beneficial to the community (compare Harner, 1982, p. 25). Becoming a shaman involves an initiatory crisis of psychic death, dismemberment and reconstitution. Shamanism is not uncommon in fantasy novels for young adults, and connects with uses of magic (see Box 9.1). Like magic, shamanism is a way of accessing other realities and thus presenting an alternative view of the world. Additionally, shamanism, like the broader category of magic, may be seen as a metaphor for maturation: the shaman's initiatory crisis and perceptual breakthrough, and consequent value to the community, dramatizes the adolescent's development of both individual subjectivity and social agency.

The uses of shamanism in Price's *The Ghost Drum* (1987) considered in detail in this chapter, but there are other children's novels in which depictions of shamanism can be explored. Philip (1981, 1997) argues for the centrality of shamanism to Alan Garner's work, and to Garner's perception of himself as a writer. In Philip Pullman's *The Subtle Knife* (1997), Will's father's shamanism, as well as scientific methods and the imaginative act of storytelling itself, are all concurrent ways of accessing alternate realities. Eileen Kernaghan's *The Snow Queen* (2000), a novel-length elaboration of Andersen's fairy tale, shows how the Saami (Lapp) young woman Ritva is empowered by her shamanism. Rosalind Kerven presents Lapp shamanism as extinct in *The Reindeer and the Drum* (1980), but indicates the resilience of animistic beliefs.

objects can facilitate transitions in space and time by functioning as a type of portal to other realities; thus the magical object acts as a metaphor for imagination.

The key magical object in Price's novel is the eponymous ghost drum, the defining signifier of the shaman: at the outset, the old witch declares that it is by 'the Ghost-drum at my back [that] you know … I am a shaman' (4). Chingis's drum is a useful, though not essential, means for her to focus her skills. When she does use it for divination, she finds that 'the future was not yet set and certain' (65), so that she is not subjected to fatalism, but rather, spurred into activity. Later, when she finds that 'The drum tells me nothing' (119), it is because Chingis – and therefore the drum, and not vice versa – cannot anticipate the tricks of her evil antagonist, Kuzma. Chingis is not ruled by her drum; rather, it is a projection of personality, an expression of her will and limitations.

The drum is ultimately dispensable when Chingis's soul achieves its own agency in communion with the other women's souls. Her 'grandmother', the old witch, commands her, 'Leave the drum, leave the house. We can take nothing from here except courage' (135). Thus it is without the drum that Chingis triumphs in the shapechanging battle with Kuzma. She counters brute force with guile, by clinging to him as 'a small, spiked seed-head' and a leech (146). Once more emphasizing her agency, she is 'in her own shape' (147) when she kills him.

In *The Ghost Drum*, the shaman's drum is a device to signify the capacities of dream and imagination, and so it *is* a security device, but not materially essential. Imagination – creating images – is essential to personality development in Jungian analytical psychology. Jung's concept of the collective unconscious assumes that all humanity has an instinct for myth-making. Universal archetypes from the collective unconscious are imaged in ways modulated by culture and personal experience. Individuals achieve wholeness by integrating into their personalities the 'otherness' of their archetypal images. Susan Price's rendering of shamanism in *The Ghost Drum* offers readers a model for developing subjectivity, which is amenable to Jungian interpretation (Box 3.1).

A Jungian analysis of the fictional shamanism of *The Ghost Drum* seems very apt, for 'Jung … took a deep interest in shamanism, and his own form of therapy has been likened to shamanic transformation of healer and patient' (Atkinson, 1992: 313). Complementarily, Michele Jamal describes 'Shamanic awakening' in Jungian terms as 'a time of individuation, when the male and female principles … come together into an androgynous whole' (1987: 175). Chingis in *The Ghost Drum* achieves personality integration with the old witch, her 'grandmother'; with Safa, her animus; and with Kuzma, her shadow.

According to Jung, the 'grandmother' archetype often 'assumes the attributes of wisdom as well as those of a witch' (1980: 102). This fits Chingis's witch 'grandmother', who passes on wisdom to her apprentice. Once Chingis's training is complete, the old witch lets herself die, and so allows Chingis autonomy. Chingis then spends an indeterminate spell alone, writing and travelling. She observes the great variety of nature, and learns that 'nothing in the world is content to be alone' (64).

Chingis is paired with Safa, who could be seen as her animus, a personification of desire who also offers new ways of seeing: Safa is beautiful to Chingis (69), and from him she 'learn[s] to see anew things which even a witch comes to think of as ordinary' (94). Chingis asserts her independence by taking Safa as 'an apprentice, though she was still so young herself. And ... a male apprentice! And one who was not new-born!' (94). At the same time as affirming her independence, Chingis is entering into a relationship of loving co-dependency, through which both she and Safa attain their own subjectivity.

A hazard of psychoanalytic criticism is that it becomes, quite literally, egocentric, with all characters being seen as aspects of one. *The Ghost Drum* is resistant to such a solipsistic reading because central to Chingis's character development is her attainment of a role in the community. When she graduates as a shaman, witches from all over the world gather to celebrate (41); but Chingis must still serve, and be recognized by, the non-witch community. She does this by freeing Safa from his confinement, and then by feeding the outlaws in the forest. To achieve the latter, she uses her drum and the power of music (the third magic her 'grandmother' has taught her) to summon the spirit of an ageing bear, which agrees to give its body in an easy death to feed the starving people. Chingis neither masters spirits, nor is she possessed by them: she negotiates with them.

A sense of community, negotiation and shared creativity are characteristics of feminist writing (see Chapters 3 and 7); these female values are not just shown to the reader through Chingis's behaviour, but are also enacted in the self-consciousness of the narrative, and its cadences of oral storytelling. As Trites observes:

> Feminist metafiction often asks the reader to think about the creation of narrative as something that occurs within a community, for the subject manipulating language to create a story usually does so for audience (i.e., within a dialogue). (1997: 123)

The turning point in Chingis's maturation as an individual subject and as an agent in the community occurs, extraordinarily, after her death. The psychic experience of shamanic initiatory death, dismemberment and reconstitution is actualized for Chingis. Kuzma murders her, cuts her up, and stakes her down. She finds herself 'already on the other side of the [Ghost World] gate. It was closed and locked behind her. No words would open it. So Chingis knew that she was dead' (130). However, her spirit allies with those of three other dead women to return to earth and possess Kuzma. The significance of this is spelled out in Stewig's study of the witch motif (see Box 9.3) in contemporary children's fantasy: 'Thus the four women working together are able to overcome Kuzma's solitary evil' (1995: 123; see also Box 9.1, point 5).

Kuzma could be regarded, in a Jungian reading, as Chingis's shadow: such an interpretation is encouraged by Susan Price (personal correspondence, 2002) when she reveals, 'In the earliest versions [of *The Ghost Drum*] Chingis was both heroine and villain, but that gradually changed, and Kuzma became the villain.' Chingis achieves integration with her shadow (Box 3.1),

BOX 9.3 WITCHES

In creating witches who are powerful, independent women from humble back-grounds, Susan Price knowingly recasts the Russian folk-tale witch, Baba Yaga, who also takes babies, has a black cat, and lives in a hut that runs around on chicken legs. Chingis's 'grandmother' witch in *The Ghost Drum* may inspire dread, but she is also a wise mentor to her apprentice. Recent picturebooks maintain that Baba Yaga is fear-some but can be out-tricked: see Katya Arnold's *Baba Yaga* (1993), Geraldine McCaughrean's *Grandma Chickenlegs* (2000; illustrated by Moyra Kemp) and Hiawyn Oram's *The Wise Doll* (1997; illustrated by Ruth Brown).

It is worth comparing Susan Price's witches with those in Philip Pullman's *His Dark Materials* trilogy (1995–2000), and Joan Aiken's *The Jewel Seed* (1997). All three writers are drawing on North Eurasian beliefs – Russian, Siberian, Saami (Lapp) and Norse – but with some differences of emphasis.

Like Price's witches, Pullman's are long-lived, and they too 'live in forests and on the tundra. . . . Their business is with the wild' (*Northern Lights*, 1995, p. 165). Pull-man's witches 'own nothing' (p. 308); Price's are born in poverty and elect to stay poor. Both types of witch are capable of invisibility, prophecy and divination. Price's witch-shamans can soul-journey; equivalently, in Lyra's world, the only people whose daemons can travel away from them are shamans and witches. What current scien-tists theorise, Price's and Pullman's witches have always known and experienced: there is a multitude of alternate worlds, including the world of the dead, which is visited in both *The Ghost Drum* and *The Amber Spyglass* (2000).

Like Pullman, Price and Mahy (in *Alchemy*), Aiken makes use of scientific ideas: 'The Jewel Seed . . . is a compressed universe' (p. 10) and the witches capture Mozart, Shakespeare, Austen, Caesar, Napoleon and others in 'a fold in time' (p. 129). These touches of physics are added lightly to what is a humorous story.

by transferring her spirit to Kuzma through a kiss on the mouth. Good and evil are fused, presenting the adolescent reader with moral complexity and doubt, again a characteristic use of magic.

In *The Ghost Drum*, becoming a shaman is a way of liberating women who are poor. When the old witch first appears, she declares, 'I know all the magics, and am a Woman of Power, yet I was born a slave too' (5). As a shaman, Chingis, born in provincial poverty and powerlessness, can challenge the central political authority. The shaman's ability to predict and control her own death, as the old witch does when she has finished training Chingis, defies the total ruler's claims to godlike power over life and death. Safa's choice of death is also a political act. He thereby renounces Czardom, and becomes something greater: 'now he is a shaman and not a Czarevich, I think there are no doors closed against Safa that he cannot open' (164). He dies to be with Chingis: love triumphs over earthly power, and over death itself.

Millicent Lenz argues that protagonists in contemporary fantasy, such as Pullman's Lyra and Will, mix and exchange traditional patterns of 'male' heroic quest and 'female' initiation (see Hunt and Lenz, 2001: chapter 4).

In *The Ghost Drum*, these patterns are inverted in Chingis's heroic quest, and conversely, Safa's emergence from confinement; Chingis's rescue of Prince Safa from the tower is a clear reversal of fairy-tale gender roles. Chingis is humbly born, and effectively orphaned when the old witch takes her away, prophesying her future, to give her a name and train her in magic. However, Chingis differs from the 'male' heroic pattern in significant ways: though she overcomes an evil adversary, she also merges with him as her Jungian shadow; though she restores justice and harmony, she does not return home, but finds a new community with her kindred spirits in the Ghost World.

Whereas shamanism is presented as being empowering in *The Ghost Drum*, its successors in the Ghost World series interrogate disempowering aspects of the shamanism created in *The Ghost Drum*. In *Ghost Song* (1992), Kuzma seems to resent having no choice about becoming a shaman, about losing his childhood, and about being alone (37). Malyuta says of his child Ambrosi: 'More treasure I have here than lies in all the Czar's storehouses!' (45), and will not allow him to become Kuzma's apprentice. Haunted by Kuzma, Ambrosi makes his own ghost drum, and becomes a hypnotic storyteller and singer. Finally, Kuzma gives Ambrosi the ultimatum of becoming a shaman or being constantly tormented by spirits. Ambrosi resists becoming a shaman to the end, choosing a third way – death.

Shingebiss, in *Ghost Dance* (1994), at first chooses not to become a shaman, because a shaman cannot change the despoliation of the Northlands (23). When she fails to influence the Czar as she would wish, she changes her mind and decides to become a shaman. She enters the Ghost World independently, without apprenticeship or tuition: 'Strength and power rushed through her' (149).

While the emphasis here has been on shamanism as a metaphor for personal growth, it is also possible to see the roles of writers and readers as shamanic. Mongush Kenin-Lopsan detects a narrative syntax to shamanic performances: 'we see that the seance is a complex and well-structured event, where one can discern a prologue, exposition, plot, author's digression, culmination, denouement, and epilogue.' Moreover, Kenin-Lopsan explains, 'shamans told their listeners of their impressions and actions. It might be said that shamans created worlds through words' (in Balzer, 1997: 110). Creating 'worlds through words' is just what writers and their readers do, so that shamanism may be seen as a metaphor for the creative acts of writing and reading.

Male magic: Margaret Mahy's *Alchemy*

Margaret Mahy's *Alchemy* (2002) contrasts with Susan Price's *The Ghost Drum*, by focusing on the maturation of a male protagonist, seventeen-year-old Roland Fairfield. Where Chingis's development echoes but revises the 'male' heroic quest, Roland's magical experiences are patterned like 'female' initiation, though with some 'male' heroic elements. His visions and transformations also express a view of the nature of reality (Box 9.1, point 6). Like Chingis, his growth can be interpreted in terms of Jungian personality integration, in this case with a trickster figure, and with his anima (Box 3.1). Critical to Roland's maturation is overcoming the prohibitions and inhibitions of his father's voice, to achieve his potential in a way his father failed to do.

Roland's interest in his reclusive classmate, Jess Ferret, is forced upon him by his teacher, who wants to keep an eye on her, but Roland becomes increasingly obsessed by Jess, to the extent that he worries that his questing after her is a kind of stalking. The narrative repeats the line from *King Lear* and Robert Browning, 'Childe Roland to the dark tower came,' signalling that Mahy's Roland is cast in a male heroic role, crossing the spiritual wasteland of a shopping mall to rescue Jess from magical entrapment in her 'dark tower' of a house.

Otherwise, Roland's development conforms to the 'female' initiatory pattern of enclosure–metamorphosis–emergence. In the dream or memory with which the novel opens, he is in a circus, enclosed in a coffin, in which he is transformed – 'Roland feels he is both a grain of dust and a great flaring sun' (11) – so that he emerges changed. This dream is played out in Roland's later encounter with the magician Quando, and is also a microcosm of his development through the novel as a whole. Both Roland's darkened bedroom and Jess's house are spaces of enclosure and metamorphosis for him. In a succession of magical experiences, what has most impact on him is being inhabited by an *eidolon*, a 'ghost' projection of Jess which is nevertheless sexless and ageless. Through it:

> He could hear the universe breathing. He was sitting still ... yet, at the same time, he was in continual motion. And every single thing in the world out there, every single solitary thing, no matter how big, no matter how small, was somehow *singing* at him.   (143)

What Roland undergoes accords with the definition of alchemy he has looked up, which explains that it is concerned with transformation and seeking '*to harmonise the human individual with the universe surrounding him*' (101). This apprehension of the universe is explicated by Jess, who says that Newton, scientist and alchemist, 'probably believed that matter and spirit were interchangeable, and in a funny way that's part of what physicists believe today, isn't it?' (184). She regards the alchemical concept that 'a spirit underlay everything' as 'a metaphor, say, of what people like Stephen Hawking are getting at when they talk about unifying the forces' (185). Jess believes that 'every grain of dust is a universe' (199) and quotes Blake's 'To see the World in a grain of sand'. Mahy in *Alchemy* and Pullman in *His Dark Materials*, use old and new science, and poetry, to explore metaphysics. The gap between what C. P. Snow, scientist and novelist, referred to as 'The Two Cultures' of science and literature is closed by these writers, and others like them (see Further Reading), who present science and storytelling, and indeed magic, as different metaphors for the same underlying reality. 'Dust' is used by both Pullman and Mahy as an image of how consciousness inheres in matter.

Roland in *Alchemy* hears the universe breathing words such as '*Breaking apart ... melting together ... feeding ... falling ... flowing ... flowering ...*

folding … singing … stalking … circling … circling … circling' (170). This unity through constant flowing and changing, and the perception of a cosmos in a particle, fits in with David Bohm's (1994) theory that matter (life and non-life) and consciousness are aspects of a 'holomovement' of limitless dimensions – 'unbroken wholeness in flowing movement'. Any one region of space or time has enfolded and 'implicated' within it the unbroken wholeness of flowing movement. Bohm uses the image of a river – a particular molecule or wave of which may be drawn to attention ('relevated'), and laws formulated for it, but it is still an inextricable part of the whole river and has the whole river implicated in itself. As the molecule is to the river, so is the reality we perceive to the holomovement. With Bohm's theory in mind, how appropriate it is that Jess's house is in a place called Riverlaw!

At the same time as Roland's perception is expanding so remarkably, he grows towards personality integration in his relationships with the magician Quando and Jess, personifications respectively of the trickster figure and the anima archetype (Box 3.1). Jung connects the trickster figure with the shadow, and it is interesting that he associates the trickster with carnival (compare Mahy's *The Tricksters*, 1986), shamanism (compare *The Ghost Drum*) and alchemy (1980:255f). Quando matches closely Jung's description of 'the alchemical figure of Mercurius' – 'his fondness for sly jokes and malicious pranks, his powers as a shape-shifter, his dual nature, … his approximation to the figure of a saviour' (1980: 255). The trickster is also 'the ape of God', and can in turn be out-tricked (255).

An example of one of Quando's 'sly jokes' is when he declares, 'I promise you that everything I do is pure trickery. Watch me closely and you'll soon see through my little deceits' (109). As Roland realizes, part of the trickery is to pretend that something is trickery when it is not, but is 'something truly magical' (110). Seeing through false magic affirms the reality of true magic (Box 9.1, point 5). As Quando exhorts Roland, and the reader, in the dream at the outset of the novel, 'it is your job to work out just where the trick leaves off and the true magic begins' (9).

Quando also represents a Jungian trickster archetype by being a shape-shifter with a dual nature, mysteriously popping up in Roland's life, and, it is revealed, having another identity, an *alter ego*. The adolescent reader can engage with the moral complexity of the metaphor of magic by contemplating Quando's ambiguous role. He is a saviour figure, facilitating Roland's maturation, but he is also the ape of God, his ambition and greed built dangerously on faulty understanding, as Jess perceives:

> I don't think he's curious about the *greatness* of things out there. I think it scares him. But he does want to be the big boss of everything. In charge! So he steals the energy out of other people and feeds it into himself. (246)

And at the climax of the story, Roland outmanoeuvres the trickster, Quando.

Roland's projection of the anima archetype, the female aspect of the male psyche, evolves from the conventional desirability of his previous girlfriend, to the complexity of Jess. Born the same day as he was, she is a kind of twin or mirror: she walks backwards and mixes words around (word magic) – 'you never know what the words are suddenly going to reveal when you toss them around' (86). On her home ground, he sees her very differently, not as a lonely and unpopular schoolgirl, but 'a creature of power' (83). This is seen, for instance, in the way that her eyes act as a magic transitional object; to Roland, they seem 'like peepholes to another universe' (61) and she opens up to him a deeply thought-provoking way of apprehending the world, central to which are 'female' qualities of sympathy, intuition, fluidity and connection.

Roland and Jess share love and laughter, which empower them both. Both of these adolescents need to mature. Like Roland, Jess's emotional development has been stuck, in her case because she is living in a house frozen by an act of magic she performed in hatred, and which has divided her personality. Magic here is simultaneously a vehicle of morality and a metaphor for maturation as love triumphs over hatred and Jess's character is reintegrated: 'Jess kissed him back with desperate, confused kisses, so that it seemed as if her inner chaos were flowing out through her lips and in between his' (240).

In order to achieve his potential, Roland has to confront his fear of 'becoming something his father might not recognise' (16); he has to overcome the urgings of his inner voice, his father's voice, to *keep clear* and *be careful*. His father ran off, he denied his gift; according to Roland's mother, he was 'Afraid of life' and 'didn't know himself' (149; 152). Roland, by becoming his 'wider self', which includes embracing his feminine and visionary side, corrects his father's mistakes and establishes a connection with him. This speaks powerfully to young people whose fathers are inadequate and absent (whether physically or emotionally). Achieving magical potential is here very evidently a metaphor for achieving real potential.

Conclusion

A key function of magic in children's fantasy fiction is as a metaphor for maturation. A fruitful way of interpreting this is in terms of the Jungian process of individuation, which involves confronting and accommodating archetypal images. Such personal growth is not solipsistic, because, as we have seen in *The Ghost Drum* and *Alchemy*, relationship with others and the world is essential to maturation.

Maria Nikolajeva observes that 'Secondary worlds in fantasy are projections of . . . particular authors' models of the world. They are also products of creative imagination and as such a matter of belief' (1988: 35). Each reading experience, whether of a 'realist' or 'fantasy' text, generates a unique virtual world from the dialogue between the reader's outlook and the author's. The ideas readers encounter may confirm, challenge or change their own. Readers may perceive inconsistencies in the writer's or their own beliefs, which they might seek to resolve, or tolerate.

We perceive our world in different ways, constructing alternate realities which vary as to how, or indeed whether, they accommodate magical thinking and the realm of the spirit. Magic can be used in fantasy, as it is in *The Ghost*

Drum and *Alchemy*, as vehicle for a world-view, in which some of its operations are presented as supernatural, wondrous and beyond reason. Indeed, 'supernatural', with its implied dualism, is not a satisfactory term – the wondrous is a part of, not apart from, the world, whether it is believed to be divine in origin, or, in the words of the epigraph to Philip Pullman's *Galatea* (1978), 'Everything is what it seems.'

WORKS CITED AND FURTHER READING

Primary Texts

Mahy, M., *Alchemy* (London: HarperCollins, 2002).
Price, S., *The Ghost Drum* (London: Faber, 1987).

Critical Texts

Harner, M., *The Way of the Shaman: A Guide to Power and Healing* (New York: Bantam, 1982; first published 1980).
Hunt, P. and Lenz, M., *Alternative Worlds in Fantasy Fiction* (London and New York: Continuum, 2001).
Jamal, M., *Shape Shifters: Shaman Women in Contemporary Society* (Harmondsworth: Penguin, 1987).
Johnston, R., 'The Special Magic of the Eighties: Shaping Words and Shape-Shifting Words', in *Children's Literature in Education*, 26(4) (1995), pp. 211–17.
Nikolajeva, M., *The Magic Code: The Use of Magical Patterns in Fantasy for Children* (Stockholm: Almqvist & Wiksell International, 1988).
Stewig, J., 'The Witch Woman: a Recurring Motif in Recent Fantasy Writing for Young Readers', *Children's Literature in Education*, 26(4) (1995), pp. 119–33.
Todorov, T., *The Fantastic: A Structural Approach to a Literary Genre*, trans. Richard Howard (New York: Cornell University Press, 1995; first published 1975).

Children's Books

Aiken, J., *The Jewel Seed* (London: Hodder, 1998; first published 1997).
Arnold, K., *Baba Yaga: A Russian Folktale* (New York: North-South, 1993).
Geras, A., *The Fabulous Fantora Files* (Oxford: Oxford University Press, 2003; first published 1988 as *The Fantora Family Files*); *The Fabulous Fantora Photographs* (Oxford: Oxford University Press, 2003; first published 1993 as *The Fantora Family Photographs*).
Gordon, J., *The Waterfall Box* (Harmondsworth: Penguin, 1978); *The Midwinter Watch* (London: Walker, 1998).
Kernaghan, E., *The Snow Queen* (Saskatoon, Saskatchewan: Thistledown, 2000).
Kerven, R., *The Reindeer and the Drum* (London: Blackie, 1980).
Le Guin, U., *The Earthsea Quartet* (Harmondsworth: Penguin, 1993; first published separately, from 1968 onwards). The Earthsea sequence continues in *The Other Wind* and *Tales from Earthsea* (both London: Orion, 2002).
McCaughrean, G., *Grandma Chickenlegs*, illustrated by Moyra Kemp (London: Doubleday, 2000).

Mahy, M., *The Tricksters* (Harmondsworth: Penguin, 1988; first published 1986).

Oram, H., *The Wise Doll*, illustrated by Ruth Brown (London: Andersen, 1997).

Price, S., *Ghost Song* (London: Faber, 1992); *Ghost Dance: The Czar's Black Angel* (London: Faber, 1994).

Pullman, P., *Galatea* (London: Gollancz, 1978); *Northern Lights* (London: Scholastic, 1998; first published 1995); *The Subtle Knife* (London: Scholastic, 1998; first published 1997); *The Amber Spyglass* (London: Scholastic, 2001; first published 2000).

Chronotopes and Heritage: Time and Memory in Contemporary Children's Literature

10

Lisa Sainsbury

KEY TEXTS

M. Anno *et al.*, *All in a Day* (1986)
A. Provoost, *Falling* (1997; first published in Dutch, 1995)
H. Scott, *Why Weeps the Brogan?* (1989)
M. Sedgwick, *The Dark Horse* (2002)

Books dealing with time, whether as a subject in its own right or as part of thematic or metaphoric explorations, comprise an important body of writing for the young, despite the fact that understanding time poses numerous problems for children – especially for younger readers. In this chapter, Lisa Sainsbury looks at how a range of texts, from picturebooks through adolescent fiction, encourage readers to engage with the conceptual and intellectual challenges involved in thinking about time; how they develop awareness of different aspects of time, and how they manage to speak about history in ways meaningful to an audience that has limited knowledge and experience of the past at any level. In doing so she draws on Bakhtin's concept of the chronotope (also discussed in Chapter 1) and current theories about the relationship between the past, memory, the heritage industry, and museums, to provide new ways of reading modern classics as well as showing how contemporary writers are reflecting current thinking about time in the content, style and structure of writing for children.

> I do not have a body
> yet I grow constantly.

Everyone wants to visit
yet no one wants to live with me.

Nobody can find me
yet in the end,

Like the stuff between the stars,
I shall be everywhere.
Riddle: Bill Herbert (no. 44, 'The Past', in
Crossley-Holland, Sail and Drew, 2000)

Introducing time and memory to young readers

Time is a difficult idea for children to understand for several reasons. As an abstract concept it is hard for the youngest of children to comprehend. Furthermore, children's relationship with time is complicated by their restricted experience of it – particularly of time past. Childhood often represents hope for the future, but young children have only limited understanding of tomorrow and yesterday for, until they are able to make cognitive sense of these concepts, they tend to live in the present. Additionally, there is a mismatch between children's knowledge of time and the language available to them to express that knowledge.

While time itself can be conceived of as a natural, scientific phenomenon with which humans must interact, the acquisition of time *sense* is actually part of the socialization process, working alongside such things as the learning of language skills or moral values. Past, present and future are cultural concepts that change in accordance with social development. As Stephen Kern observes in *The Culture of Time and Space, 1880–1918*:

> From around 1880 to the outbreak of World War I a series of sweeping changes in technology and culture created distinctive new modes of thinking about and experiencing time and space. Technological innovations including the telephone, wireless telegraph, x-ray, cinema, bicycle, automobile, and airplane established the material foundation for this reorientation; independent cultural developments such as the stream-of-consciousness novel, psychoanalysis, Cubism and the theory of relativity shaped consciousness directly. The result was a transformation of the dimensions of life and thought. (1983: 1–2)

While children (and probably most adults) will be unaware of the impact of such developments on concepts of space and time, Kern's argument that our perception of them is culturally constructed is compelling. In 'Narrative Time' (1981), Paul Ricoeur also asserts that perceptions of time are structured; that we make sense of our state 'within time' through language or narrative. His approach to time borrows from the ideas of the German philosopher Heidegger (1889–1976), who proposes that humans are naturally placed 'within time' and that signs (words) such as 'now', 'then', 'when', 'past', 'tomorrow' allow us to come to terms with and understand our state within time. Unsurprisingly then, developmental progress is intimately tied with mastery of time, as Appleyard observes:

> We know that children organize their world spatially before they can do it temporally, and that the acquisition of a time sense during the concrete–operational period requires that they de-center from their dependence on a spatially concrete understanding of the world. (1994: 72)

Time in picturebooks

There are many ways in which young children may be introduced to the notion of time, but perhaps the most basic lessons are concerned with teaching children to read clocks and to distinguish between different times of day, as can be seen in *All in a Day* (1986), by Mitsumasa Anno with a group of international artists, which introduces children to the twenty-four-hour day and its division into worldwide time zones. *All in a Day* might be described as a 'concept book' (see Chapter 13), since it is designed to teach children that 'their activities are related to the very different conditions of time and climate that exist in various parts of the earth', as Anno reveals in an explanatory note. Anno also states that 'Peace is the theme of this book', but this implicit message is an authorial intention that will not necessarily be uncovered by young readers; the overt representation of time and cultural context is more difficult for readers to overlook. Conceptually, this might seem a simple book, but in fact, the temporal dynamics at work are rather sophisticated.

Each double-spread in *All in a Day* depicts eight tableaux of children from around the world, distinguished by place, date and time (see Figure 8). New Year, according to Greenwich meantime, is the starting point for chronological organization on the first page, so, in the USA, Tom awaits New Year, since the USA (Chicago specifically) is six hours behind Greenwich, England, where James is fast asleep at midnight, as is the Kenyan Jomo at 3.00 am. Individual tableaux are illustrated by artists from the relevant country (with the exception of the illustrations of Kenya, done by a pair of American illustrators), so that the British artist Raymond Briggs is responsible for the Greenwich scenes, Nicolai Ye. Popov for the Muscovite images, and so on. Each tableau is stylistically distinctive, adding to the exploration of cultural diversity central to this project.

This stylistic variation also calls to mind Bakhtin's notion of chronotope (Box 1.2). The words labelling a single tableau, situate it in time and place, but the illustrations are purely spatial, conveying action within a clearly defined space. As Perry Nodelman suggests in *Words about Pictures*, 'stories, which are about movements and changes, necessarily take place in time, whereas most pictures depict only how things look at one moment separated from the flow of time' (1988: 158). The particular combination of time (verbal) and space (visual) in Anno's picturebook thus accentuates *the unity* of time and

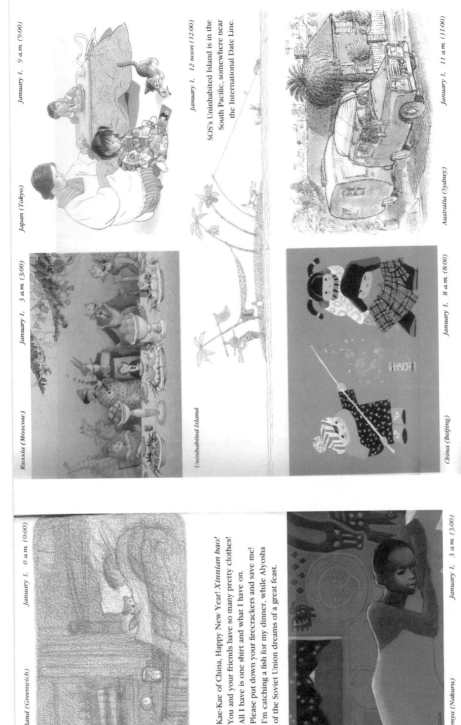

England (Greenwich)   January 1,   0 a.m. (0:00)

Russia (Moscow)   January 1,   3 a.m. (3:00)

Japan (Tokyo)   January 1,   9 a.m. (9:00)

January 1,   12 noon (12:00)

SOS's Uninhabited Island is in the South Pacific, somewhere near the International Date Line.

Uninhabited Island

China (Beijing)   January 1,   8 a.m. (8:00)

Australia (Sydney)   January 1,   11 a.m. (11:00)

Kenya (Nakuru)   January 1,   3 a.m. (3:00)

Kae-Kae of China, Happy New Year! *Xinnian hao!*
You and your friends have so many pretty clothes!
All I have is one shirt and what I have on.
Please put down your firecrackers and save me!
I'm catching a fish for my dinner, while Alyosha
of the Soviet Union dreams of a great feast.

Figure 8   Parallel times shown in *All in a Day* by Mitsumasa Anno

space suggested by Bakhtin's concept. Additionally, an understanding of chronotope allows us to appreciate the idea that although these tableaux all represent the same moment in time, the unique relationship between time and space in each one signifies a different chronotope. In this way, readers encounter different chronotopes, though all are linked because they are concerned with the same moment. Anno's text effectively works with a range of chronotopes that are in dialogue with each other, confirming that the term 'chronotope' refers to more than a suggestion of historical period. Chronotopes can indicate cultural difference, as in *All in a Day*, and, as Maria Nikolajeva suggests, 'specific forms of chronotope are unique for particular genres', though these may be reinterpreted over time (Holquist, 1990; Nikolajeva, 1996: 121) and so the chronotope becomes a way of recognizing and exploring ideology and narrative structure. Nikolajeva underplays the unstable nature of the chronotope as a concept and critical tool, though she is right to emphasize the useful ways in which it allows readers to distinguish narrative experience in terms of time and space.

Like the concept of chronotope, the notion of dialogism can also be attributed to Bakhtin. As Pam Morris explains, for Bakhtin, 'There is no existence, no meaning, no word or thought that does not enter into dialogue or "dialogic" relations with the other, that does not exhibit intertextuality in both time and space' (1994: 247). Following this line of thought, the contrasting chronotopes in *All in a Day* could be described as dialogic 'voices', all competing for attention. How, then, does Anno ensure that young readers will not be lost in the midst of these disparate voices?

Anno draws together the separate tableaux on each page through his representation of an 'Uninhabited Island', which is 'in the South Pacific, somewhere near the International Date Line'. Uninhabited Island is a peritextual addition to the central images, situated on the recto (Box 13.1). Its lack of frame and muted colours allow it to float behind the tableaux, and thus it occupies a unique space on the page. It is also the location of Anno's first-person narrator, a shipwrecked child, Sailor Oliver Smith (dubbed SOS), who directly addresses the children depicted in the surrounding tableaux.

SOS's narration constitutes a unifying voice, suggesting that while experience differs in space and time, common humanity might be grounds for experience shared and for the ideological notion of Peace expressed in Anno's closing note. This fantasy element of the text also serves to emphasize the realistic experiences depicted in the tableaux, and thus SOS's imaginary narrative conveys a message of real relevance to young readers.

Having mastered some of the basic tools (yesterday, now, tomorrow) of time management, children can begin to move through time conceptually and to organize experience chronologically, and it is here that the articulation of remembered experience comes into play. In *Past, Space and Self*, John Campbell suggests that self-consciousness entails the ability to construct stories around 'one's past life' (1995: 1). Obviously, this is problematic for young children, who, quite apart from cognitive restrictions, have only a limited 'past life' compared with adults. Accordingly, Campbell suggests that:

one of the most basic kinds of social interaction, from a developmental point of view, is the sharing of memories between parent and child. This kind of social bonding seems to be part of what explains the evolutionary benefit, the selection value, of autobiographical memory.   (1)

Of particular interest here is Campbell's allusion to shared memory; the social bonding which is implicitly necessary to subjective development. Although outside the scope of Campbell's argument, the degree to which this bonding can be perceived as a reciprocal sharing of memory must be questioned. Given children's limited access to a past life or sustained temporal perspective, it is likely that the adult becomes the dominant contributor in the construction of autobiographical memory; children are more likely to share in adults' perception of past life than vice versa. This is not to say that children have no memories, rather that their ability to express remembered experience chronologically is limited, as is their access to historical, public knowledge. There are numerous picturebooks – such as Michael Foreman's three linked works *Jack's Fantastic Voyage* (1992), *Grandfather's Pencil and the Room of Stories* (1993) and *Jack's Big Race* (1998) – that explore the way in which memory, both personal and public, locates children in time and that demonstrate the significance of the past in our conception of the present.

A brief history of time in children's literature

Of course, all narrative is shaped through time and, as Paul Ricoeur observes, 'narrativity and temporality are closely related' (1981: 165). In the realms of children's literature, movements backwards and forwards in time have become increasingly popular since the early twentieth century, when a number of scientific theories, such as Einstein's 'Special Theory of Relativity' (1905) and J. W. Dunne's *An Experiment with Time* (1927), central to the explanations of time given by Uncle Alan in Philippa Pearce's *Tom's Midnight Garden* (1958) (Pearce, 1990: 70–4), attracted public attention. H. G. Wells's post-Darwinian fantasy *The Time Machine* (1895) is one of the earliest examples of the time-travel genre, while E. Nesbit, in *The Story of the Amulet* (1906), and Rudyard Kipling, in *Puck of Pook's Hill* (1906), were among the earliest children's writers to manipulate time for the purposes of historicized adventure. Moving on through the twentieth century, time travel has been used increasingly by writers to emphasize the changes wrought by adolescence; the rupture in time frequently mirrors pre-pubertal or adolescent anxiety, as exemplified in *Tom's Midnight Garden*, *A Wrinkle in Time* (1962) by Madeleine L'Engle, *Charlotte Sometimes* (1969) by Penelope Farmer, and *Playing Beatie Bow* (1980), by Ruth Park. For a number of children's writers, such as Alan Garner in *Elidor* (1965) and William Mayne in *Earthfasts* (1966), human relationships resonate deeply and darkly with the past, as characters in the present struggle to understand themselves and the world around them. Playing with time also preoccupies inventive, postmodern writers such as Diana Wynne Jones in *The Homeward Bounders* (1981) or *The Tale of Time City* (1987), Peter Pohl in

Johnny, My Friend (1985), Aidan Chambers in *Dance on My Grave* (1982), and Pauline Fisk in *Midnight Blue* (1990), who encourage readers to think about the relationships between time, fiction and lived experience (also see the suggestions for Further Reading at the end of this chapter).

The popularity of historical fiction is enduring, but Valerie Krips points to a shift in representations of the past from the literature of 'heritage' which 'is determined to show the past "as it really was" (1999: 178) – exemplified by such writers as Rosemary Sutcliff or Geoffrey Trease – to books that challenge this authoritative and finite notion of the past. These texts stress the mutable and idiosyncratic nature of time, particularly as it is shaped through memory, and explore the relationship between self-knowledge and the passage of time. The remainder of this chapter looks at three such books for young people which share an interest in the nature and expression of memory, but that explore memory from contrasting perspectives in time and for different purposes. Set in a 'distant past' that might roughly be estimated as the time of the Viking invasion and colonization of Europe in AD circa 700, *The Dark Horse* (2002), by Marcus Sedgwick, makes interesting use of narrative chronology, emphasizing the way in which memory is manipulated in the telling of stories. Conversely, Anne Provoost's powerful and disturbing novel *Falling* (1995) is set in contemporary France. It explores the resonance of private and public memories as they shape perceptions of past, present and future. Finally, Hugh Scott's *Why Weeps the Brogan?* (1989) is a dystopian fable set, ambiguously (4 years 81 days from hostilities – see p. 18), some time in the future and which challenges the relevance of authorized versions of history to children's experience of the present. Through their past, present and future settings, each of these novels examines the significance of memory in terms of both narrative structure and lived experience, thus expanding readers' comprehension of time and memory.

Memories of the past

Though Sedgwick does not identify a specific historical period for his setting of *The Dark Horse*, his numerous references to Norse mythology and his selection of Scandinavian names for place and character indicate that his novel is located at a time of Viking invasions. However, it is not the historicity of the text that is of primary interest here; while this has an impact on the lexical tone of the narrative and Sedgwick's choice of imagery, the dual voice of Sedgwick's narrative is more significant. The first chapter opens in a straightforward manner, making use of a third-person narrator:

> It was Mouse who found the box. She was trotting along the tide-line. ...
> Looking for sea cabbage washed up in the black sand after last night's
> storm, because the fishing had been bad again. They were half a day from
> home. (3)

Although written in the past tense, the text relates to events that seem to be unfolding in the present. The reader apparently witnesses proceedings as they happen, rather than from the distance suggested by the use of past tense and the historical setting. The narrative perspective – the children, Mouse and Sigurd, are observed by a detached narrator – also adds to the sense of watching these characters in the present: readers observe the children alongside the narrator. The chapter closes with the children's removal of the mysterious box and the narrator's observation that: 'neither of them noticed the man lying still amongst the rocks ...' (4). This confirms that the narrator is omniscient and so able to access information unavailable to the characters. This narrative structure is typical of many books; it is the transformation of narrative structure in the second chapter that makes Sedgwick's text unusual.

Having established itself as a seemingly conventional narrative, the second chapter then disrupts the reader's perspective:

> I remember better than anyone. I remember better than anyone the day we found Mouse. ... I was the only child there, and I *was* a child then. It was my eleventh or twelfth summer; I can't remember. I was a part of the games Horn and Father played. (5–6)

Any reader expecting a continuation of the third-person narration is likely to be disorientated by this passage. At first it is unclear who is speaking, until eventually the narrator identifies himself to be Sigurd. That this is a different narrator from that in the first section is confirmed, for Sigurd himself is observed in the first chapter. The perspective from which Sigurd narrates is also uncertain. His opening words, 'I remember' ...', suggest that his narration is an evocation of memory; that he is relating events from his past. Even at the end of the book, it is unclear from exactly which point in time Sigurd is looking back, but it is evidently some years after the events related in the book's central narrative. Unusually then, this is a narrative structure which proceeds from two distinctive chronotopes; it is told *from* (it is not *about*) two different moments in space and time. Although the space (a tribal village by the sea) of Sigurd's experiences with Mouse in the past is geographically the same as the space from which he remembers, it is clearly reshaped through the passage of time and is perceived differently by characters and readers alike. The unity of space and time is particular to each narrative, and thus they can be identified as distinct chronotopes in dialogue with each other.

The Dark Horse is essentially Mouse's story. It is the tale of a strangely gifted child, discovered by the Storn (a Norse tribe of fishermen) in a cave inhabited by some wolves. Mouse is adopted into Sigurd's family, and it soon becomes clear that she has an affinity with nature, animals in particular. She and Sigurd discover a strange box on the beach, causing disharmony within the tribe when it cannot be opened. It transpires that Ragnald, the stranger on the beach, was bringing the box to Mouse, though it is not until the Storn have nearly been destroyed by the powerful 'Dark Horse' tribe that the box's true significance is revealed. As the tale reaches its climax, Mouse betrays the remaining members of the Storn tribe, including Sigurd, leading them directly to the Dark Horse. Finally, Sigurd discovers that Mouse is actually a lost princess of the Dark Horse, and Ragnald has been sent to her with a box of her memories. Significantly, then, this is a story *about* memory, relayed through memory.

The Dark Horse recounts a period in the Storn's history relating to the appearance and eventual departure of a young girl called Mouse. It is told through a dual narrative which switches after each chapter; the pattern of third person, first person, is maintained throughout the book, and finally gives Sigurd the last word. The third-person narrative is conveyed chronologically, in a linear direction by a distanced narrator. Sigurd's narrative is retrospective and starts (it transpires) four years prior to Mouse and Sigurd's discovery of the box on the beach. Sigurd's narrative eventually seems to dovetail with the omniscient narration (thus Sedgwick avoids alienating his readership with an overly disruptive narrative structure), moving into the same period and adopting a chronological ordering of events.

Sigurd's retrospective account, however, is a useful tool for introducing suspense, as Sedgwick peppers Sigurd's narrative with ominous observations: 'It was all for nothing' (136); 'As it fell, I was right to worry' (148). The reader is thus encouraged to anticipate and look forward; to move toward the point from which Sigurd tells his tale. As Ricoeur observes, even the simplest stories escape ordinary notions of linear time, for each new story event involves new contingencies and possibilities to be reckoned with by the reader. Plot cannot evolve in a temporally linear fashion, because the reader is constantly engaged in the process of modification and expectation (Ricoeur, 1981: 170). Sedgwick seems purposely to intervene in this process, and uses it to move his reader backwards and forwards in time; to engage in a complex relationship with his central narrative and its status as memory.

At times, Sigurd too withdraws from the past moment of his narrative and reflects from his place in the future: 'I remember, how could I forget? I will remember the words he said next until the day I die' (88). He thus draws attention to the constructed nature of his narrative and to its status as a past event. That he is engaged in the act of reconstructing the past attests to the intrinsic value of that period in time. This is evidently an episode in Storn history that is worth relating; one that has consequence for future generations.

The Dark Horse addresses time at the deepest level, as it is played out through structure and theme, but it is not until the closing pages that the thematic significance of memory becomes obvious. Mouse and Sigurd are torn apart by the enmity of their respective tribes, but on parting they heal their sibling bond and Mouse asks Sigurd to: 'Keep my memories, for me ... when you find them' (184). When the narrative reaches the moment from which Sigurd has told his story, he reflects on the aftermath of the Storn's decisive battle with the Dark Horse and Mouse's place in it:

And Mouse? ... though I hadn't understood her last words to me at the time, it wasn't long before the meaning was revealed. As we struggled through that first winter, we ate our way through the pile of grain where Ragnald had died. And one day, as the mound grew yet smaller, the box of memories appeared from where it had been hidden, I guessed by Mouse. So I keep her memories for her, the memories of who she truly was, though who she truly was is something I do not like to think of. And the years have come and gone, and I think of my own life, and I realise that many of my own memories are memories of blood. (187)

Sigurd's observation that his memories are 'of blood' suggests multiple meanings. Certainly his memories have included those of bloodshed, but they are also the fabric of life (blood), and are central to familial heritage (blood). Mouse was stripped of identity when she lost her memories in the wolves' cave, an idea which the box comes to represent. Literally, the box once held her memories, but it also works as a metaphor for Sigurd's engagement with the memory of her story; the box becomes a route back to the past for him, but it is his act of remembering that enables her tale to be told. On this level, the dual structure of the tale itself also becomes a figure for the working of memory as it fluctuates between past and present, manipulating time as it tells us stories which allow us to make sense of ourselves.

Memories in the present

It is to the aftermath of World War II and its implications for contemporary children that Belgian writer Anne Provoost turns in her challenging novel *Falling* (1995). Since I am discussing the English translation (by John Nieuwenhuizen, 1997), I will not attempt to consider the intricate details of narrative structure and language, which might have altered in the process of translation. Rather, Provoost's broader treatment of the past and memory forms the basis of discussion.

Falling is set in contemporary France, in the imaginary town of Montourin, and focuses on the experiences of Lucas Beigne during the summer after his grandfather's death. During the course of the novel, Lucas gradually becomes aware that a secret from his grandfather's past has long been kept from him and it is his uncovering of this secret that initiates his 'fall' from childhood innocence. Early in the novel, as he attempts to come to terms with the summer's tragic sequence of events, Lucas reflects:

Going back over it all, I can see that this was the moment everything started to go wrong – but of course that's easy to say with hindsight. At times, I lie on the bed with my face in the pillow. I scratch my head and want to reverse time, but it's impossible. I can no longer wake up innocent, as I was that morning. Only in my dreams can I believe that it was all a bad dream. (28)

As this extract indicates, *Falling* is in many ways an exercise in 'going back', of filtering the present, or at least recent events, through memory in the hope that a new perspective might change the outcome; change the present. As Lucas realizes, this is impossible – what is possible is a new understanding of those events as they are absorbed and altered 'with hindsight'.

A brief summary is necessary before discussing the text. Lucas and his mother spend the summer in his deceased grandfather's house in the hills of

Montourin. Lucas soon befriends Caitlin, an enigmatic young dancer, who is staying with her mother as the guest of Soeur Béate at the old convent next door. A series of burglaries, blamed on immigrant Arabs working in the town, leads Lucas to Benoît, a charismatic extremist who involves Lucas in his racist schemes by repeated inferences about Lucas's grandfather's mysterious reputation. Meanwhile, obscure references are made to the fate of Jewish children once kept at the convent and it eventually transpires that Felix Stockx (Lucas's grandfather) betrayed them to the Nazis after the death of his own daughter through possible malnutrition. Caitlin's mother, it is also revealed, was one of the children who survived, while several of her friends died at Auschwitz. As his relationships with Caitlin and Benoît progress, Lucas becomes embroiled in a circle of divided loyalties and a cycle of guilt and blame. When Caitlin becomes trapped in a burning car he is forced to make a terrible choice which implicates him as the inheritor of his grandfather's actions. In order to free her, he decides to cut off her foot and *Falling* charts his attempts to come to terms with this decision through reference to the past, both recent and distant.

As Lucas's retrospective narrative suggests, the chronology of *Falling* is not straightforward. It opens at the chronological end of the story, as Lucas waits for Caitlin to return home from hospital, where it seems that she has had her foot amputated. The reader can have no understanding of the implications of Caitlin's injury at this point in the novel and thus is immediately engaged in a process of anticipation and retrospective revisioning, mirroring Lucas's position in the text. In order to understand Lucas's connection to Caitlin, the reader must, like Lucas, return to 'the very beginning of it all … back in time … to last winter' (22). What soon becomes clear, however, is that Lucas's attempts to locate 'the beginning' of his story are futile, since events in the present are shaped by events from his grandfather's past and beyond.

It is obvious, however, that Felix Stockx's death is the catalyst for an opening up of the past, giving Lucas a way in to the unknown events which influence people's perception of him. As Lucas tells Caitlin, 'I'm discovering all sorts of things … now that my grandfather is dead, everybody is beginning to talk' (136). It is as if his grandfather's death has catapulted Lucas into William Blake's world of experience (Blake's *Songs of Innocence and Experience*, 1794, depict a cruel adult world distanced from God's love, as opposed to the world of innocence enabled by the child's proximity to God), whereas he previously enjoyed the innocence made possible by his mother's, indeed the whole town's, silence. However, it was an uneasy and unnatural innocence, embalmed, as Lucas suggests, in a desire to suppress and thus not deal with the past: 'My feet are tangled up in something, but I don't know what. This town feels as if it's preserved in formaldehyde' (96).

It is almost as if Lucas himself becomes a *lieu de mémoire* (site of memory) as he becomes the focus for the blame or sympathy of the townsfolk. Krips adopts the notion of *lieux de mémoire* from Pierre Nora, explaining that,

> the sites of memory of which Nora writes, come into being because memory fails. They are the sites at which what remains of collective

memory is constellated, where, in other words there is an intention to remember.   (2000: 17)

This concept usually refers to objects or memorials; artefacts that focus attention on a past moment. In Provoost's hands, however, Lucas becomes the object of admiration or disdain as people respond to a specific, and terrible, moment in their history. Their own culpability is thus distanced from them, and Lucas is left to struggle with this unasked for inheritance. This is not to say that Lucas is any longer innocent himself; his actions in the present may have a bearing on the past, but Provoost makes it clear that finally he must take responsibility and choose. As he struggles to free Caitlin from the car, Lucas recognizes that 'There was nobody to ask for advice ... I felt infinitely alone and knew that, no matter what I did, that feeling would be with me for ever' (235).

As Provoost herself has observed of *Falling*, however, 'more important than the question of who is guilty is the problem of inherited versus personal guilt, and the awareness that different kinds of guilt are there, also in other lives and in other situations' (Provoost, 2003). In *Falling*, the nature of guilt, both public and private, is intimately tied to the act of remembering and thus to the nature of human relationships formed in the present. The only way to deal with such terrible and complex memories is to translate them into the present and move forward; the nostalgia figured in so many representations of the British war experience is simply not an option when confronted with an almost unmanageable burden of public and private guilt (see also Chapter 5).

Caitlin, it seems, is wrong when she states that the events at the convent are unrelated to Lucas and herself in the present: 'it doesn't really upset me, all that. I mean it's a long time ago. It has nothing to do with us and our time' (137). Caitlin initially refuses to take part in the process of blame and justification engaged in by Soeur Béate and Felix Stockx, welcoming Lucas as a friend. By the end of the book, however, she is unable to separate the Lucas before her from the boy who destroyed her future career as a dancer: 'When I think of my foot I think of you ... I want to do everything I can to remember you as my rescuer, not the person who mutilated me. That's not easy' (284). Caitlin comes to realize that the past does have an impact on the present and that children must come to terms with the past as handed down by adult authorities. Provoost suggests that children can certainly take possession of that past and move forward, but that the past defines them just as much as the present. In order to move into the future, this truth must be accepted. Perhaps less comforting for Provoost's readers is that, finally, moving forward is not always possible, a message implied by Caitlin's loss of her leg and career.

Memories for the future

The museum setting of Hugh Scott's dystopian novella *Why Weeps the Brogan?* is crucial to understanding the ways in which Scott's post-Holocaust story interrogates the status of 'the Museum' (as a cultural concept) and its relationship with the past. Indeed, *Why Weeps the Brogan?* could be described as an articulation of 'Museum Theory', which recognizes the ways in which adult representations of and attitudes to the past affect future generations. In his provocative work of museology, *The Representation of the Past*, Kevin Walsh attacks the stasis of museum displays and the heritagization of history as effected by battle re-enactments or 'the cult of the country house'. He argues that the 'powerful gaze' elicited by historical attractions does not in fact empower the individual observer. Rather, it empowers the authority behind the display, the expert voice which labels the past so neatly. The museum visitor *seems* to respond to a past inherent within auratic objects – referring to the auras Walter Benjamin ascribed to powerful works of art (see below, and Benjamin, 1969) – but *actually* responds to an ideologically bound, contrived representation. The process is mirrored in historical fiction, which seems to relate readers to a moment of 'real' past which too is only a narrative construction.

Children are particularly vulnerable to displays which appear to supply reliable knowledge about times completely out of their reach, for, as Walsh points out in a discussion of open-air historic sites:

> The most dangerous consequence of this type of museum is its effect on those who can not remember. For them, their nostalgia is often second-hand. Their parents or grandparents can pass on their own nostalgia, and before long, a generation will exist whose heritage lies with the heritage industry.   (1992: 99)

Walsh does not suggest that museums must necessarily be detrimental to the child's construction of the past; rather he regrets the distancing of the past from daily life, resulting in a denial of ongoing historical process. He argues for a contextualization of history in which the museum visitor plays an active role, and provides the framework for a 'new museology', which 'must concern itself with involving the public, not just during the visit to the museum through interactive displays, but also in the production of the past' (1992: 161). This museology activates localized environments in which history is recognized as an ongoing process created by individuals in the present.

That children's literature also has a role to play in this is confirmed by writers such as Provoost, but *Why Weeps the Brogan?* specifically takes on the role of the museum in children's response to past and future. *Why Weeps the Brogan?* is almost generically postmodern (Boxes 6.3; 11.1), and refuses complete explanations or resolution. Scott's narrative is revealed in an uncannily fragmented fashion, which simulates the ruined and collapsing museum in which it is set.

Scott tells the story of Saxon and Gilbert, siblings mysteriously incarcerated in a vast museum; apparently they are the lone survivors of war, destined to an indoor life of perpetual fear. The children's solitary existence is broken only by the sparrows living in the museum's dome, deadly spiders which the children are forced to destroy and, most significant, the Brogan. The Brogan lives in the museum's shadows and is fed by the children with a ritualized regularity; they do so out of an ambivalent mixture of fear and pity, which stirs the memories lingering at the back of Saxon's mind. Snapshots of the children's past existence are provided by tentative allusions to a possible outside world, but Scott refuses a complete picture of the events leading to their incarceration, even after the powerful revelation at the end of the book.

The implied reader of this book is placed in a strange relationship with the protagonists, at once distanced from and involved in narrative developments. Significantly, though, this paradoxical perspective is sustained through received conceptions of museum culture. The reader is alerted to the fact that the children are inside a museum through such ubiquitous signs, appearing in upper case throughout the text, as: ARMS AND ARMOUR, MINEROLOGY, COFFEE SHOP, PRIVATE and JANITOR. The implied reader is expected to recognize these signs and, accordingly, to discern that some refer to exhibits and others to more functional locations within a building, probably located in a town or city, known as a museum. It is precisely this kind of external knowledge that distances the reader from Saxon and Gilbert. The children's regimented existence is founded on their conviction that the museum constitutes a complete universe, or at least that 'outside' consists only of dust and darkness. The enlightened reader is thus led to interpret the children's beliefs as false or misconceived. Gradually, the children come to suspect that there is, in fact, a world of light outside the museum and this is confirmed by their eventual release at the end of the story. Furthermore, the reader's superior knowledge of 'reality' is seemingly vindicated.

However, this vindication is destabilized through the narrative disruption of signification. Although the children's reading of signs appears mistaken, it soon becomes clear that their relocation of meaning is a matter of survival. For instance, their ability to differentiate between spears from various lands and times is forged by necessity; as Scott reveals: 'Empty hooks reminded Saxon of their first search for weapons; many weapons were displayed throughout the world, but only African spears were light enough' (47). In Saxon's utilitarian terms, weapons are classified according to portability and destructive capability. In their desperate struggle for survival, the children have little need for the dictates of history and geography; such concepts are rendered useless. Therefore, when Saxon is moved by a display of fossilized tree stumps, it seems unlikely that Scott is responding to Walter Benjamin's notions of auratic beauty:

> She sat alone in the kitchen while the bread baked; breathing its smell, thinking of the fossil tree stumps. She wondered at their shape – not measured into straight lines and perfect curves like the world, but – she smiled – like Gilbert, and the sparrows. And the spiders.
>
> How strange that she could divide creation in two: that which is measured, and that which is not. (56)

Certainly, Saxon is brought to recognize the latent chaos of nature, thus enabling this differentiation between the natural and the fabricated, between reproduction and reality. However, her attraction is enabled not so much through the inherent aura of the object itself, but through the memories of life outside and previous to existence in the museum. Saxon's identification with the artefact, then, relies on her own experience; her sense of the thing is activated through reference to herself and the outside environment into which she was born. As Saxon increasingly comes to realize, there is little point in names, labels and classifications unless they have some reference to individual experience. Saxon has to claim a past for herself that bears no relation to the original signification of museum exhibits and the past they evoke; she has no access to the public time described by Kern, and thus the concept of the Museum as a *lieu de mémoire* is necessarily alien to her.

The children have difficulty remembering their surname because they have lost contact with the people and places that once lent it meaning. Equally, their attempt to learn the names of each museum exhibit is a futile exercise, since their only point of reference is a dictionary; they soon learn that there is no natural affinity between object and label. Their efforts to classify and name are without apparent motivation, but it is implied that they are acting out the earliest lessons of childhood rendered futile in their social and cultural isolation. Finally, Saxon is forced to reach within herself in order to locate her past; she must face her innermost fears if she is ever to make sense of the world which once was hers. As the Brogan falls to her death, as the passing (past) of death rushes to meet the present, so Saxon is able to recognize her mother:

> And they lay weeping, Saxon and Gilbert, weeping for something found then lost in a heartbeat, and Saxon suddenly knew many things. A great stone falling. A young woman on the steps of the museum. The stone touching her place as it came down, striking her legs. A red shoe, and two children obeying instructions spoken only a moment earlier. 'Get inside. Whatever happens don't come out!' And she fled with Gilbert inside, and whatever happened she hadn't come out. Despite the screams, she hadn't come out. (101–2)

Of course, the children are not alone in their re-evaluation of signification. At this moment, or perhaps at an earlier moment of realization, the reader is forced to reconsider the title of the book. 'Why Weeps the Brogan?' no longer implicates a terrifying creature as its subject, rather a family destroyed through tragedy. The monster that Gilbert and Saxon have feared for so long is actually their mother; a mother who sacrifices herself in order that her children might have a future.

Like Provoost, having revealed the painful secrets of the past, Scott is unwilling to promise his readers a rosy future; such a closure would compromise the complexity of his exploration of identity as constructed through past, present and future (and would undermine the implied political message warning against the devastating consequences of nuclear combat). Ultimately, both authors confirm that we construct ourselves through time, but that this construction is a difficult, often painful process, and that while the past should not be privileged over the present (in the exercise of nostalgia), neither should we expect too much from a future overburdened with a painful past.

Conclusion

It is clear that time permeates children's literature on a number of levels. It manifests itself as a fundamental aspect of narrative, a fact which writers have increasingly manipulated through postmodern techniques (such as Sedgwick's dual narrative structure, or Provoost's achronological framework) that destabilize and challenge readers' relationships with time and history. As a necessary aspect of lived experience, time is also explored on a thematic level in these books. Writers frequently explore the resonance of memory and the various ways in which children might come to terms with an unknown past as they attempt to make sense of present experience in preparation for the future.

Marcus Sedgwick and Hugh Scott suggest that the past, and more specifically memory, is accessible through objects. However, in line with museum theorists, they suggest that the past cannot be *contained* within objects such as Mouse's box, as Sigurd's narration of Mouse's tale puts her memories to use (they are no longer trapped within the box). Furthermore, *The Dark Horse*, *Falling* and *Why Weeps the Brogan?* all recognize the relationship between individual development and an understanding of time past, present and future. Memory might be inscribed with the past, but it also has a hand in shaping action, response and identity in the present and for the future. Our memories – either the stories we tell ourselves about the past, or those we are told – influence our actions, emotions and responses in the present. Significantly though, these memories can be created and altered by those around us, or by our own variable moods and perceptions; they are not stable and thus we can change, as Lucas does in *Falling*, in response to these retrospective shifts. Essentially, recent books for children suggest that children must be taught to 'reckon with time' in Heidegger's terms, and to look to their own place in time if the past is to have any relevance to self-knowledge and growth.

WORKS CITED AND FURTHER READING

Primary Texts

Anno, M. *et al.*, *All in a Day*, tr. Kuso-Kubo (New York: PaperStar, 1986).
Provoost, A., *Falling*, tr. John Nieuwenhuizen (St Leonard's, NSW: Allen & Unwin, 1997; first published in Dutch, 1995).
Scott, H., *Why Weeps the Brogan?* (London: Walker Books, 1991; first published 1989).
Sedgwick, M., *The Dark Horse* (London: Orion Children's Books, 2002).

Critical Texts

Benjamin, W., 'The Work of Art in an Age of Mechanical Reproduction', in *Illuminations*, ed. H. Arendt, trans. H. Zohan (New York: Schocken Books, 1969).
Campbell, J., *Past, Space and Self* (Cambridge, MA, and London: MIT Press, 1995).
Crossley-Holland, K., Sail, L. and Drew, S., *The New Exeter Book of Riddles* (London: Enitharmon Press, 2000).
Holquist, M., *Dialogism: Bakhtin and his World* (London: Routledge, 1990).

Krips, V., 'Presencing the Past', *Signal*, 90 (September 1999), pp. 176–86.

Krips, V., *The Presence of the Past: Memory, Heritage and Childhood in Postwar Britain* (London and New York: Garland, 2000).

Pearce, P., 'Time Present', in *Travellers in Time: Past, Present and to Come – Proceedings* (Greenbay: Children's Literature New England, 1990), pp. 70–4.

Piaget, J., *The Child's Conception of Time*, trans. A. J. Pomeras (London: Routledge & Kegan Paul, 1969; first published 1927).

Ricoeur, P., 'Narrative Time', in W. J. T. Mitchell (ed.), *On Narrative* (Chicago and London: University of Chicago Press, 1981).

Walsh, K., *The Representation of the Past* (London: Routledge, 1992).

Websites

Provoost, A., 'If Goblins Don't Exist . . .' at: www.anneprovoost.com/English/Essays/Essays Goblins.htm (accessed 7/11/03).

Children's Books

Foreman, M., *Jack's Fantastic Voyage* (London: Andersen Press, 1992); *Grandfather's Pencil and the Room of Stories* (London: Red Fox, 1995; first published 1993); *Jack's Big Race* (London: Andersen Press, 1998).

Garner, A., *Red Shift* (London: Collins, 1973).

Lively, P., *A Stitch in Time* (London: Mammoth, 1994; first published, 1976).

Newbery, L., *The Shell House* (Oxford: David Fickling, 2002).

Wiesner, D., *Tuesday* (New York: Clarion Books, 1991).

Postmodernism, New Historicism and Migration: New Historical Novels

11

Pat Pinsent

One of the most rapidly growing areas in children's literature in recent decades is fiction that deals with the experiences of young people, past and present, who for a variety of reasons find themselves caught between cultures. Often these are accounts of children and adolescents whose families have been forced to migrate to new countries as a consequence of war, economic necessity, or oppression. Some reflect the experiences of those whose countries have been invaded and/or colonized. At the best of times, because they lack economic and political power as well as being in the process of acquiring the education and sense of identity normally associated with those who give public voice and shape to experience, children constitute a muted group. When they lose their language and culture this situation is exacerbated, yet often children in these circumstances acquire language and otherwise adjust to new circumstances more rapidly than the adults in their families, and the attendant repercussions on domestic power dynamics and relationships can be profound and unsettling. Traditionally such experiences have largely been left out of official histories, but under the general heading of postcolonial writing and criticism, new kinds of narratives and new ways of reading and interrogating the past are proliferating. In this chapter, Pat Pinsent considers a range of such texts, using critical tools developed by New Historicists, Cultural Materialists, and those working in the area of Postcolonial Criticism. As this is a less-established area of study than some of those considered in this book, there are fewer critical works to which students can be directed for this chapter than there are for most other chapters; to balance this and provide representative coverage of issues, kinds and sources of new histories, this chapter uses more key texts than others. If it is being used as part of a course of study, it would be advisable to concentrate on two or three of the key texts, or to use the chapter as the basis for reading other texts using some of the ideas and approaches it explains and illustrates.

Written history throughout the ages has generally been created by historians who have viewed events from the perspective of those possessing power, the representatives of the dominant culture. Unsurprisingly, until relatively recently, historians of the British Empire have been likely to display, explicitly or implicitly, completely different attitudes towards those exerting dominion over subjugated peoples from those they reveal towards the members of the subject peoples themselves. This phenomenon is evidenced also in literature, so that nineteenth-century historical novelists treating the theme of empire for a young audience, such as R. M. Ballantyne (1825–94) and G. A. Henty (1832–1902), were far more likely to present the action through the eyes of the imperialist adventurers rather than through the 'natives' whom they encounter. Although a few twentieth-century authors, notably Geoffrey Trease and Rosemary Sutcliff, attempted to portray life from the perspective of a marginalized or suppressed group, this trend remained a minor one in comparison to material, particularly in comics and boys' magazines, which still adopted a superior attitude towards the majority of the inhabitants of 'the colonies'.

Not until relatively recently have novels set in the past, as well as those depicting present-day situations, virtually taken as a norm that marginalized and oppressed groups provide as interesting a focus as characters from the majority group. This foregrounding of marginalized groups appears to result from a more widely embracing understanding and empathy with the underprivileged; though today's society is no more guiltless of the persecution of minorities than were those of the past, the break-up of empire and the development of mass communications makes it more difficult for writer and reader alike to be oblivious to the plight of the disempowered.

The texts to be discussed in this chapter represent an attempt on the part of children's authors, whether themselves inside or outside such communities, to foreground the experiences of immigrant or minority groups, or in some cases disempowered indigenous communities, in lands where there are strong, western-derived, majority cultures. These books tend to be characterized by the recognition on the part of the authors of the need to give a voice to the voiceless and to relativize the role of those in power by presenting a perspective other than theirs. This contrasts with much of the earlier British children's literature set in outposts of empire, which, however sympathetic the author might be to the under-privileged, automatically presented the perspective of the imperial colonizer. Justice and beneficence were preached in such books, but today such an approach can all too easily appear patronizing. By contrast, in books currently being written on such topics, frequently set in the past, there is a tendency to portray disempowered characters who quite naturally take on such strategies as learning the oppressor's language, or profiting from educational opportunities in order to acquire autonomy, both for themselves individually and for their communities. Such a phenomenon may be recognized in the history of the development of colonial regimes throughout the world, and is increasingly portrayed in the literatures of the United States, Canada and Australia, as well as of Britain itself.

Associated with this assimilation, both in books and in real life, is the tendency for the powerless to internalize the structures which keep the empowered group in authority, so that these no longer need to be imposed externally. Children may grow up to accept not only the language, but also the culture of the dominant group, rejecting their own. This is the almost inevitable result of liminality; marginalized people who are on the threshold of a more powerful group may strive to be part of such a group. Alternatively, they may seek by subversive means to raise the status of their own community while trying to retain some vestiges of their own identity. The books discussed in this chapter foreground language, education and culture as sites for such processes. In particular, they often emphasize the ways in which religion, song and folk tale serve as means to preserve, or even re-create, a culture potentially subversive to the mainstream.

Critical approaches

All the novels considered here have a strong relationship to history, generally the submerged and almost forgotten history of people regarded as marginal to the main areas of human progress. The approaches to history in these books, although quite varied, all emphasize the personal element, whether that of a first-person narrator or a single focal character, or, in the case of the works of Gary Crew (1947–), that of late twentieth-century characters being exposed to the events of a remote period. In tackling such material, certain critical approaches seem to offer the possibility of most insights: those of New Historicism, Cultural Materialism, and because of the settings of the novels, Postcolonialism (see Boxes 11.1 and 11.2). As will be seen in the analyses of individual novels, it is not always easy to distinguish between the literary-critical approach employed in looking at the texts, and the historio-critical techniques used by the writers concerned. For instance, in *Strange Objects*, Gary Crew's postmodern (Boxes 6.3 and 11.1) creation of apparently 'factual' material to be set against the narrative passages involving his protagonist, is putting the reader in the position of a New Historicist critic faced with 'real' material. Similarly, the experience of characters learning the majority language and culture tends to encapsulate the development of postcolonial literatures generally: Adopt, Adapt, Adept (Barry, 1995: 195 – see also Box 11.2).

BOX 11.1   POSTMODERNISM AND NEW HISTORICISM

In *Working with Structuralism*, David Lodge cites a number of characteristics of post-modern texts, such as the defiance of any notion of continuity between ideas, and the creation of a sense of randomness. Particularly apposite to the texts under discussion here, especially the work of Gary Crew, is what he identifies as 'combining in the one work the apparently factual and the obviously fictional, introducing the author and the question of authorship into the text, and exposing conventions in the act of using them' (1981: 15).

Barry (1995: 172) defines New Historicism as 'a method based on the *parallel* reading of literary and non-literary texts'. He suggests that it detaches the literary text from the 'accumulated weight of previous literary scholarship' and focuses attention 'on issues of State power' and its maintenance. Significantly, New Historicism is not a theory and is not theorized; it treats texts from all domains (though particularly archival material and historical documents) as part of culture, artificially separated into separate areas. It abhors the separation of history and text, regarding all texts as historical documents and all historical documents as texts.

It is easy to see the similarity between the concerns of postmodern writing and New Historicism as a critical approach: when the author sets real or apparent historical sources in parallel with the sections of narrative involving plot and characters, the result is the novelistic creation of what appears to be a New Historicist discourse. Without any label, this practice has been employed frequently in historical fiction, from Sir Walter Scott onwards.

In creating a number of what appear to be primary historical sources, Crew is highlighting a dilemma always latently there in the historical novel: the challenge to the reader to be aware of the fictionality of most of the narrative, as opposed to the historicity of the basic situation. As Stephens observes: 'The distinction between what is real and what is fictive is often difficult for young readers to make, so the authority with which fictive events are invested by their interaction with actual events will be intensified' (1992: 209). Thus, although the actual events which provide the background of these texts are often only present in a shadowy way, by their factuality they nevertheless invite the young reader to believe in the fictional characters and events within the novels. There is for the reader a delicate balance between, on the one hand, regarding the characters and the specific situations in which they are involved as typical of the experience of members of disempowered communities, and on the other, of being subject to the force of the narrative and actually believing that the novelists' inventions are 'true'. It invests the author with a high degree of responsibility, lest young readers, once they are disabused of literal belief that the novel itself is history, carry from the experience too high a level of scepticism about what actually happened as well as about the fictional account. The extent of the success of this process in these novels is examined below.

BOX 11.2   CULTURAL MATERIALISM AND POSTCOLONIALISM

Cultural Materialism developed in Britain as a response to the premises of New Historicism. It too is interested in demonstrating that texts and history cannot be separated, but rather than focusing on the way combining texts and historical documents helps to understand the past, Cultural Materialists insist that the process is in fact about understanding the present, 'revealing the politics of our own society by what we choose to emphasize or suppress of the past' (Barry, 1995: 184). Jonathan Dollimore and Alan Sinfield, two of the founders of this approach, explain: 'insistence on the process through which a text achieves its current estimation is the key move in cultural materialism' (1994: 28).

Postcolonialism foregrounds the way in which European cultural traditions have been taken as the norm, marginalizing the language and mores of original inhabitants and minority groups. Edward Said's work emphasizes how non-western cultures have been seen as 'other' or exotic. Barry (1995: 195) suggests that all postcolonial literatures seem to go through a process of 'Adopt', the unquestioning acceptance of the authority of European models; 'Adapt', when they transmute these to their own subject matter; and 'Adept', a re-making of the forms to their own specifications. He also suggests that '[an] emphasis on identity as doubled, or hybrid, or unstable is a ... characteristic of the postcolonial approach' (195), something which clearly relates to the dual language and culture accessible to people in the post-colonial situation.

Equality, anti-racism and multiculturalism

During the 1960s and 1970s, many people in Britain and America began to be increasingly conscious of the importance of children's literature in the process of giving minority groups a more equal role in society. It could help make future citizens aware not only of past oppression, but also of how literature itself had been complicit in this oppression, both by using language, characters and situations which took it for granted, and by rendering such groups invisible. The examination of children's literature was bi-focal; first there was a reappraisal of children's classics of the past in order to determine how characters from minority ethnic groups had been portrayed, and secondly and more relevant here, new works of fiction were written with the object of informing white readers about the oppression of other races.

Initially such books were widely welcomed. William Armstrong's *Sounder* (1969), with its account of the brutal treatment and imprisonment of a poor black sharecropper, won the US Newbery Award, while Theodore Taylor's *The Cay* (1969), in which a young white boy is disabused of his racial prejudice by being shipwrecked on an island with a wise but illiterate elderly black seaman, was highly praised. During the 1970s, however, critics began to question the legitimacy of writers who did not belong to the minority group concerned 'usurping' the role that properly belonged to members of these groups, and in effect ventriloquizing through the characters as if they were little more than puppets. There was also censure of what critics saw as the collusion by authors such as Armstrong and Taylor in the depiction of passivity and lack of individual identity in the characters they created, though the justice of these charges has never totally been conceded. Another relevant objection is the fact that it is impossible for those outside a culture fully to understand its literature; Clare Bradford's analysis of some Aboriginal picturebooks (2003: 65–77) makes very explicit some of the pitfalls to which readers from a western background are liable.

Paula Fox's *The Slave Dancer* (1973) has been a particularly controversial text. Its narrator, Jessie, is a young boy who is kidnapped in New Orleans so that he can play his pipe for the slaves aboard a slave ship, the *Moonlight*, to dance to. This exercise is intended to ensure that they are relatively healthy when they arrive in America to be sold. The slaves are, however, cast overboard when the ship is confronted by an anti-slavery patrol, their deaths happening only slightly in advance of the wreck of the ship itself with nearly all its crew. Jessie survives, together with a slave boy, Ras. Jessie's experiences leave him psychologically scarred for life, but he has learned enduring lessons about humanity. Like *Sounder*, this book won the Newbery Award, initially being praised for its indictment of the slave trade. Before long, however, black critics in particular savaged its depiction of the slaves on board the vessel as passive and effectively complicit in their own servitude. Stephens describes it as a text which 'expresses attitudes which are now considered undesirable but are defended on grounds of historicity' (1992: 205).

Crucial to the debate are passages such as this, where Jessie confronts his feelings towards the slaves when they are brought on deck:

> I found a dreadful thing in my mind.
> I hated the slaves! I hated their shuffling, their howling, their very suffering! I hated the way they spat out their food upon the deck, the overflowing buckets, the emptying of which tried all my strength. ...
> I would have snatched the rope from Spark's hand and beaten them myself! (78)

Since readers have probably been identifying with the first-person narrator, Jessie, empathizing with his feelings of powerlessness, the question arises as to whether they will automatically share his hostility to the slaves. Although his hatred could be seen as a form of self-loathing, given that the slaves' passivity is an extreme version of his own lack of opposition to either his or their servitude, young readers may not immediately recognize it as such. The extent to which this negative reaction is overridden by Jessie's growing friendship with Ras is debatable, especially as Ras's character remains only sketched in. It may be that at the period when the book was written, authors were more intent on making white readers recognize their own complicity in the guilt of the slave-trade, and less concerned about the desirability of showing the slaves as dignified human beings themselves, figures with whom both black and white child readers might identify.

A further issue is that of the inarticulacy of the slaves, who are seen as either silent or muttering in an unintelligible language. The most heightened instance of this is the figure of a slave who accompanies a Spanish slaver and is dressed in finery, but for some undisclosed reason has had his tongue cut out. He could be seen as an image of the way in which silent compliance with the white man's wishes could lead to advancement, though at the cost of heritage and culture. The beginnings of hope may nevertheless be seen in the fact that by the time they part, Jessie and Ras are beginning to communicate, and Jessie's regard for Ras has increased, signified by the fact that once he sees him in respectable clothes, he finds that Ras seems 'taller' (134). Fox's intentions are clearly indicated in a passage near the end of the book, when the adult Jessie muses on his subsequent life:

> When I passed a black man, I often turned to look at him, trying to see in his walk the man he had once been before he'd been driven through the dangerous heaving surf to a long boat, toppled into it, chained, brought to a waiting ship all narrowed and stripped for speed, carried through storms, and the bitter brightness of sun-filled days to a place, where if he had survived, he would be sold like cloth. (140–2)

The silence and passivity of the slaves in Fox's book may be contrasted with their agency in a later work, also by a white author, Gary Paulsen's *Nightjohn* (1993). The title character is a young black man who continually risks mutilation and death in order to bring literacy to groups of slaves. Not only is he articulate and active, but he also has obviously succeeded in both educating and raising the consciousness of the narrator, a young slave girl, who is also the titular character and narrator of Paulsen's later book *Sarny* (1997). The events of *Nightjohn* are seen from her perspective, so that we no longer have voiceless victims, but rather individuals who, despite their suffering, have dignity. Nightjohn is punished for illegally teaching the slaves to read, having confessed his guilt in order to get one of the other slaves re-leased from a beating. A toe is cut off from each of his feet, and the defiant silence with which he receives this punishment is very different from the silent cowed submission of the slaves in Fox's text: 'They hold the foot to the block. John he still not making any sounds, but his face is stiff. Like it's carved out of rock' (50). The force of this image only becomes apparent at the end of the book in an afterword, when Paulsen describes the lives of two slaves owned by Thomas Jefferson (1743–1826), a great exponent of human rights, who seemed less aware of his responsibilities to the slaves in his employ. Of one of these, a carpenter, who built the house where Jefferson lived, Paulsen says, 'His face is not on Mount Rushmore,' the mountain on which the faces of US presidents are carved out of stone. For Paulsen, it would appear, those who deserve to be immortalized in this way are people like this carpenter, Isaac, and disseminators of learning such as Nightjohn himself.

By its nature, children's fiction tends to focus on individuals rather than communities, as a more effective way of capturing the interest of the reader. Nevertheless, to make an effective statement about people who are marginalized, the role of the community is generally vital, particularly since the result of oppression is often the fragmentation of communities. Mildred Taylor's *Roll of Thunder, Hear my Cry* (1976), another Newbery Medal winner, while centred in the consciousness of the young black narrator Cassie, equally firmly roots her experience within the Mississippi community in which she comes to maturity. Taylor's sureness of touch in depicting the community results from the fact that, as she admits, both the incidents and the characters are based on the experience of her own father, who grew up in the Southern States and benefited by inheriting stories from past generations.

Books such as *Roll of Thunder* show how it is possible to create in young readers a combination of a sense of otherness and an empathy with the characters. On the one hand, this alterity is essential so that readers can appreciate how different the lives and settings portrayed are from their own lives; without this the understanding, the plight of people disadvantaged by prejudice cannot be conveyed. Unless this insight is combined with an empathetic sharing in the experience of the characters, however, readers may lack the involvement which creates in them an ownership of such experience; as a consequence they may be too detached from the outcomes to engage with the issues being raised. Taylor achieves both alterity and empathy throughout the book by describing incidents accessible to children of any background, though for most, inconceivable as a part of everyday life. Examples range from the initial description of Cassie, her siblings and other local children walking to school, with her little brother's anger at being splashed by the bus which is taking the privileged white children to their superior school, through the children's resentment at being handed down schoolbooks in poor condition and regarded as fit only for 'nigras', to Cassie's fury at being pushed off the sidewalk by the father of a white girl.

Cassie's mother's presentation of the history of the oppression of black people in America (chapter 6) brilliantly summarizes what readers, like Cassie herself, need to know about this subject for the book to have its maximum effect. The aspect of community is kept to the fore, particularly in the scene set at the church (187), where the 'revival' is much more than simply a religious occasion; it also shows how the church is the centre of the community. This is reinforced by what Cassie's mother has to say about the way in which the slave-owners taught Christianity:

> They didn't teach us Christianity to save our souls, but to teach us obedience. They were afraid of slave revolts and they wanted us to learn the Bible's teaching about slaves being loyal to their masters.   (106)

Yet the function of the church in maintaining community is apparent, while the role of prayer in Cassie's mother's life is not minimized (107). Members of the oppressed community have transformed and made their own the sacred narratives of the oppressors.

Literature of immigration and postcolonialism

The phenomenon of the displacement of individuals and communities from their native countries is certainly not a new one. The very spread of the human race from its origins in Africa to the whole surface of the globe must have involved this kind of movement. Events such as the creation of empires and the consequent flight of refugees from powerful invaders have happened throughout the ages. The major differences between earlier movements of people and those in today's world are probably the scale and speed of migration, as well as the extent to which modern communications inform virtually everyone in the world about the process. Accompanying this process has been the emancipation of erstwhile colonial peoples into autonomous nations. Inevitably both processes have formed the subject matter of children's fiction, some of this interest being triggered by the need for newer communities to find their voices, while the acceptability of such narratives for publication for children has been increased by the awareness in privileged western societies of the racism which is now generally latent but in periods as recent as World War II was actually enforced by law.

It is noticeable that contemporary children's fiction tends to a greater extent than in the past to make readers aware of the migrant community or the emerging, previously disempowered, indigenous group, rather than to represent protagonists either as (often aberrant) individuals or as members of the empowered group. Thus an awareness is created of the lack within such communities of the advantages taken for granted by those who possess power. A consequence is the realization of an ambivalence within the displaced or subordinate groups about the preservation of their culture and language, as well as their subjection to concomitant problems about employment, and resulting failures in self-image, particularly for adult men.

Those children's books which have focused on the plight of migrant communities could be seen as providing something of a bridge between texts (like those discussed in the preceding section) which focus on racial issues or on divisions between long-established minority groups and the hegemonic majority, and texts which can be more accurately described as 'postcolonial', being set in what would once have been termed the outposts of empire, or written by people historically from them. Like the former category, books featuring migrant groups foreground equality issues, while like the latter, they often suggest that the culture of the subordinate group is strange, even exotic, to the majority population. Unlike a great deal of earlier colonial literature, however, they also pinpoint the strangeness of the majority culture as seen by the immigrant group, thus succeeding in relativizing it for the reader. This mutual 'otherness' may simply take the form of differing foods, but quite often it relates to customs, especially those concerned with sex, notably the position of girls faced with a dichotomy between the standards of home and of neighbourhood. Whether or not such books depict the past, a degree of alterity is created by the misunderstandings of the incomers about behaviour in the host community, as well as by a description of their own customs.

A frequently used strategy is to present young characters who find it difficult to understand why they are forbidden participation in the activities of the host community which their schoolmates regard as normal. They also display the need to find a balance between retaining relationships within their communities and attempting to 'get on' in the new society. Another recurring feature in several of these books is what might be termed the emasculation of the father figure. He is shown as all too often incapable of fulfilling the role of breadwinner in the new society, with his consequent frustration leading him to resent the much easier integration experienced by his children.

Jeanne Wakatsuki Houston and James Houston's first-person narrative *Farewell to Manzanar* (1974) is presented as an autobiography rather than a novel, being described as 'A true story of Japanese American experience during and after the World War II internment'. The Wakatsuki family and many other Japanese Americans were removed from their homes, which were regarded as too dangerously near a US naval station, and interned in a half-finished and over-crowded camp which all too inadequately provided for their physical and emotional needs, with its 'bare floors, blanket partitions, one bulb in each compartment dangling from a roof beam' (28). The father of the family is arrested on a charge of which he is eventually found innocent, but only released after nine months of imprisonment; during this period his health and self-respect are irremediably damaged. The narrative is prefaced by a foreword which describes the research for the book, and again stresses that 'this is a true story'. Nevertheless, there is a constant tension between the factual and the fictive, which is most apparent when the authors present, verbatim and at length, conversations which could not possibly have been remembered in such detail. Even more obviously fictional are chapters which re-create scenes that Wakatsuki Houston could not have witnessed, such as the interrogation of her father at his place of imprisonment, Fort Lincoln (chapter 7). There is often a tension between the young child's perceptions and the adult writer's interpretations, as when she first describes how her father continued to use a cane which gave support to an injured leg even when he no longer needed it: 'I see it *now* [my emphasis] as a sad, homemade version of [a] Samurai sword' (47). When after more than three years they are allowed to find their own living accommodation again, the protagonist has internalized the 'shame for being a person guilty of something enormous enough to deserve that kind of treatment' (185).

Linda Crew's *Children of the River* (1989), set in the 1970s, focuses on Sundara, who has escaped with her aunt's family from the Khmer Rouge in Cambodia, leaving her parents behind. She struggles both in adapting to American society in Oregon and in coming to terms with the death of the baby niece for whom she has been a main carer. Crew, while not of Cambodian origin, writes out of her personal acquaintance with Cambodian refugees, so while the events are based on real happenings, this book, narrated in the third person, is more overt in its fictionality than is the case with the other texts discussed in this section. The main emphasis in *Children of the River* is on the clash of cultures, particularly with regard to relationships with the opposite sex. Sundara's struggle to comply with her aunt's prohibition against friendship with Jonathan, the son of a doctor, is matched by the boy's total incomprehension of the impossibility for Sundara even of going to the cinema with him. Finally Sundara takes control of her own life by spending a day with Jonathan's family, and her aunt comes to understand some of the alien cultural elements.

Both differences in understanding and cultural clash within the family because of friendships with American classmates also feature strongly as elements in An Na's *A Step from Heaven* (2001), a first-person account of the process towards integration into American society as experienced by a Korean girl, Park Young Ju. One of her first experiences is being introduced in a classroom and hearing the teacher's word 'welcome' as 'Wah ko um'. The school is very different from the more rigid setting to which she is accustomed, but is likely to be more familiar to the majority of readers than would Young's former school. Thus the strangeness experienced by the character, together with the empathy which has probably already been generated in the readers, may enable them to see the problems faced by the characters as if they were their own. While Young is becoming a competent and confident member of American society, she witnesses the disintegration of her family, triggered by her father's violence, a consequence of his low status and dependence on his wife, who works all available hours to support the family. Deprived of his traditional role as provider, he replaces it by the tyranny of forbidding Young to have American friends, even of the same sex. At the same time, she is conscious of the differences between her status in the family and that of her younger brother.

No easy resolution is offered: the father returns to Korea while Young finds some consolation in remembering his role early in her childhood in establishing her confidence by teaching her how to swim. The autobiographical element in *A Step from Heaven* appears to be strong; Na, like her protagonist, was born in Korea and came as a child to America, and met with academic success. An instance of the literary approach of this novel is the way in which the sometimes fragmentary nature of the text, particularly in the early chapters, mirrors the incomplete understandings of the developing child – a technique recalling, for instance, James Joyce's *A Portrait of the Artist* (1916). The book begins:

> Just to the edge, Young Ju. Only your feet. Stay there.
> Cold. Cold water. Oh. My toes are fish. Come here. Fast. Look.
> What is it, Young Ju?
> See my toes. See how they are swimming in the sea? Like fish.
> Yes they are little fat piggy fish.   (9)

The usage is strikingly different from the long paragraphs and more cohesive style at the end of the book.

Despite the different settings and periods of time concerned, these three books have a great deal in common. In all but one instance the authors are drawn from the minority communities depicted, and portray the focal characters as going through the stages that in all probability they themselves as children experienced, first learning the language of the empowered group, then employing it to describe their own culture, and finally becoming so proficient as to appear to be in transition to the majority group. This process is analogous to Barry's summary of the development of postcolonial literature: 'Adopt, Adapt, Adept.'

Wakatsuki Houston and Houston's text could be seen as nearer to the 'adopt' phase; throughout *Farewell to Manzanar*, the protagonist reveals ambivalence about her own culture, almost to the point of rejection, spurred on by her hostility to her father. She is deracinated to the extent of initially being terrified of other Japanese (11) and talking about them as if she were not part of the group, as in: 'There is a phrase the Japanese use in such situations ...' (16). Towards the end of the book she discloses, 'I was the first member of our family to finish college and the first to marry out of my race' (186). Her revisiting of the scene of her childhood internment appears to be therapeutic rather than related to any pride in her background or desire to pass it on to her own children.

The situation in the more recent books is more complex. Park Young and Selda both certainly become 'adept' in the western language and culture in which they are immersed, and it could be argued that the characters are to some extent rejecting their own cultures. In *A Step from Heaven*, the father's return to Korea, meaning that he virtually loses touch with the family, signifies for the rest of the family a severing of their Korean roots. Nevertheless the strong attachment between mother and daughter suggests some desire to retain the positive elements of the culture. In particular, it evinces Na's wish to 'remake the [literary] form to [her] own specification' (Barry, 1995: 195) rather than simply to 'adapt' it to her own subject matter. In addition to Na's innovative mirroring of her protagonist's mental state throughout the text, she shows her command of symbol by her final image of Young's mother's scarred and workworn hands. The response to the girl's wistful 'I wish I could erase these scars for you' is:

> Uhmma gently slips her hands from mine. She stares for a moment at her callused skin and then says firmly, These are my hands, Young Ji. Uhmma tucks a wisp of my long, straight black hair behind my ear and then puts her arm around my waist. We continue our walk along the beach. (155–6)

The mother's claim to her total past and her care for the girl's very characteristically Korean hair, together with the setting on the beach, serve as metonyms for the acceptance of both cultures. All these books, in their various ways, indicate how migration stories probably work most effectively when a balance is achieved, both by the characters concerned and in the actual writing, between assimilation into the new culture and an acknowledgement of the influence and value of the old.

Postcolonial literature has much in common with these migration novels, in particular in its response to representations of the non-European as 'other'.

Creative writers who are either from minority cultures or have attempted to depict them positively have therefore frequently sought to 'normalize' non-European characters. This process is to be seen in Beverley Naidoo's work; though she herself, as a white South African, would have potentially been a member of the hegemonic group, in her writing and in political action she has allied herself with the oppressed black underclass. In both her early novels, *Journey to Jo'Burg* (1985) and *Chain of Fire* (1989), she presents events entirely from the perspective of the young black children who are sufferers from the government's *apartheid* policies; in the first book we see them having to live in a distant township while their mother works 300 kilometres away in Johannesburg, and in the second they have been uprooted from their village to live in a bleak 'homeland'.

A problem for the writer who uses a perspective very different from that of the majority of her readers is to make the unfamiliar not only comprehensible but also ordinary, a particularly difficult task where, as in *Journey to Jo'Burg*, the expected audience consists of children under ten years old. Naidoo attempts to achieve this by prefacing the novel with two short annotated newspaper cuttings, dated 1981, which make clear that the following first scene is not set in the distant past:

> Naledi and Tiro were worried. Their baby sister Dineo was ill, very ill. For three days now, Nono their granny had been trying to cool her fever with damp cloths paced on her little head and body. ... 'Can't we take Dineo to the hospital?' Naledi begged, but Nono said Dineo was much too sick to be carried that far. The only hospital was many miles away, and Naledi also knew they had no money to pay a doctor to visit them.   (11)

Most young readers in western countries are likely to be so accustomed to the ideas that the doctor can be called freely and that a sick child will be carried to the hospital by ambulance or if necessary private car, that the situation presented here could be quite difficult to understand, but in this instance, as throughout the book, Naidoo creates a strong element of identity between the viewpoints of the two young children and the young reader.

Naidoo's more recent *No Turning Back* (1995) is based on the experiences of street-children in Johannesburg, while *Out of Bounds* (2001) is a collection of short stories, one for each decade from the 1940s to the beginning of the twenty-first century. The penultimate story, 'The Playground', is set in 1995, shortly after Nelson Mandela became South African president. It explores the experiences of a young black girl, Rosa, when she moves from the overcrowded and inadequate school for black children to become the first black pupil at a previously all-white school. In this process she undergoes several shifts in identity (see Box 11.2). The transition from being socially invisible and a victim of school bullying to finally arriving at recognition and resolution, epitomizes much of the colonial and post-colonial experience.

The Australian experience

The history of Australia is quite different from that of most of the colonies which made up the British Empire, a fact that has had considerable influence on the many children's books which in one way or another reflect this history. At a considerable distance from the motherland, and in its early years used as what Niall Ferguson (2003: 103) describes as 'a dumping ground for criminals' and notorious for its sexual licence, Australia paradoxically became for much of its history a notably loyal part of the Empire. Ferguson suggests that this may have been because the policy of transportation in effect liberated the petty criminals who were sent there, to a much greater extent than would have been possible in England. This sense of liberation, later to be shared by those suffering, for instance, from the 'clearances' in the Scottish Highlands, was fostered by the enormous empty spaces, while, less happily, the presence of aboriginal inhabitants at a lower level of technology meant that the new settlers developed an attitude towards them that had all the hallmarks of racism. Australian children's fiction has consequently been characterized by its exploration of how the land has shaped its people, both the white settlers and the Aborigines.

Many of the approaches considered above in relation to equality, migrant communities, and postcolonialism are also relevant to Australian children's fiction, while the whole issue of fact and fictionality is one of its major themes, as can be seen in the unconventional use of history by one of the most acclaimed recent Australian novelists, Gary Crew. His *Strange Objects* (1991) could be described as a clever collage of different types of (largely narrative) sources. In creating a 'New History', Crew presents readers with the kind of puzzles that an assembly of 'real' historical sources would pose: 'Is this reliable?' 'Did the person who wrote this know from the inside or the outside about the events described?', and, most of all, 'What really happened?' Thus readers are in effect asked to take on some of the disciplines of New Historicist criticism (Box 11.1), in which all kinds of texts are given equal status.

As well as two main fictional narratives, the sources include a foreword and afterword by Dr Hope Michaels, from the semi-fictional Western Australian Institute of Maritime Archaeology; she also intervenes in the main story with letters and articles at various points in the text. There are many allusions to existing reference books about the history of Western Australia, interspersed with passages from apparently equally credible sources which only an experienced reader, who observes that no credit is given for copyright to these texts, would realize are part of Crew's invention. The narrative which has the closest link with fact is that concerning two seamen from the *Batavia*, a ship from Amsterdam bound for the Dutch East Indies, which was wrecked off the Western Australian coast in 1629. The 'Commandeur', Francisco Pelsaert, succeeded in reaching Java in an open boat, but on his return after fourteen weeks to rescue the 260 surviving passengers and crew, discovered that over 120 of them had been murdered by a small group of malcontents. Pelsaert ordered seven of these to be hanged, but sentenced two others, a seventeen-year-old boy, Jan Pelgrom, and a soldier, Wouter Loos, to be cast off in an open boat (32). All this is recorded history, but as Mike Dash (2002) states in his historical account of the wreck, there is little evidence related to their actual survival on the mainland, and none of any contact with aboriginal inhabitants.

Much of *Strange Objects*, however, consists of the (fictional) journal of Wouter Loos, recording his and Pelgrom's encounter with what he describes as 'black Indians', and also describing a white girl, Ela, who, it would appear, has survived from an earlier wreck, that of the *Tryal*, a British ship lost in 1622. The journal, which is made to appear more authentic by its many lists and its use of dates throughout, records the men's attempts to trade with the toys which Pelsaert (really) gave them for this purpose, and the obsessive love which Pelgrom has for Ela, to whom he gives a gold ring which he took from a Spaniard (132), and by whom he appears to have had a child (173).

This ring, and Ela's mummified hand, are buried with Loos's journal, in a cauldron, which is discovered in 1986 by the youth who recounts the other main (and entirely fictional) narrative source, Steven Messenger. The teenager becomes obsessed with the ring, refusing to give it up despite Dr Michael's pleas. At one stage an almost supernatural impression is created when Steven has a dream about Ela (74–8). The events he dreams of seem to correspond with what later is disclosed as something that 'really' happened. Finally Steven leaves home, never to be seen again. Questions are raised as to what has happened to him: should readers accept his own interpretation of events, which involves another 'Steven Messenger' character and the possibility of intervention from a mythical figure termed the 'Hitchhiker'; should they see him as suffering from a form of schizophrenia, as Dr Michaels suggests (180); or has his disappearance something to do with the death of his father some months previously, as his mother opines? Readers are not given any answer to this conundrum, a situation consistent with the position in which they have been placed throughout the novel, where no guidance is given as to what is 'true' and what is fictional. Rather, an air of authenticity is conveyed to the fictional material, be it the history of *Batavia* survivors or the events leading up to the boy's disappearance, by the use of the kind of material which is normally factual, such as reference books and newspaper articles.

This deliberate conflating of factual and fictive sources raises the possibility, as suggested by Stephens (1992: 209), that the author's ideology, which underlies the fictional events, achieves a greater effect on the reader because actual historical events are also included. A problem may also lie in the fact that Crew's handling of issues of racism makes heavy demands on the readers' sophistication. A very strong sense of the otherness of the Aboriginal culture is created in the 'historical' sections, where Loos reflects on the childishness of the 'black Indians', displayed by their interest in the tawdry toys he has with him and their superstitious fright at some white stockings; additionally, Pelgrom frequently expresses his (totally unfounded) fears that they may be cannibals. Twentieth-century Steven Messenger is little better, though because of his greater knowledge, he is more reprehensible. He despises Charlie Sunrise, the repository of wisdom for the local Aboriginal group, talking about Charlie's 'filthy pants' (149) and describing his own discomfort when Charlie sits next to him in the car. While it is clear that Steven is a highly unreliable narrator, and greater authority is given to the opinions about Charlie held by the local community, it could be difficult for young readers to dissent from the view of a main character with whose thought processes they are involved. This complex text certainly demands reading and re-reading. It also raises questions about whether texts of this nature need to include introductory material to help young readers tease out the differences between fiction and 'real history'.

Conclusion

This discussion has inevitably been selective, concentrating to a greater extent on innovative texts which have raised questions about the portrayal of minority groups from a variety of different types of communities, than on the more traditional novels which have continued to present events from the perspective of imperialist adventurers. In looking at texts of both types, a postcolonialist perspective is often helpful. It is all too easy for readers familiar with, for instance, Captain Marryatt (1792–1848), Ballantyne, Henty and Rudyard Kipling (1865–1936) to accept rather than to question the imperialist assumptions of these and later authors, at least for the duration of the story. Alternatively, readers may reject this kind of writing, regarding it as too polluted by out-of-date views of empire, and expecting writers to be ahead of their time in criticizing such ideas. Looking at earlier writers in the context of non-literary texts, which serve to display the assumptions taken for granted in the period (as in New-Historicist approaches), can often provide salutary evidence that authors indeed represented the views of their own time. Cultural Materialism is another approach which can also provide an invaluable perspective on the 'wisdom' of the present – what we regard as enlightened is likely to be seen as barbarous by later generations!

Reading texts from groups which until recently did not have the kind of literary traditions that in western culture we take for granted can be particularly informative. In this context, the work of Clare Bradford on Aboriginal picturebooks (2002; 2003) is especially illuminating, showing the ways in which 'Aboriginal textuality engages with Western forms and practices in order to interrogate the assumptions and ideologies of the dominant culture ... [and affirming] the centrality of country to narrative traditions' (2003: 76).

WORKS CITED AND FURTHER READING

Primary Texts

Crew, G., *Strange Objects* (Rydalmere, NSW: Hodder Headline, 1998; first published 1991).

Crew, G. and Gouldthorpe, P., *The Lost Diamonds of Killiecrankie* (Port Melbourne: Lothian Books, 1999; first published 1995).

Fox, P., *The Slave Dancer* (London: Macmillan, 1974; first published 1973).

Wakatsuki Houston, J. W. & Houston, J. D., *Farewell to Manzanar* (New York: Bantam Doubleday Dell, 1995; first published 1973).

Na, A., *A Step from Heaven* (London: Allen & Unwin, 2002; first published 2001).

Naidoo, B., *Journey to Jo'Burg* (London: HarperCollins, 1987; first published 1985).

Paulsen, G., *Nightjohn* (Basingstoke: Macmillan, 1994; first published 1993).

Taylor, M., *Roll of Thunder, Hear my Cry* (London: Gollancz, 1977).

Critical Texts

Barry, P., *Beginning Theory: An Introduction to Literary and Cultural Theory* (Manchester: Manchester University Press, 1995).

Bradford, C., *Reading Race: Aboriginality in Australian Children's Literature* (Carlton South: Melbourne University Press, 2001).

Bradford, C., 'The End of Empire? Colonial and Postcolonial Journeys in Children's Books', *Children's Literature*, 27: 4 (2002), pp. 8–25.

Bradford, C., 'Aboriginal Visual Narratives for Children: a Politics of Place', in M. Styles and E. Bearne (eds) *Art, Narrative and Childhood* (Stoke-on-Trent: Trentham Books, 2003).

Dash, M., *Balavia's Graveyard* (London: Weidenfeld & Nicolson, 2002).

Dollimore, J. and Sinfield, A. (eds), *Political Shakespeare: New Essays on Cultural Materialism* (Manchester: Manchester University Press, 2nd edn, 1994).

Ferguson, N., *How Britain Made the Modern World* (London: Allen Lane, 2003).

Lodge, D., *Working with Structuralism* (London: Routledge, 1981).

McGillis, R. (ed.), *Voices of the Other: Colonisation and Children's Literature* (London and New York: Garland, 1999).

Pinsent, P., *Children's Literature and the Politics of Equality* (London: David Fulton, 1997).

Pinsent, P., ' "Bone and Blood a Slave": the Construct of the Slave and Slavery in Historical Novels for Children', in *The New Review of Children's Literature and Librarianship*, 2002.

Children's Books

Armstrong, W., *Sounder* (London: Gollancz, 1971).

Caswell, B. and Phu An Chiem, D., *Only the Heart* (St Lucia, Queensland: University of Queensland Press, 1997).

Cooney, C. B., *Mercy* (Basingstoke: Macmillan, 2001).

Creech, S., *Walk Two Moons* (Basingstoke: Macmillan, 1994).

Crew, L., *Children of the River* (New York: Bantam Doubleday Dell, 1989).

Gavin, J., The Surya Trilogy (London: Mammoth, 1995).

Hiçyilmaz, G., *The Frozen Waterfall* (London: Faber and Faber, 1993).

Marsden, J. and Tan, S., *The Rabbits* (Melbourne: Lothian Books, 2001).

Marshall, J. V., *Walkabout* (Harmondsworth: Penguin, 1963; first published as *The Children*, 1959).

Mayne, W., *Drift* (London: Cape, 1985).

Naidoo, B., *Chain of Fire* (London: HarperCollins, 1990; first published 1989).

Naidoo, B., *No Turning Back* (Harmondsworth: Penguin, 1996; first published 1995).

Naidoo, B., *Out of Bounds* (Harmondsworth: Penguin, 2001).

Namioka, L., *Yang the Youngest and his Terrible Ear* (New York: Bantam Doubleday Dell, 1992).

O'Neill, J., *So Far from Skye* (Harmondsworth: Penguin, 1993; first published 1992).

Smith, R., *Sumitra's Story* (London: Bodley Head, 1982).

Taylor, T., *The Cay* (London: Bodley Head, 1970; first published 1969).

Zephania, B., *Refugee Boy* (London: Bloomsbury, 2001).

Language, Genres and Issues: the Socially Committed Novel

12

Pat Pinsent

Since the late-1960s, children's literature in the West has maintained a commitment to making young people aware of some of the topical debates taking place in society and especially those concerned with human rights, equal opportunities, and social injustices, past and present. In this chapter, Pat Pinsent explores a selection of texts that have dealt with material of this kind and how it is presented to a juvenile audience. There are tensions inherent in this strand of children's literature arising from the fact that many of those involved in writing, publishing and purchasing books for the young are also concerned to preserve what they regard as characteristics of childhood: innocence, lack of experience, and an optimistic attitude to the future. It could be argued that texts which explore topics such as racism, substance abuse, bullying, divorce, death and disability in realistic ways, require their readers to acquire kinds of knowledge that impinge on innocence and make optimism seem naive and misplaced. By approaching discussion of selected texts through a combination of close reading, knowledge of genres, and setting them in their social and historical contexts, this chapter is designed to provoke questions about writers' ideological agendas, the extent to which children's literature is capable of dealing with complex social problems, and the role such texts may play in shaping social understanding and modelling ideas about the future.

Historical background: children's novels and social didacticism

Since its earliest beginnings, children's literature has been used by authors to influence young readers to adopt those attitudes and that behaviour considered in any period to be desirable. Didacticism has never been confined to helping readers to accumulate factual knowledge; rather, books have commonly also been used in the attempt to inculcate acceptable morals and ethics. Until relatively recently, however, children have seldom been confronted with themes related intrinsically to social issues. For instance, most British children's novels from the first half of the twentieth century, if they touch at all on social issues, do so in order to provide background for the characters. Most children's writers, whatever their political convictions, were themselves very firmly of middle-class origin (as in the case of the Fabian socialist, Edith Nesbit). This means that however good their intentions, they inevitably either employed middle-class protagonists, sometimes afflicted by genteel poverty, as in Noel Streatfeild's *Ballet Shoes* (1936 – see Chapter 2), or succumbed to the danger of making lower-class characters somewhat comic, as in Eve Garnett's *The Family from One End Street* (1937 – also discussed in Chapter 2).

It was not until the 1970s and the beginnings of legislation dealing with issues of discrimination in society that significant numbers of children's authors began to take on board issues of equality. During this period there was an increasing awareness of how literature could affect social attitudes. In its first stages, such awareness tended to concentrate on how children's books from the past portrayed (or in many cases, failed to portray) females, the working classes, and minority ethnic groups. At the same time, the growth of the academic discipline of socio-linguistics during this period led to a greater sensitivity about the way language was often used in books to disempower characters from minority groups or render them invisible. The initial period of detecting bias was followed relatively speedily by the production of fiction designed to ensure that readers' attitudes towards such groups were compatible with contemporary views about equality.

Although most children's authors prior to this period had not overtly used literature as an instrument to disseminate their views about society, their work often reflects their own preconceptions on this subject. In all periods, writers' views will, directly or indirectly, have been conveyed to their young readers by such means as characterization and plot situations as well as by language. British children's fiction advocating social change, however, became more significant during the last quarter of the twentieth century because of two main factors: the increasing attention which society had been forced to give to the voices of women, and the effect of large-scale immigration into Britain from the Commonwealth. Factors such as these led to social changes which could not be ignored, at least in realistic fiction. This situation was recognized by, for instance, the founding in 1975 of the 'Other Award' by the Children's Rights Workshop; its aim was, as

Robert Leeson puts it, to 'encourage new writing free from sex, race or class bias' (1985: 136).

Concerns about bias began to be treated explicitly in children's books, though in some cases it is possible to detect that authors' prejudices, possibly unrecognized even to themselves, may run counter to the views that the writers intend to convey. Novels with a powerful message of equality need to be analysed to determine if there is any tension between the explicit ideology proffered by their authors and any aspects of the texts which suggest implicit acceptance of less enlightened values. Peter Hollindale (1988) provides a useful series of questions designed to aid readers in the task of detecting the ideology of writers who may not have been entirely conscious of it themselves. Interrogation of the ending of a book, for instance, may show that it reaffirms values which much of the text has held in question.

In the case of picturebooks, ideological messages conveyed by the text may be reinforced, or in some instances contradicted, by the pictures, which in the case of books for younger children can be even more powerful in their effects. Although it is not possible here to give attention to this area, some relevant books are listed at the end of this chapter.

Critical approaches

In looking at the books to be discussed in this chapter, account will be taken of how narrative stance affects the reader's positioning in relation to the development of plot and character. Stephens (1992: 136) notes how different modes of narration, such as the use of an 'omniscient' narrator, the employment of first-person, possibly 'unreliable', narrative, or the focus provided by the perspective of a single main character, can in different ways be powerful means of conveying ideology. It is interesting, therefore, to observe the modes of narration employed in the novels which will be discussed here.

Another key feature that affects the manner in which a novel can influence social attitudes is its use of intertextuality (see Box 12.1): the insertion into a novel of themes, or references to named or unnamed existing texts, or the use of genres which derive from related or even unrelated fields. For those who are familiar with these earlier texts, references to them may cause a kind of resonance which has a significant effect on their responses to the books which make these intertextual references.

Central to any discussion of literature, but perhaps particularly significant in considering social issues, is an awareness of the ways in which language is used. In many instances, the differences between the dialects and registers employed by characters from different kinds of social backgrounds are foregrounded by the authors, generally in an attempt to influence the attitudes of the young reader. This is certainly the case in several of the novels to be discussed here.

BOX 12.1   INTERTEXTUALITY

While this term was only coined by Julia Kristeva in 1966 as a way of describing the interactions and interdependences between texts (her examples typically deal only with works for an implied audience of adults), as a phenomenon, it has been present in children's literature at least since the eighteenth century, with children's books consciously assuming knowledge of other texts (a famous nineteenth-century example is Louisa May Alcott's use of *Pilgrim's Progress* in *Little Women*) in their readers. Intertextuality refers not simply to the use of quotation, allusion and reference, but to the whole network of ways in which one text is read in relation to all the others that reader and writer have read and will read.

While earlier ways of describing relationships between texts assumed a hierarchy in which newer texts were seen as making use of, and so subservient to, works from earlier epochs, Kristeva argued that intertextuality was based on a relationship between equals. All texts depend on other texts for their meanings – and indeed, for their readers' abilities to decode them. This dynamic is particularly relevant to the use and function of intertextuality in children's literature since young readers are necessarily at the start of their literary histories and so have less of a reservoir of literary texts on which to draw – though they are likely to have a greater knowledge of non-literary texts such as television programmes, commercials, popular music, illustrations, films and cartoons. Moreover, with the increasing numbers of books available, including those which are deliberately intertextual, the order in which texts are encountered by the reader may not be as intended by the writer. For instance, many children today encounter Jon Scieszka's *The True Story of the Three Little Pigs* (1989) before they know the original tale. According to intertextual theory, the order in which the texts are read is unimportant: both will act on and overlay both each other and other texts whenever they are encountered.

Stephens (1992, chapter 3) distinguishes usefully between the *focus* text (the text being read) and seven categories of *intertexts* (texts that are deliberately interpolated, referred to, quoted or otherwise evoked in the focus text). Included in this list are *pre-texts*, or specific earlier texts to which the focus text is consciously and significantly related; for example, the fairy tale *The Three Little Pigs* and Scieszka's retelling of it.

Race, class and the dystopian novel: Robert Swindells's *Daz4Zoe* and Malorie Blackman's *Noughts and Crosses*

Both Blackman and Swindells use a combination of two well-established genres, the romance (see Box 12.2) and dystopia (see Box 12.3), as a way of confronting contemporary social problems. Romance is one of the oldest literary genres, being particularly prevalent during the Middle Ages, but showing its vitality by its continuing appearance in popular films, television, magazines and books. Both Blackman and Swindells adhere to the convention that love conquers all, even when the lovers belong to antagonistic groups.

BOX 12.2 ROMANCE

The term 'romance' is often used to describe two kinds of writing. Its oldest form and meaning date back to the thirteenth century and refer to fictional works, usually concerned with the world of the court and involving quests, heroic deeds, the separation and reuniting of lovers (including parents and children), and often elements of the supernatural. Early romances tended to make up story cycles, and indeed, the individual stories were usually circular in nature, with protagonists ending up where they began and order being restored. From these roots has grown a contemporary genre, often dismissed as slight and escapist, known as romance fiction, written for both adult and teenage (usually female) readers. While preoccupied with the trials, tribulations and thrills arising from romantic relationships rather than heroic deeds, these works nevertheless retain many of the elements from earlier romances, even to making up cycles of stories – many of the most popular examples of romance fiction belong to series, such as Sweet Valley High, Point Romance and the Boyfriend Club. Some sources specifically dealing with adolescent romance fiction include:

- John Calweit, *Adventure, Mystery and Romance: Formula Stories as Art and Popular Culture* (Chicago: University of Chicago Press, 1976).
- Linda K. Christian-Smith, *Becoming a Woman through Romance* (New York: Routledge, 1990).
- Mieke Desmet, 'Love Forever? Teenage Romance Series in the Nineties', unpublished MA thesis, University of Surrey Roehampton, 1999.
- Dave Jenkinson, 'The Young Adult Romance: a Second Glance (Sigh!)' *Emergency Librarian*, 11 (May–June, 1984), pp. 10–13.
- Mike Peters, 'Sweet Hearts and Couples: Teen Romance and the School Library', *School Librarian*, 38(3) (August 1990).

The love in Blackman's novel, between Sephy (a Cross, a member of the dark-skinned, socially dominant class) and Cal (a Nought, one of the low-ranking whites), has developed gradually from their childhood, when the social factors separating them had not yet become fully operative. In Swindells' book, the attraction between Daz and the wealthy Zoe begins at their first sight of each other, and is mutual and all-absorbing.

The dystopia is also very evident in both these novels, set in worlds where society is more polarized than it is today. Swindells has taken to extremes the already existing (in 1990) divisions between the suburbs and the inner cities. The use of established genres does not in any way diminish the originality of Blackman and Swindells, nor indeed does the possibility that, in its use of a romance theme to interrogate a divided society, *Noughts and Crosses* may itself have been influenced by the slightly earlier *Daz4Zoe* diminish the quality of Blackman's response to this subject.

The two novels have much in common, touching on areas such as membership of illegal organizations and the possible justification for terrorism in

---

BOX 12.3 DYSTOPIAN FICTION

The word 'dystopia' was formed by analogy with the well-established 'Utopia' (literally meaning 'nowhere') from the Greek prefix *dys*, meaning 'bad', and *topos*, meaning 'place'. Dystopian fiction is usually set in an imagined, possible, unpleasant future, which has much to say about the writer's and the reader's present. Interestingly, in the closing decades of the twentieth century, dystopian writing for young people increased noticeably, with the element of futurity being diminished. In other words, perhaps in response to social changes associated with 'Thatcherism' and 'Reaganism' and particularly their emphasis on market forces and the needs/rights of the individual rather than society, future dystopias began to be set ever-closer to the time of writing, and the worlds they portray tend to be little different from the reader's own. What makes them conform to the genre of dystopian fiction is that in these works current problems are taken to their logical conclusion, to the detriment of community, environment and personal happiness. The impact of dystopian fiction for juvenile audiences is often undercut by offerering improbably optimistic endings, usually conceived and engineered by young people.

---

an unjust society; in both books, members of the families of the protagonists are victims of judicial execution. There are also certain similarities between the respective family relationships, those between siblings in particular. But perhaps the most significant resemblance, from the literary point of view, is that both novels divide the narration between the two central characters, drawn from opposing ranks of society. Particularly in *Daz4Zoe*, this approach not only intensifies the contrasts between the two characters concerned, but also throws into question the perceptions of both the narrators, possibly leading the reader towards the realization that an objective account of events is impossible.

In *Daz4Zoe*, the difference between the reader's world and the fictional location created by the polarization of society is more evident within the inner city environment of Rawhampton than in the affluent suburbs. Daz has relatively little to say about his background, because it is so familiar to him, but the reader sees the surroundings through Zoe's eyes. Of the Blue Moon club, Daz simply says: 'Nite club. Bands and strippers and pool and that' (14), but Zoe's view is more detailed:

> I looked out and saw what looked like a poky old shop in a dilapidated row. Its window was boarded up and somebody had daubed 'Blue Moon' across the boards with blue paint. ... [we went into] a large, crowded room ... the atmosphere was ninety percent smoke and there was a nauseating smell whose cause I didn't want to think about. (17–19)

Her own perceptions are, however, changed as, under the influence of several 'lobotomisers', she begins to enjoy the atmosphere.

Zoe's sensitivity to smell provides Swindells with a means of guiding the reader's response in the description provided of her view of Daz's home in the tallest block in the town. First she finds herself in a 'dim' lobby outside the flat; it is covered with graffiti, unpleasant puddles bedeck the floor, and she nearly gags on the smell. When she enters the flat, however, her perceptions seem to be influenced by her love for Daz; the flat is significantly cleaner and though she observes the need for repainting, the smell, 'like toadstools', is less repulsive (124–5). Daz has already stated that his mother is suffering from depression: 'Our Mam been down a longtime ... wiv the dulleye' (3), and Zoe's perception of her is scarcely flattering. Although she is no more than forty-five, she appears elderly, and with her dull and worn clothes, she virtually matches the 'saggy, colourless armchairs'. '[Her] Grey hair hung in greasy rat-rails [sic] to her shoulders. White bony fingers gripped the armrests of her chair and she gazed at her son with lustreless eyes' (125–6). The association between the sagging armchair and the woman with her uninspiring garments and physical features, culminating in the 'lustreless' eyes, encourages the reader to share Zoe's low expectations about her. However, there have already been some correctives to this negative view, particularly in the wit which she occasionally displays in her remarks to her son: 'Wear you bin our Daz, sez Mam. no wear Mam, i sez. that's just wear you sed you was going, she sez. she's dry, our mam' (111). Consequently we are not entirely surprised when, despite the negative image, she is instrumental in Zoe's escape by swapping jumpers, wearing the discarded one to prevent it being discovered in a search.

This interplay between the perceptions of Daz and Zoe enables Swindells to relativize the descriptions, forcing the reader towards judgements not only about the settings but also about the people who live in them. The possible initial assumption that nearly all the Chippies are, by their own choice, unwashed and correspondingly unintelligent, is subverted, replaced by admiration for the resilience of those who maintain human values in such an unfavourable environment. The contrast between the living conditions of Blackman's Noughts and Crosses is by no means so extreme, nor does she individualize the perceptions of her narrators to the same extent as Swindells.

As with most children's writers, both Blackman and Swindells are adults writing for a younger audience, and as writers, they almost inevitably espouse middle-class values, a situation of some complexity concerning their positioning as implied authors. While revealing the defects in the education system of the underclass (and, implicitly, because of its bias, also that of the overclass), both novels nevertheless make the humanitarian assumption that the way towards greater equality is through the gradual recognition by members of both groups that their supposed enemies are human beings, a process to which education is essential. Both imply that the actions of illegal organizations with terrorist aims, such as Swindell's DRED and Blackman's Liberation Militia, are likely to be self-defeating, while FAIR, led in Silverdale by Zoe's elderly grandmother, achieves much more positive objectives.

Both writers tend to assume that their teenage readers will share their belief in the essential equality of all humans, while added complexity is supplied by

Blackman's deliberate reversal of power roles within western society. Not only does she make the dark-skinned Crosses the dominant rank, but also she attributes to them many of the worst characteristics of rulers throughout the world, whether black or white. As a black writer, she is clearly on dangerous ground; for oppressed groups, it is always more congenial to claim that if 'we' were in power, society would be much more just than it is when 'they' are in power.

Another situation of some complexity is that regarding romantic love, which is experienced as an irresistible force. The young people who feel this emotion are seen as right to keep their confidences from their parents, an assumption that is likely to appeal to the young reader. Readers who are familiar with the genres of romance and dystopia may form certain expectations about closure, but these may not necessarily be met by the endings of the novels, an aspect which again may throw light on the authors' ideologies. Similarly, those who know, for example, Shakespeare's *Romeo and Juliet* and Orwell's *Nineteen-Eighty-Four* will be aware that romances, and to an even greater extent dystopias, do not necessarily end happily; in this regard the fortunate implied escape of Daz and Zoe at the end of Swindells' book may in fact challenge credibility, though by affording some hope for the human race the author is acceding to the conventions of literature for young people.

While the language used in Blackman's novel is not significantly differentiated between the two main characters, and her originality lies less in her linguistic usage than in her narrative strategy, the language in Swindells' book demands more direct attention. An unusual aspect is Zoe's use of a joke to introduce herself: 'Hi, I'm Zoe. Zoe May Askew. Or Zoe may not. (Joke)' (4). Stephens suggests that such jokes may reflect 'an attempt to subvert what is perceived as the dominant discourse' (1992: 93). It certainly implies that Zoe is likely to question the values of the subby society in which she has been brought up. Her use of language is, however, relatively conventional by comparison with Daz's. In the quotation below, his first utterance, I have used upper case for phonetically spelt words, and italics for coinings:

> Daz THAY call me. 2 years back WEN I COM 13 Del that's my BROVVER THAY catch IM raiding WIV the Dred. Top IM don't THAY, and IM just GON 15.
>
> 2 *lornorders* COM TEL our mam, 1 WUMIN, 1 man, nor THAY don't come TIL after THAY DUNNIT NEEVER. Our Mam been down a longtime FORE then WIV the *dulleye*, and she just sort of STAIRS don't she, TIL THAY go OF, and its not TIL NITE she CRYS.
>
> She SEZ don't you never go OF WIV no Dred, our Daz. No Mam, I SEZ, but I never CROST my HART. Don't COWNT LESS you CROST YOR HART, RITE? (3)

It is easy to see that most of the effect is conveyed by the phonetic spelling, though the coined words, often related to contemporary slang, are an attractive feature. Non-standard syntax also figures largely. Another usage, less obvious in the passage above but evident even in the title of the book, is the use of numbers for words: the numeral 2 meaning 'to' and 'too', and 4 representing 'for'. This device, together with some aspects of the spelling, seems somewhat prescient of the text-messaging popular with twenty-first-century teenagers. It makes it less likely that Daz's use of a form of language very far removed from Zoe's standard English will downgrade him for the reader, or render belief in his status as romantic hero more difficult, though the question remains as to whether he is truly so attractive, or just Zoe's 'bit of rough'. It is significant that at the end of the book, in parallel with the final sentence, 'It was impossible to tell where the city ended and the suburb began,' his language style has fused with hers. Despite its relatively optimistic ending, *Daz4Zoe* has its quota of gritty realism in the picture of the tower blocks, the depressed mother and the difficulties of family relationships.

Gender and disability: Jean Ure's *Cool Simon*

During the 1970s and early 1980s, the focus of equality legislation, and consequently of socially committed children's fiction, tended to be on class, race and gender, but in subsequent years, other issues, notably those of age and disability, have also become significant. Jean Ure's *Cool Simon* integrates an emphasis on gender with a treatment of the subject of disability, to the extent that the disabled title character ultimately becomes instrumental in action against the sexism of some of the other characters – an aspect which in itself reverses the way in which disabled characters seldom have agency and tend to appear largely as objects of pity.

During the 1970s, when authors began to be confronted by issues of racism in British society, the topic of ethnic bias, as distinct from that of slavery, had not received a great deal of attention in earlier children's literature this side of the Atlantic. The issue of gender had, however, inevitably been present earlier. Before about 1960, the omission of black characters from books set in Britain could be justified by the relative rarity of non-indigenous people among the British population, but the omission of female characters from adventure stories, or their casting into secondary roles when they did appear, had always been possible.

Another genre in which gender issues are inevitably raised is the school story (see Chapter 1). By the 1970s, the long tradition of single-sex boarding-school fiction no longer appeared so immediately appealing to children as it had done in the past, though it has subsequently experienced some degree of revival. The mixed day-school environment provided a setting very suitable for dealing with gender bias, as can be seen in Gene Kemp's *The Turbulent Term of Tyke Tiler* (1977) and Anne Fine's *Bill's New Frock* (1989), while Bernard Ashley's *The Trouble with Donovan Croft* (1974) was one of the first books to exploit the potential of the genre for tackling racism.

Writers committed to social change, however, have gradually become aware that other issues also need to be presented to young readers. The 'Grange Hill' TV series (1978–), including its book spin-offs, confronted themes inescapable in a school setting, such as bullying, but also to a lesser extent disability.

Children's literature has had a long history of portraying disabled people as objects for pity, though sometimes they have been demonized, as in the instance of Blind Pew in R. L. Stevenson's *Treasure Island* (1883). At other times, a happy conclusion to the book has demanded a near miraculous cure, as in Susan Coolidge's *What Katy Did* (1872). Gradually, however, the recognition has dawned that to reflect society properly, the position of disabled children needs attention in its own right, particularly as legislation has made them more numerous within mainstream education. Jean Ure, whose output includes a number of books about Woodside School, clearly appreciates the potential of the school setting as a means of confronting prejudice against disabled children. *Cool Simon* (1990) combines the disability theme, in the form of a deaf boy in mainstream education, with that of gender and social isolation, as focalized through a female character, Sam. An incidental added point is that Simon is black; although the race issue is in no way foregrounded in this book, the fact that Simon is an active and attractive character means that anti-racism is indirectly reinforced.

Unlike the two novels discussed above, the narratorial stance in *Cool Simon* is omniscient, though the all-knowing narrator also relies on direct speech from a variety of different voices. The reader is allowed access to places where the children would not be permitted, notably, in chapter 1, the staffroom, where the comments of the teachers establish details about the various pupils, a scene which is followed by the rather differing perceptions vouchsafed by the children themselves, and interspersed by authoritative third-person description. The first of the two central characters to whom the reader is introduced is Samantha Swales, described by the teaching staff as a 'problem' and by her classmates as 'a *pain* [sic]' (3). The description which follows displays the alternation of different voices; I have commented alongside the quotation on the source of the judgement:

> 'Look at her!' Alison Webb ... tossed her hair irritably over her shoulder. 'Great butch thing!' [Child observation]
>
> ... Samantha slouched through the gates. She was dressed just the same as everybody else, in a blouse and skirt, but still she managed to look more like a boy than a girl. It was something to do with the way she had her school bag slung over one shoulder [3rd person narrator] – 'Like a cowboy,' as Shirin had once scornfully said, 'without his horse.' [Child observation]
>
> Sam stood, scowling, just inside the playground. [Another pupil] accidentally brushed against Sam as she went past. You would have thought, from the way Sam furiously chopped at the air with the side of her hand, that it had been some kind of deliberate attack. Sam was *aggressive*. You could tell she was aggressive, just by looking at her. Her face was all scrumpled and pursed from being in a state of permanent crossness. ... (4)

The final section of this quotation, from 'Sam stood' onwards, is all seen from the perspective of the third-person narrator, but the direct address to the reader as 'you' gives the impression of a voice which is no more sympathetic than Alison and Shirin, but rather more sophisticated in use of imagery. The fact that the third-person narrator seems to endorse the negative judgements made by Sam's classmates might be thought to engender dislike of the character, but experienced readers are likely to anticipate that these adverse verdicts will eventually be reversed.

It seems to be Sam's defiance of female stereotypes that most infuriates her classmates; her desire to join the boys' football team rather than playing the gender-approved netball becomes the crux of the plot, and a central image of the resentment she feels against the whole human race, experienced, we learn, ever since her father left home.

Sam's own voice, incidentally, is not heard until her character has been well established by these other voices, and, significantly, when she first speaks it is to point out how useless it is for anyone to shout at Simon. Her friendship with him seems to result from a combination of her implicit realization that, like her, he is an outsider in the class, together with the fact that she has a cousin who is partially deaf. The book, however, reverses the reader's likely initial expectation that it will be Sam who manages to help Simon to achieve his true potential – rather, the disabled character is the means of ensuring that the 'helper' can find her way towards her own goal (literally!). His negotiation of relationships with the other children, largely through his interest in the school rabbit, in fact precedes his own integration into the class and is the means of hers. His success at his previous school has given him enough confidence to rise above the mixture of sympathy ('Poor deaf child, thought Miss Lilly,' 8) and hostility ('Eh! You! What d'you say your stupid name was?') with which he is confronted, though he is still less than happy that the sports master seems to assume that the only position in which a deaf boy can play is goal, whereas at his previous school he had played midfield. After he triumphs through his courage in rescuing the school rabbit from a fire, he obtains agency, not only achieving a midfield position in the football team for himself but also being able to insist that Sam too is allowed to play. In the context of narration it is significant that his is the final voice we hear in the text: 'I goo Dimon an' you my fred ...' (154); by now, readers, like his classmates, are able to understand his use of language. It is clear that despite Simon's being the eponymous hero of the book, it is Sam's isolation that has been the real issue; paradoxically, Simon, despite deafness being a notoriously isolating condition, has never been as alone as Sam.

Ure's technique of using a diversity of voices tends to undercut any authority given to the omniscient narrator, and is likely to leave the reader uncertain about the 'correct' attitude to take towards Sam (though it is generally clear that Simon's character should be seen positively). This has the effect of communicating Sam's feeling of uncertainty, even exclusion, and making the final reversal, when Simon insists on her being included in the team, all the more powerful. It also means that it would be difficult to state categorically which is the strongest theme of the book – gender, race, disability or, indeed, the effect on a child of emotional distress and the way that this may isolate her from her classmates.

Sexuality and religion: Virginia Euwer Wolff's *True Believer*

Children's fiction from the mid-1970s until near the end of the twentieth century was often criticized for being too 'issue-laden', leaving children no escape from confronting social problems. Certainly a number of authors seem to have been driven by their social consciences to make children aware both of issues involving the environment and of the situation of under-privileged people within otherwise prosperous societies. The creation of future worlds was seen as one way of alerting young readers to the effect of pollution and climate change on the environment (as in Peter Dickinson's *Eva*, 1988, and Lesley Howarth's *Ultraviolet*, 2001), while a number of writers, including Robert O'Brien (*Z for Zachariah*, 1974), Robert Swindells (*Brother in the Land*, 1984) and Louise Lawrence (*Children of the Dust*, 1985), have grappled with the theme of nuclear holocaust. (See also, the section on Further Reading at the end of the chapter.)

Other writers, however, seem to have felt that portraying their characters within a 'real' world was more appropriate to the consideration of immediate social problems such as drugs (Maureen Stewart's *Out of It*, 1995, and Melvin Burgess's *Junk*, 1996) and pre-marital pregnancy (Berlie Doherty's *Dear Nobody*, 1991; Kate Cann's *In the Deep End*, 1997 and Sue Welford's *Nowhere to Run*, 1999). Many of the novels of Jacqueline Wilson deal with social problems: inadequate parents (*The Story of Tracey Beaker*, 1991, *The Illustrated Mum*, 1999); poor housing (*The Bed and Breakfast Star*, 1994); and the repercussions of divorce (*The Suitcase Kid*, 1992). Jean Ure, as well as confronting issues such as environmental pollution and disability, has treated the difficult subject of a child dying (*Becky Bananas: This is your Life*, 1997), as has Lois Lowry in *A Summer to Die* (1977).

True Believer, a recent book by the American writer Virginia Euwer Wolff, depicts the economic struggles of people marginalized by affluent societies; it also includes two main additional areas of social comment. One of these, the problematization of the small religious sects which are particularly attractive to people whose personal circumstances render them powerless, is relatively uncommon in contemporary British children's fiction. The other, the disclosure of the homosexuality of one of the significant characters, is a theme which is becoming more prominent in children's fiction as social legislation insisting on equality in relation to sexual preferences becomes more frequent in western countries.

Rather unusually, Wolff's novel, like *Make Lemonade* (1995), its predecessor in a trilogy focusing on the same first-person narrator, a female high-school student named LaVaughn, is written in what might be described as a kind of prose poetry. Although this is without rhyme or any regular pattern of rhythm, its presentation on the page in short lines and use of saturated language creates emphasis and allows for the foregrounding of certain words and images. The beliefs of the 'Joyful Universal Church', in which, for reasons related to their poor home backgrounds, LaVaughn's two friends have sought emotional refuge, appear all the more threatening when expressed in this mode. La Vaughn's straightforward view that there is a force responsible for creation is contrasted with the more threatening ideas of her friends:

> Myrtle & Annie and me went all through this subject before.
> But now they have new news.
> Myrtle & Annie say all Muslims and Jews and Hindus
> and other religions will go to Hell
> along with criminal and sexual teenagers
> and all tribes of foreign lands
> that have not come to Jesus and the Bible
> which they say God wrote.   (18)

The way the reader's eye needs to pause momentarily and revert to the left-hand margins means that particular emphasis is conveyed to the significant words at the ends of the lines, highlighting the intolerance expressed. Wolff's hostility to the rigid tenets of this church is evident, though it is also apparent that what has attracted the two girls to it is the sense of community, together with that of being 'special' as members of the 'chosen', while the rest of humanity will be damned.

Unlike her friends, LaVaughn is blessed in having a stable home background, even though her mother is a single parent; indeed, her mother's effective campaigning and care for the underprivileged make her a strong role model for LaVaughn. Readers feel confident that the girl's resilience and intelligence will prevent her from being perpetually mired in the adverse environment in which she currently lives. Her school in particular, which runs language-based special classes for pupils who have academic potential, is portrayed as an effective agent for change. One of the teachers, Dr Rose, outlines her belief in the potential of all her pupils, and that, despite the statistics, 'they can make a difference in the vast and terrifying and magnificent world' (170).

Like most of the other novelists discussed here, Wolff uses language as an indicator of social status and frequently as a means of directing the reader's attitudes towards the characters. The social presumptiveness of Lester, the boyfriend of LaVaughn's mother, whose falsity they both eventually detect, is shown by his pronunciation:

> Lester says eyther and nyther
> in addition to vahze. I asked my mom.
> 'Well, Lester has high standards,' she explains.   (111)

Other linguistic variations are shown in the elaborate games played between LaVaughan and her classmate Patrick with scientific language, such as 'endoplasmic reticulum' (126).

Despite their occasional shared jokes, LaVaughn takes little notice of Patrick's obvious interest in her, for she is blinded by her romantic yearning for Jody, a boy she knew when they were both younger, who is now for her the acme of perfection. Much of the plot concerns her elaborate plans about how she may meet up with him while giving the impression the meeting was a chance one – a situation familiar to many teenagers! When he is ill and away from school, at a time when she feels rejected by her two friends, she resolves to take Jody in his neighbouring apartment some 'get-well cookies' that she has baked and placed in an elaborate pattern on a plate. She enters the apartment, worried about protecting her pattern, but sees

> ... two people, just their heads
> partly hidden behind the [fish] tank.
> Like they were whispering to each other ...
> and I recognized Jody but not the other one,
> I only noticed it was a boy.
> I stood ice-still and I saw their mouths go together and stay
> and I froze.
> The plate of cookies went straight onto the rug
> and my lifetime jumped upside down.   (193)

In its heightened descriptions and perhaps particularly the way in which the broken cookies image LaVaughn's fragmented illusions about romantic love, this passage provides ample evidence that dealing with social issues does not imply that an author will make use of impoverished language.

The message of this novel is one of tolerance for people's differences, given form in a complex final scene at the birthday party where LaVaughn becomes reconciled to Jody's sexuality, and also realizes that she has been punishing Patrick 'for not being Jody' (263). Finally the presence of Myrtle and Annie, and of two children, whom LaVaughn had previously looked after for their needy single-parent mother, provide her with an element of hope:

> I feast my eyes on this amazing birthday
> and I think I can live with the way life is.   (264)

Asylum seekers and Beverley Naidoo's *The Other Side of Truth*

Another area that has recently received a good deal of attention is the plight of people excluded from everyday society, a theme which in different ways has always preoccupied Beverley Naidoo. Her fiction is more strongly politicized than that of many children's writers, perhaps because her identity as a white South African did not allow her to shirk the issue of inequality. In a personal account (in Pinsent, 2001), Naidoo describes the evolution of her novels. Her best known earlier novels, *Journey to Jo'burg* (1985) and *Chain of Fire* (1989), are set in South Africa before apartheid finished, while *No Turning Back* (1995) reveals that its end did not immediately bring a good life to street children in Johannesburg (see Chapter 11). Naidoo's *The Other Side of Truth* is mostly located in Britain, and is one of the most hard-hitting children's novels dealing with the plight of asylum seekers.

Like the other socially committed fiction discussed here, the narratorial stance and the use of intertextuality in this novel reward attention. When Sade and Feme, escaping from Nigeria where their mother has been assassinated, are abandoned at Victoria Station by Mrs Bankole, who should have taken them to their uncle, their plight has an inescapable similarity to that of the 'Babes in the Wood' or 'Hansel and Gretel'. Since she was standing in for their own dead mother, Mrs Bankole is something of a wicked stepmother, and the resemblance is reinforced by a reference to the way in which the huge buildings nearby 'loomed over the narrow pavements like a thick forest of brick, concrete and glass' (48). For the reader who detects it, this parallel may, however implicitly, work as a promise of an ultimately happy ending.

The urban environment has other threats, also presented intertextually; in the sequence where the children are lost, they encounter a figure who robs them, whom Sade sees as 'Darth Vader of the alley looming up above them, his arm sweeping away their holdall' (58), thus referring to a *Star Wars* character who is the 'dark lord' of an 'evil empire' (Carpenter and Prichard, 1984: 495). The reader nurtured on fairy tale and space fiction will certainly have been expecting monsters and ogres to loom out of the darkness and cold, yet here again the intertextual reference serves to remind us that in such tales, good almost always ultimately triumphs.

A rather different variety of intertextuality is supplied by the tortoise story (191–3) which their father tells Sade and Femi in a letter he writes to them. As he points out, this story, derived from African folklore, represents the tortoise as being artful, cunning, sensible, wise, courageous and daring. Threatened by Leopard and allowed only five minutes before he is devoured, Tortoise marks the earth deeply, so that the struggle between them will be remembered. As well as being a very appropriate story to be told by a journalist who wants the world to know about evils in his country, the story suggests survival (will the leopard in fact be able to penetrate the tortoise's shell?); it also serves to remind the child characters, and thus the reader, of the richness and complexity of the African folk-tale tradition, in which the tortoise is often portrayed as a lovable trickster. The tortoise is again referred to near the end of the novel, as an image for the forced mobility of the family: 'Wherever they went, they would have to become like tortoises who carry their homes on their backs. [Sade] thought of Papa's brave tortoise and hoped that at least they would not have to meet any more leopards' (222).

The narrative approach of *The Other Side of Truth* differs from that of the other books which have been discussed, yet it too bears a close connection with the way in which Naidoo conveys her message. The focal character is Sade, and access to the thoughts of other characters is generally only available if mediated through what they say to her. The narrative is generally conveyed to the reader through Sade's consciousness; this is often signalled by the use of expressions that only she would use, as in the words I have italicized here: 'The *Brass Button* officers at the airport would be on alert for *Papa* himself' (75). Frequently, Sade's perceptions are presented conditionally, as if the third-person narrator is speaking ventriloquially: 'She [Mrs King] seemed quite tall but that might have been because her thick grey hair was piled up high' (99);

certitude is no more available to the narrator than to Sade, who has presumably made this judgement. Naidoo frequently uses images to elucidate thoughts and situations; such images may be attributed directly to Sade's thought processes: 'Sade imagined a string pulling up her head like a puppet' (99). Quite often, however, there is a degree of uncertainty as to whether or not Sade has actually made the comparison: 'Sade watched in horror, her own silent tears trapped within her, like in a stone. Grief burst around them like a pierced boil' (3). The effect of this technique is that there is a centrality to Sade's perceptions, together with the impression that a more knowledgeable adult is both approving them and working outwards through them.

Additional insights are offered in two main ways, both signalled by changes of typographical font. Sade's father's letters, like Sade's to him and her grandmother, and her class teacher's to her, are printed to resemble type-writing, which inevitably singles them out as carrying a different kind of authority from the rest of the text. They reveal thoughts and events that are not accessible to Sade, unlike other passages, which are italicized to give a kind of dream-like effect, often harking back to earlier scenes thus recalled to Sade's consciousness. The murder scene (chapter 1) is not only repeated almost verbatim (chapter 11), but it is also distorted by a dream (117) where Sade's fear of the school bullies is conflated with her anguish at her mother's death and her feelings of guilt that her tardiness in getting ready for school had delayed their departure and made the family more vulnerable.

Another variant on the nearly exclusive use of Sade's consciousness is the story of her friend Mariam, which is recounted without any access to Sade's response being interspersed (140). This technique gives this chapter a greater impression of objective reportage than is carried by the rest of the book.

Looking at Naidoo's approaches to narrative reveals that this book, which may appear to be a relatively artless production, is in fact a complex tissue of different modes. These enable the reader to take different subject positions and to be encouraged towards forming what feels like an 'objective' judgement, while still remaining close to the perceptions of the focal character.

Conclusion

The extent to which literature can influence attitudes remains a debatable issue, though children's authors from time immemorial have accepted without question that it does so, something which advertisers and writers of newspaper leader columns also continue to assume. Beverley Naidoo herself has done some important research into the extent to which children's literature can influence attitudes; this is presented in *Through Whose Eyes: Exploring Racism: Reader, Text and Context* (1992). More recently, in a talk at University of Surrey Roehampton, Naidoo spoke explicitly about her intentions in writing her books, all of which, as she says, 'deal with – and reveal – the impact of the political world on the lives of young people' (14). She described how her books were an attempt to 'win the heart', to make her own and other fortunate children aware of human suffering, adding:

I have always believed in the power of fiction and story. ... Whether readers' responses emerge from imaginative empathy or a sense of identification with one or other of my characters, what is most important to me is that their imaginations have been fired, emotions and intellects stirred. That knowledge is surely one of the best rewards that a writer can receive. (15; 20)

Authors such as Swindells, Blackman, Ure, Wolff, Naidoo and many others have made their social commitment explicit, both within and outside their work. The ways that they seek to fire the imagination of their readers are undoubtedly more subtle than is the case with earlier children's writers, but they are all the more likely therefore to appeal to young readers, who would probably be resistant to over-explicit ideology.

WORKS CITED AND FURTHER READING

Primary Texts

Blackman, M., *Noughts and Crosses* (London: Transworld, 2001).
Naidoo, B., *The Other Side of Truth* (London: Puffin, 2000).
Swindells, R., *Daz4Zoe* (London: Puffin, 1992; first published 1990).
Ure, J., *Cool Simon* (London: Orchard Books, 1990).
Wolff, V. E., *True Believer* (London: Faber, 2001).

Critical Texts

Booktrusted News, issue 2 (Autumn 2002), featuring disability.
Hollindale, P., *Ideology and the Children's Book* (Stroud: Thimble Press, 1994; first published 1988).
Keith, L., *Take up thy Bed and Walk* (London: The Women's Press, 2001).
Leeson, R., *Reading and Righting* (London: Collins, 1985).
Naidoo, B., *Through Whose Eyes? Exploring Racism: Reader, Text, Context* (Stoke-on-Trent: Trentham Books, 1992).
Pinsent, P., *Children's Literature and the Politics of Equality* (London: David Fulton, 1997).
Pinsent, P. (ed.), *The Big Issues: Representations of Socially Marginalized Groups and Individuals in Children's Literature, Past and Present* (London: NCRCL, 2001).
Saunders, K., *Happy Ever Afters: A Storybook Guide to Teaching Children about Disability* (Stoke-on-Trent: Trentham Books, 2000).

Children's Books

Ashley, B., *The Trouble with Donovan Croft* (Oxford: Oxford University Press, 1974).
Burgess, M., *Junk* (London: Andersen Press, 1996).
Cann, K., *In the Deep End* (London: Livewire, 1997).
Dickinson, P., *Eva* (London: Gollancz, 1988).
Doherty, B., *Dear Nobody* (London: Hamish Hamilton, 1991).
Fine, A., *Bill's New Frock* (London: Methuen, 1989).

Garnett, E., *The Family from One End Street* (first published 1937; Harmondsworth: Penguin, 1967).

Gleitzman, M., *Sticky Beak* (London: Macmillan, 1994).

Howarth, L., *Ultraviolet* (Harmondsworth: Puffin, 2001).

Jung, R., *Dreaming in Black and White*, trans. from the German by Anthea Bell (London: Mammoth, 2000).

Kemp, G., *The Turbulent Term of Tyke Tiler* (London: Faber, 1977).

Lawrence, L., *Children of the Dust* (London: Bodley Head, 1985).

Lowry, Lois., *A Summer to Die* (London: Granada, 1977).

Naidoo, B., *No Turning Back* (London: Viking, 1995).

Naidoo, B., *Out of Bounds* (London: Puffin, 2001).

O'Brien, R., *Z for Zachariah* (London: Collins, 1974).

Stewart, M., *Out of It* (Harmondsworth: Puffin, 1995).

Swindells, R., *Brother in the Land* (Oxford: Oxford University Press, 1984).

Ure, J., *Becky Bananas: This is your Life* (London: Collins, 1997).

Welford, S., *Nowhere to Run* (Oxford: Oxford University Press, 1999).

Westall, R., *Future Track 5* (Harmondsworth: Kestrel, 1983).

Wilson, J., *The Story of Tracey Beaker* (London: Transworld, 1991); *The Illustrated Mum* (London: Transworld, 1999); *The Bed and Breakfast Star* (London: Transworld, 1994); *The Suitcase Kid* (London: Transworld, 1992).

Wolff, V. E., *Make Lemonade* (London: Faber, 1995).

Picturebooks with Socially Committed Themes

Burningham, J., *Granpa* (London: Cape, 1984).

Burningham, J., *Oi! Get Off Our Train* (London: Random House, 1991).

Glen, M., *Maggie* (London: Random House, 1990).

Guy, R., *Billy the Great*, illustrated by Caroline Binch (London: Gollancz, 1991).

Hathorn, L., *Way Home*, illustrated by G. Rogers (London: Andersen Press, 1994).

Hoban, R., *Mole*, illustrated by J. Pienkowski (London: Jonathan Cape, 1993).

Hoffmann, M., *Amazing Grace*, illustrated by Caroline Binch (London: Frances Lincoln, 1991); *Grace and Family* (London: Frances Lincoln, 1995); *An Angel Just Like Me*, illustrated by Cornelius van Wright and Ying-Hwa Hu (London: Frances Lincoln, 1997).

Rosen, M., *This is Our House*, illustrated by Bob Graham (London: Walker, 1996).

Schermbrucker, R., *Charlie's House*, illustrated by Niki Daly (London: Walker, 1989).

Sendai, M., *We're All in the Dumps with Jack and Guy* (New York: Michael DI Cap Books and HarperCollins, 1993).

Wheatley, N., *My Place*, illustrated by D. Rawlins (Sydney: Collins Dove, 1988).

Wilkins, V., *Boots for a Bridesmaid*, illustrated by Pamela Venus (Camberley: Tamarind, 1995).

Reading Contemporary Picturebooks

Judith Graham

Picturebooks are a distinct and diverse area of children's literature that offers contemporary artists, illustrators, designers and book-makers a unique art form combining narrative (whether or not words are used) and image. Reading picturebooks well requires readers to be alert to different elements from those associated with novels or illustrated books; not least the book as an object. As Judith Graham explains in this chapter, the best picturebooks are usually complete designs, incorporating covers, end papers, layout, typography, format, and size. They also pay attention to the potential for dramatic effect in each turn of the page.

Perhaps more than most areas of book production, the creation of picturebooks has been closely linked to developments in printing technology, with illustrators and printers working together to push technology to new limits. In recent decades picturebooks have been transformed by the use of colour throughout, and also through their interactions with new media.

Picturebooks are almost invariably the first books that children encounter. This means that they shape aesthetic tastes, and introduce the principles and conventions of narrative. In all these ways picturebooks are a vital part of artistic and literary culture, but they are also witty, entertaining and part of the child's world of play. This chapter, and the case study of Raymond Briggs that follows, reflect all these aspects of the form and offer practical ideas for working with picturebooks.

Note: There is a problem for critics discussing picturebooks because it is common to find that the pages and spread are unnumbered. In this chapter and Chapter 14, whenever specific pages and spreads are referred to and the original text is unnumbered, numbers have been provided by counting pages, starting with the title page, which becomes page 1. This includes the usual page of publisher's information, since this often also carries textual material of a variety of kinds.

Illustration is everywhere; not only in children's books but in books for all ages; in comics and magazines; in advertisements, on posters, on food and other packaging, in brochures and on the television and computer screen. Though many of these outlets for illustration seem utterly contemporary, illustration has been around for a long time, perhaps over three thousand years if we think of Egyptian papyrus rolls, and it pre-dates printing by one thousand five hundred years. In its purist sense, illustration is a series of pictures connected to a text and 'illuminating' it in every sense of that word. Illustration in children's books may be simply decorative, but more often it aims to interpret or supply narrative meaning that is not present or accessible in written text alone. Two succinct definitions of picturebooks (rather than illustrated books) are useful to hold in the mind.

> A picturebook is a text, illustrations, total design; an item of manufacture and a commercial product; a social, cultural, historical document; and foremost an experience for a child. As an art form, it hinges on the interdependence of pictures and words, on the simultaneous display of two facing pages, and on the drama of the turning page.   (Bader, 1976: 1)

> Picturebooks – books intended for young children which communicate information or tell stories through a series of many pictures combined with relatively slight text or no text at all – are unlike any other form of verbal or visual art.   (Nodelman, 1988: vii)

Bader and Nodelman define the picturebook; the illustrated book usually has a written text that, whilst it may be enhanced by the illustrations, can survive without them and indeed may have existed without them for a great many years. Few, if any, picturebooks are republished with a different set of illustrations; illustrated texts frequently reappear with new illustrations, with *Alice's Adventures in Wonderland* perhaps topping the charts as the most frequently re-illustrated children's book. Though both are equally valid art forms and both have contributed significantly to children's literature, this chapter is primarily concerned with the picturebook rather than the illustrated book.

It would be wrong to imagine that reading a picturebook is a simple operation. When John Burningham's *Come Away from the Water, Shirley* was first published in 1977, it was apparent that many adults, expecting pictures to duplicate the written text, were bemused by the apparent mismatch and failed to see the more subtle interaction going on between word and picture. In this book, as in many picturebooks, the words are few and can be read in a short space of time, but the pictures need more time and scrutiny if their detail and meaning are to be perceived. Becoming alert to the way a written text constantly pushes the reader while a picture stops us in our tracks and slows down the reading is the first requirement for students in their appreciation of picturebooks. As Nodelman puts it: '[The] sort of ironic relationship between the sequential storytelling of words and the series of stopped moments we see in a sequence of pictures is, I believe, the essence of picturebook storytelling (239).

It is also important to appreciate how very varied the picturebook can be. Pictures in reading schemes may intentionally show what the written text indicates ('here is a dog'; 'here is a ball') but most illustrators are more ambitious than that and will aim for the unusual or unexpected, a secondary story, a running gag, a surreal embroidering, incongruity, ambiguity and irony, even in books aimed at the youngest audience. Writers will also want to focus on what words can do best (what things and people are called, what people say and think, when things happen, what happened earlier or later – off-stage as it were) and eliminate language made superfluous by the illustration. Illustration is better suited to creating mood and atmosphere, using colour, tone, light and dark; showing characters' clothes, faces and expressions of feeling; or representing their spatial relationship to one another and what places look like.

A popular picturebook, *Handa's Surprise* (1994) by Eileen Browne, exemplifies some of these points and is a good example of how the picturebook medium can be effectively exploited. As with Pat Hutchins' well-known *Rosie's Walk* (1968), it is a perfect example of the written text and the pictured text being balanced to provide different information. Handa is preparing a present of seven delicious fruits to take to her friend Akeyo in the next village. Off she goes, basket on head, speculating on which fruit Akeyo will like best. Unknown to her, and uncommented on by the narrator but seen by the reader, the pieces of fruit are filched from the basket by seven different animals.

Just as Handa arrives at Akeyo's village with her now empty basket, a goat breaks free from its tether and, after a series of small frames showing his headlong charge, butts a tangerine tree. The tangerines conveniently fall into the basket (the mound breaks through the frame to draw the reader's attention). Akeyo's delight at the gift of tangerines, her favourite fruit, is only matched by Handa's surprise. The delight that young readers experience in realizing what is happening ahead of Handa and of the narrator bonds them to the book and makes each re-reading an exciting experience. In this book, and this is different from *Rosie's Walk*, the written text does something that it is difficult for pictures to do: it gives us Handa's thoughts. 'Will she like the spiky-leaved pineapple, the creamy green avocado or the tangy purple passion fruit?'

With such a wealth of picture and illustrated books available, it is necessary to try to impose an order if newcomers to the field are to have any chance of finding a way through. I have chosen to divide the field into four categories and within those categories to discuss a few titles in detail.

Books of pictures

Into this category come those books with minimal written text, which are designed particularly for the inspection and enjoyment of the pictures. The written text is not only minimal; it is frequently a 'given', with little or no variation possible, as in the case of most alphabet and counting books. Concept books, designed to teach colours, shapes, materials, animals, and much else, also come into this category. Whilst there are obvious restrictions in terms of what may be done with the written text in such books, the very constraint seems to attract and inspire illustrators. There are ABCs dating from the mid-eighteenth century (which is when we can say children's books began), and several of those created in the nineteenth century (those of Edward Lear and Kate Greenaway, for instance) are still obtainable. Currently, there are thousands of alphabet books and thousands of counting books and probably tens of thousands of concept books. Many of these are extraordinarily inventive and even approach being works of art. Many of the most talented illustrators are drawn to create an alphabet at some point in their careers and the originality on show is impressive.

These books may appear to be produced for the youngest children, but it should not be forgotten how much readers know and need to know if they are to enjoy books. The 'rules', codes and conventions for reading words and pictures have to be learned (technical terms describing this process, which is unconscious in most readers, are found in Box 13.1). At six months, babies tend to chew their books, explaining why 'rag' books have come into being. They may hold their books the 'wrong' way round, they may turn the pages from back to front and possibly turn several pages at a time. This is not only a question of manual dexterity; the appreciation that stories have a logical sequence, requiring readers to start at the beginning and look from top to bottom and from left to right (though not in all scripts), is a necessary aspect of a child's learning. Many children's books tell their stories through double-page spreads, which may not obviously be organized on the principles of left and right, so learning how to read these has to be mastered too.

Many other intellectual/perceptual challenges face the young child. Looking out of a window, the view could be considered to make a picture. Yet it is utterly different from a printed image, particularly because everything is moving. How do we come to accept static representations? How do we learn that objects shown in two dimensions, sometimes far too small, occasionally too big, stand for those objects in real life? Why do we accept heavy lines drawn around items, the incompleteness of some items, the fact that back-grounds may be absent so that the characters appear to float in space?

A further challenge is that the child is asked to accept things that are never normally encountered in life. Perhaps more than half the output of children's books features animals or toys as characters, often in clothing, usually speaking, living in recognizable human houses and behaving rather as humans do. And then there is a whole cast of witches, monsters, dragons, goblins and others who are pictured for us but which have parallels, if at all, only in our heads. Even when children are the main characters, they may seem to exist without adults to care for them, and they often do impossible things. Of course, such books appeal to children for a variety of reasons to do with their inner lives and their delight in topsy-turvydom; nevertheless, the taking on board of these facets of picturebooks has to be learned.

Helen Oxenbury is an author and illustrator who, in the thirty-plus years that she has been at work, has created several classic books for babies and several award-winning books for older children. Her *ABC of Things* (1967) encapsulates many of the characteristics of the book of pictures. The organizing principle of the alphabet is probably lost on most of the children who are looking at the book, though naming the pictured items will certainly

BOX 13.1   VISUAL TERMINOLOGY

Bleed   A picture in a picturebook 'bleeds' or is 'bled' to the very edge of the paper when it has no frame and leaves no margin. The effect is to pull the reader more actively into the picture (cf: 'frame').

Closure   Of particular relevance to comic strips, this refers to the way in which readers must make sense of (interpret) the gaps in information left between one frame and the next (McCloud, 1994: 60–93).

Double-page spread   An opening in a picturebook where the image spreads over the two facing pages (cf: 'page opening').

Endpapers   The pages (in hardbacks) which are immediately inside the front and back covers. The story in a picturebook often starts or ends here, though the illustrator may use the endpapers decoratively or symbolically. Paperback picturebooks are sometimes, regrettably, published without the original endpapers.

Format   The physical size and shape of the book. 'Portrait' format is taller than it is wide; 'landscape' is wider than it is tall. The choice should be influenced by the nature of the illustration, with portrait more commonly used when a focus on character is required and landscape for when the setting is more important.

Frame   The border around an illustration, which may simply be the white margin of the page or can be a printed line, a drawn free-hand line or a decorated band. Often the separate illustrations on a page are called separate frames. When a picture bursts through a frame ('breaks' the frame'), extra momentum and significance is added. 'Frame' is also used occasionally in a very different sense to indicate everything about a book that is not the text; in other words, those elements, such as author's and illustrator's names, title, blurb, typographic aspects, publishing details, etc. which surround the book and package it (cf: 'peritext').

Gutter   The grooved space at the centre of a book, created by the binding, where pages abut; the space between frames in a comic strip or between different frames on one page of a picturebook.

Page opening   Where the picture on the left is distinct from the picture on the right.

Page turn   Turning the page in a picturebook is a different experience from turning over the page in an unillustrated text; it requires the reader to pause and peruse the picture. At the same time, the written text (if there is one) – especially if the turn comes in the middle of a sentence – impels the reader to turn over. The text may sometimes foreshadow the next picture so that the reader is in a state of high anticipation as the page is turned. Turning the page may also reveal surprising information or effects. All of this creates a typical picturebook rhythm for the reader, whether reading aloud or silently.

Peritext   All the material that is not the text itself (cf. 'frame' above). In a picturebook where the illustrations and written text together count as text, the peritext does not include the illustrations, though a case could be made for the peritext to include the cover illustration. Typically, the peritext is not in the author's nor in the illustrator's control and is the domain of designers, typographers, publishers, publicity and marketing people.

Pictorial/Iconic sequence   Of particular relevance to comic strips, this refers to pictorial or iconic frames placed in a narrative sequence (as opposed to the self-contained frames you might find in illustrations).

Recto   The right-hand page of a book.

Speech bubble   Typically found in comic strips and graphic texts, this refers to dialogue contained within a stylized 'bubble' and which is usually superimposed onto pictorial images. Speech bubbles frequently break frames (see 'frames') and can be used to indicate who is speaking, or to convey sound.

Tone   The level of brightness, lightness or darkness used in coloured images.

Verso   The left-hand page of a book.

Viewpoint   The position from which the reader views the illustrations. There may be a static viewpoint, where the illustrations are seen from the same point throughout, or the illustrator may change the viewpoint from, perhaps, a high position where the scene is surveyed from above, to a low viewpoint, where the image dominates.

be a game that develops. The primary interest is the pictures. The left-hand page shows the upper and lower case letter 'A', the right-hand page shows a large, exquisitely drawn apple with an ant crawling on it. The words, 'ant' and 'apple' are given at the bottom of the left-hand page. So far, so ordinary, though a lesser illustrator might have been content with just the apple.

But Helen Oxenbury is a narrative illustrator, and even in that first simple image, which combines the items, there is the germ of a story. 'B' follows, with 'baby', 'badger', 'baker', 'bear' and 'bird'. The image shows the weariest of bakers submitting to the other creatures, who swarm all over him. Oxenbury is guiding the child to see cause (four demanding creatures) and effect (fatigue), a skill that will be necessary in reading texts in the future. 'C' has a cow and a cat waiting in pleasant anticipation, bibs in place, for a crow to bring a cake with candles. And so we go on. Every now and again the image covers the two pages of an opening, changing the rhythm of the book agreeably. There is no connection between pages, so making narrative links between the openings is not required of the young reader. But the book goes beyond the average ABC book in terms of the narrative interest within each picture, in the surprising combinations, the humour and the careful draughtsmanship.

Counting is something children do even before they learn the alphabet, so inviting a child into the world of numbers and counting interests illustrators. Mitsumaso Anno is one of Japan's leading illustrators and designers and, as well as an ingenious alphabet book, which has the designated letter apparently but impossibly fashioned from wood, he has produced *Anno's Counting Book* (1977). There is a simplicity to the design of this book, with each double-page spread exemplifying the numerals up to twelve. As you can see in Figure 9, each picture, neatly framed and drawn and therefore read from a fixed position, shows a landscape bisected by a river, but, as the numbers increase, so do the numbers of children, adults, birds, buildings, trees, animals and much else. Child beholders need to bring what they have counted, sorted,

Figure 9   Mitsumasa Anno's *Anno's Counting Book* – spot the builders with their plans

classified or grouped from one picture to the next. So, on page one, the reader identifies a single sun, a single house, a single boy and a single girl, but for the number two, the memory of what has happened on the previous page needs to be evoked so that when the picture shows that a church has been built, it is now necessary to talk about two *buildings*. Similarly, the boy and the girl now count as two *children*, and Anno has helpfully grouped them together. Frequently, as the numbers mount, the image shows, for example, two cats facing three cats, so that there is an opportunity not only to count but also to add. As well as one-to-one correspondences, groups and sets, there are the changing seasons, and human activities to observe. Those familiar with Anno's wordless travel books will know that it is worth poring over every picture to detect additional narrative details. For instance, just before the page turns from '7' to '8', readers can spot the builders who will construct building number eight, looking at their plan.

An intriguing concept book, which could also be discussed in the category of wordless picturebooks below since the title is the only written text, is *The Colors* (1991) by the Swiss illustrator Monique Felix. Some readers will already know the small mouse, who is the main character in Felix's previous titles where, trapped in the books, he needs to nibble his way to freedom. In *The Colors*, he nibbles his way *into* the book (the hard cover has a tangible hole and teeth marks) and through the page to find he is alongside the art materials of a young girl who we can see leaving the room. Colours, first of all the three primary colours, are introduced to the reader by the small mouse, who squeezes oils from the tubes of paint and then runs over to the empty left-hand page with his loaded paintbrush. With great effort, he squeezes two tubes together to make green, then orange and then purple. He dunks himself in the jam-jar of water and escapes through his hole in the page just before the girl returns – with a cat who looks as if she can smell mouse!

The series of pictures is enjoyable on many levels: the conceit of eating through the very pages that the reader is turning; the use of the pages as the mouse runs between paint box on the right and empty page on the left; the tension that builds up as we see the mess the mouse is making; the astonishment, mischief and delight present in the mouse's expression. Playing with the very form of the book in this way and telling a story, without the use of words, gives this concept book great added value.

In addition to the understanding about how pictures and books work, which children need to have acquired in order to enter a text, they must also realize that here, although the mouse is shown several times in a single picture, this does not mean that there are several mice in the story. Moreover, there are gaps between the pictures: not every race across the page is shown; children must fill in the unpictured events. The perspective has to be understood: the door through which the girl disappears and reappears is tiny as the angle of viewpoint is on the nearby table top. Perhaps most challenging is the conceit of the drawn hole that the mouse has nibbled. Child readers cannot poke a finger through it (as in Eric Carle's *The Very Hungry Caterpillar*, 1968) but must read the delicate pencil lines as representing a hole.

Novelty books

Into this category come those books where the reader lifts flaps, pulls tabs, spins discs, reveals three-dimensional panoramas on the turn of the page, removes items from integrated pockets or envelopes, unfolds hinged pages, looks through holes, turns over half-pages and engages with the book in many another active way. 'Movable' is the more accurate term for those books where the reader physically manipulates a device in the book. Such books come closer to toys than other books, though these are often more fragile than toys, and the best of such books are those in which the paper engineering is not merely clever, but closely linked to the story.

Some of the most successful novelty books are designed for very small children and have simple flaps, holes or half-pages. Rod Campbell's *Dear Zoo* (1982), Jan Ormerod's *Peek-a-boo!* (1997), and Lucy Cousins's *Where Does Maisy Live?* (2000) are all small masterpieces, principally because the folded paper flap is integral to the story. So, each animal that is sent to the narrator in *Dear Zoo* arrives in its own crate/box/basket, and the reader must reveal its occupant before sending it back. Jan Ormerod's babies are playing the timeless game of peep-bo and so, to see their faces, the reader must peel back the towel, the dress, the quilt, the teddy, the gloved hands, the bib. Looking for Maisy involves opening up the henhouse, pigsty, kennel, and stable before she is found in her house.

The Ahlbergs, with *The Jolly Postman*, created a hugely significant, multi-layered novelty book which seemed to have everything to engage the reader: rhyming text, fairy-tale characters, extra story to pore over in the illustrations, jokes – both visual and verbal – and, above all, a wonderful series of letters, circulars, little books, postcards, birthday cards, even paper money that can be extracted from the pages, which are folded to resemble envelopes. Knowing the textual references increases pleasure in this book, as then, such details as Baby Bear's repaired chair or Jack's paper plaster can be searched for in the illustrations, but the book and its sequels also create a curiosity about these traditional stories which a parent or teacher can satisfy. The Ahlbergs conceived of this book after noting their daughter's keen interest in the mail that came through the door every morning; the book nicely builds on this cultural activity.

In the same vein as the Ahlbergs' work, though in no sense derivative, is Cressida Cowell's *Little Bo Peep's Library Book* (1999). A replica of a date-stamping page is on the first endpaper, fixed at the top as in all the best library books, and by the end of the book readers have taken down from the shelves several real books: a cookery book, *Basic Little Girl Cookery*, which interests the wolf, who has his eye on Bo Peep; *Who Stole the Tarts?*, which the Queen is sadly studying; and *How to Find Sheep* (by A. Shepherd). Each of these little books is fully developed and by the end, Bo Peep has had her library book stamped, has returned home, read it and found her sheep (observant readers will have seen that the sheep follow Bo Peep to and through the library, where they deal with the wicked wolf). Cultural and literary references and jokes abound, and understatement (the wolf's tail is trailed before we see him) and overstatement (*scores* of sheep follow Bo Peep home) add to the richness of the text. Once again, the novelty book is able to draw on literacy, and cultural events and activities, to engage young readers; perhaps for those who are not library users, this book might even establish the practice.

One problem with novelty books is that a tension can be created between the narrative, which wants to go forward, and the need to lift flaps and explore other effects. Certainly, the Ahlbergs' and Cowell's books require readers to interrupt the narrative to read the letters and the little books that are inserted into the body of the texts. But because, as with all picturebooks, which by their very nature require pausing to inspect images, these books are usually revisited frequently by their readers, the disturbance to the narrative flow may only be a problem on the first reading. In addition, it may be that the very interruptions build a facility in the reader for putting narrative on hold and then picking up the threads again. For these reasons, such books are read rather differently from other books; the insertions may be read later – or even before a straight run-through of the book. We don't know enough about how these books are read by their child readers to be categoric about their impact on the reading process. We do know that the books are treasured and that their 'loose parts' are not lost, as was initially feared, indicating both care for the books and a recognition that such parts are integral to the narrative.

Wordless books

Picturebooks with no words other than the title form a small fraction of the sum total of picturebooks, but they are a sub-genre that repays attention. Many illustrators are drawn to the wordless book, perhaps because they rise to the challenge to tell a story using only images, and perhaps because they enjoy the prospect that their books will be bought and read by those who respect and enjoy close examining of pictures. Because there are no words to alert readers to what is significant or absent in the pictures, the reading of wordless books is not as straightforward as is often assumed. Until children are experienced with story structures, they may perceive the task of recounting the story of a wordless book as detailing everything that is taking place, which is both confusing and exhausting. Work that I have done (Graham, in Evans, 1998) with books such as Quentin Blake's *Clown* suggests that narrative in-experience rather than visual literacy is the problem for children who try to reconstruct the narratives they see in words.

The inexperienced reader–viewer cannot always perceive significance and sequence and does not, for instance, group various pictured activities and say 'the woman is spring-cleaning'. With experience comes the ability to recognize both the general point being made and its place in the narrative. That said, visual literacy is certainly important; illustrators of wordless books frequently employ a language that owes much to comic strip, film and animated cartoons that use a pictorial sequence (Box 13.1). Thus a wordless picturebook may use many more frames than one with words in order to close narrative gaps. Use may also be made of a variety of 'shots' – long, medium and

Figure 10   From *Sunshine* by Jan Omerod

close-up – in order to focus the reader on the wider scene, the significant element and then the key emotions or transactions. The viewpoint will also
change frequently, according to what needs to be emphasised, and colour may
be used more deliberately than in a book with words in order to mark mood
and atmosphere.

The wordless book *Sunshine* (1981) by Jan Ormerod contains 70 different
pictures. Eighteen small frames alone go to showing a young girl, whose
parents are finding it difficult to get up, dressing herself in the morning (see
Figure 10). That such a sequence enchants the reader is a tribute to Ormerod's
accurate observation and shrewd decisions of how to keep the images lively;
for instance, many of the child's garments spill into an adjacent frame.
To indicate movement, Ormerod shows her characters *against* a frame rather
than *in* one, so that they seem to be forever leaving or entering the stage.
In order to keep variety in the text, the illustrator also has several full-page
pictures, usually of something relatively static, such as the parents asleep in
bed. Other wordless picturebook creators who proceed through the use both
of many small frames and intermittent much larger scenes, as if the camera has
pulled back, are Peter Collington, Philippe Dupasquier, Shirley Hughes and
Raymond Briggs (see Chapter 14).

Monique Felix's wordless books about mice trapped in books, *The Story of
a Little Mouse Trapped in a Book* (1980) and *Another Story of a Little Mouse
Trapped in a Book* (1983), use the whole (admittedly small) page, not the
frame, to convey the wordless story. The mouse nibbles away at one side and
pulls the detached page across to the left to reveal his coveted destination.
By folding his detached page into an aeroplane or boat depending on terrain,

the mouse effects his escape. The fact that my description at this point is somewhat clumsy indicates how difficult it is to encapsulate the ingenuity of these books; playing with the book as physical object in order to tell of the mouse's escape makes Felix's titles nicely postmodern.

Australian illustrator Jeannie Baker has a different method again in her wordless book *Window* (1991). Each page turn (until the very last double-page spread) has the reader looking both at and through the same window, but the years are passing and gradual changes are recorded; the accumulative effect is sobering as nature gives way to an urbanized world. Baker's photo-graphed collage constructions use several visual devices to indicate the passage of time – a child growing up (birthday cards on the widow ledge, toys deteriorating and changing) as well as the changes beyond the window, where are shown, amongst other environmental destruction, the trees opposite felled and a sign appearing advertising firewood for sale.

David Wiesner is an American illustrator who has come to be associated with the wordless (or practically wordless) picturebook. *Tuesday* (1991) is typical of his work. It is perhaps useful to pause for a minute and consider how the threshold into a book such as this is crossed. It may begin with noting the high quality of this production: large, landscape format; loose book jacket and elegant binding; fine quality paper and picture reproduction. Knowledge of the author–illustrator and of his previous wordless books may also be brought into play. Perhaps the starting point comes from the title, *Tuesday*, in its upper-case boldness, and linking it to the clock on the cover showing nine o'clock – what is meaningful about this exact time? At one level the gold 'Caldecott Medal' superimposed on the cover may be registered, alongside the solemn blurb: *The events recorded here are verified by an undisclosed source to have happened somewhere, U.S.A., on Tuesday. All those in doubt are reminded that there is always another Tuesday.* Aspects such as these comprise the peritext – the textual context for the story – and certainly influence entry into the book. *Tuesday* uses a cover illustration that is not one of the illustrations in the story, though, once the book has been read, it's clear where it belongs in the narrative and we know how to read it, something impossible before the story has been digested. A cameo illustration on the back cover appears – again before the story is known – to be an innocent frog on a lily-pad on a pond. These peritextual elements surround and promote the text and are frequently worth analysing in order to account for the overall impact of a book.

With *Tuesday*, the story begins before the title page (illustrators often need to exploit every one of the thirty-two pages a standard picturebook allows) as frogs begin to rise from the surface of a lake, each on its own lily-pad magic carpet. Through the eyes of a passing turtle (images zoom in on the turtle's astonishment over three horizontal frames), the reader infers that this is indeed a surreal event. The frogs increase in number, become a flying flotilla, and have a wild night on the town. Against a double-page spread of the night, with birds resting on telegraph wires, Wiesner superimposes three horizontal frames of the frogs' increasing relish. Later, he uses three vertical frames against a full double-page spread of a clapboard house to show the frogs (one of whom flies like batman after an encounter with laundry hung out to dry) entering an open sitting-room window and coming down a chimney. The page turn reveals them settling in (hovering actually) to watch TV around a sleeping granny (and a nonplussed cat). One of the frogs uses his prehensile tongue to change channels on the remote control. An encounter with a dog is also told in three horizontal strips, enabling the incident to keep its momentum and movement. Then, when the magic fades with the dawn, three vertical strips again, against a larger picture showing the sun rising and illuminating the landscape, show the frogs falling, diving into their pond and then wondering what on earth all that was about. Two endings are offered. The first shows morning, and the countryside strewn with limp lily-pads; the police and the media are out in force to investigate. The second, identified as the following Tuesday, depicts sunset and the shadow of a flying pig on the gable end of a barn. The final image is of pigs cavorting in the sky, visually spelling out that pigs might fly. The book repays study not only in its full range of cinematic techniques, but also in its understated, humorous detail, magical use of night-time colour and witty references to science fiction and super-hero literature.

Picture storybooks

Two recent titles, *Beegu* by Alexis Deacon (2003) and Lauren Child's *Who's Afraid of the Big, Bad Book?* (2002), illustrate a number of points. Some children's picturebooks can engender real tension and be profoundly moving; some can be created principally for humour and pleasure; some picturebooks leave readers reflecting on a sober message; some work well with no message at all. Some picturebooks form a composite text, with words and pictures sharing the telling; others retain a written text that is self-sufficient and use the illustrated text to add extra effects. Some picture books include painterly illustrations that could be framed and hung on a wall; some illustrators make skilful use of digital means to add photographic and other textures to the line drawing. In other words, this is a versatile medium capable of conveying narrative at a variety of levels and to different effect.

Beegu is the story of a forlorn little yellow three-eyed alien who crash lands on Earth and finds herself rejected or ignored by all save a playground of children. Ultimately her parents arrive from space to rescue her, and Beegu reports that any hope for Earth creatures lies with the small ones. The themes of this story are not uncommon in children's literature: abandonment, loneliness, rejection and separation. The device of placing a child character (or equivalent) alone in an alien environment enables an author to present the isolation from a viewpoint familiar to young readers who know what vulnerability feels like. In addition, in this story, there is the theme of isolation through not being able to communicate – Beegu's language is not understood by the adults on Earth. Together they make this story function on several levels, including as a metaphor for the condition of refugee children.

In a story of fewer than 150 words, and without reverting to sentimentality, Alexis Deacon uses his illustrations to do three (at least) important things.

First, he creates interest and concern in his reader for his main character. This starts with a striking cover where the luminous and distinct Beegu appears rather like a sticker applied against a background of dark sky and skyscrapers. Could she be a toy left out on the roof? When seen again on the title page, she is sleeping (or is she dead?) in a bleak and empty landscape, her spacecraft smouldering in the background. The mood is dark. It is a relief when she wakes with the dawn on the next opening; having been beguiled by her three eyes and floppy ears, the reader is prepared to accompany her through the book. She stands out on every page in her glowing yellowness; the mostly dark and sinister backgrounds increase our sympathy.

Deacon also needs to ensure that his illustrations indicate the desired mood. In *Beegu* this is achieved with a palette of dark turquoise and navy blue, textured backgrounds in grey and brown, line drawing that is also soft and textured, lots of space around the lonely creature. The pace is calm and measured, with page after page underlining, through repeated incidents, the themes of search and despair.

Finally, the author–illustrator uses his illustrations to extend the minimal written text. Thus the words 'No one seemed to understand her' are followed by three illustrations showing Beegu trying to talk to rabbits (who vaguely resemble her), to a single tree, whose branches perhaps echo her long ears, and to leaves which seem to have life as they whirl around. An uncaptioned full-page illustration ('bled' to the very edges of the page to increase the sense of involvement) shows a most dejected Beegu on a city pavement, in a sea of grey-trousered legs.

When at last she finds some friends, her happiness is short-lived. Pictures alone show the sourest of all school teachers come to remove the alien creature. Where the text says that the children 'want to say goodbye' (Figure 11), the pictures show her playmates squeezing through the school railings, and offering her their hoop. Beegu's ears stand up straight, as they do when she is happy, and later the hoop intrigues Beegu's father aboard the rescue spacecraft.

Who's Afraid of the Big, Bad Book? conceives the picturebook in an entirely different way. Herb has the misfortune to fall asleep over a book of fairy tales. What's more, they are fairy tales whose illustrations he has previously added to – a moustache on a princess here, a pair of glasses on a king there – and defaced (Prince Charming was cut from his story for a birthday card for his mother). These actions would have made his visit to the stories uncomfortable enough (most of those at the royal ball demand restitution), but as you can see in Figure 12, he also has to cope with a petulant Goldilocks who is furious that he has infiltrated her story.

Later in the story, we meet Cinderella who, despite having been deprived of her Prince Charming, comes to Herb's rescue, and, by clambering up the text, Herb escapes back to his bedroom. The story-book characters have their unsightly extras erased and Prince Charming is prised off the birthday card and sticky-taped back into position, though 'his dancing would never quite be the same again due to severe leg creasing'. Goldilocks, however, is punished

'Wait!'

Her friends
wanted to say goodbye.

**Figure 11   Beegu says goodbye to her earth-friends: from Alexis
Deacon's *Beegu***

for her shrill meanness with a wig of mousy brown hair, and the three bears
(who had been very courteous to Herb) have their cottage door protected with
a carefully drawn padlock.

Those familiar with Lauren Child's work will know how much fun she has
with the words, pictures, layout, fonts and the whole physical object that is the
book. The collage effect in her pictures – there is much inspired sticking and
pasting and use of photography – complements the cartoon style of her line
drawing, and though the pages may strike readers initially as crowded, messy
and rather difficult to read, familiarity allows her skill and wit to be
appreciated. In any case, child readers probably have the edge on adults here
as their reading of such pages is finely honed by contact with screen pages.
Kress usefully discusses multi-modal texts and the different 'reading paths' that
are taken through a text such as this, and the demands made on readers by the
screen-organized 'display' genre that he believes is replacing traditional text:
'Reliance on simple linearity is certainly not a useful approach to the reading
(of such texts)' (in Styles and Bearne, 2003: 146).

Figure 12   From Lauren Child's *Who's Afraid of the Big Bad Book?*

The use of varied fonts is inspired: the gothic script for Hansel and Gretel's rebuff to Herb ('Get lost!' they shout when he warns them not to eat the gingerbread house); the twirly curlicues applied to the speech of the royals; the uppercase print on a stone tablet reminiscent of tombstones.

Child's playful bending and breaking of literary rules and conventions puts her work firmly in the postmodern camp, where effects are achieved by challenge to and parody of traditional forms of storytelling, and by highlighting the very form of the book. Perhaps surprisingly, her written text stands independently of the pictures, but this does not detract from *Who's Afraid of the Big, Bad Book*; indeed the book has so much going on that it is probably a wise decision. There's much else to enjoy – a double pull-out page, a cut-out in the palace floor, spotting the Little Bad Wolf from an earlier Child book.

Conclusion

In between the two very different texts discussed above, there are tens of thousands of picture storybooks. Undoubtedly, age and personal taste guide choice. The three-year-old who introduced me to *Beegu* is left perplexed by *Who's Afraid of the Big, Bad Book?* Six-year-old twins spent an hour giggling over the Lauren Child and long to own all her equally inventive books. Adults studying children's picturebooks will form similar preferences; the qualities of the picturebooks are revealed by repeated, patient and close looking and analysis, by sharing readings and responses with others and by keeping an open mind.

WORKS CITED AND FURTHER READING

There are so many excellent picturebooks available that it is impossible to provide a meaningful list here. Other works by the writers and illustrators discussed in this chapter are worth exploring, as are those discussed by the works listed below.

Children's Books

Ahlberg, A. and J., *The Jolly Postman, or Other People's Letters* (London: William Heinemann, 1986).
Anno, M., *Anno's Counting Book* (London: Bodley Head, 1977).
Baker, J., *Window* (London: Julia MacCrae, 1991).
Browne, E., *Handa's Surprise* (London: Walker Books, 1994).
Burningham, J., *Come Away from the Water, Shirley* (London: Jonathan Cape, 1977).
Campbell, R., *Dear Zoo* (London: Abelard-Schuman, 1982).
Child, L., *Beware of the Storybook Wolves* (London: Hodder Children's Books, 2000).
Child, L., *Who's Afraid of the Big, Bad Book?* (London: Hodder Children's Books, 2002).
Cousins, L., *Where Does Maisy Live?* (London: Walker Books, 2000).
Cowell, C., *Little Bo Peep's Library Book* (London: Hodder Children's Books, 1999).
Deacon A., *Beegu* (London: Hutchinson, 2003).
Felix, M., *The Story of a Little Mouse Trapped in a Book* (London: Methuen/Moonlight, 1980).
Felix, M., *Another Story of a Little Mouse Trapped in a Book* (London: Methuen/Moonlight, 1983).
Felix, M., *The Colors* (New York: Stewart, Tabori and Chang, 1991).
Hutchins, P., *Rosie's Walk* (London: Bodley Head, 1970).
Ormerod, J., *Sunshine* (London: Kestrel Books, 1981).
Ormerod, J., *Peek-a-boo!* (London: Bodley Head, 1997).
Oxenbury, H., *ABC of Things* (London: William Heinemann, 1967).
Wiesner, D., *Tuesday* (New York: Clarion Books, 1991).

Critical Texts

Arizpe, E. and Styles, M., Children Reading Pictures (London: RoutledgeFalmer, 2003).
Bader, B., *American Picturebooks from Noah's Ark to the Beast Within* (New York: Macmillan, 1976).
Bang, M., *Picture This: How Pictures Work* (New York: SeaStar Books, 1991).
Doonan, J., *Looking at Pictures in Picturebooks* (Stroud: Thimble Press, 1993).
Evans, J., (ed.), *What's in the Picture? Responding to Illustrations in Picturebooks* (London: Paul Chapman, 1998).
Graham, J., *Pictures on the Page* (Sheffield: NATE, 1990).
Lewis, D., *Reading Contemporary Picturebooks* (London: RoutledgeFalmer, 2001).
Martin, D., *The Telling Line* (London: Julia MacRae, 1989).
McCloud, S., *Understanding Comics* (New York: HarperCollins, 1994).
Meek, M., *How Texts Teach what Readers Learn* (Stroud: Thimble Press, 1988).
Nikolajeva, M. and Scott, C., *How Picturebooks Work* (New York: Garland, 2001).
Nodelman, P., *Words about Pictures: The Narrative Art of Children's Picturebooks* (Athens, GA, and London: University of Georgia Press, 1988).
Schwarcz, J. H., *Ways of the Illustrator* (Chicago: American Library Association, 1982).

Sendak, M., *Caldecott & Co* (London: Reinhardt Books, in association with Viking, 1989).

Sipe, C., 'How Picturebooks Work: a Semiotically Framed Theory of Text–Picture Relationships', *Children's Literature in Education*, 29 (1998), pp. 97–108.

Stephens, J. and Watson, K. (eds), *From Picturebook to Literary Theory* (Sydney: St Clair Press, 1994).

Styles, M. and Bearne, E. (eds), *Art, Narrative and Childhood* (Stoke-on-Trent: Trentham Books, 2003).

Watson, K. (ed.), *Word and Image – Using Picturebooks* (Sydney: St Clair Press, 1997).

Watson, V. and Styles, M. (eds), *Talking Pictures* (London: Hodder & Stoughton, 1996).

Whalley, J. I. and Chester, T. R., *A History of Children's Book Illustration* (London: John Murray and the Victoria and Albert Museum, 1988).

Picturebook Case Study: Politics and Philosophy in the Work of Raymond Briggs

14

Lisa Sainsbury

KEY TEXTS

Selected work by Raymond Briggs

This chapter is intended to be read in conjunction with Chapter 13, and makes use of the terminology set out in Box 13.1. Lisa Sainsbury adopts a case-study approach to provide both a practical demonstration of how to discuss pictures, and a model for considering the work of one person. While the emphasis here is on Raymond Briggs as a creator of visual texts, he is in fact a writer–illustrator, and attention is paid to both dimensions of his work. The case-study approach can be used in a variety of ways: to construct a particular argument, to zoom in on a specific aspect of an individual's work, or to provide an overview. Raymond Briggs's entire career as a children's writer–illustrator is encompassed in this study, which also looks thematically at key texts to assess Briggs's contribution to children's literature. In order to make the most of the ideas and material contained in this chapter, it is advisable to have a representative sample of Briggs's work beside you as you read it.

From the mundane reality of toilet cleaning in *Gentleman Jim* (1980) to the grotesque fantasy of *Fungus the Bogeyman* (1977), Raymond Briggs's vibrant corpus embraces a wide range of literary genres, artistic styles and narrative structures; a diversity which is united through themes and characters that are constantly revisited and reworked. His books are by turns philosophical and political, but they share an ideological outlook that accepts and conveys the brutal reality of human experience while investing a humanist faith in the restorative power of love. This tendency to explore related issues through different media (including illustrated stories, wordless books and comic strips) and for the benefit of different audiences (the youngest of readers can enjoy *The Snowman* (1978), while the harrowing vision of nuclear war in *When the Wind Blows* (1982) invites a much more sophisticated teenage/adult readership) makes Briggs's work well-suited for a case-study approach. While this chapter is a thematic study of Briggs's texts on one level, it is also concerned with the way in which pictures and words communicate ideas in his books. Briggs frequently expresses meaning through shifts in style, and an understanding of these structural dynamics is crucial to any analysis of his work.

Raymond Briggs is probably best known for *The Snowman*, which has spawned a long line of spin-off texts, including picturebooks, pop-ups, toys and an animated film. He has twice won the UK's Kate Greenaway Prize for illustration: first for *Mother Goose* (1966) and then for *Father Christmas* (1973). While Raymond Briggs is now recognized as a pioneer of the comic-book form in the United Kingdom, it took him some time to develop his unmistakable style and to win critical recognition. He has been forced to battle against a cultural prejudice which marginalizes the comic strip. While graphic novels and comics are taken seriously in many other countries, particularly across mainland Europe and in Japan, Briggs suggests that there is,

> a snobbery in England that goes back to the days of the monastery. When they were doing these illustrated books and things, the people who wrote them were looked on as intellectuals and the people who did the pictures were looked on as painters, the way you look on a house-painter today. I'm sure it stems from that. ... Certainly with strip cartoons, on the continent it's looked upon as a proper art form equal to film. And they have huge conventions which I'm supposed to go to but never do where they all meet and have their lectures and talks. Big tomes are published. It's looked upon as a perfectly serious art form which it should be really ... as a medium it's fantastic.   (Achuka interview, 2001b)

Clearly the comic-strip medium is crucial to much of Briggs's work, though as Philip Pullman points out, he stumbled on the format in a moment of serendipity. Originally conceiving *Father Christmas* (1973) as a picturebook, Briggs found that he had too much material and discovered that the comic-strip format allowed him to accommodate a more full and complex pictorial/verbal narrative (Pullman, 1998: 124). Although Briggs is now best known for his use of the comic strip, he constantly experiments with a range of styles and formats, incorporating, for example, line drawings and double-page spreads as he adapts his visual palette to the demands of narrative development/structure. His early work as an illustrator for the publishing house Hamish Hamilton is mostly rendered in simple line drawing; a style which Briggs returns to for emotive and political impact in later work such as *The Tin-pot Foreign General and the Old Iron Woman* (1984).

Briggs's first excursion into picturebooks came in 1969, when he collaborated with Elfrida Vipont in *The Elephant and the Bad Baby*. It is easy to forget that Briggs is not the sole author of this book, since so many elements of his later work can be located in this almost satirical homage to Victorian morality tales. Briggs has confessed that he has no interest in the 'sweet innocent pink and blue baby stuff' (in Moss, 1979: 28) that is frequently offered to children, and thus it is not surprising that a *bad* baby should become the hero of this early picturebook. The baby's red hair marks him out as a Briggsian protagonist, a visual tag confirming early on that his characters might have experiences in common. Indeed, Briggs seems more interested in social circumstance or the way in which human experience acts upon the individual, than he does in character development. Thus he takes a recognizable generic character and places him/her in different environments or situations.

Close examination of Briggs's body of work reveals recognizable patterns and a recurring network of themes (though each time these themes appear they are reconsidered and developed). It could even be argued that some of his texts can be arranged as series, so close are they in terms of narrative development and thematic structure, and it is these series of texts that are explored in the remainder of this chapter.

The visitors

The first identifiable sequence of texts includes Briggs's most popular fantasies, *The Snowman* (1978), *The Bear* (1994) and *The Man* (1992), involving the nocturnal appearance of magical or enigmatic beings into the lives of individual children. Each text makes use of different stylistic elements, but each explores the central relationship between child and visitor; between child and newly discovered other.

The process of balancing self and other is central to an understanding of this series, as protagonists try to come to terms with these strange and demanding encounters. Piaget's theory of adaptation (Box 14.1), incorporating the process of assimilation and accommodation, is helpful here.

Piaget suggests that cognitive maturity is achieved through the ability to integrate environment/experience with self, while simultaneously adapting self to environment/experience. While, according to Piaget, the very young child indulges primarily in assimilative play, as children mature, there is an increasing capacity to equilibrate this process of assimilation and accommodation. As Appleyard suggests, the growing child repeatedly seeks 'opportunities for dealing expertly with the world', which 'correspond to changes in the child's inner sense of self' (1991: 59). While Piaget's emphasis is on the child's experience of the physical or sensory world, his theory is extended here to consider the emotions involved in human relationships, so that Piaget's ideas become a metaphorical vehicle for understanding the processes at work in Briggs's sequence. Accordingly, I am suggesting that each of Briggs's texts in this sequence deals with the process of adaptation on some level, as his central

BOX 14.1 PIAGET'S THEORY OF ADAPTATION

In *The Origin of Intelligence in the Child* (tr. 1953), Piaget suggests that human intelligence is a process of *adaptation* (3). This process of adaptation is necessary if *equilibrium* is to be achieved between the child and her/his environment, and Piaget asserts that, 'adaptation is an equilibrium between assimilation and accommodation' (6). Throughout his discussion of adaptation, Piaget stresses that *assimilation* and *accommodation* are complementary aspects of the adaptive process and must work together if equilibrium is to be achieved.

Assimilation   Piaget explains that 'intelligence is *assimilation* to the extent that it incorporates all the given data of experience within its framework' (6). Thus, assimilation can be described as the process by which the child attempts to deal with the environment by forcing it to fit in with her/his own experience of the world.

Accommodation   During accommodation, Piaget suggests, 'intelligence constantly modifies' its 'earlier schemata ... in order to adjust them to new elements' (6–7). Accommodation is, then, the process by which the child adjusts her/his own experience of the world to allow for new knowledge of her/his environment.

characters are confronted with relationships which lead from the self, into realms of otherness (representing the world outside the home), and back again.

In the context of the 'Visitors' sequence, *The Snowman* is unique in the stability of its style. The story is primarily rendered in wordless, comic-strip format, and uses muted shades of pastel throughout. The frames vary in size, sometimes allowing for a shift in viewpoint, and the images are generally contained within the gently curving sides of each frame – contributing to the idea that the text itself is non-confrontational and welcoming to young readers. The frames are only broken three times in the whole book – twice by the Snowman's head and once by his hat – and these breaks all occur while the boy is building the Snowman. This might be a figurative indication of the manner in which the Snowman is to disrupt the boy's life, both literally, during their magical night together, and emotionally, after his departure. Indeed, *The Snowman* engages the reader in something of an emotional roller-coaster ride, apparently endowing the red-haired boy (with whom identification is encouraged) with feelings of excited anticipation, joy, desire, love and finally devastating grief. The comic-strip format is also dispensed with briefly for the duration of the flight, throughout which Briggs uses full-page plates and double-page spreads to convey the magnitude of this experience and the expanse of space covered, as boy and Snowman fly across the Sussex landscape.

Briggs's wordless text also demands to be read at a different pace from more traditional picture books, and it is worth taking a moment to look at this closely, focussing on the last four frames of the first page. The early frames in *The Snowman* convey the boy's growing enthusiasm as it begins to snow.

In this pictorial sequence, forward movement impels readers through each of the four frames, complementing the left-to-right visual progress. In the first frame, the boy seems to point outside (as suggested by his pointing finger, but readers must perform an act of closure to make this connection). In the second, though the boy leans backwards, his eyes look ahead and his boots point forward. In the third frame, the boy pulls his hat onto his head while staring straight ahead, while in the fourth, extended frame, he begins to run into the action on the next page, ignoring the hat, which he has now lost in his eagerness to play in the snow. Thus, the directed movement allows readers to digest the sequence rapidly, reflecting the emotional tone of the text; the boy's excitement over the snow is mirrored in the structural flow of illustrations.

The Snowman tells the tale of an (apparently) only child who escapes from loneliness into a fantasy world offered up to him by the Snowman he has lovingly made. The fantasy takes place at night (cf. Chapter 8) and seems to fill some unspoken need, figured in the boy's longing gaze out of his bedroom window at the Snowman he has built earlier in the day. That this desire is to be only fleetingly fulfilled surely adds to the poignancy of the Snowman's eventual demise.

The boy's relationship with the Snowman is primarily positive (largely because it is so short-lived and the pair do not attempt to live together as do the characters in *The Man* and *The Bear*), culminating in a magical flight over the snow-covered landscape of Brighton, in the south-east of England, where Raymond Briggs lives. It is a balanced relationship, in which the two friends offer each other invitations into the heart of their respective worlds. Briggs differentiates between these worlds stylistically, rendering the boy's home in soft shades of red and brown, while the Snowman's flight is dominated by colder whites, blues, greys and greens. The boy shows the Snowman around his home, revealing the wonders of electricity, television, clothes and his favourite toys. However, it is clear that the new-found friends will never be able to share anything other than a temporary bond, as the boy's world is fraught with danger for the Snowman. They are allowed to enjoy the strangeness of each *other*, but Briggs suggests that the adaptive process necessary for a long-term relationship is impossible for boy and Snowman (perhaps because the boy is not yet ready to disrupt the security of self and home). Indeed, the loss to come is anticipated early in the book when the Snowman shrinks from the heat of the fire in the boy's home, confirming that he cannot adapt to, or exist within, the boy's environment.

The film's considerable success, typified by the fact that it is regularly shown at Christmas in the UK, means that *The Snowman* has become associated with a 'feel good' factor. But to conceive it in nostalgic terms is to misread a book which, fundamentally, is about death and loss. Ultimately, Briggs confronts this loss head on, with one of the most haunting images in children's literature (see Figure 13). Readers are offered no reassurances at this point, apparently in line with Briggs's belief that children should not be shielded from the darker aspects of human experience. Although retaining the style of previous frames in this final image, Briggs places the small frame at the centre of an otherwise empty, white page; indeed, the image is lost in space, just as the boy is lost in

Figure 13   Final image from *The Snowman* by Raymond Briggs. Briggs refuses to insulate his readers from the realities of death and loss.

grief. The reader's gaze is thus focused on the loss encapsulated in the boy's hunched shoulders and the diminished lump of snow before him.

Although, chronologically, *The Bear* is the third in the 'Visitors' series, in terms of thematic and stylistic development, it comes second, forming a stepping stone to the more complex relationship between man and boy in *The Man*. Though Briggs makes use of wordless frames in *The Bear*, he also uses a combination of speech bubbles and lengthy dialogue, perhaps indicating that he wants to explore the relationships in this book on a different level from those depicted in *The Snowman*. Briggs also makes use of plates and double-page spreads in order to convey the enormity of the Bear and the over-powering nature of his presence in his little-girl protagonist, Tilly's, life.

In none of these three books does Briggs resolve the question of whether the visitor is imagined or not. In *The Bear* and *The Man*, readers see the visitors before the sleeping children wake to discover them, suggesting that they have a presence beyond the child characters' imagination. Indeed, on the first page of *The Bear*, the Bear's arrival dominates the pictorial sequence, as Briggs achieves a shift in focus from Tilly, her mother and their conversation about Tilly's inanimate teddy, to the emergent figure outside Tilly's window. Finally, the Bear's dark presence fills the window (perhaps ominously), blotting out the snowscape through which he has travelled, before climbing through the window and intruding into Tilly's room (see Figure 14). His arrival seems to be for the benefit of the reader alone (though it might be argued that Tilly's 'wise old' teddy is a silent witness to events, since he seems to reach out for the Bear's paw as he enters the room), since Tilly sleeps through the process and does not wake. Furthermore, the blocking out of light suggests a movement from day to night; from snowscape to dreamscape. Clearly there is a tension at

Figure 14   Tilly sleeps through the Bear's arrival in this sequence from *The Bear*.

work here which Briggs does not resolve. It is certainly possible that Tilly is dreaming (fuelled by her conversation about Teddy), but the Bear's apparently distant presence while Tilly is still asleep, seems to belie this interpretation.

Of all the visitors, the Bear's presence is the most questionable, and it is less clear than in *The Snowman* or *The Man* whether Briggs has constructed a fantasy domain. This is because Tilly's parents clearly cannot see the Bear and interpret Tilly's descriptions of him as the arrival of an imaginary friend. When Tilly describes the Bear to her parents in minute, gruesome detail: 'And his claws! They're all black and curved like hooks. He could easily tear me to bits and eat me,' her father responds with a predictably flippant comment: 'Aaah! The wonderful world of a child's imagination' (14). For Tilly, however, he is real, and seems to be the manifestation of the desire for a companion to love more deeply than she can her teddy bear; for a companion who lives and breathes. That the reader can also see the Bear encourages identification with Tilly and an investment in her version/perception of reality. Thus, the overwhelming and unavoidable pictorial/physical presence of the Bear suggests that the narrative perspective is at the level of child experience.

Tilly's Bear is massive and, ultimately, overwhelming. This is figured in the way he takes over the illustrated frames, breaking up the pattern of Briggs's comic strip (see Figure 15). The Bear's disruptive influence is also signalled by a gradual change in style, as Briggs shifts from comic-strip format, to a looser combination of dialogue and image. Unlike the stable comic strip of *The Snowman*, neither image nor dialogue is neatly framed, suggesting the unmanageable nature of the Bear's presence and his disruptive impact on family life. Though she is initially delighted with the Bear, he soon upsets Tilly's routine and breaks the taboos of her limited experience when he defecates in the hall and urinates on the bathroom floor; mess that Tilly is forced to clear up and that elicits her anger. Tilly shouts at him, calling him a 'BEAST', thus drawing attention to his otherness, and tells him: 'You are awful! I hate you. Don't you dare do it again' (27). Tilly seems unable to accommodate the Bear's behaviour, suggesting that, like the boy in *The Snowman*, she is not ready to change herself for the benefit of others outside her environment. Consequently,

Figure 15   The Bear's physical reality seems irrefutable (*The Bear*)

Tilly is unsuccessful in trying to assimilate the unwieldy, clumsy creature into the unsuitable environment of her home and becomes increasingly exasperated with the Bear's cumbersome presence. In a refinement of the uncomplicated relationship portrayed in *The Snowman*, Briggs also suggests that love and desire are less than easy to handle, however necessary to human experience.

Indeed, as can be seen in Figure 16, it is love that has the final word in *The Bear*, as in so many of Briggs's texts. Immediately prior to his departure, Tilly declares her love for the Bear while sleeping between his paws: 'I love you Bear, with all my heart . . .' (37). Finally, Tilly seems ready to accept the Bear, perhaps even to begin the process of adaptation described by Piaget. Maybe

Figure 16   Tilly sits in the Bear's lap (*The Bear*)

Figure 17   The Bear leaves a bereft Tilly alone in bed (*The Bear*)

this readiness to confront and deal with strange experiences, implied in Tilly's affirmation of love, indicates that the Bear has served his purpose for he immediately leaves her alone in bed. The sleeping child looks entirely bereft (Figure 17), and once again Briggs refuses to shield his readers from the reality of love and loss. However, while he leaves *The Snowman* at this intense moment of grief, he allows Tilly (and the reader) the comfort of her father's reassurance, thus showing that grieving is a process that can be overcome. Furthermore, *The Bear* moves away from the moment of loss entirely, depicting the Bear's return to an ice-capped domain under the warm red of a sunset sky. Briggs's hazy pastel tones distance the reader from Tilly's loss, while simultaneously validating the Bear's existence outside of Tilly's dreams. This closing scene also stresses the fact that the reader's perspective is different from that of the characters depicted in the book and that what the reader sees is of primary significance in Briggs's narrative structure.

The epigraph printed at the beginning of *The Man*: 'After three days, fish and visitors begin to stink' (Chinese Proverb), provides an indication that this is the most complex of the three texts and also confirms that it too explores the concept of visitation and its impact. *The Man* can be read in both political and philosophical terms and its thematic complexity is reflected in its hybrid style, making use of long snatches of dialogue. That *The Man* relates to earlier Briggsian themes and texts is suggested in its intertextual references, evoking pre-texts in a literal manner. For example, the note which first appears in *Jim & The Beanstalk* (1970) reappears in *The Man*, and *The Snowman*, an earlier visitor, is figured on John's mug, supporting the notion that these books are thematically linked.

In a change from the earlier texts, the Man does not seem to be a manifestation of longing and desire, or a response to loneliness. He imposes

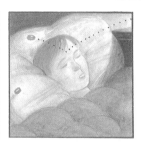

Figure 18 The Man announces his presence by throwing jelly beans at the sleeping Boy (*The Man*)

himself upon John in quite a brutal fashion (see Figure 18) and, although the boy comes to love him, his behaviour is frequently less than lovable or cute (epithets which both Snowman and Bear invite). The comic-strip format introduced on the first page is soon dispensed with as the Man makes his presence felt through dynamic dialogue, differentiated from John's voice though contrasting typeface; the Man's voice is rendered in a smaller and bolder font than John's, perhaps indicating the forceful nature of this diminutive individual. As in *The Bear*, images frequently lack frames, bleeding into sections of dialogue and thus signalling the lack of control John has over his own feelings (and over the Man himself).

It also seems significant that this visitor is, despite his miniature stature, a man, rather than an animated, magical snowman or anthropomorphized bear. His relationship with John, despite their struggles to understand one another, is essentially human and is thus invested with the difficulties of human relationships. The proportionally large amount of dialogue in *The Man* also indicates that this book is primarily about the way in which people make sense of themselves and of the world through language. Briggs suggests (Achuka interview, 2001b) that the tensions between this pair stem from differences in class and education, tensions that Briggs explores in many of his books. The relationship between Man and John, or Boy, as the man calls him, is also reminiscent of that between Arrietty and the Boy in *The Borrowers* (1952 – see Chapter 6) and Briggs makes specific reference to Norton's text, suggesting a thematic level of intertextuality (Box 12.3) as ontological issues are explored. The boy asks the Man:

Where do you come from?

What do you mean, where do I come from? Where do *you* come from?
I live here.

Yes, but you don't *come from* here, do you? Here is just a house.
Yes, I – um ...

So where do you *come* from then?
I ... well ... I don't know ... my parents ... gave birth to me, I suppose ...

So did mine.
Yes, but –

Look, you were born. I was born. Let's leave it at that, shall we?
I've got it! Yes! You're a Borrower!

A what?
A Borrower.

Don't approve of credit.
You live under the floorboards! You do, don't you?

Live under the floorboards? What a barmy idea. It would be filthy. Cobwebs, spiders, mice, electric wiring – disgusting. How dare you suggest I live under the floorboards! You are prejudiced, aren't you? Just because I'm smaller than you, you think I must live in small, dirty places – like a rat!
No, no, sorry ... I didn't mean – I thought you were a Borrower, that's all. They're in a famous book. Borrowers are very good people. It's a great story.

Pah! Stories! I hate them. (8)

This exchange demonstrates John's struggle to understand the Man and to assimilate his presence into his own perception of the world. Such conversations are typical of books inviting a more mature readership than that implied by *The Snowman* or *The Bear* and which involve protagonists on the cusp of adolescence. As Appleyard suggests, adolescent experience 'can be viewed as an attempt to come to grips with a philosophical truth about existence – that inside and outside differ and can be at odds' (1994: 97). This neatly describes the struggle at the centre of *The Man*, though it is a struggle that is finally unresolved. The notion of prejudice is also flagged up in this passage, and there is no doubt that Briggs has extended his interest in otherness to include the wider ramifications of prejudice and its damaging potential to individual and society. The politicization of the theme, which, in the other Briggs texts discussed, related to the social development of the young child, further emphasizes that this text implies an older and more mature readership. So, it is through this type of antagonistic discussion that John begins the process of accommodation. Failing to assimilate the Man into his life, he reluctantly begins to make changes to his own routine (for example, buying expensive marmalade of which his mother disapproves) in an effort to build a positive relationship with this small intruder.

In *The Man*, Briggs also introduces a theme running through many of his books (particularly through the 'Everyman' series, also discussed in this chapter), pitting the diminutive individual against authoritative institutions and thus aligning Man with Briggs's working-class Everyman. Motivated by his fear of 'the Authorities', the Man extracts from John a promise never to tell anyone about his existence, and later threatens John's life when the boy vows to call the Authorities. Man and boy label each other murderers as the strains in their relationship reach crisis point. Man's alienation from John's apparently comfortable world is indicated by a number of images – the front cover is a good example of this and comments peritextually on Man's social position as an outsider – in which he is depicted from a distance, gazing in pensive silence at a world which denies (or at least challenges) his existence.

Like Tilly, John's relationship with Man is ambivalent, veering from irritation, and even dislike, to love as John takes on the nurturing role of provider (Figure 19). Eventually, the relationship breaks down and though John regrets its loss – in the final image (see Figure 20), which, like that of *The Snowman* and *The Bear*, is haunting and emotive, suggesting an ambivalence towards the departed visitor – Briggs implies that the breakdown was inevitable.

Figure 19   The Boy rocks Man as a father might rock his child (*The Man*)

Figure 20   As in *The Snowman*, Briggs ends *The Man* with a sombre image of the Boy after Man's departure

In his provocative closure Briggs appears to be making two main points, one essentially philosophical and the other political. In philosophical terms, Briggs seems to be suggesting that though there are many people who cannot fend for themselves and must rely on others for support, humans are social animals who respond best to those who contribute to society's structure, and find it difficult to make lasting relationships with those who do not contribute in any way (or at least that it is difficult for us to befriend or understand people outside of our own social class). Accommodation of the marginalized other is only possible up to a point. John certainly comes further down this path than *The Snowman*'s boy or Tilly in *The Bear*, but finally he is unable to maintain a healthy relationship with this creature who threatens the sanctity of his home (see Figure 21). In political terms, Briggs appears to be attacking a welfare state which does little to change the living conditions of those unable to support themselves – inadequate handouts from limited funds do little to bolster self-esteem, and keep these people on the outside of society looking in.

It is clear that these books grow in maturity, manifested through stylistic development and through increasingly complex narrative structures and themes, which demand progressively more advanced levels of literacy from their readers. The balance between word and picture also changes, as Briggs

**Figure 21   Divided literally by circumstances and figuratively by the
gutter, Boy and Man occupy different worlds**

seems to reflect a complexity of ideas through increased use of dialogue; thus
the verbal text of *The Man* is more weighty than *The Snowman* (obviously!)
and *The Bear*. Briggs's tendency to experiment with illustrative techniques, also
allows for greater detail in *The Man* and *The Bear*, as 'watercolour overlaid
with crayon ... allows him to express graduations in tone and form' (Pullman,
1998: 126). Though these are works of fantasy, each of these texts explores

dark and difficult issues of the real world through a lens of realism which refuses to cosset young readers and to hide the fact that if human experience includes joy and love, then it must also embrace loss, anger and pain.

Everyman

Familiarity with the body of Briggs's work reveals that he works with a fairly limited range of characters. Many of his male characters – young and old – are red-headed and share the name Jim or James. Aside from nominal/visual similarities, however, the most common bond between Briggs's characters is that they exemplify 'Everyman', and it is Everyman who provides the key to understanding many of his books. As Douglas Martin observes:

> his working-class, 'like most of us', values are the absolute bed-rock of his personality, and, I'm convinced, provide the most serviceable key towards an understanding of his skill as a communicator. In the process of learning to become middle class, he neither rejected nor complained about his heritage, as was becoming fashionable at the time. (1989: 229)

It should be stressed, however, that Briggs's Everyman is born out of very specific social conditions, for though he appears in a variety of guises, from Fungus the Bogeyman, to Father Christmas, to Jim in *Gentleman Jim* and *When the Wind Blows* and most recently *UG: Boy Genius of the Stone Age* (2001), he is always recognizably British and working class. Many of these characters have miserable lives because they are not educated and have no power to change their circumstances. As Jim says when he searches for a new career in *Gentleman Jim*:

> It's these Levels all the time in these adverts ... I wonder what they are? I bet it's all to do with Education – that's what it is. ... They give them these things at school nowadays. All we got at school was a bible and a thick ear. (5)

Characters such as Jim, a toilet cleaner, long to escape their mundane existences but are bewildered by the authoritative structures that hem them in. While Briggs is obviously not mystified by 'the powers that be' (as Jim and Hilda refer to them in *When the Wind Blows*) as are his frustrated protagonists, his view of authority in all its guises is unremittingly negative. Briggs's politics are rooted in British socialism of the 1950/60s (as played out by Briggs's father in *Ethel and Ernest*) and can usefully be explored through the Marxist theories of Louis Althusser. Peter Barry provides a helpful explanation:

> Althusser makes a useful distinction between what we might call state power and state control. State power is maintained by what Althusser terms *repressive structures*, which are institutions like the law courts,

prisons, the police force, and the army, which operate, in the last analysis, by external force. But the power of the state is also maintained more subtly, by seeming to secure the internal consent of its citizens, using what Althusser calls *ideological structures* or *State ideological apparatus*. These are groupings such as political parties, schools, the media, churches, the family, art (including literature) which foster an ideology – a set of ideas and attitudes – which is sympathetic to the aims of the state and the political status quo. Thus, each of us feels that we are freely choosing what is in fact being imposed upon us. (1995: 164)

Briggs's depiction of Althusser's 'repressive structures' is always savage, and characters associated with them are frequently dehumanized. In *Gentleman Jim*, the policemen are stylized caricatures of Adolf Hitler (see Figure 22), while the courtroom judge takes on a crazed, bestial appearance. Obviously, this serves to accentuate the humanity of Jim and his fellow Everymen, but Briggs also suggests that it is the very inhumanity of these structures that makes them impenetrable for the likes of Jim and Fungus. Of course, we should not forget that these exaggerated characters are a source of humour in Briggs's books, and it is this irreverence which implies that all is not lost; that there are ways of undermining 'the powers that be'. One of Briggs's most vicious attacks comes in an overtly political, adult picture book, *The Tin-Pot Foreign General and the Old Iron Woman*, in which General Galtieri and Margaret Thatcher are derisively lampooned. Briggs uses contrasting styles to convey his pacifist message in this book, juxtaposing a full colour spread

Figure 22   Briggs's 'powers that be' are exaggerated, stylized caricatures, serving to emphasize the humanity of his Everyman characters (*Gentleman Jim*)

of Thatcher's mechanized breasts (as instruments of nurture become those of destruction) with the soft line drawings of families mourning for their dead. Once again Briggs demands that the Everyman take centre stage, for the powerful silence of these images is all the more dramatic for its proximity to the outrageous cartoons, which seek to steal the limelight.

Briggs's work clearly holds *relative autonomy*, suggesting that 'in spite of the connections between culture and economics, art has a degree of independence from economic forces' (Barry, 1995: 163). In this way, it is possible to suggest that the tentative discontent voiced by the likes of Jim and Fungus is a way of challenging 'the powers that be'; of suggesting that literature has a powerful role to play in upsetting the more insidious influence of Althusser's Ideological State Apparatus (ISA). While Jim and Fungus do not understand the root cause of their dissatisfaction with life, they do at least understand that they are in some way repressed. While methodically carrying out his job of terrifying humans (or 'Drycleaners' in Bogey terminology), Fungus reflects:

> I'm a very lucky Bogey, really ... Nice damp dump [house]. Never dries out ... Always full of flies ... Good smelly dumpling [wife] keeps the house filthy ... Steady job ... No prospects ... but then – what *are* the prospects for Bogeyman?   (24–5)

For many of Briggs's characters such philosophizing is the limit of their escape from the drudgery of life-long routines. The muddy, snot-green palette of *Fungus* emphasizes the world-weariness experienced by Fungus himself as, visually, Briggs brings his characters down to earth. The peritextual backdrop behind frames in *Fungus* also comments on the worn-down monotony of Fungus's existence; cracked bathroom tiles, oozing, slug-infested walls and torn wall-paper all contribute to the ideal of Bogey domesticity, while simultaneously reflecting Fungus's frustration. Stylistically, *Fungus* is probably the most sophisticated of Briggs's texts, refusing a central narrative and instead detailing the day-to-day routines of a discontented Bogeyman. It is an exquisitely detailed text, incorporating a complex Bogey language, editorial asides, philosophical dialogue, annotated diagrams and graffiti scrawled upon the angry landscape of Fungus's domain. Though ostensibly destructive, this graffiti (for example, 'the woods decay', p. 24) is another example of *relative autonomy*; it is an art form (though some might debate this point) that speaks from the outside, commenting on the shortcomings of social order.

The dissatisfaction expressed both verbally and visually in *Fungus* is certainly a key to change, but few of Briggs's characters find the appropriate lock. In *Gentleman Jim*, Jim actually considers a series of alternative lifestyles, from cowboy to soldier, before finally opting for the romantic life of a highwayman, which lands him in prison by the end of the book. This might seem to suggest that Everyman is basically miserable (that they are Bogeys all); as Briggs explains to Elaine Moss: 'I'm noticing all my characters now are sad old men or, rather sad middle-aged men, which is what I am probably. Life is sad really but there's always love which makes life worth living' (Moss, 1979: 31).

Figure 23   Fungus's existential angst is soothed by the presence of Mildew, his 'first dear love and early wife' (*Fungus the Bogeyman*)

Significantly, it is largely this faith in the human capacity for love that prevents Briggs's work from remaining bleak in outlook as most of these texts close with an affirmation of its importance and impregnability. In what can be described as an essentially humanist outlook, Briggs suggests that this capacity for love is universal and enduring. The powers that be are never depicted in the closing stages of Briggs's books; rather, as is seen in the closing image from *Fungus* (Figure 23), this space is reserved for the loving wives and families who comfort their disillusioned Everymen.

Briggs's characteristic conjoining of love and humour is a reassuring force in even the most harrowing of his Everyman books. Alongside satire, a less overt and ubiquitous source of humour comes from Briggs's treatment of Everyman, whom he observes in a voyeuristic manner from an exterior and superior position. The implied author clearly knows far more about the world than these simple characters, whose ignorance and unworldliness is frequently thrown into comic relief. It is this humour that permeates *Ethel and Ernest: A True Story* (1998), Briggs's groundbreaking biography of his parents, and while some might suggest that this narrative perspective is patronizing, it could be argued that Briggs represents honestly the gap between his parents' life experience and his own. Indeed, in this comment on *UG: Boy Genius of the Stone Age*, Briggs suggests that his treatment of Ethel and Ernest is inevitable:

In *The Man* as well as in this new book it's a younger boy who is more intelligent than the parents, like I was a bit more intelligent than my mum and dad, not that they were stupid or anything, but they hadn't had the benefit of education, which I had, and so I was potentially more intelligent.

A lot of that happens in *The Man*. A middle-class, educated, artistically-minded boy talking to a kind of working-class Man. And it's the same here, the boy is somewhat exasperated by them and they're exasperated by him. Because they're both living in different worlds really.   (Achuka interview, 2001a)

Briggs inhabits a different world from that experienced by his parents, and consequently, he is forced to recall their experience from a perspective that is often at odds with it.

Figure 24   The first page of *Ethel and Ernest*

As a biography, *Ethel and Ernest* clearly differs from Briggs's fictional Everyman books, but in many ways it can be seen as the culmination of this series, as many of the themes and characters overlap with Briggs's earlier texts. Of course, *Ethel and Ernest* can be read as a personal family record, but it also serves as a historical document, charting the considerable social changes which have transformed people's lives in the twentieth century. A full discussion of *Ethel and Ernest* is beyond the scope of this chapter, but a close reading of the opening sequence, in which Ethel and Ernest first meet, demonstrates the power and economy of Briggs's comic-strip narrative and establishes the ideological perspective and social conditions that dominate the whole text.

The pictorial sequence on the first two pages is wordless, apart from the dates which place the text historically (1928) and personally (Monday, Tuesday, Wednesday), as it transpires that this week represents a turning point for both Ethel and Ernest. In this early sequence, Briggs frames his parents in a series of close-ups, first depicting Ethel in a maid's uniform, cleaning a table, and then switching to Ernest cycling up the street outside (see Figure 24). The ninth frame is broken by Ethel's duster as she shakes it out of the window, thus catching Ernest's attention as he cycles past, and he raises his cap (again breaking the frame) in response. That the duster should first break the frame of Briggs's sequence is significant since it indicates, first, the blossoming of a romance which is to shape the rest of Ethel's life, and secondly, her liberation from servitude. It should be stressed, however, that the duster has a wider importance in the context of Ethel's experience, since in marriage and motherhood she is largely restricted (though not unwillingly) by the domestic realm and, indeed, the duster soon makes a reappearance as Ethel and Ernest settle into their new home (180).

Having made contact, Ethel and Ernest look out for each other on a daily basis. The first moment of dialogue comes from Ethel's employer, impatient with her distracted maid. This impatience is conveyed through Briggs's use of upper-case typeface, 'ETHEL! FOR HEAVEN'S SAKE! WHERE **ARE** YOU?' (5) and the use of a speech bubble with jagged edges to invoke screaming urgency. On Friday, Ethel waits for Ernest, framed by imposing, austere windows, gradually realizing that he is not going to appear. Interestingly, Briggs has extended these frames so that they are longer, and he has altered the perspective so that we see Ethel from a greater distance. Thus Ethel seems diminished, even trapped within the windows and, by association, the job which (it is soon clear) she longs to give up. By comparison the 'Saturday' sequence bursts with colour as Ernest presents Ethel with flowers and asks her out for the first time; the vibrant oranges and reds contrast loudly with the dark plum and grey of the preceding frames.

As Briggs has pointed out, 'there is not a word of narration, only speech bubbles' (2002, web page) in *Ethel and Ernest*, but the narrative perspective is none the less clear. For instance, at this point, sympathy undoubtedly lies with Ethel, rather than 'Madam', the harsh, disembodied voice that disrupts the peaceful and positive sequence of events thus far, and so the worker is championed over the employer.

Once Ethel and Ernest begin courting, it is soon clear that they do not quite share the same world-view. While Ernest is not ashamed of his working-class roots, he recognizes that his childhood home, 'full of diddicois and coster-mongers ... scrap iron, rag and bone men' (7) is not Ethel's 'cup of tea'. The final sequence of frames in this section lapses into comedy, as Ethel frets over leaving her employers, who Ernest labels as 'Bloated plutocrats' (8). Ethel misunderstands and, nose in air, admonishes Ernest for swearing before retorting that she was '**NOT** a skivvy!', as Ernest suggests, but 'a **LADY'S MAID!**' (8). Thus, Briggs sets the pattern for his parents' relationship, in which Ernest, the committed socialist, is keen to advocate the rights of his fellow workers, while Ethel repeatedly militates against his working-class pride in her dogged desire to be recognized as middle-class. Significantly, however, the final image is one of unity, as Ethel and Ernest happily contemplate married life. In this moment of joy, they are unframed and walk towards the next page in anticipation of a happy life together. Of course, Briggs soon demonstrates that 'happiness' is relative and that marriage is more complicated than this hopeful image suggests. *Ethel and Ernest* is essentially about the basic cycle of life and death, charting the agonies, loves and sorrows that make up human experience. In many ways it is typical of the books discussed in this chapter in its powerful expression of that experience through a carefully constructed combination of word and image.

Conclusion

This journey through the work of Raymond Briggs emphasizes some of the common philosophical and political threads that draw together his books. I hope, however, that this has not served to suggest that Briggs's repertoire is either narrow or shallow. There is enormous scope for further research into Briggs's work; for example, his depiction of war or construction of gender, his integration of fantasy and realism, or the tendency toward the car-nivalesque and grotesque that informs his work. Any of these avenues would surely reveal an author–illustrator who always pushes at the boundaries of what literature can do and say, while constructing and marking out his unique world.

WORKS CITED AND FURTHER READING

Primary Texts

Briggs, R., *Fungus the Bogeyman* (London: Puffin, 1990; first published 1977).
Briggs, R., *Gentleman Jim* (London: Hamish Hamilton, 1980).
Briggs, R., *The Snowman* (London: Puffin, 1980; first published 1978).
Briggs, R., *The Man* (London: Red Fox, 1994; first published 1992).
Briggs, R., *The Bear* (London: Red Fox, 1996; first published 1994).
Briggs, R., *Ethel and Ernest* (London: Jonathan Cape, 1998).

Briggs, R. and Vipont, E., *The Elephant and the Bad Baby* (London: Puffin, 1971; first published 1969).

Briggs, R., *Jim and the Beanstalk* (London: Puffin, 1973; first published 1970).

Briggs, R., *Father Christmas* (London: Puffin, 1974; first published 1973).

Briggs, R., *When the Wind Blows* (London: Penguin, 1983; first published 1982).

Briggs, R., *The Tin-Pot Foreign General and the Old Iron Woman* (London: Hamish Hamilton, 1984).

Briggs, R., *UG: Boy Genius of the Stone Age* (London: Jonathan Cape, 2001).

Briggs, R. and Ahlberg, A., *The Adventures of Bert* (London: Viking, 2001).

Briggs, R., *The Puddleman* (London: Bodley Head, 2004).

Critical Texts

Doonan, J., *Looking at Picture Books* (Stroud: Thimble Press, 1993).

Jones, N., *Blooming Books: Raymond Briggs* (London: Bodley Head, 2003).

McCloud, S., *Understanding Comics: The Invisible Art* (New York: Harper Perennial, 1994).

Martin, D., *The Telling Line* (London: Julia MacRae, 1989).

Moss, E., 'Raymond Briggs: On British Attitudes to the Strip Cartoon and Children's-Book Illustration', *Signal*, 28 (January 1979), pp. 26–33.

Pullman, P., 'Picture Stories and Graphic Novels', in K. Reynolds and N. Tucker (eds), *Children's Book Publishing in Britain since 1945* (Aldershot: Ashgate, 1998), pp. 110–32.

Websites

Achuka (2001a) 'Raymond Briggs Interview: Part Two: www.achuka.co.uk/guests/briggs/int03.htm (accessed 28.2.02).

Achuka (2001b) 'Raymond Briggs Interview: Part Five: www.achuka.co.uk/guests/briggs/int06.htm (accessed 28.2.02).

Briggs, R. (2002) 'Why I'd Like to be a Proper Author', *Guardian Unlimited*: http://books.guardian.co.uk/review/story/0,12084,824023,00.html (accessed 10.11.03).

Electronic Texts and Adolescent Agency: Computers and the Internet in Contemporary Children's Fiction

Noga Applebaum

The majority of this study has been concerned with conventional print media; in this final chapter, Noga Applebaum looks at the interactions between prose fiction in book form, and electronic narratives, including those developing on the Internet. While Chapter 13 considers some of the ways that picturebook readers and makers are adjusting their expectations about the organization of space and narrative in response to the icon-based organization of the computer screen, this chapter looks at both the ambivalence surrounding electronic narratives – and, indeed, the whole domain of the Internet – and their potential to facilitate political action in the young. Judith Butler has pointed out that agency is 'always and only a political prerogative' (1992: 13); the problem for the young is that for the most part they lack the tools of agency (public platforms, economic influence, individual experience), and in recent years particularly, many forces at work in culture, not least corporate capitalism, have worked to make them apolitical. If young people are to acquire political agency in tandem with maturity, they need narratives that require them to engage with topical issues and which require them to position themselves. Such narratives must resist the use of the conventions of classic realism (Box 6.1) and demand that readers are consciously involved in and aware of the narrative process. As this chapter shows, the innately non-linear nature of electronic narratives may offer useful ways forward for writers who seek to urge their readers towards positions of agency.

In the last decade, Information Technology (IT) has become a part of everyday life, so much so that it is hard to imagine the world running smoothly without it. Millions of people worldwide use computers to work as well as to surf the Internet in order to find information, buy different products, entertain themselves with games and even pay bills. Many stay in touch using email, and a considerable number of people meet new friends and form online relationships. Not only do computers make our pace of life quicker and our communication abilities broader and more efficient, they also change the way we think and interpret the world around us. Distances diminish, information is more readily available to more people rather than to a selected few, and networking across geographical divides empowers marginalized groups to draw the public's attention to their needs and interests.

The Internet, advanced computer games and virtual reality environments also create an exciting tension between the real and the virtual body, as users can adopt new online personas and may alter any components of their real selves, from age to gender identity. The new technology allows for fresh and intricate stylistic forms as well. Internet and virtual reality (VR) environments are non-linear and enable users to become authors of their own narratives, exploring and creating versatile, sometimes limitless, storylines.

Ambivalent attitudes

Although the Internet is here to stay, and more people get connected each year, it seems that there is still a general fear of the new technology. A recent survey showed that although more than 16 million Britons are regular Internet users, over half of all adults in the UK still believe that the Internet undermines the morality of the nation (*Which? Online Annual Internet Survey, 2001*). Other surveys show that a significant proportion of computer and Internet users is composed of children and young adults (*2-in-10 Are Connected Kids*, 2003). However, a quick look at titles published in the last ten years shows that children's books in which protagonists send owls are increasingly prevalent, while it is still rare to find books in which they send emails.

Adults' attitudes towards young people's use of computers and the Internet are ambivalent. While most western parents believe that information technology contributes to their children's education, many still fear that online activities might expose them to harmful influences and even put them in physical danger (*Safe and Smart*, 1999). These fears exist despite the evidence showing that most young Internet users would not give away personal information online, and that only a small minority encounters frightening or upsetting information on the Web (*Kids Wise Up to Cyberspace Danger*, 2002).

A less widespread concern is that teenagers, especially males, will actively search the Web for pornography. However, while researchers into online sexual addiction recommend that parents do not install a computer in their child's bedroom, they also admit that they are uncertain as to the potential of teenagers to become sexual compulsives as a result of their online sexual behaviours (Freeman-Longo, 2000: 86–9).

Another popular adult fear is that surfing the Web, or generally spending time in front of the monitor, can damage young people's social skills, distract them from activities considered more healthy, such as reading and sports, and turn them into recluses (*Which? Online Annual Internet Survey, 2001*). In their appraisal of online communities, Wellman and Gulia respond to these allegations, asserting that

> Such fears are misstated in several ways. For one thing, they treat community as a zero-sum game, assuming that if people spend more time interacting on-line they will spend less time interacting in 'real life'. Second, such accounts demonstrate the strength and importance of on-line ties, and not their weakness ... strong, intimate ties are capable of being maintained on-line as well as face-to-face. (1996: online at www. acm.org/ccp/references/wellman/wellman.html)

One of the main reasons for these fears is the technological gap existing between parents and their children, as it is often children who bring the technology into the home and explore its potential while the parents' online time is limited to sending a few emails (Wallace, 1999: 246). The vast circulation of child-pornography-related stories in various media contributes to parents' fear (34–5), while policy decisions regarding internet regulation also reflect adult fears about children's activities and presence on the Web by constructing children as passive victims, and focusing on protecting them from harmful online material. They seem to offer parents greater control and reinforce adult authority and power over children, and so policies submit to adult fear rather than hearkening to the needs of the young (Oswell, 1998: 271–91). With this background in mind, it is not surprising that children's and young adult literature, written and published by adults and bought by parents, reflects the same ambivalence towards young people's use of the Internet and computers.

On the other hand, as publishers have realized, computers exert a powerful allure for children and teenagers, who are technology's most avid fans. For this reason, images of monitors and Internet jargon increasingly appear on the covers of children's books, even when their content is only remotely related to IT. *Yo! Dot UK* (2001) uses a website address as a title, setting up expectations that the text will involve the Internet; in fact, the only connection to the Web is an Internet café where a group of teenagers often meet. *Love Bytes* (1997), the first of the teen-romance series @café, also uses both Internet jargon ('bytes') and design ('@') on the cover, yet in the book itself, Internet activities are limited to personal columns published on a cyber-café's website by a group of teenagers employed there. The plots of these two books remain very much in the realm of real life. *PS Longer Letter Later* (1998) revolves around a series of letters exchanged between two girls. In the sequel, the correspondence continues; however, it is now sent by email, and the novel is entitled *Snail Mail No More* (1999), again using popular Web jargon. It is clear that this change is an attempt to increase the book's allure by tapping into contemporary technological culture; significantly, the format of the sequel is virtually identical to that of the original, showing how superficial the change has been. These books, and others like them (see Further Reading), often reflect the ignorance of publishers and authors; ignorance that prevents them from incorporating current technology into a children's book in a manner that does more than pay simple lip service to popular culture in the service of increased sales.

For some years the Web was regarded as 'the preserve of the nerdy 15-year-old boy closeted in his bedroom', a notion which is contradicted by the overwhelming numbers of children of all ages and walks of life that use the Internet today (Clarke, in *Kids Wise Up*, NOP Research Group, 2002). However, 'nerdy' boy characters are abundant in the children's books that incorporate elements of IT to some degree or other. It seems that while adult authors may be keen to hop on the cyber wagon, they shy away from making their central characters too computer literate. Instead they construct loyal sidekicks to the main protagonist in the form of minor characters, unpopular amongst their peers, yet wizards when it comes to computers. These 'nerds' embody parental concerns that the Internet will isolate children from the community. They may also reflect the way in which adults writing for children choose to deal with the feeling that information technology poses a threat to their own profession as a result of the alleged competition between surfing and reading.

The protagonist of John Larkin's *Ghost Byte* (1994) is Brendan, a witty, popular teenager who has a beautiful girlfriend, and whose main interests are swimming and surfing. In contrast, his friend Brains is constantly picked on: 'Brains came wandering across the quadrangle with kids kicking him up the backside as he walked along' (31). Brains, as the nickname suggests, is very clever; however, he is branded a 'geek', and even his best friends wonder: 'Why are we friends with him? ... Shouldn't we have some sort of standards?' (33). Unlike the healthy image of boys his age, Brains hates playing sports and his chief interests are maths and computers. Although Brendan dismisses Brains' 'techno tangents' (85), he still confides in him when a strange ghost starts haunting his computer.

In a similar manner, Louise Cooper provides a computer-literate sidekick to Leo, the hero of her book *Incy Wincy Spider* (2000). Mikey is known as 'the class brainbox' (2), and his chief interests are computers and space. Like Brains, Mikey dislikes sports. He is also the shortest child in his year and wears glasses. As sport is usually associated with a healthy lifestyle, providing children with strength and stamina and involving going outdoors and working in a team, Mikey and Brains' dislike of athletic games reflects the popular fear that a child in front of a monitor is (or will become) unhealthy and weak. Although Mikey saves the day by beating the vicious computer game that Leo downloaded from the Web, Cooper chooses the latter, a 'normal' child, to narrate the story, thus turning Leo into the focal point of her novel and implying that he is the character with whom children should identify.

The situation is summed up succinctly by Adamina, an Internet message board user in Catherine Jinks's *To Die For* (2000), who describes the average Web user thus:

> The Internet is for antisocial losers. ... People who hardly ever emerge from their dark, untidy rooms. People who don't have any real friends. People who don't play sport, who are addicted to computer games, and who are either (a) cursed with enormous IQs together with disfiguring acne, or (b) planning to massacre half the kids at their school.   (14)

In truth, the other users of the board *are* all social outcasts, perverts, or in one case, snowed in. Similar associations between unpopularity and computer literacy can be found in Malorie Blackman's *Computer Ghost* (1997), and Caroline Plaisted's *e-love* (2001).

As mentioned earlier, one of the prominent fears of parents regarding their children's use of the Internet is that an ill-meaning adult will approach their children online, or that they will encounter harmful material. Examination of a range of children's books shows that not only parents, but also authors subscribe to the notion that the Internet gives evil free access to young people.

In Blackman's *Computer Ghost*, Jade, who has recently lost her father, begins to receive emails from him from beyond the grave. He implores Jade to help him but not to tell anyone of their correspondence: 'no one must know about me but you ... don't even tell your mum' (117). To the adult ear, this type of request sounds alarming, as child abusers often emotionally blackmail their victims into silence. Jade, however, being an inexperienced and trusting child, replies to the emails, promising to help the sender, who she believes to be her dead father (19). Luckily, she decides to consult her friends, who raise doubts as to the authenticity of the emails. When the sender asks Jade to search her house for a package and drop it off in a litter bin, her friends point out that: 'if it really was your dad, he'd have known where the package was from the beginning ... and since when does a ghost need a package to be dropped off in a bin ... ?' (137). After some clever detective work, the children discover that the emails were sent by a corrupt work colleague, who is trying to obtain an advanced computer game, developed by Jade's father. Once caught, the criminal and her accomplice declare that they are 'not in the least bit repentant' (199) for manipulating Jade's feelings. Although the crime committed in the book is not of a sexual nature, the fear that the Internet opens a door through which ill-meaning adults can abuse children resonates throughout the novel.

Evil worming its way through the monitor is also at the centre of *Incy Wincy Spider*. Leo downloads from the Web a new computer game called Incy Wincy Spider. The game turns out to be a vicious virus that causes Leo's computer to crash. The trouble does not end here, for the virus crosses the border between the real and the virtual, and the spider from the game emerges from the back of the computer, begins growing at a terrifying rate, and starts spreading cobwebs all around Leo's house. An email from a friend in the USA reveals what is in store for Leo, for it tells of other teenagers who have fallen victim to the spider; their families have had to leave their homes as giant spiders have invaded them (94). Although all ends well, it is not difficult to see the spider and its cobwebs as a metaphor for the amazing speed at which the World Wide Web has established itself as a powerful global medium. The fact that teenagers were responsible for letting the dangerous spider into their family homes further emphasizes how this text reflects perfectly the fears discussed earlier. At the conclusion of this book, Leo declares that: 'He could do without computers for a while. Quite a long while' (148), showing *Incy Wincy Spider* to be a product of the ambivalent attitudes described above. Although she has written a novel revolving around computers, Cooper seems to advise teenagers that they are better of without them.

Unlike Cooper's novel, Caroline Plaisted's *e-love* seems to prefer the direct approach, rather than metaphors, to convey a warning that the Internet is a danger zone. The novel is narrated by Sam, a bright and popular teenager who visits chat rooms only to gossip with her friends because it is cheaper than using the phone (and despite the fact that she believes that anyone using chat rooms to make new friends must be 'a geek' and 'a sad case' (12). Sam warns the readers about the danger that lurks online: 'I know that you have to be a bit careful about what you give away to people when you're on-line. I mean we've all read in the papers about those weirdos out there, haven't we? You know, all those dirty old men who try and chat to young kids' (26). Sam's tone resembles that of an adult lecturing a child rather than a teenager speaking to her peers. Plaisted does not seem to be content with one warning, for it is later repeated by Sam's best friend, as well as by her mother:

> We've read all about those perverts who prey on people via the Internet in the paper. ... You have to be really careful with these people. We've all read about people posing as someone perfectly innocent and then turning out to be truly dangerous. (84–5)

Even Sam's teacher demonstrates her concern for innocent teenaged Internet users: 'Mrs Jones has been telling us all about the nutters that the police reckoned were out there surfing the net and trying to whisk us away' (41). To seal the matter, Sam meets a pervert online. One day, while she is waiting for Dan to log on, she is approached by someone who identifies himself as Steve. After asking 'Do you prefer bikinis or swimsuits?', Steve gets wiped off Sam's screen, 'presumably by whoever was monitoring the chatroom', to Sam's evident relief (61).

However, after constantly warning the reader not to chat to strangers online, Sam does just that. She falls in love with Dan, a boy that she meets in a chat room. Plaisted's novel is equivocal, as it is trying to tell a modern love story that will appeal to teenagers and reflect their own online experiences, while simultaneously embedding within it adult fears in the form of repetitive warnings. The result is a confusing 'don't try this at home' plot that ends, in line with parental morals, with the conclusion that online romance cannot lead to a real and satisfying relationship (141).

Similar warnings about the dangerous potential of the Web can be found in *To Die For*. Neville, the only adult on an Internet message board, constantly warns young users not to give any email addresses or personal details online and to check with their parents before contacting anyone. He reminds them that 'it is easy to lie on the Internet' (79), and asks them not to log on to unknown sites, which may turn out to be obscene. Neville refers to his co-users as 'you girls' (113) and 'a nice girl' (87) when he issues these warnings. Together with the fact that he remains a 'good guy' throughout the book, this establishes his position as a protective adult who only has the children's best interest in mind. However, Neville himself posts his own email address on the message board (14), thus exposing society's double standards when it comes to online conduct for children and adults.

The children's book market does not ignore the information revolution; on the contrary, at times it is keen to exploit computer technology's appeal. However, it has still to resolve the tension between young people's fast-growing technological interest and the fears it evokes in the adults surrounding them. As of yet, this tension continues to be reflected in many books written for children and young adults.

Narrative forms

Computer games, CD-ROMs and MUDs (Multi-User Dungeon or Dimension: a text-based online virtual world created for gaming or social purposes), are all VR (Virtual Reality) environments that challenge the traditional narrative form by dismissing the linear story, which has a beginning, middle and end. Sherry Turkle, a MUD expert, uses terms borrowed from the literary world to describe the attractions of this particular environment:

> There are parallel narratives in the different rooms of the MUD; one can move forward or backward in time. ... The MUDs are authored by their players, thousands of people in all, often hundreds of people at a time, all logged on from different places. (1994: 158–67)

Unlike a reader of a book, a VR player is not merely an observer, but an active participant in the creation of a narrative. Although some VR games, mainly those marketed on CD-ROMs, have an official 'end' – a mission the player needs to accomplish – there are many ways to complete the game, and much of its enjoyment derives from the time spent exploring the different options on offer. MUDs and MOOs (MUD Object Oriented) are more radical, as they usually do not have a starting or an ending point at all.

The interactive nature of these technological gaming environments blurs the boundaries between what is considered 'real life' and what is termed 'virtual'. VR is not merely a 'text' to be 'read'; it is a parallel world, existing simultaneously with the physical one. For example, a VR user can be walking with a friend in a busy virtual street while physically sitting at home alone. Moreover, gamers in MUDs can form relationships and even get virtually married while maintaining similar partnerships in real life. As virtual identities and physical bodies mingle and shift, the very essence of what is 'real' is questioned.

Although many VR environments are based on literary works (such as games based on *The Lord of the Rings* or the Harry Potter series), and despite the fact that young people are more likely than adults to be immersed in VR activities (Wallace, 1999: 246), not many books written for this audience have taken on board the radical literary styles that VR has to offer. However, two novels that do incorporate narrative forms undoubtedly influenced by VR are Lesley Howarth's *Ultraviolet* (2001), and William Sleator's *Rewind* (1999).

Howarth's novel is set in the not-too-distant future, when planet Earth becomes an ecologically damaged world in which, for ten months of the year, the sun's radiation makes it impossible to go outside. Complex, all-immersive VR environments are designed to compensate for outdoor activities. Vi, the protagonist, like many of her teenaged friends, is spending most of her time in Quest – a sophisticated multi-levelled VR adventure game, which includes 'feelies' – physical props to enhance the sensation of reality. Quest also allows gamers to 'paste in' elements of their own life into the gameplan (15).

However, Vi is tired of being cooped up and decides to 'leak', slang for going outside. She undergoes many adventures and meets a charismatic 'leakers' gang-leader named Jope. Jope convinces Vi to betray her father, who works for a corporation manufacturing expensive anti-radiation material, by breaking into his computer files and disclosing the location of his secret factory, so that the 'leakers' can raid it. The plot unfolds through the first half of the book, at which point Vi's father rips the headset off her head and Vi, and the reader, discover that she has been Questing for months and all her adventures have taken place in Virtual Reality. This surprising turn of events makes the reader reconsider the narrative told so far. As Vi tries to piece together her story, separating what was real and what was virtual, the reader must do the same in order to understand what has happened and what is about to happen. Howarth does not overtly signal the shift between the reality of the game and the reality of her protagonist (there are clues, but many readers will only notice these on a second reading). Thus the fluid boundaries between the physical world and the virtual one is experienced at first hand.

The second half of the book includes a section in which Vi and her father seem to go on a journey; however, the experienced reader knows that the episode may well be virtual. Vi and her father create a rosy future scenario, one which they both agree is 'a bit over the top' (242). The plot continues; however, at this point the reader is already supplied with one version of an end.

Howarth successfully conveys the playfulness of the virtual narrative, not only the one played by Vi, but also the one held by the reader. By the end of the book, Vi produces a manuscript printed off the Net. It is entitled *Ultraviolet*, and it is the result of her questing. She declares it is 'at least my fifth different ending' and that 'it leads back to itself' (243–4). The reader is therefore holding the looped product of a VR journey and is invited to re-read the complete text in a new light. Howarth is unusual in striking a balance between new and old narrative technologies; she suggests that a handheld book can be regarded, and function, as a kind of Virtual Reality, and that computerized Virtual Reality games are just as valid as other forms of narrative (Stratton, in Porter, 1997: 259–64).

Unlike *Ultraviolet*, the novel *Rewind* does not engage in a computer-driven plot. However, the structure of the narrative implies that the author was influenced by Internet and computer games, for it is non-linear and includes several beginnings, middles and endings. Peter is an eleven-year-old whose adoptive parents are expecting their first natural child. The fear of being unwanted brings the conflict between artistic, temperamental Peter and his down-to-earth parents to a tragic climax when the boy runs out of the house and is killed by a passing car. Once dead, Peter is given various opportunities to change his life story in ways that would prevent his death. He is given the power to go back in time, to a moment of his own choosing, to make different decisions. If he fails, he knows his death will become permanent. Peter does fail, twice, but as he moves backwards and forwards in time, he learns new things about himself and his relationship with his parents and friends, things which help him to succeed on his third and final attempt.

Rewind resembles a computer game in a number of ways. There is a task to accomplish, and many possible paths to achieve it. However, a wrong move leads to the termination of the game. The player can then start again, benefiting from information gathered in previous attempts. There are crossroads along the way, where decisions must be made that can easily affect the outcome of the game. In this manner, Peter's reaction to the same, seemingly insignificant, event, such as the new assignment in his favourite art class, can lead to his failure or success. Moreover, while an ordinary computer game has one starting point, *Rewind* has several, as in each attempt Peter chooses to go further and further back in time.

Sleator supplies his reader with a multi-stranded narrative. Following each strand separately introduces the reader to a linear, stand-alone story, but together they encompass a rich variety of options, implying that other ways to succeed or fail in the mission still live beyond the written text.

Ultraviolet and *Rewind* are both unusual examples of the influence of Internet and VR narrative styles on literature written for young people. It seems that authors of prose fiction have not yet come to grips with these radical influences, and there is still much confusion about the ways VR's narrative forms may be adopted into the written text. Undoubtedly this confusion will be resolved in the future, as the next generation of authors, who have grown up with electronic narratives as well as those in print and other media forms, begin to write of their own technological experiences.

Internet and politics

The Internet is a meeting place for people from all walks of life. Unlike other media, such as television or newspapers, which typically broadcast the opinions of a minority to a silent, absorbing majority, the Internet offers an unsupervised, interactive arena where people may voice their opinions and debate them publicly. It is therefore potentially a powerful democratic tool. Furthermore, the Internet cuts across geo-physical boundaries, and its users interact with each other on the basis of shared interests rather than common cultural denominators. This allows marginalized groups, which were formerly oppressed by either state or culture, to network globally and make their voices heard. Young people, having been denied the right to vote or be elected, and thus being dependent on adults to represent their political and social needs, may be one of the chief groups to benefit from this online alternative political sphere. However, the open nature of the Web is a cause for concern, not only for nation-states, democratic or non-democratic (Haselton: online at <www. peacefire.org/info/why.shtml>), but also for parents and teachers. There have been many attempts to regulate and supervise the Internet, and as the debate about online censorship goes on, it becomes clear that it has much to do with adults' attempt to control minors' Internet activity. Although the discourse revolves around protecting the vulnerable, it is clearly a struggle for control, which perhaps reflects adults' fear of young people's potential political power. Indeed, teenagers have already founded an online organization to fight blocking software often used by parents to prevent their children from accessing parts of the Web (Lockard, in Porter, 1997: 228).

The debate about censorship is not the only political discourse surrounding information technology. The Internet is frequently referred to as the 'global village', as many believe that it can bridge the gap between different cultures and help create a multicultural, more tolerant, society. However, experts such as Joseph Lockard claim that this potential is yet to be fulfilled. Lockard criticizes the Web for engaging in a pseudo-multicultural discourse that is in fact dominated by western culture (Lockard, in Porter, 1997: 228). The fact that getting connected is still a luxury, and that the necessary equipment is beyond the means of many, reinforces Lockard's criticism. Furthermore, as most of the information and communication on the Net is available exclusively to English speakers, it seems that there is a long way to go before the dream of the democratic global village will come true.

A small number of novels for children and young adults capture the main themes of this wider debate regarding the Internet as an alternative public sphere. They echo the discourse of Internet liberalism – of its potential to promote multiculturalism, freedom of speech and the possibilities for minors' online political activism. *Amongst the Hidden* (1998) and *Weather Eye* (1995) are two such novels depicting young people's attempts to transcend their inferior political status by networking online to gain recognition and change society. However, they differ in their attitudes towards such networking.

Margaret Haddix's *Amongst the Hidden* tells the story of Luke, a secret third child living under a totalitarian regime that forbids families from having more than two children, because of food shortages. Cooped up, scared and lonely, Luke spends his time spying on the new houses built near his parents' farm. One day he discovers Jen, the third daughter of a neighbouring high-ranking government official. Jen is streetwise, and while Luke and his family fear the authorities, Jen already reckons that 'everybody knows the Government's not that competent' (48). She knows that the government's declaration that public television and the Internet are monitored is nothing but 'propaganda stuff' (54), and she sets up a secret chat room for third children. Using the web, Jen plans a rally to free the shadow children, an open challenge to mainstream political power. Through Jen, Haddix begins to confront issues such as propaganda and human rights. Jen believes that it is up to her and the other children to change their fate. She believes that 'action's the only thing that counts' (89), and thus she represents the rebellious child who challenges adult authority, in this case using information technology as a revolutionary tool.

Unlike Jen, Luke is cautious. He refuses to join her rally and finds out later that she and sixty other children who dared to show up were shot dead by the police. Luke escapes using fake papers and makes his own plans for helping the shadow children, all of which involve finishing his studies and becoming an adult first (116).

Although the Internet in Haddix's novel is constructed as a place of free speech, where children may create political and social networks, Jen's bitter fate suggests that child power is a problematic issue for the adult writer. Luke is the one who remains alive to carry on to the next book in what is planned to be a trilogy. Thus it is implied that if children wish to challenge adult authority, they need to do it slowly and individually, and preferably grow up first.

Lesley Howarth's *Weather Eye* also engages with an online network of socially aware children. Written before the end of the millennium, it predicts violent global weather during 1999. Telly lives on a wind-farm in England. She is an active member of Weather Eye, an online international club for young meteorologists. She realizes something is wrong with the weather and that the adults around her are too afraid to admit it: 'there would be no adults in Weather Eye Club, because they didn't want to see what was going on' (55). The online network of environmentally aware children is thus constructed as superior to the adults, and their actions are almost subversive.

Following a near-death experience, Telly realizes that the weather reflects society's violence. She hatches a plan to calm things by posting a picture of a tree on the Web and asking Weather Eye members to meditate on it every evening at 7.00 pm their time. The campaign, under the motto 'One Safe Haven in Our Mind' (96), is successful. It mobilizes other children to campaign for environmental awareness in their localities. The children announce their supremacy online: 'Kids, active on all fronts. Adults, brighter later' (171). Telly, satisfied, declares 'Kids could make a difference' (173). Indeed, by the end of the book, the adults admit that children do have something to teach society.

Weather Eye is a song of praise to the Internet as a political domain for children. The website's diverse members, all from different cultural backgrounds, connect online to make a real difference. Howarth's text strongly reflects the notion that the Web creates positive opportunities for children to be heard globally. The adults in her text are anachronistic and weak, afraid to make changes, and online activity gives young people the chance to network behind their backs and challenge their authority and experience. In this sense Howarth is different from Haddix as she is aware of the permanent gap between adults and children and chooses to celebrate the potential of children's solidarity, independent of adults' authority and control. Haddix, in contrast, perpetuates the rift by questioning children's ability to mobilize themselves as a unified political force.

Conclusion

Information technology plays an integral part in young people's lives, and is slowly finding its way into the books written for them; however, at the time of writing, representations of computers and the Internet in books for young readers are characterized and burdened by confusion and fear, as a consequence of the technological gap between adult authors and their constantly evolving young readers. The likelihood is that in the near future, books for children and young adults will make more sophisticated use of non-linear narrative formats and exploit the tension created between the virtual and the physical body. The recognition of IT's literary potential will perhaps lead to a cease-fire in the war between surfing and reading.

WORKS CITED AND FURTHER READING

Primary Texts

Blackman, M., *Computer Ghost* (London: Scholastic Hippo Paperback, 1997).
Cooper, L., *Incy Wincy Spider*, 'Creatures', no. 8 (London: Scholastic, 2000).
Craft, E., *Love Bytes* (New York: Archway, 1997).
Danzinger, P. and Martin, A. M., *Snail Mail No More* (London: Hodder, 1999).
Haddix, M., *Amongst the Hidden* (London: Red Fox, 2001).
Howarth, L., *Weather Eye* (London: Walker, 1995); *Ultraviolet* (London: Puffin, 2001).
Jinks, C., *To Die For* (London: Macmillan, 2002).
Larkin, J., *Ghost Byte* (Sydney: Random House, 1994).
Meres, J., *Yo! Dot UK* (London: Picaddily, 2001).
Plaisted, C., *e-love* (London: Piccadilly, 2001).
Sleator, W., *Rewind* (New York: Puffin, 2001).

Critical Texts

Freeman-Longo, R. E., 'Children, Teens and Sex on the Internet', *Sexual Addiction and Compulsivity: The Journal of Treatment and Prevention*, 7(1–2) (2000), pp. 86–9.
Lockard, J., 'Progressive Politics: Electronic Individualism and the Myth of Virtual Community', in D. Porter (ed.), *Internet Culture* (New York: Routledge, 1997).
Mackey, M., *Literacies Across Media: Playing the Text* (London and New York: Routledge, 2002).
Mackey, M., 'Playing in the Phase Space: Contemporary Forms of Fictional Pleasure', *Signal*, 88 (January 1999), pp. 16–33.
Oswell, D., 'The Place of "Childhood" in Internet Content Regulation: a Case Study of Policy in the UK', *International Journal of Cultural Studies*, 1(2) (August 1998), pp. 271–91.

Stratton, J., 'Cyberspace and the Globalization of Culture', in D. Porter (ed.), *Internet Culture* (New York: Routledge, 1997).

Turkle, S., 'Constructions and Reconstructions of Self in Virtual Reality: Playing in the MUDs', *Mind, Culture and Activity*, 1(3) (1994), pp. 158–67, and online: ‹web.mit.edu/sturkle/www/constructions.html›.

Wallace, P., *The Psychology of the Internet* (Cambridge: Cambridge University Press, 1999).

Wellman, B. and Gulia, M., 'Net Surfers Don't Ride Alone: Virtual Communities as Communities', in P. Kollock and M. Smith (eds), *Communities in Cyberspace* (Berkeley: University of California Press, 1996), and online: ‹www.acm.org/ccp/references/wellman/wellman.html›.

Websites

CyberAtlas, *Population Explosion!*, online at: http://cyberatlas.internet.com/big_picture/geographics/article/0,1323,5911_151151,00.html›.

Girls Catch Boys as Three-Quarters of Kids Use Internet (NOP Research Group, 16 August 2001), online: ‹www.nopres.co.uk/›.

Haselton, B., *Why We Do This: A Note to People who Think we Suck*, online: ‹www.peacefire.org/info/why.shtml›.

Internet Upsets Kids (NOP Research Group, 1 November 1998), online: ‹www.nopres.co.uk/›.

Kids Wise Up to Cyberspace Danger (NOP Research Group, 18, January 2002), online: ‹www.nopres.co.uk/›)

Neilsen Net Rating, *13 Million Kids Using the Internet across Europe*, online at: www.neilsen-netratings.com/pr/pr_030930_UK.pdf.

Safe and Smart — Research and Guidelines for Children's Use of the Internet (National School Boards Foundation, USA, 1999), online: ‹www.nsbf.org/safe-smart/full-report.htm›.

Turow, J., *The Internet and the Family: The View from the Family, the View from the Press* (the Annenberg Public Policy Center of the University of Pennsylvania, 1999), online: ‹http://appcpenn.org/internet/family/rep.227.pdf›.

Which.net Annual Internet Survey, 2001, online: www.which.net/surveys/findings.htm›.

2-in-10 Are Connected Kids, online at: ‹http://cyberatlas.internet.com/big_picture/demographics/article/0,1323,5901_3110071,00.html›.

Children's Books

Blackman, M., *Hacker* (London: Corgi, 1993).

Brown, E., *Untouchable* (London: Dolphin Paperback, 1997).

Cooper, S., *The Boggart* (London: Puffin, 1994).

Cross, G., *The Prime Minister's Brain* (Oxford: Oxford University Press, 1990).

Gibbons, A., *Shadow of the Minotaur* (London: Dolphin Paperbacks, 2000).

MacLeod, K., *Cydonia* (London: Dolphin Paperbacks, 1998).

Rubinstein, G., *Space Demons* (London: Dolphin Paperbacks, 1997).

References

(Also see the works cited and suggestions for further reading at the end of each chapter.)

Abrams, J. (ed.) (1991) *Reclaiming the Inner Child* (London: HarperCollins).

Agnew, K. and Fox, G. (2001) *Children at War: From the First World War to the Gulf* (London: Continuum).

Agnew, K. et al. (2001) 'Historical fiction', in V. Watson (ed.), *The Cambridge Guide to Children's Books in English* (Cambridge: Cambridge University Press), pp. 335–8.

Ann, M. and Imel, D. (1995) *Goddesses in World Mythology* (New York: Oxford University Press).

Appleyard, J. (1991; paperback 1994) *Becoming a Reader: The Experience of Fiction from Childhood to Adulthood* (Cambridge: Cambridge University Press, 1990).

Arizpe, E. and Styles, M. (2003) *Children Reading Pictures* (London: RoutledgeFalmer).

Atkinson, J. (1992) 'Shamanisms Today', *Annual Review of Anthropology*, 21, pp. 307–30.

Attebery, B. (1992) *Strategies of Fantasy* (Bloomington and Indianapolis: Indiana University Press.

Auchmuty, R. (1992) *A World of Girls: The Appeal of the Girls' School Story* (London: The Women's Press).

Bachelard, Gaston (1994) *The Poetics of Space* (Boston, MA: Beacon Press).

Bader, B. (1976) *American Picturebooks from Noah's Ark to the Beast Within* (New York: Macmillan).

Balzer, M. (ed.) (1997) *Shamanic Worlds: Rituals and Lore of Siberia and Central Asia* (New York: M. E. Sharpe).

Banham, D. (1992) *Monasteriales Indicia* (Hockwold-cum-Wilton, Norfolk: Anglo-Saxon Books).

Barry, Peter (1995) *Beginning Theory: An Introduction to Literary Cultural Theory* (Manchester and New York: Manchester University Press).

Bassnett, S. (1993) *Comparative Literature: A Critical Introduction* (Oxford: Blackwell).

Batho, B. *et al.* (1998) *War and Peace in Children's Books: A Selection* (Brighton: University of Brighton).

Bawden, Nina (1994) *In My Own Time: Almost an Autobiography* (London: Virago).

Belsey, C. (1980) *Critical Practice* (London Methuen).

Benjamin, W. (1969) 'The Work of Art in an Age of Mechnical Reproduction', in *Illuminations*, ed. H. Arendt, trans. H. Zohan (New York: Schocken Books).

Bettelheim, B. (1991) *The Uses of Enchantment* (London: Penguin).

Bohm, D. (1994) *Wholeness and the Implicate Order* (London: Routledge).

Booktrusted News, issue 2, Autumn 2002.

Bradford, C. (2003) 'Aboriginal Visual Narratives for Children: a Politics of Places', in M. Styles and E. Bearne (eds), *Art, Narrative and Childhood* (Stoke-on-Trent: Trentham Books).

Bull, Angela (1984) *Noel Streatfeild* (London: Collins).

Butler, J. (1992) 'Contingent Foundations, Feminism and the Question of Postmodernism', in J. Butler and J. Scott (eds), *Feminists Theorize the Political* (New York: Routledge).

Campbell, J. (1995) *Past Space and Self* (Cambridge, MA and London: MIT Press).

Cantor, N. (1991) *Inventing the Middle Ages: The Lives, Works, and Ideas of the Great Medievalists of the Twentieth Century* (New York: Morrow).

Carpenter, H. (1978) *The Inklings* (London: HarperCollins).

Carpenter, H. and Prichard, M. (1984) *The Oxford Companion to Children's Literature* (Oxford and New York: Oxford University Press, 1984).

Carr, E. H. (1986) *What is History?* (Harmondsworth: Penguin).

Carter, J. (1999) *Talking Books: Children's Authors Talk about the Craft, Creativity and Process of Writing* (London: Routledge).

Cleverley, John and Phillips, D. C. (1986) *Visions of Childhood: Influential Models from Locke to Spock* (New York and London: Teachers College Press).

Collins, F. and Graham, J. (eds) (2001) *Historical Fiction for Children: Capturing the Past* (London: Fulton).

Cott, J. (1983) *Pipers at the Gates of Dawn: The Wisdom of Children's Books* (Harmondsworth: Viking).

Crossley-Holland, K., Sail, L. and Drew, S. (1999) *The New Exeter Book of Riddles* (London: Enitharmon Press, 2000).

Cunningham, H. (1996) *Children and Childhood in Western Society since 1500* (London and New York: Longman).

Dash, M. (2002) *Batavia's Graveyard* (London: Weidenfeld & Nicolson).

Dollimore, J. and Sinfield, A. (eds.) *Political Shakespeare: New Essays in Cultural Materialism* (Manchester: Manchester University Press).

Donaldson, M. (1978) *Children's Minds* (Glasgow: Fontana).

Doonan, J. (1993) *Looking at Pictures in Picture Books* (Stroud: Thimble Press).

Dusinberre, J. (1987) *Alice to the Lighthouse: Children's Books and Radical Experiments in Art* (Basingstoke: Macmillan).

Eagleton, M. (ed.) (1996) *Feminist Literary Theory: A Reader* (Oxford: Blackwell).

Eagleton, T. (1983) *Literary Theory: An Introduction* (Oxford: Basil Blackwell).

Egoff, S., Stubbs, E. T. and Ashley, L. F. (eds) (1980) *Only Connect: Readings on Childern's Literature*, 2nd edition (Toronto: Oxford University Press).

Erikson, E. (1968) *Identity, Youth and Crisis* (New York: W. W. Norton).

Evans, J. (ed.) (1998) *What's in the Picture? Responding to Illustrations in Picturebooks* (London: Paul Chapman).

Ferguson, N. (2003) *How Britain Made the Modern World* (London: Allen Lane).

Fowles, J. (2000) *The Tree* (London: Random House).

Fox, C. *et al.* (eds) (2000) *In Times of War: An Anthology of War and Peace in Children's Books* (London: Pavilion).

Freeman-Longo, R. E. (2000) 'Children, Teens and Sex on the Internet', *Sexual Addiction and Compulsivity: The Journal of Treatment and Prevention*, 7 (1–2), pp. 86–9.

Freud, S. (1963) 'Symbolism in Dreams' (1916) in the Collected Works, vol. XV (London: Hogarth Press).

Freud, S. (1990) 'The Uncanny', *The Penguin Freud Library*, vol. 14, *Art and Literature* (London: Penguin).

Fried, Kerry (2003) 'Amazon.com: Darkness Visible: an Interview with Phillip Pullman', Internet WWW page at (accessed 14 October 2003).

Fry, D. (1985) *Children Talk about Books: Seeing Themselves as Readers* (Milton Keynes: Open University Press).

Furlong, M. (1991) *A Dangerous Delight: Women and Power in the Church* (London: SPCK).

Gantz, G. (trans.) (1976) *The Mabinogion* (Harmondsworth: Penguin).

Garner, A. (1971) *The Voice that Thunders* (London: Harvill Press).

Gavin, A. and Routledge, C. (eds) (2001) *Mystery in Children's Literature: From the Rational to the Supernatural* (Basingstoke: Palgrave).

Gillis, John R. (1974) *Youth and History* (New York and London: Academic Press).

Golden, C. et al. (2000) *Buffy the Vampire Slayer: The Monster Book* (New York: Pocket Books).

Graham, J. (1990) *Pictures on the Page* (Sheffield: NATE).

Guroian, V. (1998) *Tending the Heart of Virtue: How Classic Stories Awaken a Child's Moral Imagination* (Oxford and New York: Oxford University Press).

Gusdorf, George (1980; first published 1956) 'Conditions and Limits of Autobiography', in J. Olney (ed.), *Autobiography: Essays Theoretical and Critical* (Princeton, NJ: Princeton University Press), pp. 22–48.

Hall, L. (1998) 'The Pattern of Dead and Living: Lucy Boston and the Necessity of Continuity', *Children's Literature in Education*, 29(4), pp. 223–36.

Hobsbawm, E. (1994) *Age of Extremes: The Short Twentieth Century, 1914–1991* (Harmondsworth: Penguin).

Hollindale, P. (1994; first published 1988) *Ideology and the Children's Book* (Stroud: Thimble Press).

Hollindale, P. (1997) *Signs of Childness in Children's Books* (Stroud: Thimble Press).

Holquist, M. (1990) *Dialogism: Bakhtin and his World* (London: Routledge).

Humble, N. (2003) 'Eccentric Families in the Fiction of Adolescence from the 1920s to the 1940s', in K. Reynolds (ed.), *Childhood Remembered* (London: NCRCL, 1998; republished by Pied Piper Publishing).

Hunt, P. (ed.) (1990) *Children's Literature: The Development of Criticism* (London: Routledge).

Hunt, P. (ed.) (1992) *Literature for Children: Contemporary Criticism* (London: Routledge).

Hunt, P. (1994) *An Introduction to Children's Literature* (Oxford: Oxford University Press).

Hunt, P. (ed.) (1995) *Children's Literature: An Illustrated History* (Oxford and New York: Oxford University Press).

Hunt, P. (ed.) (1996) *International Companion Encyclopedia of Children's Literature* (London: Routledge).

Hunt, P. and Lenz, M. (2001) *Alternative Worlds in Fantasy Fiction* (London and New York: Continuum).

Jackson, R. (1995) *Fantasy: The Literature of Subversion* (London and New York: Routledge; first published 1981).

Jameson, F. (1991) *Postmodernism: or Cultural Logic of Late Capitalism* (London: Verso).

Jamal, H. (1987) *Shape Shifters: Shaman Women in Contemporary Society* (Harmondsworth: Penguin).

Johnston, R. (1995) 'The Special Magic of the Eighties: Shaping Words and Shape-shifting Words', *Children's Literature in Education*, 26(4): 119–33.

Jung, C. (1980) *The Archetypes and the Collective Unconscious*, trans. R. F. C. Hull (Princeton: Princeton University Press).

Jung, C. (1990) *The Basic Writings of C. G. Jung*, trans. R. F. C. Hull, ed. V. S. De Laszlo (Princeton, NJ: Princeton University Press, 1990; first published, 1959).

Jung, C. (1991) 'The Psychology of the Child Archetype', trans. R. F. C. Hull, in J. Abrams (ed.), *Reclaiming the Inner Child* (London: HarperCollins).

Kern, S. (1983) *The Culture of Space and Time, 1880–1918* (London: Weidenfeld and Nicolson).

Kimmel, E. A. (1977) 'Confronting the Ovens: the Holocaust and Juvenile Fiction', *The Horn Book Magazine*, vol. LIII, no. 1, pp. 84–91.

Kirkpatrick, R. J. (2000) *The Encyclopaedia of Boy's School Stories* (Aldershot: Ashgate).

Krips, V. (1999) 'Presencing the Past', *Signal*, 90 (September), pp. 176–86.

Krips, V. (2000) *The Presence of the Past: Memory, Heritage and Childhood in Postwar Britain* (London and New York: Garland).

Lathey, G. (1999) *The Impossible Legacy: Identity and Purpose in Autobiographical Children's Literature Set in the Third Reich and the Second World War* (Berne: Peter Lang).

Lathey, G. (2003) 'Time, Narrative Intimacy and the Child: Implications of the Transition from the Present to the Past Tense in the Translation into English of Children's Texts', *Meta Translators' Journal*, 48(1–2), pp. 233–40.

Leeson, R. (1985) *Reading and Righting* (London: Collins).

Le Guin, U. (1989) 'The Child and the Shadow', in U. Le Guin, *The Language of the Night: Essays on Fantasy and Science Fiction* (London: The Women's Press), pp. 49–60.

Lesnik-Oberstein, K. (1994) *Children's Literature Criticism and the Fictional Child* (Oxford: Clarendon Press).

Lewis, D. (2001) *Reading Contemporary Picture Books* (London: RoutledgeFalmer).

Lockwood, M. (1992) '"A Sense of the Spoken": Language in *The Owl Service*', *Children's Literature in Education*, 23(2).

Lodge, D. (1981) *Working with Structuralism* (London: Routledge).

Lurie, A. (1990) *Don't Tell the Grown-Ups: Subversive Children's Literature* (London: Bloomsbury).

McCallum, R. (1999) *Ideologies of Identity in Adolescent Fiction: The Dialogic Construction of Subjectivity* (New York and London: Garland).

McGillis, R. (1997) *The Nimble Reader: Literary Theory and Children's Literature* (New York: Twayne).

Mackey, M. (1999) 'Playing in the Phase Space: Contemporary Forms of Fictional Pleasure', in *Signal*, 88, pp. 16–33.

Mackey, M. (2002) *Literacies Across Media: Playing the Text* (London and New York: Routledge).

Magnusson, M. (ed.) (1990) *Chambers Biographical Dictionary*, 5th edition (Edinburgh: Chambers Harrap).

Mallan, K. and Pearce, S. (eds) (2003) *Youth Cultures: Texts, Images, Identities* (Westport, CT: Praeger).

Manlove, C. N. (1983) 'Fantasy and Loss: T. H. White', in *The Impulse of Fantasy Literature* (Kent, OH: Kent State University Press).

Martin, D. (1989) *The Telling Line* (London: Julia MacRae).

Maund, K. (1997) 'History in Fantasy', in J. Clute and J. Grant (eds), *The Encyclopedia of Fantasy* (London: Orbit), pp. 468–9.

McCloud, S. (1994) *Understanding Comics* (New York: HarperCollins).

Meek, M. (1988) *How Texts Teach what Readers Learn* (Stroud: Thimble Press).

Meek, M., Warlow, A. and Barton, G. (eds) (1997) *The Cool Web: The Pattern of Children's Reading* (London: Bodley Head).

Mitchell, J. (2000) *Psychoanalysis and Feminism: Radical Reassessment of Freudian Psychoanalysis* (Harmondsworth: Penguin; first published 1974).

Molson, F. (1981) 'Children's Fantasy and Science Fiction', in M. B. Tymn (ed.), *The Science Fiction Reference Book* (Mercer Island, WA: Starmont House).

Morris, P. (ed.) (1994) *The Bakhtin Reader* (London: Edward Arnold).

Moss, E. (1979) 'Raymond Briggs: On British Attitudes to the Strip Cartoon and Children's-Book Illustration', *Signal*, 28 (January), pp. 26–33.

Nelson, C. (2003) 'The *Unheimlich* Manoeuver: Uncanny Domesticity in the Urban Waif Tale', in K. Mallan and S. Pearce (eds) *Youth Cultures: Texts, Images, and Identities* (London and Westport, CT: Praeger).

Nikolajeva, M. (1996) *Children's Literature Comes of Age: Toward a New Aesthetic* (New York and London: Garland).

Nikolajeva, M. (1988) *The Magic Code: The Use of Magical Patterns in Fantasy for Children* (Stockholm: Almqvist and Wiksell International).

Nikolajeva, M. and Scott, C. (2001) *How Picturebooks Work* (New York: Garland).

Nodelman, P. (1988) *Words about Pictures: The Narrative Art of Children's Picture Book* (Athens, GA and London: University of Georgia Press).

Nodelman, P. (1996) *The Pleasures of Children's Literature* (New York: Longman).

Olney, J. (ed.) (1980) *Autobiography: Essays Theoretical and Critical* (Princeton, NJ: Princeton University Press).

Olsen, L. (1987) *Ellipse of Uncertainty: An Introduction to Postmodern Fantasy* (New York and London: Greenwood Press).

O'Malley, A. (2003) 'Mary Norton's *Borrowers* Series and the Myth of the Paternalist Past', in *Children Literature*, 31, pp. 71–89.

O'Neill, T. (1980) *The Individuated Hobbit* (London: Thames & Hudson; first published 1979).

O'Sullivan, E. (1990) *Friend and Foe: The Image of Germany and the Germans in British Children's Fiction from 1870 to the Present* (Tubingen: Gunter Narr Verlag).

Oswell, D. (1998) 'The Place of "Childhood" in Internet Content Regulation: a Case Study of Policy in the UK', *International Journal of Cultural Studies*, 1(2) (August), pp. 271–91.

Pascal, R. (1960) *Design and Truth in Autobiography* (London: Routledge).

Paul, L. (1987) 'Enigma Variations: What Feminist Theory Knows about Children's Literature', *Signal*, 54 (Sept. 1987), pp. 186–201.

Paul, L. (1992) 'Intimations of Imitations: Mimesis, Fractal Geometry and Children's Literature', in P. Hunt (ed.), *Literature for Children* (London: Routledge), pp. 66–77.

Pearce, P. (1990) 'Time Present', in *Travellers in Time: Past, Present and to Come – Proceedings* (Greenbay: Children's Literature New England), pp. 70–4.

Philip, N. (1981) *A Fine Anger: A Critical Introduction to the Work of Alan Garner* (London: Collins).

Philip, N. (1997) 'England's Dreaming', *Signal*, 82 (January), pp. 14–30.

Piaget, J. (1953) *The Origin of Intelligence in the Child*, trans. M. Cook (London: Routledge).

Pinsent, P. (1997) *Children's Literature and the Politics of Equality* (London: David Fulton).

Pinsent, P. (ed.) (2001) *The Big Issues: Representations of Socially Marginalized Groups and Individuals in Children's Literature, Past and Present* (London: NCRCL).

Power, E. (1922) *Medieval English Nunneries, c. 1275–1535* (Cambridge: Cambridge University Press).

Porter, D. (ed.) (1997) *Internet Culture* (New York: Routledge).

Pullman, P. (1998) 'Picture Stories and Graphic Novels', in K. Reynolds and N. Tucker (eds), *Children's Book Publishing in Britain since 1945* (Aldershot: Ashgate), pp. 110–32.

Rahn, S. (1991) 'An Evolving Past: the Story of Historical Fiction and Nonfiction for Children', *The Lion and the Unicorn*, 15, pp. 468–9.

Reynolds, K. (1994) *Children's Literature in the 1890s and 1990s* (Plymouth: Northcote House).

Reynolds, K. (ed.) (2001) *Frightening Fiction* (London: Continuum).

Reynolds, K. and Tucker, N. (eds.) (1998) *Children's Book Publishing in Britain since 1945* (Aldershot: Scolar/Ashgate).

Richards, J. (1988) *Happiest Days: The Public Schools in English Fiction* (Manchester: Manchester University Press).

Ricoeur, P. (1981) 'Narrative Time', in W. J. T. Mitchell (ed.), *On Narrative* (Chicago and London: University of Chicago Press).

Rose, J. (1984) *The Case of Peter Pan, or, The Impossibility of Children's Literature* (Basingstoke: Macmillan).

Rowland, S. (1999) *C. G. Jung and Literary Theory: The Challenge from Fiction* (Basingstoke: Macmillan).

Rowntree, B. S. (2000; first published 1901) *Poverty: A Study of Town Life* (Oxford: Polity Press).

Royle, N. (2003) *The Uncanny* (Manchester: Manchester University Press).

Rudd, D. (2000) *Enid Blyton and the Mystery of Children's Literature* (Basingstoke: Macmillan).

Russ, J. (1995) 'Introduction' to A. Williams and R. Jones (eds), *The Penguin Book of Modern Fantasy by Women* (Harmondsworth: Penguin).

Rustin, M. and M. (2001) *Narratives of Love and Loss: Studies in Modern Children's Fiction* (London: Verso, 1987; revised edition, London and New York: Karnac).

Scott Littleton, C. (ed.) (2002) *Mythology: The Illustrated Anthology of World Myth and Storytelling* (London: Duncan Baird).

Sebeok, D. and T. (1987) *Monastic Sign Languages* (New York: Mouton de Gruyter).

Shavit, Z. (1986) *The Poetics of Children's Literature* (Athens, GA: University of Georgia Press).

Shavit, Z. (1988) 'Die Darstellung des Nationalsozialismus und des Holocaust in der deutschen und israelischen Kinder- und Jugendliteratur', in M. Dahrendorf and Z. Shavit (eds), *Die Darstellung des dritten Reichs im Kinder- und Jugendbuch* (Frankfurt: dipa).

Sims, S. and Clare, H. (2000) *The Encyclopaedia of Girls' School Stories* (Aldershot: Ashgate).

Sinfield, A. (ed.) (1983) *Society and Literature, 1945–1970* (London: Methuen).

Smith, D. (2001) *Dear Octopus* (London: Samuel French).

Snow, C. P. (1993) *The Two Cultures* (Cambridge: Cambridge University Press; first published 1959).

Spock, B. (1946) *Baby and Child Care* (New York: Pocketbooks).

Spufford, F. (2002) *The Child that Books Built* (London: Faber and Faber).

Stephens, J. (1992) *Language and Ideology in Children's Fiction* (Harlow: Longman).

Stephens, J. and McCallum, R. (1998) *Retelling Stories, Framing Culture: Traditional Stories and Metanarratives in Children's Literature* (New York and London: Garland).

Stephens, J. and McCallum, R. (2001) ' "There are Worse Things than Ghosts": Reworking Horror Chronotopes in Australian Childrens Fiction', in A. E. Gavin and C. Routledge (eds), *Mystery in Children's Literature: From the Rational to the Supernatural* (Basingstoke: Palgrave Macmillan), pp. 165–83.

Stewig, J. (1995) 'The Witch Woman: A Recurring Motif in Recent Fantasy Writing for Young Readers', *Children's Literature in Education*, 26(4), pp. 119–33.

Stonehill, B. (1988) *The Self-Conscious Novel: Artifice in Fiction from Joyce to Pynchon* (Philadelphia: University of Pennsylvania Press).

Stratton, J. (1997) 'Cyberspace and the Globalization of Culture', in D. Porter (ed.) *Internet Culture* (New York: Routledge).

Styles, M. and Bearne, E. (2003) *Art, Narrative, Childhood* (Stoke-on-Trent: Trentham Books).

Swinfen, A. (1984) *In Defence of Fantasy* (London: Routledge).

Todorov, T. (1995) *The Fantastic: A Structural Approach to a Literary Genre*, trans. Richard Howard (New York: Cornell University Press).

Tolkien, J. R. R. (1983) 'On Fairy-Stories', in C. Tolkien (ed.), *The Monsters and the Critics and other Essays* (London: George Allen & Unwin; originally the Andrew Lang Lecture, given at the University of St Andrew's, 8 March 1939).

Tolkien, J. R. R. (1968) 'Foreword' to *The Lord of the Rings* (London: George Allen & Unwin; first published 1954–5).

Tonkin, B. (2002) 'Entropy as Demon: Buffy in Southern California', in R. Kaveney (ed.), *Reading the Vampire Slayer: An Unofficial Critical Companion to* Buffy *and* Angel (London and New York: Tauris Parke, 2002), pp. 37–52.

Townsend, J. R. (1990) *Written for Children* (London: Bodley Head).

Trites, R. (1997) *Waking Sleeping Beauty: Feminist Voices in Children's Novels* (Iowa: University of Iowa Press).

Tucker, N. (1981) *The Child and the Book: A Psychological and Literary Exploration* (Cambridge: Cambridge University Press).

Tucker, N. and Reynolds, K. (eds) (1997) *Enid Blyton: A Celebration and Reappraisal* (London: NCRCL).

Turkle, S. (1994) 'Construction and Reconstructions of Self in Virtual Reality: Playing in the MUDs', *Mind, Culture and Activity*, 1(3), pp. 158–67.

Ungerer, T. (1993) *Die Gedanken sind bei: Meine Kindheit im Elsass* (Zürich: Diogenes).

Ungerer, T. (1998) *Tomi: A Childhood Under the Nazis* (London, Boulder: Roberts Rinehart).

von Franz, M. (1996) *The Interpretation of Fairy Tales* (Boston: Shambhala Publications; first published 1970).

Wall, B. (1991) *The Narrator's Voice* (London: Macmillan).

Wallace, P. (1999) *The Psychology of the Internet* (Cambridge: Cambridge University Press).

Walsh, K. (1992) *The Representation of the Past* (London: Routledge).

Watson, K. (ed.) (1997) *Word and Image – Using Picture Books* (Sydney: St Clair Press).

Watson, V. (ed.) (2001) *The Cambridge Guide to Children's Books in English* (Cambridge: Cambridge University Press).

Watson, V. and Styles, M. (eds) (1996) *Talking Pictures* (London: Hodder and Stoughton).

Wellman, B. and Guila, M. (1996) 'Net Surfers Don't Ride Alone: Virtual Communities as Communities', in P. Kollock and M. Smith (eds), *Communities in Cyberspace* (Berkeley, CA: University of California Press).

Westall, R. (1979) 'How Real do you Want your Realism?', *Signal*, 28, pp. 34–46.

White, H. (1973) *Metahistory: The Historical Imagination in Nineteenth-Century Europe* (Baltimore and London: Johns Hopkins University Press).

Wilkie, C. (1998) 'The Garden, the Wolf and the Dream of Childhood: from Philippa Pearce to Gillian Cross', in K. Reynolds (ed.), *Childhood Remembered* (London: NCRCL), pp. 91–105.

Wilkie-Stibbs, C. (2002) *The Feminine Subject Children's Literature* (New York and London: Routledge).

Zipes, J. (2001) *Sticks and Stones: The Troublesome Success of Children's Literature from Slovenly Peter to Harry Potter* (London: Routledge).

Index

NB: Page numbers in **bold** denote boxed items; page numbers in *italics* denote illustrations